Global Supply Chains, Standards and the Poor

How the Globalization of Food Systems and Standards Affects Rural Development and Poverty

Global Supply Chains, Standards and the Poor

How the Globalization of Food Systems and Standards Affects Rural Development and Poverty

Edited by

Johan F.M. Swinnen

www.cabi.org

CABI is a trading name of CAB International

CABI Head Office	CABI North American Office
Nosworthy Way	875 Massachusetts Avenue
Wallingford	7th Floor
Oxon OX10 8DE	Cambridge, MA 02139
UK	USA
Tel: +44 (0)1491 832111	Tel: +1 617 395 4056
Fax: +44 (0)1491 833508	Fax: +1 617 354 6875
E-mail: cabi@cabi.org	E-mail: cabi-nao@cabi.org
Website: www.cabi.org	

© CAB International 2007. All rights reserved. No part of this publication may be reproduced in any form or by any means, electronically, mechanically, by photocopying, recording or otherwise, without the prior permission of the copyright owners.

A catalogue record for this book is available from the British Library, London, UK.

A catalogue record for this book is available from the Library of Congress, Washington, DC.

ISBN-13: 978 1 84593 1858

Typeset by Columns Design Ltd, Reading, UK
Printed and bound in the UK by Cromwell Press, Trowbridge

Contents

Contributors		ix
Preface		xv
1	Introduction J.F.M. Swinnen	1
Part I	Global Supply Chains and Standards	3
2	The Globalization of Private Standards and the Agri-food System L. Fulponi	5
3	Public and Private Food Quality Standards: Recent Trends and Strategic Incentives J.J. McCluskey	19
4	The Costs and Benefits of Compliance with Food Safety Standards for Exports by Developing Countries: the Case of Fish and Fishery Products S. Henson and S. Jaffee	26
5	The Dynamics of Vertical Coordination in Agri-food Supply Chains in Transition Countries J.F.M. Swinnen	42
6	Trade Liberalization and Rent Distribution in Vertically Related Markets S. McCorriston and I. Sheldon	59
7	Contracting, Competition and Rent Distribution in Supply Chains: Theory and Empirical Evidence from Central Asia J.F.M. Swinnen, M. Sadler and A. Vandeplas	75

Part II Empirical Studies on Changes and Effects   89

ASIA

8   Growth in High-value Agriculture in Asia and the Emergence of Vertical Links with Farmers   91
    A. Gulati, N. Minot, C. Delgado and S. Bora

9   Small Traders and Small Farmers: the Small Engines Driving China's Giant Boom in Horticulture   109
    X. Dong, H. Wang, S. Rozelle, J. Huang and T. Reardon

10 Quality Control and the Marketing of Non-staple Crops in India   122
    M. Fafchamps, R. Vargas-Hill and B. Minten

LATIN AMERICA   133

11 Supermarkets and Small Horticultural Product Farmers in Central America   135
    J.A. Berdegué, T. Reardon, F. Balsevich, L.G. Flores and R.A. Hernández

AFRICA   145

12 Global Supply Chains, Poverty and the Environment: Evidence from Madagascar   147
    B. Minten, L. Randrianarison and J.F.M. Swinnen

13 High-value Supply Chains, Food Standards and Rural Households in Senegal   159
    M. Maertens, L. Dries, F.A. Dedehouanou and J.F.M. Swinnen

THE FORMER SOVIET UNION   173

14 Transformation and Contracting in the Supply Chains of the Former Soviet Union: Evidence from Armenia, Georgia, Moldova, Ukraine and Russia   175
    M. Gorton and J. White

15 Agro-holdings: Vertical Integration in Agri-food Supply Chains in Russia   188
    E. Serova

CENTRAL AND EASTERN EUROPE   207

16 Restructuring Market Relations in Food and Agriculture of Central Eastern Europe: Impacts upon Small Farmers   209
    C. Csáki and C. Forgacs

17 The Impact of Retail Investments in the Czech Republic, Slovakia, Poland and the Russian Federation   228
    L. Dries, T. Reardon and E. Van Kerckhove

18 Vertical Coordination in the Dairy Sector: a Comparative Analysis of Romania and Slovakia   241
    S. van Berkum

	PART III THE POLICY AGENDA	257
19	Global Supply Chains, Standards and the Poor: some Conclusions and Implications for Government Policy and International Organizations *J.F.M. Swinnen and M. Maertens*	259
20	The Role of the Public and Private Sectors in Commercializing Small Farms and Reducing Transaction Costs *P. Pingali, Y. Khwaja and M. Meijer*	267
21	Building Capacity for Compliance with Evolving Food Safety and Agricultural Health Standards *K. van der Meer*	281
22	Public Sector Initiatives to Facilitate Small Farmer Access to International Marketing Channels: Lessons from Marketing Assistance Programmes in Armenia *H.R. Gow and J. Cocks*	295
	Index	311

Contributors

Fernando Balsevich is a PhD candidate at Michigan State University (MSU), USA, where he joined the Master program in 2000 as a Fulbright Fellow. His applied research work combines development and agribusiness topics linking farmers to dynamic markets. At MSU he served as teaching assistant of the course International Agrifood Markets and Industries and worked as a research assistant for the PFID-F&V project. Before 2000 he worked in the financial sector and in consulting companies such as PriceWaterhouseCoopers in his home country Paraguay. E-mail: balsevic@msu.edu

Julio A. Berdegué is Chairman of Rimisp-Latin American Centre for Rural Development (http://www.rimisp.org). He holds a PhD in Social Sciences from Wageningen University, Netherlands. His recent areas of interest include non-farm rural employment, small farmers' economic organizations, the rise of supermarkets and its impact on agri-food systems and the development of a territorial approach to rural development in Latin America. E-mail: jberdegue@rimisp.org

Saswati Bora is a Senior Research Assistant in the Markets, Trade and Institutions Division of IFPRI, Washington, DC, USA. Her current research focuses on small farmers and high-value agriculture, agricultural market reform, vertical linkages between farms and firms and the role of institutions in agriculture markets. Previously, she worked for the United Nations Development Programme in Nepal and New York and as a journalist in India. A citizen of India, Bora has a Masters in International Economic Policy from Columbia University, USA. E-mail: s.bora@cgiar.org

Jack Cocks is Partner and Consultant at AbacusBio Ltd, Dunedin, New Zealand. Previously, he was Lecturer of Business Management at the Agribusiness Training Centre at the Armenian Agricultural Academy. He holds a MSc in Agribusiness Management from the University of Illinois at Urbana-Champaign, USA and BCom(Ag). in Farm Management from Lincoln University, New Zealand. His research and consulting focuses on farm production management, entrepreneurship and innovation management in the global agri-food sector and transition economies. E-mail: jcocks@abacusbio.co.nz

Csaba Csáki is Professor of Agricultural Economics and Department Head at the Budapest Corvinus University. He is a member of the Monetary Board of the Hungarian National Bank, former rector of BUES and former President of the International Association of

Agricultural Economists. He was Senior Advisor on Agriculture and Rural Development at the World Bank, and principal author of the World Bank's new rural development strategy. He is a leading expert on agricultural transition and development. He has edited, authored or co-authored numerous books and articles. E-mail: csaba.csaki@uni-corvinus.hu

Fidèle Ange Dedehouanou is a Research Associate at the Consortium pour la Recherche Économique et Social (CRES) at the University Cheikh Anta Diop in Dakar, Senegal. He is a collaborator in LIRGIAD – the Leuven Interdisciplinary Research Network on International Agreements and Development. He has a MSc degree from the University Cheikh Anta Diop in Dakar and received the Belgian Prize for Development Cooperation in 2003 for his research. E-mail: dfidelus@yahoo.fr

Christopher Delgado is currently Advisor, Rural Strategy and Policy, at The World Bank, Washington, DC, USA. His contribution was received during his previous role as Director of the Joint International Livestock Research Institute/International Food Policy Research Institute Program on Livestock Market Opportunities, where he conducted research on the structural and policy factors that exclude poor people and poor countries from participation in high-value agricultural markets. A US citizen, Delgado received his PhD in economics from Cornell University, USA. E-mail: c.delgado@cgiar.org

Liesbeth Dries is Assistant Professor at the Centre for Agricultural and Food Economics at the Catholic University of Leuven, Belgium. She has a MSc degree in Agricultural Sciences and a PhD in Economics from that institution. Her research focuses on vertical coordination in supply chains in Central and Eastern Europe. E-mail: liesbeth.dries@biw.kuleuven.be

Marcel Fafchamps is Reader in the Department of Economics and Professorial Fellow in Mansfield College at the University of Oxford, UK. He has served as deputy director of the Centre for the Study of African Economies since 1999. Formerly, he taught for 9 years at Stanford University, USA. He holds degrees in Law and in Economics from the Catholic University of Leuven, Belgium, and a PhD from UC Berkeley, USA. From 1981 to 1985 Marcel worked for the International Labour Organization in Ethiopia. His current research interests focus on market institutions, social networks and geographical isolation. E-mail: marcel.fafchamps@economics.ox.ac.uk

Luis G. Flores completed his Masters in Agricultural Economics at Michigan State University, USA, and is a current PhD Student at the department of Community, Agriculture and Resource Studies at that university. He has been involved with the agribusiness export sector in Central America since 1998 and has worked as a country coordinator since 2002 for Guatemala and Nicaragua in the project Partnerships for Food Industry Development, Fruits and Vegetables (PFID-F&V) – a USAID-funded project managed by Michigan State University. E-mail: floreslg@msu.edu

Csaba Forgacs is Professor at Corvinus University, Budapest. He has several degrees in economics from Karl Marx University, Leipzig, Germany. He was Vice-rector of Budapest University of Economics and President of the European Association of Agricultural Economists. His major fields of teaching and research include agricultural economics, agricultural policy and rural development. He was a coordinator or partner in many international projects and is responsible for numerous publications in these fields. E-mail: csaba.forgacs@uni-corvinus.hu

Linda Fulponi is a Senior Economist at the OECD, Paris. Her current work focuses on the use of private standards in the global food system and their implications for trade. She holds a PhD in Economics from the University of Pennsylvania, USA. Currently, she is on the editorial board of the *European Review of Agricultural Economics* and *Cahiers* *d'Économie et Sociologie Rurales* and is Vice-president of the European Society for Agricultural and Food Ethics. E-mail: fulponi@oecd.org

Matthew Gorton is Lecturer at the School of Agriculture, Food and Rural Development, University of Newcastle-upon-Tyne, UK. His research focuses on the restructuring of the agri-food industry in Central and Eastern Europe. He has contributed to several research projects, funded by the European Union, OECD, World Bank and FAO. E-mail: matthew.gorton@newcastle.ac.uk

Hamish R. Gow is an Assistant Professor of International Agribusiness and Marketing and Director of the International Business Immersion Program at the University of Illinois Urbana-Champaign, USA. He is also Research Associate at the LICOS Center for Transition Economics, Catholic University of Leuven, Belgium. He holds a PhD in Agricultural Economics from Cornell University, USA. His research focuses on international food marketing strategies, global value chains, marketing channel design, inter-organizational relationships and entrepreneurship in subsistence and transforming markets. E-mail: hgow@uiuc.edu

Ashok Gulati is Director in Asia, based in New Delhi, for the International Food Policy Research Institute (IFPRI). His areas of research include agricultural markets, agricultural trade liberalization and the WTO, globalization and its impact on smallholders, vertical linkages between farms and firms, input subsidies and the role of infrastructure and institutions in making markets function efficiently. A citizen of India, Gulati received his PhD in economics from the Delhi School of Economics, India. E-mail: a.gulati@cgiar.org

Spencer Henson is Professor in the Department of Food, Agricultural and Resource Economics at the University of Guelph, Canada. His research interests focus on the economics of food safety and quality, with a particular emphasis on the implications of food safety and quality standards for developing countries. He has undertaken research in numerous industrialized and developing countries globally and worked with organizations such as the World Bank, FAO, OECD and WHO. E-mail: shenson@uoguelph.ca

Ricardo A. Hernández is a PhD student in Agricultural Economics at Michigan State University, USA, working as a research assistant in Partnerships for Food Industry Development for Central American and Nicaraguan projects. He was working in the agricultural export sector in his home country, Guatemala, from 1997 to 2003. Previously, he obtained his BS degree in agricultural sciences at EARTH University in Costa Rica. His research interests includes finance, production economics and international development. E-mail: hernan79@msu.edu

Jikun Huang is the Director of the Center for Chinese Agricultural Policy (CCAP) and a Professor at the Chinese Academy of Sciences in Beijing. He is visiting Professor of Economics at Zhejiang University in Hangzhou and Nanjing Agricultural University and vice president of the Chinese Association of Agro-Technology Economics. He holds a PhD from the University of the Philippines in Los Banos and a MSc from Nanjing Agricultural University, China. He is associate editor of *Agricultural Economics* and on the editorial board of several Chinese academic journals. E-mail: jikhuang@public.bta.net.cn

Steven Jaffee is Senior Economist in the World Bank's International Trade Department. He was lead author of the World Bank's global study on emerging agri-food standards and their impact on exports from developing countries. He co-manages a programme seeking to improve the World Bank's analytic and investment support to clients related to trade and standards management. His field experience has been in Africa, South Asia, Eastern Europe and the Caribbean. He has a DPhil in Agricultural Economics from Oxford University, UK. E-mail: sjaffee@worldbank.org

Yasmeen Khwaja is a Lecturer in economics at the American University of Rome. She is a visiting professor at the University of Rome (Tor Vergata) and the University of Malta. Formerly, she was a lecturer at Queen Mary College, London and Brunel University, London. Her research focuses on migration, poverty and food security. She has been a consultant to the FAO and IFAD, working on issues of globalization, poverty and livelihoods. E-mail: yasmeen_khwaja@yahoo.co.uk

Miet Maertens is Senior Economist at the LICOS Centre for Institutions and Economic Performance at the Catholic University of Leuven, Belgium. Her research focuses on development in Africa and South-east Asia. She worked as a consultant for the World Bank. She has a MSc in Economics and a MSc in Agricultural Sciences from the University of Leuven and a PhD from the Georg-August University in Göttingen, Germany. She received the Josef G. Knoll Wissenschaftspreis 2004 for her doctoral thesis. E-mail: miet.maertens@econ.kuleuven.be

Jill J. McCluskey is Associate Professor and Chair of Graduate Studies in the School of Economic Sciences and Food Policy Fellow at the IMPACT Center at Washington State University, USA. Her research focuses on food and environmental quality. She is associate editor of the *American Journal of Agricultural Economics* and the *Journal of Industrial Organization Education*. She serves on the Executive Board of the American Agricultural Economics Association. She received her PhD in 1998 from UC Berkeley, USA. E-mail: mccluskey@wsu.edu

Steve McCorriston is Professor of Agricultural Economics and currently Head of the Department of Economics at the University of Exeter in the UK. His main research interests relate to international trade and industrial organization. He has served as an Associate Editor of the *American Journal of Agricultural Economics*, and is on the editorial boards of the *European Review of Agricultural Economics* and the *Journal of Agricultural Economics*. He has published widely in both agricultural economics and general economics journals. E-mail: s.mccorriston@exeter.ac.uk

Madelon Meijer is an Economist at the Agricultural and Development Economics Division at FAO. She has a MA in Economics from the University of Amsterdam and a MSc in Agricultural Development Economics from the University of Reading, UK. She works on 'making markets work for the poor', analysing the impact of changing food systems on small farmers. She previously worked in Latin America (Bolivia and Peru), studying marketing systems and advising on improving linkages of small farmers with markets and strengthening farmers' organizations. E-mail: madelon.meijer@fao.org

Nicholas Minot is a Senior Research Fellow in the Markets, Trade and Institutions Division of IFPRI, Washington, DC, USA. He has carried out research on the agricultural market reform, fertilizer policy, fruit and vegetable markets and the spatial patterns in poverty. He is the leader of a research programme on strategies for promoting the participation of small farmers in high-value agricultural supply chains. A citizen of the USA, Minot has a PhD in agricultural economics from Michigan State University, USA. E-mail: n.minot@cgiar.org

Bart Minten is a Senior Research Fellow at the International Food Policy Research Institute, based in New Delhi (India). He holds a PhD in agricultural and resource economics from Cornell University, USA and an engineering degree from the Catholic University of Leuven, Belgium. He has worked on issues related to agricultural marketing, technology adoption, agricultural productivity, environmental degradation, poverty, crime and social service delivery in developing countries and has published many articles and books in this area. He has worked also at the World Bank, Cornell University and KU Leuven. E-mail: b.minten@cgiar.org

Prabhu Pingali is the Director of the Agricultural and Development Economics Division of the Food and Agriculture Organization of the United Nations, Rome. He is the current President of the International Association of Agricultural Economists (IAAE). He is a Fellow of the American Agricultural Economics Association. An Indian national, he earned his PhD in Economics from North Carolina State University, USA, in 1982. Prior to joining FAO he worked at CIMMYT, in Mexico (1996–2002); IRRI in the Philippines (1987–1996); and the World Bank in Washington, DC, USA (1982–1987). E-mail: prabhu.pingali@fao.org

Lalaina Randrianarison is a consultant in Madagascar working on the impacts of liberalization on the agricultural sector, contract farming and rural development issues. Previously, she worked as economist for the Ilo Programme of Cornell University in Antananarivo, Madagascar, and worked on the economic impacts of soil conservation, agricultural and non-agricultural income sources and food security issues. She holds a postgraduate degree from the Economics Department of the University of Antananarivo. E-mail: rhl@wanadoo.mg

Thomas Reardon is Professor of Agricultural Economics at Michigan State University, USA. From 1986 to 1991 he was Research Fellow at IFPRI in Washington, DC, USA, and from 1984 to 1986 he was a Rockefeller Foundation Post-doctoral Fellow attached to IFPRI, posted in Burkina Faso. He received his doctorate from UC Berkeley, USA. His work focuses on links between the consolidation of the food industry (in particular the rise of supermarkets and large-scale processing) and on the rise of private food safety and quality standards and its impact on development. E-mail: reardon@msu.edu

Scott Rozelle is the Helen Farnsworth Professor in the Institute of International Studies at Stanford University, USA, and Chair of the International Advisory Board of the Center for Chinese Agricultural Policy. He has a BSc from UC Berkeley, MSc and PhD from Cornell University and was Professor at UC Davis. He is on the editorial board of *Contemporary Economic Policy*, *China Journal*, and the *China Economic Review*. His research focuses on China and deals with agricultural policy, markets and transition institutions, poverty and inequality. He has published extensively in leading scientific journals on these issues. E-mail: rozelle@primal.ucdavis.edu

Marc Sadler is currently a consultant for the World Bank in Central Asia, the Caucasus and Turkey on supply and value chain development in the agricultural sector. He has a Masters in Jurisprudence from Oxford University, UK, and worked for the past 13 years in Central Asia. He worked for 7 years in cotton trading, and later as an investment and political risk consultant to the private sector throughout Central Asia. E-mail: sadlermp@aol.com

Eugenia Serova is the Head of the Agrarian Policy Division at the Institute for Economy in Transition in Moscow. She has a PhD in Economics from Moscow State University and is Professor and Head of the Chair on Agricultural Economics at the Higher School of Economics. During the first 4 years of the Russian reforms she was economic advisor to the Minister of Agriculture. Her research focuses on agricultural economics and policy, cooperatives, land tenure and agrarian reform. E-mail: serova@iet.ru

Ian Sheldon received his PhD in Economics from the University of Salford, UK in 1981. He served as a Lecturer in Economics at the University of Exeter, UK, from 1982 to 1990 before becoming a Professor at the Ohio State University, USA, in 1990. He has published widely in the fields of economics and agricultural economics, and recently completed a 4-year term as editor of the *American Journal of Agricultural Economics*. E-mail: sheldon1@osu.edu

Johan F.M. Swinnen is Professor of Economics and Director of the LICOS Centre for Institutions and Economic Performance at the Catholic University of Leuven, Belgium. He is Senior Research Fellow at the Centre for European Policy Studies (CEPS) in Brussels and coordinator of the European Network of Agricultural and Rural Policy Research Institutes (ENARPRI). He was Lead Economist at the World Bank (2003–2004) and Economic Advisor at the European Commission (1998–2001). He has a PhD from Cornell University, USA, and has published extensively on institutional reform, globalization, agriculture and development. E-mail: jo.swinnen@econ.kuleuven.be

Siemen van Berkum is a Senior Researcher at the Agricultural Economics Research Institute (LEI) in The Hague (Netherlands). He has a PhD in Economics and extensive experience in (European) agricultural policy and international market and chain analysis. He has worked in many Central and East European countries and in the Balkan countries and Turkey. E-mail: siemen.vanberkum@wur.nl

Anneleen Vandeplas is a PhD researcher at LICOS Centre for Institutions and Economic Performance at the Catholic University of Leuven, Belgium. Her research focuses on the role of competition in contracting and supply chains. She has a MSc in Agricultural Sciences and a MSc of Advanced Studies in Economics from the University of Leuven, and a MA in International and Development Economics from the University of Namur (FUNDP), Belgium. E-mail: anneleen.vandeplas@econ.kuleuven.be

Kees van der Meer is a Senior Economist in the World Bank's Agriculture and Rural Development Department. He studied agricultural economics at Wageningen University, Netherlands, and gained a PhD in Economics at the National University at Groningen, Netherlands, in 1981, where he subsequently taught agricultural and development economics as an associate professor until 1988. Before joining the World Bank in 1999, he had worked in the Netherlands Ministry of Agriculture with responsibilities for policy and management of research and technology. E-mail: cvandermeer@worldbank.org

Elke Van Kerckhove is a Research Associate at the Centre for Agricultural and Food Economics at the Catholic University (KU) of Leuven, Belgium. She has a MSc in Agricultural Sciences. E-mail: elke.vankerckhove@biw.kuleuven.be

Ruth Vargas-Hill is a consultant at the World Bank, Washington, DC, USA. She received a PhD in Economics from the University of Oxford, UK, in 2005. Her PhD thesis examined the impact of global price volatility on coffee farmers. Her recent research work analyses trader and farmer behaviour in crop markets in Africa and India. She was a member of the 2001 Human Development Report core team and served as a consultant for the 2005 Human Development Report. E-mail: ruth.vargashill@gmail.com

John White is a Principal Lecturer in Marketing at the University of Plymouth, UK. He has coordinated two EU INTAS research projects on agricultural supply chains in Eastern Europe. His research focuses on supply chain relationships and relationship satisfaction. He has undertaken research for EU INTAS, FAO and the World Bank. E-mail: john.white@plymouth.ac.uk

Preface

The production and publication of this book were financially supported by the Flemish Science Foundation (FWO) and the KU Leuven Research Council. Anneleen Vandeplas, Bert Van Landeghem and Thÿs Vandemoortele provided excellent editorial assistance.

Jo Swinnen
Leuven, Belgium
November 2006

1 Introduction

J.F.M. Swinnen

The past decade has witnessed an effective globalization of supply chains and an unprecedented increase in foreign investment in agricultural commodities and food markets worldwide, the rise of food quality and safety standards in the rich countries and the spread of these standards – often set by private companies – to developing and transition countries and a dramatic growth in high-value food exports from developing countries.

One of the most striking features of these developments has been the dramatic rise of investments by global retail chains ('supermarkets') in emerging, transition and developing countries. Most recently, Russia, China and India were the top three destinations of foreign investment flows by multinational retail companies.

Not surprisingly, these changes in the global food system are having important effects on farmers, fishermen and households in developing and transition countries. In the wake of foreign investments or through global trading relationships, high standards for quality and safety of agricultural and food commodities have been imposed on their production systems. In several cases these changes in standards and investments are coinciding with a growth in vertical coordination in these modern supply chains, contributing to access of the local producers to inputs, credit, technology, etc. as part of contracts with companies that purchase the commodities they produce. The combination of these developments is causing dramatic changes in the supply chains in developing, emerging and transition countries, and the production circumstances for local producers – and particularly poor, often rural, households.

However, there is a lot of debate on the impact of these developments on developing and transition countries, and in particular on the poor households in these countries. Some have pointed at the benefits from these developments as farmers have gained access to high-value international markets and to inputs, credit, technology and output markets, and thereby to higher productivity and higher incomes. Others argue that these developments are likely to lead to a further marginalization of the poor as small, poorly educated and weakly capitalized farmers are likely to be excluded from these new markets, with their traditional markets being taken away from them.

Up till this moment in time, many arguments were based on both case studies and non-representative interviews with food processing and retail companies and a series of producers in various countries.

The weakness of both the conceptual analyses and the empirical evidence is a serious constraint in this debate.

The overall objective of this book is to contribute to filling this gap in our knowledge by bringing together some conceptual frameworks for understanding these changes and evaluating them and, especially, an extensive amount of new empirical evidence in this area, based on more thorough and rigorous empirical methodologies and data collection.

The book tries to combine quantity and quality. By bringing together a large set of studies we have tried to bring a comprehensive viewpoint on the changes that are occurring across the globe in poorer countries. For each of the topics, regions and countries the chapters are written by leading researchers in these areas. Several of the chapters in this book summarize key findings from large, international studies organized by leading international institutions such as the World Bank, IFPRI, the OECD and IIED/DFID. Other chapters are based on studies by highly respected academic researchers. By presenting the results of these studies together for the first time it will be possible to draw important general conclusions on the impact of the globalization of supply chains and standards, and on structural changes in these chains on local producers, growth and poverty.

Many of the chapters summarize key findings and evidence from more elaborate studies which have much more details on empirical methodology, collected data, statistical methods and measured effects than could be included in the chapters in this book. In these cases, there is explicit reference to the full studies and background reports for further details. Further, the authors of the various chapters have been asked to make the presentation of the material and the argumentation in the chapters understandable for non-specialists in order to make the book and its insights accessible to a broad audience.

The book has three parts. The chapters in Part I: (i) identify global changes in food standards and supply chains; (ii) explain their emergence and relevance for today's trade and development debate; and (iii) present a series of conceptual frameworks necessary to understand the changes and their effects. Part II contains a large set of new empirical studies, organized by region, which present new quantitative information on the effects of globalization and vertical contracting in modern supply chains in developing, emerging and transition countries. Part III has four chapters which discuss the implications of these developments for the international policy agenda.

Part I

Global Supply Chains and Standards

2 The Globalization of Private Standards and the Agri-food System

L. Fulponi[1]

Introduction

The agri-food system in most OECD economies has been undergoing significant change, with a shift in market power from manufacturing to retailing, an increasingly stringent regulatory environment, a stronger voice of consumers and civil society and the globalization in supply and distribution systems. Advances in information and communication technologies (ICT) and cost-reducing supply logistic systems have, furthermore, altered behaviours in management as well as in the organization of the food system. The development and use of private voluntary standards by lead retailers more recently can be viewed as a governance tool in the food chain and a new way of managing product and process attributes within a global sourcing strategy.

Consumers expect a great deal from the food system: safety, quality, variety, convenience and service – as well as low prices. Increasingly, they are also demanding that production and processing methods be environmentally sustainable, animal friendly and obey recognized labour and social standards. These newer demands overlay the already ongoing transformation of food demand due to changes in labour market participation, demographics, rising incomes, information technologies and the leisure home-production trade-off.

Consumer demand is now considered the main driver in the food system, and with almost 70% of food consumed being purchased in supermarkets, economic power in the system has shifted to retailers. As the main link between consumers and the food chain, retailers are responsible for translating consumer demands back up the chain and for organizing the flow of products back down to consumers. These tasks challenge the supply and distribution systems to deliver 'desired' products in an increasingly competitive market, where competition has shifted from price to price-and-quality.

What strategies or management tools can ensure that consumer demands are met, regulatory requirements fulfilled and competitive positions maintained, while sourcing either domestically or globally? Private voluntary standards can be viewed as a tool to permit firms to respond to consumer demands and to ensure that regulatory requirements are satisfied. In a business to business (B2B) context these can ensure and communicate given safety, production process and quality attributes. But private standards can also be used as instruments for product differentiation and market segmentation if communicated to consumers.

Over recent years, lead retailers have attempted to harmonize specific elements of their private standards through collaboration in the definition of core attributes and procedures. These private voluntary standards are characterized by a quality management system approach, with third party audits to certify conformity and represent a fundamentally different approach from simple product controls. Furthermore, these private standard schemes are used frequently in a B2B context, similar to the use of government standards which are required for doing business but not necessarily communicated to consumers. These schemes may cover not only food safety, but also a wider set of credence attributes such as animal welfare, environmental sustainability, social standards and market ethics.

This chapter focuses on private voluntary standards developed and implemented by lead retailers in a B2B context. It describes the evolving economic and regulatory environment that may have generated incentives for their development and then presents the results of interviews with retailers concerning the development and use of their private standards in sourcing. It also discusses the potential influence that these may have on the shaping of the food system.

Evolving Economic and Policy Environment as Incentives for Private Voluntary Standards

Evolving consumer demands

Food demands have been changing with the evolution of lifestyles, demographics and rising incomes. Quality and safety remain key food attributes for consumers; however, specific product attributes as well as the processes by which they are produced are growing in importance. For instance, consumers' animal welfare concerns – as well as citizens' – have generated legislation in the EU as to how laying hens are to be treated and housed, with similar rules in place for other farm animals.

Concern for environmental sustainability related to agriculture is also reported to be increasing, as society holds farmers, manufacturers and government accountable for negative externalities generated in food production. In addition, the increasingly important role of NGOs in informally monitoring sourcing behaviours of retailers both at home and abroad is an important incentive for firms to attempt to ensure that their suppliers operate within acceptable norms and standards for these consumer concerns.

These demands are influencing ways of doing business along the food chain (Kinsey, 2003). The use of private standards and third party certifications are examples of the significant changes underway in how retailers now source products. Any mishap in the food chain can have deleterious consequences for the reputation of a retailer, given its likely media coverage, and thus efforts on developing tools to prevent the mishap or to correct it rapidly have been given priority. Sourcing of only standards-conforming products is seen as a way of avoiding mishaps and of protecting their reputation, their intangible capital.[2]

Consumer attitudes towards government and private industry responsibilities still emphasize government responsibility in the food sector. In a survey of consumer concerns in the food area, done through representative consumer associations, results indicate that food safety, environmental effects and health were major concerns. When asked who should be responsible for determining setting standards or behavioural rules over food safety, quality, environmental effects, labour standards and animal welfare, all consumer associations felt that it was the government's role to regulate all these areas.

Only in the area of quality did consumers

concede a slight advantage towards industry self-regulation or private–public partnerships, the meshing of government regulations and industry monitoring via quality management systems is a significant step. To the extent that consumers may be willing to concede 'regulation' of these issues at least partially to the private sector, the trend in private voluntary standard schemes for the food sector could provide impetus for government and industry collaboration to avoid task duplication and to better delimit their responsibilities.

Evolving food retailing

Retailers are not only gatekeepers to shelf space for foods, thus deciding what is or is not available to consumers, but are also managers and guarantors of food attributes in the distribution processes (Dobson and Waterson, 1999; Grievink, 2003). Food retailing in many industrialized countries has become quite concentrated. In Europe, firm retailer concentration averaged over 50% in 2000, with some countries reaching close to 80%. Even in emerging economies such as Chile, Argentina and Brazil, supermarket concentration is above the 50% mark and rising (Dobson, 2003; Reardon and Timmer, 2007).

Not only is increased market size associated with substantial selling power, but it is also often associated with buying power, including the ability to impose product requirements and standards on suppliers. In many cases this power has increased, with the consolidation of procurement procedures through buyer associations, and the growth in such cross-border associations accentuates this trend. According to Dobson Consulting, these 'illustrate the various degrees of collaboration between firms on price information and acting as a single purchasing unit as well as collaborating on the sourcing of private label products' (Dobson, 2003, p. 5). Given the turnover size of these associations they are able to bargain for concessions, which in turn leads to cost concessions over rivals, reduction of consumer prices and larger market shares.

Asymmetric market power vis-à-vis small and medium suppliers permits retailers to impose specific requirements on them without having to bear the ownership risk. Given their economic importance, retailers can dictate conditions of sale/product attributes with their suppliers. Frequently, these then sub-contract out production, thus creating a hierarchy of suppliers who must follow the retailer requirements. In this context, private standards can be seen as a way of governing the network of firm hierarchies along the food chain.

Moreover, private standards are becoming global tools in governing the food chain, in as much as the lead retailers source products around the globe (Humphrey and Schmitz, 2003). In addition, these may be diffused to non-lead retailers in both developed and developing countries, though compliance in the latter is often not rigorously controlled. If harmonization of these private standards among lead retailers and manufacturers occurs, this could be the basis of a global food standards system with the potential to determine who produces what, where and when (Humphrey and Schmitz, 2001; Reardon and Berdegue, 2002; Reardon and Farina, 2002; Reardon and Timmer, 2007).

However, substantial logistical support through codified information flows, planning and record keeping, transportation and storage systems is also needed to make these private standards systems operative and economically efficient, flexible and profitable. These changes have been accompanied by a proliferation of audit and certification systems necessary to conformity assessment. In a global sourcing setting, continued innovation and technological advances in supply logistics, in standards implementation procedures – along with greater rigour in audit/certification systems – have raised the entry requirements to lead retailer supply chains. This increased use of private standards, along with more exacting management and strategic requirements of value chains, are shaping the agri-food system, making it more capital, technology and management skill dependent. As standards requirements continue to shift from product to process perspectives, these latter elements become even more important.

This growth in retail sector bargaining power, coupled with innovations and technological advances in information systems, tracking and tracing systems, transportation, cold chain and storage operations, has yielded new ways of monitoring foods 'from farm to fork' and has given rise to new forms of marketing and distribution systems. For instance, the computerized information and logistics systems business model introduced by Wal-Mart has spread among retail groups throughout the globe.

These approaches include the Just in Time and Efficient Consumer Response systems of inventory management, which often place additional demands on producers, but also stimulate innovation in technology and provide financial incentives to more finely manage flows of products, as well as quality and safety throughout the system. These new ways of doing business have brought intense competition to retailing, but have also stimulated greater communication and interaction between the lead firms in finding ways of dealing with essential issues such as food safety.

However, it would be incorrect to interpret these developments in the lead retailer environment as characterizing all food distribution systems. These may be more heterogeneous than appears so at first glance. Recent work in this area indicates that in emerging economies such as Brazil – but also in mature markets such as the USA – at least two types of retailers can coexist: the core or lead retailers and the medium-scale fringe retailers (Chen, 2003; Farina *et al.*, 2004).

Suppliers to the fringe are not necessarily kept to the same standards as are core supermarkets. It is also widely recognized that the application of standards schemes, even by lead firms, is often adapted to local environments, because of lack of both adequate suppliers and consumer purchasing power. While the standards of the core are likely to diffuse down to other retailers over time, at present there is still room for those who need time to upgrade. These 'fringe markets' provide access for a wider set of producers, not only in domestic but also in international markets, a factor that needs to be reconsidered in a development-oriented framework.

Evolving regulatory environment

Retailers are legally required to ensure that all foods meet domestic regulations. In most countries liability laws make sellers legally responsible for damage or harm resulting from a product sold by them. In case of dispute, the manufacturer or retailer must prove that all necessary precautions – within their capacities – were undertaken to ensure that the product sold or manufactured by the firm was safe. Such liability laws can be a potent incentive to follow government regulations and recommendations – or even go beyond them – as a margin of defence (Caswell and Hooker, 1996).

Some countries have gone further, in particular the UK, where the food safety issue has taken on particular importance with the passage of the 'due diligence clause' of the Food Safety Act, 1990. This clause states that: 'It shall be a defence for the person charged to prove that he took all reasonable precautions and exercised all due diligence to avoid the commission of the offence by himself or a by a person under his control …'

Firms, and those responsible for food safety, must provide evidence that they undertook all possible steps to prevent the product from causing harm or contamination. Though few other countries have a 'due diligence clause' per se, the EU legislation has been drafted in the same vein as that of the UK. This has stimulated many lead food retailers to consider what an appropriate strategy might be to insure against their liability.

The potential to influence future government standards may also be an incentive for self-regulation at levels sufficiently high to avoid the government setting even higher levels. Firms may decide to exceed mandatory standards if, in doing so, they can influence future regulations. The timing of government and firm decisions is likely to be of importance here (Ronnen, 1991; Arora and Gangopadhyay, 1995; Lutz et al., 2000). If high-quality firms decide to adopt a standard above current and expected levels before governments do, then regulators may be influenced to set lower MQS (Minimum Quality Standards) than they would have done otherwise. This pre-emption strategy can reduce social welfare compared to the situation where the government would have moved first (Lutz et al., 2000). Private standards sometimes also end up being adopted into the government's regulatory framework, in which case the government catches up with industry. This has been the case for animal welfare and certain environmental guidelines for agriculture.[3]

Where governments are first movers, a minimum quality standard often induces certain firms to raise even further their quality to relax price competition, but quality differences are never fully restored so prices may fall and welfare rise (Shaked and Sutton, 1982; Ronnen, 1991). In certain cases firms over-comply or exceed required standards in order to further enhance their reputation of offering high-quality products. Since over-compliance may improve reputations, public knowledge of a firm's behaviour provides incentives for over-compliance. Such a situation may arise when there are informational asymmetries, as is the cases of food safety or environment (Arora and Gangopadhyay, 1995; Boom, 1995; Lehman-Grube, 1997; Lutz et al., 2000).

Private Standards

Retailer coalitions

What is new in the private food standards arena setting is the rise of private standards-setting coalitions among major players.[4] These are industry grassroots harmonization efforts (Casella, 2001). They operate to secure and to promote competitive advantage of member firms where this is understood as being the ability to manage the network of firm linkages, connecting activities from production to distribution (Porter, 1990; Casella, 2001; Dolan and Humphrey, 2001). Such a development may signal a new strategy in managing the supply chain.

Important examples of a standards-setting coalition in the food sector are Global Food Safety Initiative (GFSI) and Eurep, where leading food retail firms have collaborated in identifying an objective of importance to the industry – such as food safety and/or sustainability – and collectively found new, cost-efficient approaches for achieving it. The collective standard is viewed as a public good by the coalition.

Management system approach

The management system approach to monitoring and evaluation of performance in the production process, rather than of only output, now characterizes private standards schemes applied in the food sector.[5] In so doing, these schemes incorporate domestic regulatory requirements for the product. These therefore help to ensure that all regulations are met and provide firms with an added margin of security. The management systems approach in the food sector attempts to govern the entire production process, monitoring for safety and quality or environment attributes at both the farm and manufacturing levels. With a systems approach, standards need not be specific to an attribute or product. This implies an approach that is more amenable to being utilized as a governance tool, coordinating and monitoring the different activities along the chain.

Business to Business (B2B) Standards

Private standards schemes are increasingly considered as business to business (B2B) standards in procurement. These standards are not usually communicated directly to consumers, so they generally have no role in product differentiation. These standard schemes build flexible links between suppliers and leading food firms. Lead firms are now developing export platforms for specific products where products will have been produced according to one of the benchmarked standards – but sourced from different countries, supplying not only the firm developing the platform, but other leading firms as well. They are used not only by major food retailers in the industrialized countries but also by a growing number in developing countries (Farina et al., 2004; Reardon and Timmer, 2007).

The role of B2B standards in governance of commodity value chains is particularly relevant for developing countries which, in spite of lower tariffs, may find themselves excluded from the important centres of economic activity. As the economic benefit of being linked to the leading food firms strengthens, so does the need to comply with the standards they impose (Gereffi, 1999; Dolan and Humphrey, 2001; Nadvi and Waltring, 2003). However, the increasing need to meet not only the production standards but also to integrate the set of supply chain logistics – which are capital- and management-intensive – raises the cost of entry to leading retail chains.

The Global Food Safety Initiative

This section presents the Global Food Safety Initiative (GFSI) and discusses the incentives, use and future developments of this private standards initiative. The findings are based on interviews with directors of food safety and quality of leading retailers; and a short survey. Faced with a growing number of firm-level food safety standards schemes, the GFSI was created by retailers in 2000 to harmonize standards, as well as to reduce the costs of achieving food safety.

Food safety standards are costly to develop and maintain – as well as to monitor. Efficiency gains were considered possible by moving towards one standard compared to each firm managing its own system. Through the development of codes of practice in agriculture, manufacturing and distribution, guiding principles were laid out for reducing food safety risks in a non-competitive fashion. The goal is to obtain one unified food safety standard which all players can comply with and upon which all can rely, even under varied legal liability requirements. Such an approach could decrease transaction costs through diminishing in-house inspections, multiple verifications and certifications. The goal of this one standard is to benchmark schemes that meet the overall GFSI guidelines.

Joint efforts under the GFSI have produced three basic standards: Good Agricultural Practices (GAP), Good Manufacturing Practices (GMP) and Good Distribution Practices (GDP). This represents a complete food safety assurance system from farm to fork. Each of these components sets out requirements not only for ensuring food safety but also for other attributes such as social conditions and the environment. Specific private standards schemes can then be benchmarked against these meta-level protocols.

The GMP code has thus far benchmarked four standards schemes: the British Retail Consortium (BRC) Standard, the International Food Standard (IFS), the SQF 2000 (Safe Quality Food), and the Dutch HACCP (Hazard Analysis Critical Control Point). All these schemes are based on quality and safety management systems and incorporate the Codex-recommended HACCP procedures. Differences between schemes arise in both the specific requirements and in the competences required of auditors. All schemes require firms to have a written policy for food safety, as well as traceability systems and monitoring in line with a Codex-recommended HACCP.

For agricultural production, only SQF1000 is officially benchmarked, though the EurepGap standard was developed by retailers and is widely used by GFSI members and others. This oddity has to do with auditing procedures and once-removed benchmarking. These standards have been formulated in response to consumer demands for safe food as well as to consumers' increasing awareness of the effects of agricultural production on the environment, labour safety and other issues. EurepGap and SQF1000 represent quality management schemes that have placed particular emphasis on food safety. However, they may also include other attribute standards, as does EurepGap, which includes an array of product process attributes such as environment, animal welfare and worker safety and health standards.

Interview synthesis

Interviews with 16 leading food retailers were undertaken to understand better the incentives, use and expected evolution of private standards in the food system. A brief survey was also administered to retailers to extract a rough quantitative estimate of their standards implementation policies. Interviews focused on GAP and GMP standards.[6]

Reputation-building and maintenance were reported as being the main incentives for providing consumers with products that meet consistent quality and safety standards that go beyond the minimum requirements in creating a margin of defence and avoidance of any mishaps. Legal liability risk was also put forth as a reason for increasing stringency of standards in about three-quarters of those interviewed. Many viewed the responsibility/liability issue as being a normal requisite of any business activity and not necessarily any more constraining for the food sector.

Both food safety and quality were considered by far the most important attributes. Food safety was key, which is to be expected since it was a main reason for the founding of the GFSI and is seen as resulting from a well-defined set of 'good practices' covering agriculture, manufacturing or distribution. Food safety failures were viewed as highly damaging to reputation and with likely negative effects on consumer confidence, sales and thus earnings. Ensuring food safety is a *sine qua non* of doing business in this sector.

About 90% of the retailers reported that the standards they required for doing business were higher than those set by public authorities, and about one-half reported that they were significantly higher (see Fig. 2.1). This result is attributed to both the safety and quality management protocols adopted and, in some cases, to the additional firm-specific requirements applied. The latter may include expanded lists of possible allergens, contaminants, packaging materials and care in transport, storage and distribution procedures.

For all firms, zero tolerance in food safety failure is the aim. However, should failure occur, then what matters is the ability to undertake immediate remedial action. In this optic, traceability and recall capacity are critical for the operation as they permit pinpointing the source of the problem in order to remedy it. Most firms had instituted traceability requirements for main food categories prior to any legislation, even if these were not operational at 100% levels for all foods. Several retailers, however, did have a 100% traceability system for all main food product categories.

Most reported requiring EurepGap or SQF1000 certification when sourcing fruit and vegetables from developing countries,

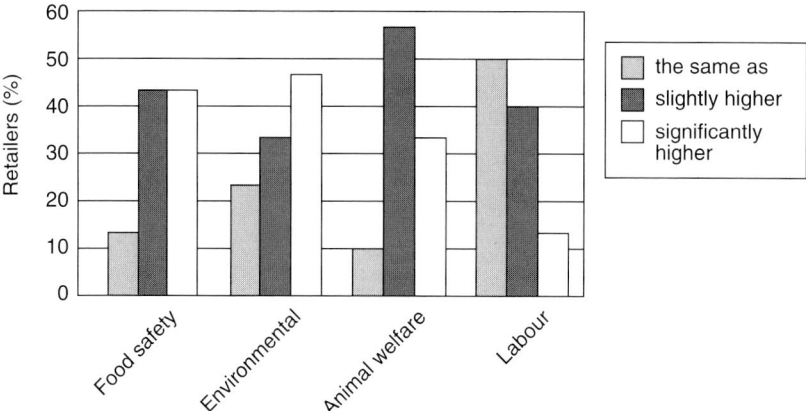

Fig. 2.1. Retailers' self-assessed standards compared to those of government.

but did not systematically require these when sourcing locally. However, the intention is to require certification even from local producers over the next 3–5 years, or sooner. The reason for the difference between local and international requirements is that firms generally know their suppliers, or at least can easily monitor at first hand the production process. They reported sourcing locally as much as possible.

According to this short survey, less than 25% of products are sourced from developing countries and this generally covers mainly off-season and tropical fresh produce. Several firms source no meat or meat products from developing countries. Some retailers noted, however, that in periods of tight supplies or lack of certified suppliers some flexibility might be applied, but products will always meet the minimum legal standards. In the case of manufactured goods, i.e. those carrying private labels, all products purchased must meet one of the benchmarked standards and be certified as such.

Quality

To satisfy increasing expectations in quality, that is organoleptic qualities and appearance in addition to food safety, a number of firms have developed high-quality product lines for which tighter product specifications are applied. These product lines generate premiums for both retailers and their suppliers, though they are likely to incur added costs for producers to meet the specifications, and not all output will usually be at the higher standard.

Social and labour standards

Social and labour standards were judged to be the most important standards after food safety and quality. In recent years, consumers and civil society have become more aware and interested in the way that retailers conduct their business, both at home and overseas. It is, however, very difficult to enforce standards outside the home country, even among European countries. It is noteworthy in this respect that there appears to be an increasing reliance on NGOs for the monitoring of firms/suppliers for these social, ethical and environmental standards. The firms interviewed found it difficult to enforce them beyond the minimum requirements and beyond one step back up the chain.

Dealing with labour conditions in developing countries is very difficult, because fewer domestic labour laws exist and those that do are often not enforced. About 50% reported meeting the minimum standard and 50% doing better than the minimum. Harmonization in the use of labour standards was viewed as a top priority but defining common criteria is difficult, given differing perceived risks to reputation as well as enforcement issues beyond international norms.

Environment and animal welfare standards

Environmental and animal welfare standards, though important, appeared less so than food safety and social standards, but the responses varied substantially according to country. Retailers in northern European countries were generally more inclined to attribute greater importance to animal welfare type issues than the southern-based firms. In spite of this, most retailers reported that their animal welfare requirements were higher than those of the national legislation. Several firms reported that they had developed animal welfare and environmental schemes that were later adopted into national legislation. This supports the possible importance that firms may invest in formulating standards, whether these are implemented in anticipation of government rules or used to influence them.

Legal liability

While all firms reported being more capable and better equipped to manage food safety and to respond faster to failures than regulatory authorities, they felt that the government should be responsible for setting the minimum standards. Due to budget cuts, the public sector has drastically reduced much of its food inspection and monitoring activities. Certain of these have been taken over by the industry, but some believed that monitoring food safety placed an extra burden on retailers, particularly given the potential legal liabilities.

The legal liability framework has had a significant influence on the structure and implementation of food safety procedures. On this issue, a number of those interviewed remarked that their main concern was: 'What do I need to show in a court of law to demonstrate that I have undertaken all possible measures to ensure product safety?' As a precautionary move, many firms have extended their list of food safety requirements, including possible allergens, food contaminants, handling and processing procedures, etc.

All firms reported a willingness to be more involved with governments in collaborative schemes to ensure food safety and even to move beyond to other attributes. Some felt there was substantial opportunity for private–public partnerships in formulating guiding principles that would promote better efficiency of the system. The industry considers governments often too cautious, cumbersome and not very efficient when problems arise that need urgent resolution. It was felt that governments must understand how the food system actually operates, in concrete terms, from the initial stages to the retail level.

Conformity assessment

To assess compliance with a given standard, retailers use a combination of in-house and third party audits. How compliance to a given standard is audited and enforced is essential to the credibility of the standards as well as to the efficacy of the standard in achieving its goals. While food safety management protocols are well known and documented, they often require specialized, experienced auditors for a given product. This renders certification and auditing difficult outside the home country, especially in those countries without long-term experience in this area.

For the newer areas such as environment, animal welfare and social conditions, the problems of certification are amplified. Few specialized auditors for social and labour standards exist and this complicates the task of setting up and enforcing such a standard. The certification issue raises the importance of accreditation bodies and their functioning, which are key factors in ensuring that imposed standards are actually met.

Henson and Heasman (1998) suggested that it is imperative to understand the compliance process of firms to be able to promulgate efficient and effective food safety regulations. Most retailers use a variety of the benchmarked schemes for certifying food products. The aim of most retailers interviewed is to have 90% of all food products certified over the next 3–5 years. This is at present required for almost all products from developing countries, but not yet for local products. The two main reasons given for the lower certification level for local producers are their long-term satisfactory relationship with the local suppliers and the lower risk nature of the products.

Future developments

All retailers interviewed expected both private and government standards to become more stringent, with more precisely identified process standards. Private standards were also expected to be extended to include labour conditions, environment and even health issues. For these to be truly effective over all supplies, they need to be harmonized. However, defining the right criteria is likely to be contentious and certainly less straightforward than for food safety, where science-based criteria and risk analysis can be used as a reference.

Retailers agreed that if food safety standards were rigorously applied, most risks could be avoided, but given a non-zero risk, greater emphasis would now be on tracing and tracking. Information and communication technology innovations are seen to continue to assist in meeting the challenges of ensuring the monitoring of the standards compliance in the food chain.

Despite difficulties in defining a common set of social and labour standards, as well as in enforcing these beyond national boundaries, this is viewed as the next major challenge for retailers. For products sourced from developing countries, labour standards have already been a source of concern given their inability to control conditions more than one step back up the chain. The increased tendency for exporters in developing countries to outsource production means that increased vigilance is needed. The negative reputation effects for failure in this area may provide incentives for another retailer-based collaborative initiative similar to the GFSI, but with labour standards as its core focus.

Environmental standards, both at the primary producer and manufacturing levels, are also expected to gain importance in the near future, but no specific programmes were cited. However, environmental standards are expected to affect manufacturing practices in energy and water use, as well as in packaging and distribution. Although animal welfare standards were also expected to increase generally, there will probably remain significant differences between countries.

With global sourcing expected to continue to rise, the need for standards and their harmonization is being felt by a majority of retailers. One of the most important benefits of harmonizing standards will be in the uniformity or equivalence of a recognized level of given attributes such as food safety, environmental effects or labour conditions. Almost all retailers would like to have one harmonized standard for each attribute. The most important – food safety – for which there is a scientific basis, has been difficult to achieve, so what can be expected for less scientifically based criteria?

Harmonization would decrease certification costs for suppliers, relieving them of the need to have separate certification for each buyer. It could also permit retailers to switch suppliers and source easily across the globe, and this could facilitate trade and increase efficiency in the food system.

Certification procedures and auditor accreditation is another area where there was an expressed urgent need to harmonize what is certified and how. The importance of certification procedures and quality of auditors was seen to be a very important issue that needed resolving in the near future in order to maintain the integrity of the entire standards system. It is important that what an auditor certifies in country A would be certified in the same way in country B. For some, this is as important an issue as defining the standard, since it is at the operational level that conformity is assessed. In the future, developing countries will be held to the same rigour in audits as are OECD countries.

Shaping the Agri-food System

Within an increasingly competitive agri-food system, compliance with specific global private standards schemes is rapidly becoming a requirement for doing business with lead retailers. This makes them important tools in potentially shaping the global food system, by determining what, how, where and with whom production occurs. From a purely economic perspective this would reduce bias of 'local or national' standards and permit greater coordination of production and distribution across the globe, with expected economies of scale and efficiency gains (Sykes, 1995).

From a simple trade perspective, this should also imply increasing flows of goods between countries. But, as there are wide divergences in supplier and country capacity in meeting these global private standards, they may exclude a wide number of potential suppliers or create two types of suppliers: those able to supply lead firms and those supplying the independent fringe.

The switch from purely product standards to process standards, along with a quality management system, presents new challenges for public and private governance at the local and global levels. Moreover, these private standards are increasingly set by private initiatives – often with the same aims as those of public authorities – and are becoming global standards as the food system becomes interlinked across the world through trade.

This evolution may weigh more heavily on small and medium farms/firms that are often unable to meet the stringent technical conditions or lack sufficient management skills. This, in turn, may generate an increasing divergence between producers within a given country, as well as between similar-sized producers between countries. Nevertheless, the technical capacity for meeting product standards at the farm level represents only the initial step in satisfying lead retailer requirements. Supplying lead retailers also requires the ability to implement modern supply logistics from farm to retail, to use technologically advanced tracking and tracing systems as well as to ensure delivery of required quantities at specific times.

Retailer requirements thus extend beyond traditional product specifications. Meeting these demands requires a well-organized, operating economy and agricultural sector with access to public physical and institutional infrastructure, including services.

For producers in many developing countries, particularly in those without well-developed infrastructures in telecommunications, energy and transport or lacking marketing assistance, these standards can be exclusionary (Humphrey, 2005, unpublished results). Countries such as Chile, South Africa or Brazil whose agricultural export sectors measure up to lead retailers requirements have access to these retailers, but how will infrastructurally poor and institutionally weak countries fare in this new system? Some do well, in spite of weak physical and institutional infrastructures, such as Peru or Kenya. These can compete with the leading suppliers across the globe. What factors have made the difference for these countries? For those who cannot meet these requirements, what are the alternatives?

Not all food consumed passes through the lead retailers: smaller chains and local markets remain important. Work by Chen (2003) underlines how independents or smaller chains are providing countervailing weight to lead retailers, even in developed economies such as that of the USA. These establishments, along with traditional small shops and open markets, do not require certification from the top-end private standard schemes. Most require only minimum legal food safety standards, with testing and approval being carried out by the government as part of a public service or by buyers. In developing countries these account for the largest share of the market. Even lead retailers, when operating in the South, do not enforce the same standards as in the North. This is often because of lack of supply of such products or less exacting consumers.

This heterogeneity in retailer demands reflects differences in consumer preferences and expenditure capacities, and thus parallel systems can exist as long as consumer heterogeneity exists (Farina *et al.*, 2004). This reasoning can also hold true for discussions regarding international trade. For some it may be more advantageous to enter markets and food distribution systems with less than the highest standards and build up management and technical competencies. While these fringe food retailers may increase their standards over time as standards diffuse from the lead to others, the present differential may provide a window of opportunity for producers to adapt gradually.

Conclusions

The development and use of the private standards discussed in this chapter is a key element in the organization of sourcing of supplies across the globe. Private standard schemes of lead retailers are the result of retailer coalitions, frequently used in a B2B context, and characterized by quality management systems. The collaboration between retailers in promoting similar goals of product safety and production process attributes signals a desire to find new ways of governing the food chain without vertical integration or coordination. Thus, in moving from a focus on the product attributes to incorporating these requirements in a wider quality management system, control over process and product is deepened, but not the financial responsibility.

Retailer private standards schemes are developed to ensure supplies meet specific criteria no matter where they are sourced and thus to increase flexibility in sourcing across the globe. This development also means that supplier costs of multiple certificates attesting to fulfilment of the same attribute or process could be reduced, as could testing and audits. They also increase supplier flexibility by permitting suppliers to sell to multiple retailers through increased product substitutability; but they may also increase competition between suppliers to provide better and cheaper standards-compliant products to retailers. Furthermore, as the outlook is for an increasing stringency in standards, this competition is likely to increase.

Private standards also require technical and managerial capacities that are often complex and costly to set up. For instance, tracing and tracking requirements to fulfil regulatory traceability requirements become capital- and technology-intensive and go beyond simple record keeping. The use of modern supply logistics has increased and may become a requirement for entry to the retailer supply system.

Since private standards of lead retailers are likely to become more stringent and expand to a variety of areas according to retailers themselves, potential suppliers seem to have little choice but to adapt to these demands if they wish to supply these retailers. The question that remains is: to what extent will lead retailer standards dominate all food markets in time, either due to the diffusion of these standards to fringe markets or to the disappearance of these fringe markets?

Notes

1 This paper is based on work for the Directorate for Food, Agriculture and Fisheries of the OECD. The opinions expressed are the sole responsibility of the author and do not reflect those of the member states of the OECD.
2 This can include such events as dealing with suppliers who exploit labour in developing countries or engaging in environmentally harmful production practices.
3 In certain industries, such as automotive or aircraft, it is normal practice for private standards to be set by industry and to be subsequently adopted by governments as regulatory requirements, or to operate within a complementary framework.
4 Both the increase in food safety incidents and a weakening of consumer confidence in regulators' abilities to deal with these have provided incentives for leading retailers to develop 'quality' management systems whose objective is to ensure the integrity, traceability, safety and quality of food. These systems and their certification procedures ensure that producers have in place an operating system that minimizes risk and ensures 'quality'.
5 Standards for products facilitate communication and reduce transaction costs for arm's-length transactions. Many products now have attributes that rely on certification or trust in labels and the management system underlying them. These include attributes such as animal welfare, organic and environmentally sustainable practices and labour conditions.
6 All products leaving the farm if packaged, boxed, washed or trimmed fall within the GMP scheme. GAP schemes deal only with production at the farm level.

References

Arora, S. and Gangopadhyay, S. (1995) Towards a theoretical model of voluntary over compliance. *Journal of Economic Behaviour and Organization* 28, 289–309.
Boom, A. (1995) Asymmetric international minimum quality standards and vertical differentiation. *Journal of Industrial Economics* 43, 101–119.
Casella, A. (2001) Product standards and international trade: harmonization through private coalitions? *Kyklos* 54, 243–264.
Caswell, J. and Hooker, N. (1996) HACCP as an international trade standard. *American Journal of Agricultural Economics* 78, 775–796.
Chen, A. (2003) Dominant retailers and the countervailing–power hypothesis. *RAND Journal of Economics.* 34, 612–625.
Dobson, P. (2003) Buyer power in food retailing: the European experience. http://webdomino1.oecd.org/comnet/agr/foodeco.nsf/viewHtml/index/$FILE/DobsonPaper.pdf (accessed 27 February 2006).
Dobson, P. and Waterson, M. (1999) Retailer power: recent developments and policy implications. *Economic Policy* 28, 134–164.
Dolan, C. and Humphrey, J. (2001) Governance and trade in fresh vegetables: the impact of UK supermarkets on the African horticulture industry. *Journal of International Economics* 10, 147–176.
Farina, E.M.M.Q., Nunes, R. and Monteiro, G.A.F. (2004) Rapid rise of supermarkets and the use of standards in their food product procurement systems in developing countries. *Working Paper, Department of Economics*, University of San Paolo, Brazil.
Gereffi, G. (1999) International upgrading in the apparel commodity chain. *Journal of International Economics* 48, 37–70.
Grievink, J.-W. (2003) The changing face of the global food supply chain. http://webdomino1. oecd.org/comnet/agr/foodeco.nsf/viewHtml/index/$FILE/GrievinkAb.pdf (accessed 27 February 2006).
Henson, S.J. and Heasman, M. (1998) Food safety regulation and the firm: understanding the compliance process. *Food Policy* 23, 9–23.
Humphrey, J. and Schmitz, H. (2001) Governance in global value chains. *IDS Bulletin* 32 (3), http://www.globalvalue chains.org/publications/ HumphreyScmitz.pdf

Kinsey, J. (2003) Emerging trends in the new food economy: consumers, firms and science. http://web-domino1.oecd.org/comnet/agr/foodeco.nsf/viewHtml/index/$FILE/KinseyPaper.pdf (accessed 27 February 2006).

Lehman-Grube, U. (1997) Strategic choice of quality when quality is costly: the persistence of the high quality advantage. *The Rand Journal of Economics* 28, 372–384.

Lutz, S., Lyon, T.P. and Maxwell, J. (2000) Quality leadership when regulatory standards are forthcoming. *The Journal of Industrial Economics* 48, 331–348.

Nadvi, K. and Waltring, F. (2003) Making sense of global standards. In: Schmitz, H. (ed.) *Local Enterprises in the Global Economy: Issues of Governance and Upgrading*. Elgar, Cheltenham, UK.

Porter, M. (1990) *The Competitive Advantage of Nations*. MacMillan, London.

Reardon, T. and Berdegué, J.A. (2002) The rapid rise of supermarkets in Latin America: challenges and opportunities for development. *Development Policy Review* 20, 317–334.

Reardon, T. and Farina, E.M.M.Q. (2002) The rise of private food quality and safety standards: illustrations from Brazil. *International Food and Agricultural Management Review* 4, 413–431.

Reardon, T. and Timmer, C.P. (In press; expected 2007>) Transformation of markets for agricultural output in developing countries since 1950: how have things changed? In: Evenson, R., Pingali, P. and Schultz, T.P. (eds) *Handbook of Agricultural Economics: Agricultural Development*, Vol. 3, Elsevier, Holland (In press).

Ronnen, U. (1991) Minimum quality standards, fixed costs and competition. *The Rand Journal of Economics* 22, 490–501.

Shaked, A. and Sutton, J. (1982) Relaxing price competition through product differentiation. *The Review of Economic Studies* 49, 3–13.

Sykes, A.O. (1995) *Product Standards for Internationally Integrated Goods*. Brookings Institution Press, Washington, DC.

3 Public and Private Food Quality Standards: Recent Trends and Strategic Incentives

J.J. McCluskey

Introduction

Food quality standards and the ability to trace food within the supply chain have become increasingly important, from both the producer and consumer sides. Historically, public food quality standards were set by the government with the objectives of: (i) safety from threats to life and health; and (ii) prevention of food adulteration and misbranding (Gardner, 2003). However, in recent years, it is the private rather than public standards that are becoming the dominant drivers of the agri-food system (Henson and Hooker, 2001).

In this chapter, the recent growth of both public and private food quality standards and the factors driving this growth are discussed, including strategic incentives for setting private quality standards. The argument is that a firm restricts itself with private standards in order to choose the form of standards. With wide-ranging possible quality standards, firms choose the private quality standards that minimize their own costs before governments or international organizations do so.

Other researchers have studied incentives for firms to push for stricter public quality regulations or to over-comply with public quality standards. In their seminal paper, Salop and Scheffman (1983) showed that a firm might want stricter regulations if complying with them is relatively costlier for its rivals. Maloney and McCormick (1982) show that an industry might lobby for tighter legal standards if tighter standards are a barrier to entry. However, neither of these articles considered establishing private quality standards or type of standard chosen. Both Arora and Gangopadhyay (1995) and Kirchhoff (2000) analyse voluntary over-compliance with environmental regulations based on an environmental premium in the market.

Self-regulation is a topic related to private quality standards and has been studied in the environmental economics literature (Arora and Cason, 1995; Maxwell et al., 2000), the agricultural economics literature (Zago, 1999) and in the law enforcement literature (Kaplow and Shavell, 1994; Innes, 1999). Malik (1993) shows that self-regulation can be beneficial to societal welfare if auditing costs and monitoring accuracy are sufficiently high.

The current chapter adds to this literature

by discussing the firm's incentive to strategically pre-empt government regulations with private quality standards by choosing the form of standards. Lutz et al. (2000) used a duopoly model of vertical product differentiation to show that if a high-quality firm can commit to a quality level before public regulations are promulgated, it induces the regulator to weaken standards. The current chapter differs because it focuses on the form or type of standards rather than the overall level of strictness.

The Recent Growth of Public and Private Food Standards

In general, both consumer expectations of food quality and concerns about food risk are increasing. Both governments and the private sector have responded. This has resulted in an abundance of food standards and certifications concerning safety, nutrition, characteristics, geographic origin, organic status and other attributes, as firms try to position their products in the market for high-value foods.

In the public sphere standards have increased and tightened, with a greater emphasis on science as a basis for standards and a systems approach. A key example is the Hazard Analysis and Critical Control Point (HACCP) food safety programme. HACCP applies science-based controls to prevent hazards that could introduce food-born illnesses at the point where the hazards initially occur. HACCP was adopted in the USA in the late 1990s and has been recognized internationally by the Codex Alimentarius commission.

Internationally, there is a growing proliferation of food standards and certifications. As Henson and Reardon (2005) discussed, quality meta-systems (such as the ISO 9000 series) are embedded in voluntary public standards at the national and/or international levels. The ISO 9000 series of quality management standards was developed to create a framework of the fundamental generic elements that would form the basis for a series of internationally recognized quality management standards (Jobwerx.com, 2006). It is in use in many countries and is increasingly becoming a requirement for food manufacturers in order to sell their products. Other quality meta-systems include good manufacturing practice (GMP) and good agricultural practice (GAP) (Henson and Reardon, 2005).

Geographical identifications (GIs) can also be thought of as food quality standards. As specialty, regional, authentic and local food products have become a more important part of consumer purchases in recent years, firms have responded by marketing food products that come from specific geographic areas. This trend has led to a greater reliance on GIs. In 1992, the European Union (EU) passed a package of legislation (EC Regulations 2081/92 and 2082/92), which provides protection of food names on a geographical basis. The categories of protected food products recognized in this regulation are protected designation of origin (PDO) and protected geographical indications (PGI), and each protected product has its own standards. These programmes promote regional and 'traditional' products in unique, value-added niche markets and help preserve traditional production that otherwise might disappear in a competitive market.

An example of a PGI is 'Galician Veal' (*Ternera Gallega*) from Spain. The quality standards for production of this product are quite strict. They include such measures as: (i) the feed must be traditional and natural; and (ii) it is prohibited to treat the animals with products that speed their growth and development (such as hormones) or provide feed derived from other animals.

As concern about genetically modified (GM) foods has increased, GM labelling standards are receiving more attention. Individual countries or groups of countries have set their own standards or thresholds for GM food products, ranging from the USA (which does not require labelling of GM products) to outright bans in some countries. The disparity in standards can and has resulted in trade disputes. The challenge of Codex will be to find the best possible set of international standards for GM food labelling that still allow fair trade, consumer choice and innovation (Kalaitzandonakes and Phillips, 2000).

Two new US laws that are currently having the greatest and most immediate impact on the food supply chain are Country of Origin Labeling (COOL) and the US Bio-terrorism and Response Acts of 2002. The COOL Act requires labelling for beef, lamb, pork, fish, perishable agricultural commodities and peanuts. The implementation of mandatory COOL for all covered commodities (except for wild and farm-raised fish and shellfish) has been delayed until 30 September 2006. Although many food industry firms were originally positive about COOL owing to the potential gains from marketing their products as 'made in the USA', many lobbied for the delay in implementation because of concern about high costs of compliance.

The US Bio-terrorism and Response Act of 2002 requires the establishment and maintenance of records by persons who manufacture, process, pack, transport, distribute, receive, hold or import food in the USA. Like HACCP, this Act creates standards in documentation and traceability in the production process.

Private standards have been evolving which address quality, environmental and social concerns. Producer groups market products which explicitly claim that the products were produced with sound environmental, animal welfare and fair labour practices. The environmentally friendly marketing movement is already successful and growing rapidly. For example, the German eco-label, Blue Angel (*Blauer Engel*), introduced in 1978, has become a successful instrument in environmental protection and marketing. Nearly 4000 certified products use it.

The Euro-ecolabel, launched in 1998, regulates and sets common standards for all eco-labels in the EU countries. In the USA, eco-labels are proliferating rapidly with programmes such as Green Seal, Scientific Certification Systems and the US Environmental Protection Agency's Energy Star Program. In addition, many regional sustainable agriculture programmes set standards to assure acceptance in regional niche markets for 'green' products.

Finally, with the expansion of premium food products (often with premium prices) in many categories from coffee to salt, it is an easy argument to make that consumers expect higher quality in their food purchases. It follows that there is a greater focus on private standards and codes of practice, which are becoming a requirement in order to do business. McCluskey and O'Rourke (2000) found an increased emphasis by major food retail buyers on product specifications. This does not necessarily mean that higher quality is being demanded. Rather, the buyers want to pay for exactly what they were receiving, and they want the product much more strictly defined than it was in the past. Further, as will be discussed below, consolidation in the food retail sector has given the major food retailers the bargaining power to define these private standards.

Reasons for the Growth in Public Food Standards

New government food regulations are being enacted as consumers are becoming more concerned about health and food safety, resource sustainability and other environmental issues. Also, as in the case of the US Bio-terrorism and Response Act of 2002, governments respond to an intentional outside threat. Consumers want to know the most basic information about 'what it is, how it was produced, and where it is from' throughout the supply chain. They want to know the origin of their food and they often prefer locally produced products. They are concerned about food safety issues, such as contaminated meat. By setting standards and ensuring accurate provision of information, governments create greater accountability for the food industry by discouraging irresponsible activities and rewarding beneficial and sustainable endeavors.

Further, public regulations can correct market failure. For example, before the US Department of Agriculture (USDA) set its national organic standards, there was no national definition of what constituted an organic food product. Under the previous system, some organic foods were certified under state and private certification programmes, and consumers were often confused about what the term 'organic' actually meant, which opens the door for 'lemons' and/or fraud. Consumers benefit if standardization and increased consumer confidence in quality cause markets to expand and to become more efficient. Finally, governments have advantages in setting public standards compared with private standards. Regulators can easily establish a single standard – such as organic – with certainty and prosecute violators under criminal law.

The Reasons for the Growth in Private Food Standards Despite the Existence of Public Standards

Flexibility in response to a changing environment

As introduced earlier, the food distribution system continues to change at a rapid rate. New formats continue to evolve, consolidation has increased among major retail food chains and new technology is constantly being introduced. A drawback of public standards is their lack of flexibility. Public standards do not adjust to changes in consumer preferences or technology.

As consumer tastes and preferences continue to change, the private sector has responded to ensure consumer satisfaction. To be successful in this new food distribution system requires retailers to display market leadership, carry strong brands, establish a good reputation for quality and price and to exhibit flexibility and adaptability.

A number of different forces are at work in the food supply chain. Among these forces are: (i) the increased level of mergers and acquisitions between retail grocery store chains; (ii) internal growth and expansion into food within both retail grocery store chains and retail discount stores; and (iii) technology and innovation. The expansion of Wal-Mart has been a catalyst for many of these changes. Wal-Mart built much of its success on the use of information technology to control costs in every part of its system, thus allowing it to sell at everyday low prices (EDLP), which drew in an ever-expanding pool of customers. Wal-Mart brought its purchasing might, logistics expertise and category management skills to the food retailing business.

The Wal-Mart threat forced traditional retailers to rethink their current mode of operation. Traditionally, supermarkets competed for customers by building ever-larger outlets, stocking an ever-increasing array of items and adding many peripheral services. They attempted to buy most items on deal (i.e. when the seller offered a discount for volume purchases) and to have extensive (and costly) inventories in the system. The first major shock to this system was when Procter and Gamble unilaterally in 1992 announced that it was switching to EDLP and would no longer sell on deal.

Traditional players in the food supply chain formed a working group to evaluate the inefficiencies of the supply chain as configured at that time and to develop strategies to improve the system to counter the competition created by the non-traditional food retailers like Wal-Mart. The outcome was the Efficient Consumer Response (ECR) initiative, which forced suppliers and retailers to work together to reduce costs and enhance profits while better serving consumers.

Vertical alliances in the food distribution system became common. It encouraged the adoption of information technology to better identify inefficiencies. Some of the applications are in category management and activity-based costing, enabling both supplier and retailer to identify opportunities for lowering costs or enhancing value to consumers. In this new food retail environment there are higher standards, by necessity, of supply chain traceability.

Strategic incentives for private standards

In this section, strategic incentives for private standard setting in order to pre-empt public regulations are analysed. This section makes arguments based on the model presented in McCluskey (2006). First, we assume that standards are multi-faceted (such as a vector of standards) and that different types of standards within this vector will affect firm revenues differently, depending on the firm's competitive advantage. The initial endowments of a firm will affect how the types of standards impinge on revenues. For example, the choice of standards for a firm located in an industrialized country might be different from the choice of standards for a firm located in a lesser developed country.

We also assume that the public's perception of desirable food quality standards is a function of its preferred characteristics that affect the product's taste, appearance, odour and texture, the number and severity of food contamination incidents and the cost of implementing these standards. We assume that the public regulator's objective is to be perceived as being fair and competent by the public and the international community. It meets this objective by minimizing the absolute value of the difference between the total standards imposed (the binding, self-imposed private quality standards plus the binding public standards) and the public's view of the appropriate standards.

Since the firm knows the public regulator's objective and is able to set the private standards first, the firm is able to minimize its costs. Therefore, if the firm sets private standards, the public regulator's additional standards are given by the maximum of the difference between the total standards imposed (the binding, self-imposed private quality standards plus the binding public standards) and the public's view of the appropriate standards and zero, which means no additional public standards.

It follows that the final quality standard is given by the sum of the public and private standards, with no distinction between the standard given by the public regulator and the private standard that the firm gives itself. However, this is important to the firm, and we illustrate this with the firm's net revenue function. The firm's revenue function is a decreasing function with respect to both public and private standards. The stricter standard the firm receives, the lower its revenues will be. However, since standards are multi-faceted, different types of standards will affect revenues differently. Since the firm can choose its private standards, it should choose the standard that marginally decreases revenue the least.

In this setup, there is an optimal set of private standards for the firm. The firm has an incentive to choose the set of private standards which results in the lowest expected final damages from standards for the firm, subject to the condition that the set must be at a level in which the public regulator will accept the standards and not add any additional standards. If the private standards have not yet reached that point, creating additional private standards will increase revenues. However, if the private standards are already stringent enough so that the public regulator will not impose additional standards, adding or increasing private standards will decrease revenue.

We can now calculate how a private standard affects the final standard. In the simple case in which there is no additional standard imposed by the public regulator, the final standard will simply be the private standard. In this case, the increase in one type of standard will have no marginal effect on other types of standards. However, if the private standards are lax enough so that the public regulator imposes additional (stricter) standards, the effects of private standards are clear. In this case, increasing one type of standard in the standards vector increases that particular type of standard in the final set of standards, but decreases the other types of standards. Therefore, since public regulators often impose additional standards, we expect private standards to increase the type of standard that it has given itself, but to decrease other types.

An example of strategic private standards from a non-food industry is the Motion Picture Association of America and its international counterpart, the Motion Picture Association, which serve as the voice and advocate of the motion picture industry. This private association sets its own private standards for film ratings, and public regulators do not rate films.

Conclusions and Discussion

In this chapter, the recent growth of both public and private food quality standards and the factors driving this growth have been discussed, including strategic incentives for setting private quality standards. It is argued that firms may set private quality standards in order to choose the form of quality standards. If firms choose their standards, they can do so in a way that minimizes their costs.

The issue of who defines the standards, of course, has implications for international trade. Unless standards do not impose a binding constraint on producers, meeting them will increase production costs. The cost of meeting the standards will differ depending on a country's comparative advantage. Consequently, firms in one country may push for standards because that would raise its rivals' costs more than their own costs, perhaps to the extent of effectively making a particular country unable to compete.

It is often the case that private standards become the industry standard. When one firm implements a voluntary standard, then all other firms may 'voluntarily' have to follow in order for supermarkets to carry their products. The end result is the same as if a public regulation had been imposed. For example, 'dolphin-safe' tuna is a purely voluntary designation, but tuna without the 'dolphin safe' label has disappeared from grocery shelves in the USA. Since the private standards can become de facto industry standards, can we trust the market to act in the public interest? Will industry standards give specific countries advantages in the international market? There are also trade-offs involved with setting public standards, including the loss of flexibility and lack of incentives for innovation.

Who defines the standards also has implications for economic development because different types of standards will affect firms' revenues differently depending on its initial endowments. Since the leading multi-national food retailers are located in industrialized countries, the private standards that become the industry standards will probably be different from the choice of standards for a firm located in a lesser developed country.

References

Arora, S. and Gangopadhyay, S. (1995) Towards a theoretical model of voluntary overcompliance. *Journal of Economic Behavior and Organization* 28, 298–309.

Arora, S. and Cason, T. (1995) An experiment in voluntary environmental regulation: participation in EPA's 33/50 programme. *Journal of Environmental Economics and Management* 28, 271–286.

Gardner, B. (2003) US food quality standards: fix for market failure or costly anachronism? *American Journal of Agricultural Economics* 85, 725–730.

Henson, S.J. and Hooker, N. (2001) Private sector management of food safety: public regulation and the role of private controls. *International Food and Agribusiness Management Review* 4, 7–17.

Henson, S. and Reardon, T. (2005) Private agri-food standards: implications for food policy and the agri-food system. *Food Policy* 30, 241–253.

Innes, R. (1999) Self-policing and optimal law enforcement when firm remediation is valuable. *Journal of Political Economy* 107, 1305–1325.

Jobwerx.com (2006) Quality systems – ISO 9000. http://www.jobwerx.com/quality/ISO9000.htm (accessed 2 March 2006).

Kalaitzandonakes, N. and Phillips, P.W.B. (2000) GM food labelling and the role of the codex. *AgBioForum* 3, http://www.agbioforum.org/v3n4/ index.htm (accessed 11 April 2006).

Kaplow, L. and Shavell, S. (1994) Optimal law enforcement with self-reporting of behaviour. *Journal of Political Economy* 102, 583–606.

Kirchhoff, S. (2000) Green business and blue angels: a model of voluntary overcompliance with asymmetric information. *Environmental and Resource Economics* 15, 403–420.

Lutz, S., Lyon, T.P. and Maxwell, J.W. (2000) Quality leadership when regulatory standards are forthcoming. *Journal of Industrial Economics* 48, 331–348.

Malik, A. (1993) Self-reporting and the design of policies for regulating stochastic pollution. *Journal of Environmental Economics and Management* 24, 241–257.

Maloney, M.T. and McCormick, R.E. (1982) A positive theory of environmental quality regulation. *Journal of Law and Economics* 25, 99–123.

Maxwell, J., Lyon, T. and Hackett, S. (2000) Self-regulation and social welfare: the political economy of corporate environmentalism. *Journal of Law and Economics* 43, 583–617.

McCluskey, J.J. (2006) Pre-empting public regulation with private food quality standards. Working Paper, Washington State University, Pullman, Washington.

McCluskey, J.J. and O'Rourke, A.D. (2000) Relationships between produce supply firms and retailers in the new food supply chain. *Journal of Food Distribution Research* 31, 11–20.

Salop, S.C. and Scheffman, D.T. (1983) Raising rivals' costs. *American Economic Review* 73, 267–271.

Zago, A. (1999) Quality and self-regulation in agricultural markets. *European Review of Agricultural Economics* 26, 199–218.

4 The Costs and Benefits of Compliance with Food Safety Standards for Exports by Developing Countries: the Case of Fish and Fishery Products

S. Henson and S. Jaffee

Introduction

Exports of fish and fishery products are widely seen as a developing country success story and a welcome contrast to the cyclical decline in markets for traditional agricultural commodities and natural resources. Over the period 1980/1981–2003/2004, exports of fish and fishery products from developing and transition economies increased from US$5.5 billion to US$37.3 billion.[1] Over this same period, the share of total agri-food exports from developing countries rose from 6.6 to 15.4%. Many developing countries are active in this trade. In 2003/2004, 20 such countries had fish product exports exceeding US$100 million per annum, while an additional 22 countries had fish exports exceeding US$25 million.

One of the major challenges facing developing country exports of fish and fishery products is progressively stricter food safety requirements, particularly in major markets such as the European Union (EU) and the USA of America (USA). Previous studies suggest that exporters in a number of developing countries have experienced problems complying with these requirements and/or incurred considerable costs in achieving such compliance (see, for example, Cato and Lima dos Santos, 1998a, b; Henson et al., 2000; Musonda and Mbowe, 2001; Rahman, 2001; UNEP, 2001a, b; Zaramba, 2002; Ponte, 2005).

In much of the prevailing debate over the impact of food safety standards on developing countries this has proved to be a contentious issue, based on perceptions that either the required measures are unnecessary or scientifically unjustified, or that they yield little or no benefit to those countries and suppliers who undertake the required changes.

This chapter explores the food safety standards facing developing country exporters of fish and fishery products supplying the EU and the USA. It argues that, while the required changes to existing control systems and investments in enhanced testing and production capacity may be considerable, the returns in terms of continued export market access are typically significant. In many countries these upgrades and investments are, arguably, long overdue. While some exporters find the associated costs of compliance prohibitive, or choose to devote their resources elsewhere, remaining firms can gain competitive advantage and/or other offsetting benefits. The cases reported below, therefore, paint a rather different picture to the 'standards as barriers' perspective that is typical of many previous commentaries on the impact of food safety standards on developing country exports.[2]

Food Safety Standards for Fish and Fishery Products

Export-oriented supply chains for fish and fishery products (hereafter referred to collectively as 'fish products') are subject to regulatory and customer requirements both domestically and in major export markets. The predominant requirements for fish products relate to food safety, in particular to standards of hygiene in production and marketing and limits on levels of microbiological contamination in the end product.

Furthermore, limits are being applied on environmental contaminants, including heavy metals and agro-chemical residues, and on the use of antibiotics in aquaculture. In some markets, grades and quality standards are also applied, although these are generally restricted to the major fish species in world trade.

Broadly, the food safety standards associated with fish products are distinct, both quantitatively and qualitatively, to those applied to many traditional agricultural commodities, often requiring fundamental changes to prevailing modes of food safety control. Given that the predominant export flows for fish products are from developing to industrialized countries, it is the latter that define the food safety control landscape in which developing country exporters must operate.

For example, the EU (on which much of the discussion below focuses) lays down harmonized requirements governing hygiene in the capture, processing, transportation and storage of fish products under Directive 91/493/EEC. EU legislation lays down detailed requirements regarding the landing of fish, structure of wholesale and auction markets and processing facilities, processing operations, transportation, storage, packaging, quality checks on finished products, laboratory testing facilities and water quality. More generally, the EU requires that fish-processing facilities undertake 'own checks', broadly based on the principle of Hazard Analysis and Critical Control Point (HACCP).

Processing plants are inspected and approved on an individual basis by a specified 'Competent Authority' in the country of origin, to ensure that they comply with these requirements. The European Commission – through its Food and Veterinary Office (FVO) – undertakes checks to ensure that the Competent Authority undertakes this task in a satisfactory manner and to ensure that provisions of Directive 91/493/EEC are complied with. Imports from non-EU countries are required to comply with requirements that are at least equivalent to those of the EU.

Furthermore, specific import conditions are established according to the particular health situation of each exporting country. In most cases the European Commission undertakes periodic inspections for the purposes of determining local health conditions and of establishing specific import conditions for the country concerned. And, within these countries, only processing establishments that are specifically approved by the Competent Authority are permitted to export to the EU.

Countries whose systems are deemed to be at least equivalent to those in the EU will have their fish consignments subjected to reduced physical inspection at EU entry points. Countries for which these procedures have not been completed, but where assurances have been given that requirements are at least equivalent to those in the EU, are permitted to export on an interim basis. Consignments must still be accompanied by a health certification.

Initially, the deadline for countries to be specifically approved by the European Commission was 31 December 1996. However, this has repeatedly been extended. This reflects not only the difficulties that a number of countries have experienced complying with EU hygiene standards for fish products, but also the considerable time and resources required for the European Commission to undertake inspections in order to establish specific import requirements.[3]

Costs and Benefits of Compliance with Food Safety Standards

The trade and other economic impacts of food safety standards for fish products are related to the incidence and level of 'compliance costs' incurred by government and the private sector. Such costs are the focus of concern that developing countries are disadvantaged in complying with such standards. In some cases, the prevailing capacity may be so weak as to require very substantial investment to attain compliance; in other cases, incremental, recurrent costs may undermine exporter competitiveness. In practice, however, the costs of compliance for developing countries have rarely even been estimated.[4] This lack of data reflects the considerable difficulties associated with such calculations.

In the context of trade, compliance costs are defined as the additional costs necessarily incurred by government and/or private enterprises in meeting the requirements to comply with a given standard in a given external market. This refers not only to the costs associated with compliance *per se* but also to the range of strategic responses to evolving food safety standards (World Bank, 2005a).

There are two key elements to this definition. First, it covers the costs that are 'additional' to those which would otherwise have been incurred by government and/or the private sector in the absence of the standard. Secondly, it refers to those costs that are 'necessarily' incurred in complying with the standard. It is these two concepts that create many of the problems associated with estimation of compliance costs.

In the case of regulatory requirements in international trade, costs are imposed on both the public and private sectors. In order to establish a 'competent authority' recognized by trading partners, government controls may need to be strengthened and institutional structures reformed. Processors may have to upgrade their procurement systems or hygiene controls in their food processes. In some cases, the actions of the public and private sectors may substitute for one another (for example, private laboratory testing instead of public testing); in other cases they may complement one another (for example, improved public testing procedures alongside better management of hygiene in processing). The costs and benefits associated with both public and private actions need to be ascertained.

An important distinction is made according to the level of recurrence of compliance costs. Non-recurring costs are the one-off or time-limited investments made in order to be able to achieve compliance (see Table 4.1). Typically, these include the upgrading of laboratory infrastructure and processing facilities, establishing new procedures and the associated training of personnel, or the costs of designing new management systems such as the HACCP system for processors. Some of these are 'lumpy' investments for which there may be significant economies of scale.

In contrast, recurring costs are borne over time and include the costs of maintaining regular surveillance and laboratory testing programmes and the additional production costs associated with enhanced food safety controls. For some functions, non-recurring and recurring costs are substitutes for one another. For example,

Table 4.1. Examples of recurring and non-recurring costs of compliance.

Tangible	Intangible
Non-recurring	
Upgrading of laboratory infrastructure	Reduced investment in new product development
Upgrading of processing facilities	Reduced investment in domestic food safety controls
Investments in upgraded boats and landing facilities to comply with hygiene standards	Reduced flexibility in production processes
Recurring	
Costs of sample collection and laboratory analysis	Reduced enforcement of domestic food safety controls
Additional procurement costs for buying raw materials that meet hygiene standards	Reduced flexibility in production processes
Additional overhead costs for implementing HACCP	Reduced enforcement of domestic food safety controls

an individual exporter can choose between using an external laboratory to undertake routine product and input testing or establishing its own laboratory facilities that permit such tests to be undertaken at a lower unit cost.[5]

Recurring and non-recurring costs can impede trade in a somewhat different manner and also influence the potential benefits that might flow from alternative strategic choices related to compliance. For example, 'first movers' might realize significant advantages if non-recurring costs are high and they have the resources to make needed investments ahead of their competitors. Yet, significant recurring costs can impede competitiveness by increasing unit production costs, especially where significant cost variations are borne by individual suppliers owing to local conditions.

A further distinction can be made between 'tangible' and 'intangible' costs of compliance (see Table 4.1). Tangible costs are easy to isolate and quantify – for example, the costs of establishing laboratory facilities and instituting routine testing programmes. Intangible costs are more difficult to identify and quantify. Indeed, in many cases they are related only indirectly to the compliance process. These include the foregone opportunity cost of investments as exporters curtail new product development or when scarce resources contribute to weakened domestic food safety controls. Most attempts to assess costs of compliance with new standards largely ignore these intangible costs, despite evidence suggesting they may be more significant than the tangible costs (Henson, 1996).

In order to estimate costs of compliance, one needs to isolate these from more general costs created by ongoing processes of change. The latter process involves evolving food safety and agricultural health controls owing to the pressure from the domestic market, or longer-term attempts to enhance capacity in line with international standards. For the individual exporter, compliance efforts need to be teased out from other competitive pressures, some of which may indirectly relate to such standards. This requires that a baseline be established that reflects the way in which food safety would be expected to evolve in the absence of the new standard.

The efficiency of compliance efforts is crucial in order to estimate the costs associated with new food safety standards. Examination of compliance costs across countries and/or individual exporters will reveal very significant differences in both non-recurring and recurring costs. Compliance can often be achieved through various technological and/or administrative means; some parties may be more efficient than others in this regard. Furthermore, countries and industries have different 'starting points' when more stringent standards are applied.

For a mature and reasonably well-developed export industry, new standards may require only incremental changes by exporters, and perhaps modest adjustments in public sector oversight. Where an export supply chain is underdeveloped, however, new standards (or better enforcement of existing regulations) may require major upgrades at the enterprise level or the consolidation of certain functions to realize economies of scale.

In addition, there is typically great variation in the efficiency with which compliance is achieved, reflecting, for example, abilities in identifying and implementing needed investments and operating procedures. Although these are themselves important management capacities, they also make it difficult to make generalizations about the magnitude of compliance costs. A key question, therefore, is whether general conclusions should be based on some 'average' of estimated costs over countries/firms or on some concept of an 'efficient' country/firm.

In assessing costs of compliance, the costs of non-compliance must also be assessed. The most explicit and direct cost is loss of market sales, due to temporary or permanent prohibitions on exports or loss of foreign market buyers. These costs can be significant for supply chains that are highly export-dependent and, more specifically, reliant on particular export markets. In extreme cases, suppliers may be forced out of the market altogether. More generally, they may take actions to diversify their market base, with which other costs will be associated. In turn, these market-based costs will be related to compliance strategy choices (World Bank, 2005a).

In addition to the costs of compliance, the associated benefits must also be identified and quantified. Until recently it was not widely acknowledged that compliance actually yields benefits, especially in international trade performance (Jaffee and Henson, 2004) and better controls over domestic food safety. Where benefits have been recognized, they have not been quantified. As a result, compliance is seen almost entirely as a cost of maintaining market access with few, if any, offsetting benefits. Although this may serve the political purpose of those advocating greater flows of technical assistance, it can also have an adverse impact on policy-makers in developing countries, steering them toward more defensive and cost-minimizing strategies rather than toward examination of the entire spectrum of strategic options (World Bank, 2005a).

Perhaps the most significant benefit, and indeed the primary driver for compliance, is continued and enhanced market access. At both the country and individual firm levels, unhindered access to markets – for example through avoidance of border detentions – may yield substantial benefits. This is especially the case where large investments in compliance-related resources have already been made. These may have limited alternative uses in the short to medium term, suggesting high 'sunk costs'. Likewise, the benefits from enhanced market access, or of lower costs due to unimpeded access, can be considerable.

As with compliance costs, the benefits associated with compliance can be recurring and non-recurring, tangible and intangible (see Table 4.2). Many of these benefits are only indirectly associated with the process of complying with a particular food safety standard and thus fall into the intangible category. Intangible benefits include opportunities to reassess the efficiency of prevailing systems of production more widely and to study the impact of stricter standards on product quality. These opportunities may improve reputation and increase customer demand over the short or long term.

Potential tangible benefits relate most directly to the impact that better food safety control systems have on costs of production, including reduced wastage and/or product

Table 4.2. Examples of recurring and non-recurring benefits of compliance.

Tangible	Intangible
Non-recurring	
Identification and containment of hygiene problems before they reach 'crisis' levels and/or major customers become aware	Opportunity to examine overall efficacy of controls Opportunity to address established production problems
Recurring	
Access to more remunerative markets and supply chains	Enhancement of product quality
Reduction in costs due to enhanced efficiency	Enhanced morale of inspection or production staff
Reduced wastage in production processes	Improved reputation of firm and/or country
Reduced level of product inspection and detention abroad	

reworking, enhanced productivity, etc. Further tangible benefits may be broader access to markets and/or particular market segments. Although the focus here is on export-oriented supply chains, spill-over benefits can also occur, through reduced wastage and enhanced safety of products in the domestic market. These benefits act to offset recurring compliance costs such that the longer-term impacts might result in lower supply costs. These benefits can be augmented if the government and firms innovate in the face of new standards, minimizing compliance costs.

Given that the costs of compliance with new food safety standards are typically more tangible (and thus more visible) than the potential benefits and that recurring benefits are typically more significant than shorter-term, non-recurring benefits, compliance is widely perceived to be costly. The failure to recognize the full extent of compliance benefits can also lead to the underestimation of rates of return on investments. In turn, this can generate a culture of delayed and reluctant compliance, which may not be the optimal strategic response to evolving food safety standards.

Measuring the Costs and Benefits of Compliance with Food Safety Standards

The preceding discussion has hinted at the problems associated with attempts to identify and quantify the costs and benefits of compliance with new food safety standards in the context of international trade. The key challenge is to identify the actions taken (or required to be taken) in order to achieve compliance, and then to quantify the cost and benefits associated with these actions. In so doing, there can be significant attribution problems that relate to the concepts of necessary costs and efficiency in the compliance discussed above.

In many cases, efforts to achieve compliance with standards are undertaken within the context of prevailing competitive challenges; the costs faced by individual enterprises may differ according to their competitive positioning and/or historic efforts to improve food safety at the national, industrial and enterprise levels. This makes it difficult to attribute costs and benefits to a particular food safety standard.

Having defined the actions attributed to a new food safety standard, the next challenge is to quantify the associated costs and/or benefits. In many cases, public authorities and private enterprises are unable to distinguish clearly the precise costs associated with compliance and, even when this is possible, may not have records of the precise quantities involved. This is particularly a challenge with recurring costs that are less discrete and liable to change over time according to both internal and external factors and ongoing learning processes.

Only as enterprises grow in size and their managerial structure becomes more sophisticated is there a possibility that quality assurance and/or food safety systems and personnel are separated out in company cost accounting. However, even in large organizations, this seems to be the exception rather than the rule.

The cost estimates reported below are based on research that attempts to take a pragmatic approach to assessing the costs of compliance with food safety standards that ensue through the process by which public authorities and individual private sector firms undertake compliance.

Thus, an in-depth questionnaire was employed that led public and private sector decision-makers through the various stages of compliance: (i) what requirements did exports have to comply with previously or compared with domestic market requirements? (ii) how have these requirements changed as a result of the new standard being implemented? (iii) what changes had to be made to prevailing food safety controls? and (iv) what were the costs of implementing these changes?

In assessing these costs of compliance, a baseline must be clearly defined against which the required changes are measured. In the case of exporters, this will depend on the specific nature and history of each enterprise. In all of the cases below, interviews were undertaken with existing exporters that were facing a new or revised food safety standard and, thus, enterprises were asked to consider the changes required in order to comply, relative to the previously prevailing standard, and the associated non-recurring and recurring costs.

The perspective adopted in the case studies below focuses on the investments the public sector and exporters make in complying with food safety standards in international trade, while ignoring how the costs of these investments are redistributed; that is, who eventually pays for compliance. This important issue should be considered alongside the flow of economic benefits from such compliance decisions. Thus, exporters may be able to pass their costs on to consumers, in foreign and/or domestic markets, through higher prices. Furthermore, the government can choose to defray some of the costs through subsidized loans or subsidies, especially if it is judged that competitiveness will be adversely affected to a significant degree. Additionally, development agencies (drawing on tax revenues from home countries) may also offset compliance costs through the provision of technical assistance, grants, etc.

Costs and benefits of compliance with food safety standards for fish and fishery products

This section brings together evidence on the costs and benefits of compliance with stricter food safety standards in international trade from a series of country- and product-specific case studies (World Bank, 2005a) in the fish product sector. These case studies, alongside the results from previous studies, throw some light on the magnitude of the costs of compliance with hygiene and other food-safety requirements set by industrialized country markets; they also reveal the ways in which these vary across source countries and individual exporters, depending on the 'initial' levels of hygiene and food safety controls, the scale of operations, the strategies adopted and other factors.

Shrimp exports from Bangladesh and Nicaragua

The variation in costs of compliance is well illustrated by the experiences of Bangladesh and Nicaragua, both of which export shrimp to the EU and USA (see Table 4.3). In the mid-1990s Bangladesh was required to make significant investments to upgrade public oversight of food safety controls through the fish products supply chain and upgrading of fish processing facilities and laboratory testing facilities. This occurred after repeated quality and safety detentions of

Table 4.3. Costs of compliance with export food safety requirements in the Bangladeshi and Nicaraguan shrimp-processing sectors (from Cato and Lima dos Santos, 1998a, b; Cato and Subasinge, 2004; Cato et al., 2004).

Costs (US$ million)	Bangladesh (1996–1998)	Nicaragua (1997–2002)
Industry facility upgrading	17.55	0.33
Government	0.38	0.14
Training programmes	0.07	0.09
Total	18.01	0.56
Annual maintenance of HACCP programme	2.43	0.29
Shrimp exports during focal periods	775.00	92.60
Average annual shrimp exports	225.00	23.20
Upgrade/focal year export (%)	2.30	0.61
Maintenance/annual exports (%)	1.10	1.26

products entering the USA and a ban on shrimp imports to the EU in 1997. The total cost is estimated to have been around US$18 million, with subsequent annual costs of maintaining the established food-safety controls of around US$2.4 million (Cato and Lima dos Santos, 2000; Cato and Subasinghe, 2004).

In the case of Nicaragua, the shrimp industry was required to improve its hygiene controls to comply with modified fish safety regulations in the USA, over the period from 1997 to 2002. However, because many Nicaraguan factories were relatively new, reflecting among other things the younger age of the sector and significant levels of foreign investment, only modest incremental investments were needed; these were estimated to have cost only US$560,000, with annual maintenance costs of only US$290,000 (Cato et al., 2004).

Although the magnitude of the costs of compliance borne with food safety standards for fish products might appear high, at least for Bangladesh, closer examination reveals that these costs are actually quite modest given the benefit of continued access to lucrative EU and/or US markets. Thus, the investments made by the Bangladeshi shrimp processing sector were equal to 2.3% of the total value of shrimp exports over the period 1996 to 1998. The annual maintenance of HACCP and regulatory systems involved costs equal to only 1.1% of the annual value of exports. Furthermore, significant tangible benefits were associated with these measures.

Thus, Bangladesh has substantially increased its shrimp exports to the EU and gained an enhanced share of overall EU imports. Furthermore, the processing sector is moving towards the production and export of value-added products (Cato and Subasinge, 2004). In recent years, Bangladesh's shrimp exports have approached US$400 million per annum, an 80% increase from the level attained in the late 1990s.

Fish product exports from Kerala

The Indian fish product sector has faced significant challenges in meeting emerging food safety requirements in the EU and USA. These challenges have been particularly pronounced in the state of Kerala, where the fish processing sector is more dependent on these markets than the rest of India and is dominated by exports of crustaceans and cephalopods (Henson et al., 2004). Historically, these problems related mainly to exports to the USA, yet by the 1990s the EU's food safety requirements – both with respect to general hygiene controls and to limits on antibiotics and both biological and chemical contaminants – emerged as the dominant concern.

The challenges faced by the fish products

sector in the face of stricter EU standards largely reflect the failure to upgrade legislative and other elements of the food safety system across India in line with developments in major export markets. Ironically, the very rigorous food safety controls implemented for agricultural and food exports by the Indian government through the 1980s were allowed to wane as a result of liberalization efforts in the early 1990s.

While this existing institutional framework may eventually have enabled the Indian government to bring about changes in food safety controls quite rapidly, it did not prevent exports to the EU being banned on the grounds of microbiological contamination. Thus, faced with restrictions on exports of fish products to the EU in the late 1990s, the Indian government responded with the dramatic imposition of quite onerous requirements intended to demonstrate it was able and willing to comply. Within a matter of months, after a rather critical inspection report from the Food and Veterinary Office (FVO), India had fully complied with EU requirements. Similarly, in 2002 when antibiotics and bacterial inhibitor residues were detected in shrimp, the Indian government swiftly imposed controls on antibiotic use.

The Export Inspection Council (EIC), India's recognized Competent Authority for the regulation of fish exports to the EU, has implemented a rigorous inspection and laboratory testing regime to monitor approved plants. This is undertaken through five regional Export Inspection Authorities (EIAs).

The laboratory facilities operated by EIA Cochin were relatively small until a series of upgrades since the mid-1990s aimed at complying with EU requirements, at a cost of US$65,000. It is estimated that the inspection and testing costs per plant are around US$6444 per annum, with the bulk of this associated with the fortnightly testing of product samples. This implies a total annual cost of monitoring EU-approved plants in Kerala of US$341,000 in 2003–2004, and a cost for the whole of India of around US$876,000. As a proportion of the value of exports to the EU, however, this is only 0.3%.

To comply with the EU's hygiene standards, fish processing facilities in Kerala have made major investments in basic infrastructure (for example flooring, walls and lighting) and control systems, including the implementation of HACCP. The changes required across the sector varied significantly among individual factories. In extreme cases, plants had to be extended or the entire layout changed.

Among the processing facilities surveyed by Henson *et al.* (2004), non-recurrent costs of compliance ranged from US$51,400 to 514,300, with a mean weighted average by volume of production of US$265,492. As a proportion of company turnover over the period 1997–1998, non-recurrent costs ranged from 2.5 to 22.5%, with a weighted mean of 7.6%. In 2001, there were 51 EU-approved facilities in Kerala, suggesting an overall non-recurrent cost across the sector of US$13,540,092. This represents around 1.7% of the value of exports from Cochin over the period 1994–1997, prior to the initial implementation of these investments.

It should be noted that these rather high numbers reflect, to a large extent, the very specific characteristics of the fish processing sector in Kerala, in particular the historic use of pre-processors that were independent of, and outside of the control of, exporting processing facilities.[6]

It is apparent that the installation of integrated pre-processing facilities was the most significant non-recurring cost of compliance borne by processors in Kerala. Traditionally, independent pre-processors sourced raw material from fish boats, which they then cleaned and peeled before sale to processing plants operated by exporters. In so doing, they played an essential role in the sourcing of raw materials and in managing the costs of pre-processing operations.

Following its inspection, however, the European Commission raised concerns over hygiene controls in these facilities. In response, the EIC prohibited the use of independent pre-processors in the case of EU-approved facilities. Thus, EU-approved processing facilities installed their own pre-processing capacity, while independent pre-processors made investments to upgrade their facilities to meet these higher hygiene standards.

While the costs of these improvements have been significant, remaining processors have highlighted the benefits. Many have recorded lower microbial counts in their end products, contributing not only to food safety but also to lower levels of spoilage. Some recognize that they now have greater control of the entire production process and expect to be able to enhance efficiency in the medium term. With their expanded chill room capacity, processors are able to store raw materials for longer periods, enabling them to take advantage of periodic gluts in supply.

Processing plants also had to implement significant changes to their operational procedures. The majority of facilities had not implemented HACCP, which was required to establish the necessary control procedures and documentation systems. Furthermore, cleaning, maintenance and pest control procedures had to be enhanced. In many cases extensive worker training programmes were required.

The cost of implementing these new procedures has been considerable, including ongoing laboratory analysis, record-keeping, ongoing staff training, maintenance of worker medical records, etc. To undertake these tasks, new technical and supervisory staff had to be employed. Monitoring fees paid to the EIA have also increased significantly.

Furthermore, the costs of pre-processing have been internalized within the processing plant; these are significantly greater than for purchasing pre-processed raw material from independent facilities. Across the surveyed processing facilities, the resultant increase in production costs ranged from 5 to 15%, with a weighted mean of 11.7%. The majority of these costs are associated with the requirement of the Indian government to have integrated pre-processing that is under the direct control of the processor.

The non-recurring and recurring costs incurred by processors in complying with these enhanced hygiene standards have varied significantly. While some firms were required only to make incremental changes to achieve compliance, others had to undertake large investments relative to their annual turnover. There was also a broad correlation between the level of fixed investment and the magnitude of recurrent costs. Firms which had to make comparatively large investments also reported greater increases in unit production costs attributable to food safety management measures. Several factors could account for this, including the depreciation costs on new equipment, relative lack of familiarity with this equipment and overall weaknesses in business management.

For whatever combination of reasons, it was precisely those firms that had incurred relatively high non-recurrent compliance costs that also struggled to compete on a cost basis within the sector. This finding suggests that the costs of compliance with food safety standards in international trade tend to exacerbate existing competitive disadvantages, perhaps reflecting historic lack of attention to the need to upgrade food safety controls.

The Marine Products Export Development Authority (MPEDA) in India has implemented various programmes to support improvements in hygienic controls and other food safety practices in the fish processing sector, both to facilitate compliance with stricter government controls and to maintain export competitiveness. The MPEDA operates a subsidy scheme to assist companies in defraying the costs of establishing quality control laboratories, integrating pre-processing facilities and undertaking other renovations.

Over the period 1996/1997–2001/2002, US$103,874 was disbursed to 98 processing units to support the installation of quality control laboratories, while 132 processing units obtained financial support – totalling US$2.5 million – for the installation of in-house pre-processing facilities.[7]

To date, the level of investment made to comply with the EU's hygiene standards for fish products in Kerala has been considerable. Although this has undoubtedly imposed hardships on many processors, in particular those that were already operating at low levels of capacity, overall it represents only 1.7% of the value of exports over the 3 years prior to the imposition of new controls by the Indian government.

Furthermore, for those processors that have managed to comply, the benefits of continued market access are considerable. They have taken advantage of restrictions placed on some of their competitors. Indeed, Keralan exporters have not faced the more recent restrictions imposed on some of their major competitors, notably China and Thailand, related to concerns over antibiotic residues in shrimp. This reflects, at least in part, the efficacy of the food safety controls implemented by the Indian government through the mid- to late 1990s and that government's willingness to take decisive action as and when food safety concerns and/or new standards in its major export markets emerge.

Nile perch export sector in Kenya and Tanzania

Industrial fish processing first evolved in Kenya in the early 1980s, and by 1987 ten factories were operational (Henson and Mitullah, 2004). At that time, no facilities had been established in Tanzania or Uganda, and Kenyan processors sourced fish in all three countries. Processing capacity continued to expand in the early 1990s, with the number of facilities peaking at 15 in 1995. The rapid growth of fish processing was motivated by the high and rising demand for Nile perch in exports markets, particularly within the EU. However, after peaking in the mid-1990s, exports began to diminish due to over-fishing and the establishment of a viable Nile perch export sector in Tanzania and Uganda.

Thus, since 1997, the Kenyan Nile perch processing sector has been operating at 55% of its 380 ton per day capacity. Today, the Nile perch processing sector in Tanzania is operating at comparable levels of capacity, while that of Uganda is operating at only 40% of capacity, suggesting significant levels of overcapacity in each of these countries in the face of (at best) static fish landings.

The Nile perch processing sector across Kenya, Tanzania and Uganda is characterized by low levels of value-addition. Most exports are in the form of block-frozen bulk packs of semi-processed or chilled fillets. The large majority of exports are directed to the EU, with some sales also made to the Middle East, North America and Asia. Some processors have explored opportunities for value-added products or have made attempts to diversify into other food sectors.

However, these initiatives remain the exception and gross margins remain both low and extremely sensitive to the landed price of Nile perch. In this context, the Nile perch processing sector across the region has become increasingly dominated by a small number of large companies that have established processing facilities in all three countries and are gaining market share through the acquisition of underperforming competitors.

Over the period 1998–2002, significant efforts were made to improve hygiene standards within the East African Nile perch processing sectors in order to comply with EU requirements. This followed a series of negative inspection visits by the FVO and the imposition of protracted restrictions on exports due to concerns about the microbiological safety of the product and the efficacy of controls on pesticide residues.

The restrictions on Ugandan and Tanzanian exports were lifted in December 2001 and January 2002, respectively, after the European Commission established that full compliance with EU standards had been achieved. Due to delayed and less effective responses, the restrictions placed on the Kenyan trade were not lifted until December 2002.

Within the industrial processing sector, major improvements were generally required to both the structure of facilities and operating procedures. Although some companies had been more proactive in starting to upgrade their hygiene controls, for example through the implementation of HACCP in the case of companies that were exporting to the USA, all had to make very considerable improvements in order to comply with the EU's requirements.

These included upgrading of the general fabric of processing facilities, rearrangement and segregation of processing operations, installation of ice, water treatment and effluent treatment plants, construction of changing rooms and toilet facilities, purchase of new tables, etc. Laboratories had to be installed or upgraded. Staff had to be trained and quality control personnel employed or enhanced in order to implement HACCP.

Henson and Mitullah (2004) provide estimates of the costs of compliance in Kenya. Non-recurring costs of compliance borne by individual processing facilities differed widely, reflecting the varying standards of hygiene that prevailed within the sector prior to the imposition of trade restrictions in 1998 (see Table 4.4).

Thus, one plant made an investment of US$128,000, while several others incurred only minimal costs. In general, costs were greatest where factories had undergone major structural change in order to improve the general facility and implement effective hygiene controls. These facilities generally had lower pre-existing standards of hygiene and/or were housed in older buildings, often converted from some alternative previous use.

The total cost of compliance for the Kenyan fish-processing sector is estimated at US$557,000. This implies an average cost per plant of around US$40,000. Although this is not a large amount given national exports valued at US$33.5 million in 2002, considering that six plants have ceased operations, a significant part of the sector has clearly derived no payout from this investment. Furthermore, there is no clear relationship between the size of fish

Table 4.4. Non-recurring and recurring costs of compliance in the Kenyan Nile perch processing sector (from Henson and Mitullah, 2004).

Plant	Number of permanent/ temporary employees	Value of exports, 2002 (US$ million)	Current operating level (%)	Non-recurring costs (US$)	Recurring costs (% production costs)
A	75/100	10.73	30	26,800	5
B	100/80	1.86	40	19,600	10
C	20/40	0.54	25	15,200	25
D	150/250	2.59	50	13,600	15
E	100/150	0.32	50	8,500	15
F	100/200	0.38	50	21,800	20
G	270/250	12.83	60	128,000	25
H	75/100	4.27	50	6,500	15
I[a]	–	0	0	80,000	30
J[a]	–	0	0	200,000	40
K[a]	–	0	0	2,100	40
L[a]	–	0	0	7,100	50
M[a]	–	0	0	19,500	25
N[a]	–	0	0	8,300	40
Total		33.52	–	557,000	–
Mean per plant		–	44	39,785	25

[a] Companies not operational in early 2003.

processing operations and the magnitude of non-recurring costs; some small processors incurred costs of the same order of magnitude as the larger firms.

Recurring costs of operating to improved standards of food safety control among the eight Kenyan plants operational in 2003 varied from 5 to 20% of annual turnover, with a mean of 16%.[8] These included the additional staff required to maintain effective hygiene controls, record-keeping, laboratory analysis, ongoing staff training, etc. Differences in the scale of operation are likely to influence compliance costs; the literature on the economics of HACCP suggests significant economies of scale (Unnevehr, 2000).

Furthermore, there were evident differences in the efficiency with which different companies adjusted to new systems of production and control. Processors differed in their ability to identify changes in production costs depending on their accounting procedures and on the degree to which written records of processing operations had been maintained.

Comparable estimates of the costs of compliance borne by the Tanzanian Nile perch processing sector have been made (World Bank, 2005b). The non-recurring company upgrade costs ranged from US$1 to 7 million, with an estimated total cost for the industry (i.e. ten operational plants) being US$24.9 million (see Table 4.5). This represented about 7% of the value of Tanzania's Nile perch exports for the period 1999–2003.

Again, this is perhaps not a huge investment to maintain access to EU markets for Nile perch.[9] Still, these investment costs may have come at the expense of working capital for some companies. One Tanzanian company ceased operations in 2004 and a further two were operating at very low levels of capacity, with uncertain prospects for the future. In Kenya, five of the 15 established Nile perch processing facilities had ceased operations in 2004.

Nile perch processors in Tanzania have also incurred significant recurring costs of compliance that have increased their production costs. It is estimated that these increases are between 10 and 15%. Given that Kenyan processors have also incurred additional costs of production and a number of the Tanganian processors are Kenyan owned, however, there is unlikely to have been a major impact on export competitiveness.

Processors have highlighted the benefits they have achieved from the enhancement of hygiene standards, including improved product quality related to the enhanced diligence of processing staff, lower risks of rejection, etc. These processors recognize the value placed on approval for export to the EU among their customers, even in non-EU countries.

The trade restrictions and required responses have also played important roles in the formation of exporter/processor associations in each of these countries. Such associations now address a broader

Table 4.5. Non-recurring and recurring costs of compliance in selected Tanzanian Nile perch processing facilities (from World Bank, 2005b).

Facility	Non-recurring costs (US$ million)	Mean turnover 2000–2003 (US$ million)	Non-recurring costs 2000–2003 (% turnover)	Recurring costs (% production costs)
A	1.0	5.0	5.0	15
B	1.5	15.0	2.5	12
C	7.0	30.9	5.7	10
D	4.1	21.8	4.7	10
E	2.0	25.0	2.0	15
F	1.5	4.0	9.5	10
G	1.5	9.3	4.0	12
H	1.3	10.0	3.2	15

range of issues and there are current efforts to form an regional umbrella association to address common concerns and also to increase the industry's representation in international forums.

In each of these countries, the difficulties experienced served as a 'wake-up call' regarding the growing importance of quality and SPS (sanitary and phytosanitary) management in international competitiveness, not only within the fish processing industry but also among a much broader set of policy-makers, other government officials and the private sector more generally.

Since the resumption of favourable market access to the EU, Nile perch exports from East Africa have increased, this growth having been been sharpest in Uganda. Over the period 1998–2001, Uganda's fish exports averaged US$43 million per annum. In 2004 and 2005, such exports exceeded US$100 million per annum.[10] Over the period 1998–2001, Tanzania's fish product exports averaged US$75 million per annum. These too have since increased considerably, averaging US$128 million per annum in 2003–2004.

Conclusions

This chapter has provided an overview of the costs and benefits of compliance with food safety standards in the context of international trade, highlighting the challenges associated with their estimation in relation to specific standards and how these vary across countries and even among firms within the same industry. Many forms of technological and organizational change are involved in the process of compliance, and different firms and countries may perform quite differently in managing these processes of change.

This, together with an array of other factors, including the initial 'starting point' for compliance, organizational and geographical structure of the supply chain, levels of intra-industry and public–private cooperation – and the strength of existing technical service industries – influences the level of compliance costs incurred by a single firm or industry.

In the case studies cited here, the costs of compliance with industrialized nations' requirements have been estimated to be in the millions or tens of millions of US dollars. This might be interpreted as a significant burden or 'barrier' to developing country trade. However, these costs (or more precisely, these investments in enhanced capacity) tend to represent only a small proportion of the value of exports in the cluster of years preceding or during the time of adjustment. Furthermore, the level of exports has tended to increase, in some cases significantly, in the years following investments in capacity and compliance.

Certainly, there are differences between the industry or national picture and that of individual companies. For some companies, the compliance challenges and costs have been relatively modest and manageable and the overall adjustment process has worked to their advantage. For other firms, compliance with (more strictly enforced) standards has proved either difficult to manage or prohibitively expensive. This has tended to be the pattern for smaller companies or for those which were already operating at low capacity or with very low margins prior to the imposition of trade restrictions and requirements for factory or operational upgrades.

While less well understood, a broad array of tangible and intangible benefits may accrue to those countries and suppliers who upgrade their food safety controls in response to evolving food safety standards. The most immediate benefit is continued access to potentially lucrative export markets. Yet compliance can also form the basis of enhanced international competitiveness, realigning firms within both the domestic supply chain and entire countries relative to international competitors.

Many of the 'compliant' companies have experienced improvements in product quality, reductions in raw material wastage and a range of benefits gained through enhanced collaboration with other industry or supply chain members. Some have utilized their upgraded factories and improved reputations to develop expanding trade in value-added fish products.

The short- or longer-term trade restrictions have certainly had adverse effects on many companies as well as fishers, factory employees and suppliers of complementary goods and services. Some companies have been unable to make the needed adjustments or recover from the adjustment process. Others have moved on, using the investments made and improved capacities and awareness as a stepping stone to improved competitiveness. In each of the cases cited, the fish industry experiences also had broader spill-over effects, sharply increasing the overall level of awareness, within both government and the private sector, about the growing importance of quality and food safety management in international competitiveness in the agri-food product trade.

Notes

1 For comparison, the combined developing country exports of coffee, cocoa, tea, cotton, sugar and tobacco rose from US$29.9 billion in 1980–1981 to US$38.8 billion in 2003–2004 (United Nations Commodity Trade Database).
2 See Jaffee and Henson (2004) and World Bank (2005a), where both the challenges and opportunities provided by standards for developing countries are assessed.
3 In the USA, while all processing plants from which fish and fishery products are imported are required to have implemented HACCP, it is the responsibility of US importers for verifying that the products they are importing comply with US regulatory requirements. This can be attained by sourcing from a country with a Memorandum of Understanding with the US Food and Drugs Administration, which documents the equivalency or compliance of that country's inspection system for fish and fishery products with US requirements or by taking 'affirmative steps' to verify that the product has been processed in accordance with US regulatory requirements. Such steps might include inspection of the exporter's processing facilities, checks on records, obtaining written assurances from exporters of their compliance with US regulatory requirements, etc. Importers are also entitled to utilize a competent third party to assist with or perform these verification procedures.
4 In industrialized countries, a much more extensive literature estimates the costs and benefits associated with various food safety, environmental and other standards. See, for example, Unnevehr (2000) and OECD (2003).
5 The distinction between recurring and non-recurring costs suggests that account must be taken of the stage in the compliance process where costs are measured. Costs can be significantly underestimated if an attempt is made to estimate costs at an early stage in the compliance process at which only non-recurring costs have been borne. Conversely, there is a tendency to overestimate costs if recurring costs decline significantly over time as exporters, for example, learn to adapt to the required controls.
6 Furthermore, these cost estimates do not include the value of lost production for plants that had to close during renovations. Many plants had to curtail production at some point in the process of upgrading hygiene standards. In cases where major construction work was required, the curtailment extended over several months.
7 MPEDA also provides and supports a number of training programmes, both in general quality control procedures and HACCP implementation and operation. Over the period 1996/1997–2001/2002, some 29,000 fishers, 20,000 pre-processing workers and 15,750 processing workers received basic quality control and hygiene training.
8 Although non-recurring costs were as high as 40% of annual turnover among plants that subsequently ceased operations.
9 The non-recurring costs of factory upgrades and the strengthening of the pertinent competent authority were of a similar proportional level for Uganda for the adjustments made over the 1997–2000 period. These investments, for the entire industry plus for upgrades in public sector regulatory capacities, amounted to some US$13–15 million, equivalent to 6–7% of Uganda's fish exports in those years. See Ponte (2005) and World Bank (2006).
10 The upgrades in factory operations and in regulatory enforcement capacities were a contributing factor, but so was the improved enforcement of restrictions on exports of raw fish to neighbouring countries, especially Kenya.

References

Cato, J.C. and Lima dos Santos, C.A. (1998a) Costs to upgrade the Bangladesh frozen shrimp processing sector to adequate technical and sanitary standards and to maintain a HACCP Program. *NE-165*, University of Massachusetts, Amhurst, Massachusetts.

Cato, J.C. and Lima dos Santos, C.A. (1998b) European Union 1997 seafood safety ban: the economic impact on Bangladesh shrimp processing. *Marine Resource Economics* 13, 215–227.

Cato, J. and Subasinge, S. (2004) *An Overview of the Bangladesh Shrimp Industry with Emphasis on the Safety and Quality of Exported Products*. World Bank, Washington, DC.

Cato, J., Otwell, S. and Saborio, C.A. (2004) *Nicaragua's Shrimp Sub-sector: Developing a Production Capacity and Export Market during Rapidly Changing Worldwide Safety and Quality Regulations*. World Bank, Washington, DC.

Henson, S.J. (1996) *The Costs of Compliance with Food Regulations in the UK*. Department of Agricultural Economics and Management, University of Reading, Reading, UK.

Henson, S.J. and Mitullah, W. (2004) *Kenyan Exports of Nile Perch: the Impact of Food Safety Standards on an Export-oriented Supply Chain*. Policy Research Working Paper, World Bank, Washington, DC.

Henson, S.J., Brouder, A.-M. and Mitullah, W. (2000) Food safety requirements and food exports from developing countries: the case of fish exports from Kenya to the European Union. *American Journal of Agricultural Economics* 82, 1159–1169.

Henson, S.J., Saqib, M. and Rajasenan, D. (2004) *Impact of Sanitary and Phytosanitary Measures on Exports of Fishery Products from India: the Case of Kerala*. World Bank, Washington, DC.

Jaffee, S. and Henson, S.J. (2004) *Standards and Agri-food Exports from Developing Countries: Rebalancing the Debate*. Policy Research Working Paper, World Bank, Washington, DC.

Musonda, F.M. and Mbowe, W. (2001) *The Impact of Implementing SPS and TBT Agreements: the Case of Fish Exports to European Union by Tanzania*. CUTS, Jaipur, India.

OECD (2003) Costs and benefits of food safety regulation. *Working Party on Agricultural Policies and Markets*. Directorate for Food, Agriculture, and Fisheries, Organization for Economic Cooperation and Development, Paris.

Ponte, S. (2005) Bans, tests and alchemy: food safety standards and the Ugandan fish export industry. *DIIS Working Paper 2005:19*. Danish Institute for International Studies, Copenhagen.

Rahman, M. (2001) *EU Ban on Shrimp Imports from Bangladesh: a Case Study on Market Access Problems Faced by the LDCs*. CUTS, Jaipur, India.

UNEP (2001a) *Country Case Studies on Trade and the Environment: a Case Study of Bangladesh's Shrimp Farming Industry*. UNEP, Geneva.

UNEP (2001b) *Country Case Studies on Trade and the Environment: a Case Study on Uganda's Fisheries Sector*. UNEP, Geneva.

Unnevehr, L. (2000) Food safety issues and fresh food product exports from LDCs. *Agricultural Economics* 23, 231–240.

World Bank (2005a) *Food Safety and Agricultural Health Standards: Challenges and Opportunities for Developing Country Exports*. World Bank, Washington, DC.

World Bank (2005b) *Tanzania's Agri-food Trade and Emerging Sanitary and Phytosanitary (SPS) Standards: Toward a Strategic Approach and Action Plan*. International Trade Department. World Bank, Washington, DC.

World Bank (2006) *Uganda, Standards and Trade: Experiences, Capacities and Priorities*. International Trade Department. World Bank, Washington, DC.

Zaramba, S. (2002) *Uganda Country Report on the Integration of Multiple Sources of Technical Assistance to Capacity Building on Improving the Quality of Fish for Export*. FAO, Rome.

5 The Dynamics of Vertical Coordination in Agri-food Supply Chains in Transition Countries

J.F.M. Swinnen

Introduction

The combination of a demand for products of high quality and safety standards and the problems which farms face in supplying such products to processors and traders has led to the growth of vertical coordination in supply chains. In transition countries (TC), market imperfections and the absence of appropriate public institutions have contributed further to the growth of private contractual initiatives to overcome these obstacles. Traders, retailers, agribusinesses and food processing companies increasingly contract with farms and rural households and provide inputs and services in return for guaranteed and quality supplies. This process of interlinked contracting is growing rapidly.

These contracts initiatives can be quite complex. They include farm management assistance, extension services, quality controls, farm input assistance programmes, trade credit and even bank loan guarantees. The programmes can generate important improvements in the credit situation of the farms, as they contribute directly to improved access to finance (e.g. through trade credit), and indirectly as they improve contracting farms' access to loans from banks or external financial institutions (through loan guarantees, enhanced farm profitability and improved future cash flows).

Arguably, the transition disruptions and contract enforcement problems have been even more severe in the rural credit markets than in other markets. In combination, the direct and indirect effects of the farm assistance programmes create important benefits for the farms and households supplying to these companies: they lead to improvements in input access, productivity, product quality and market access. There is growing evidence that these processes have been an engine of growth in the agri-food supply chains of the most advanced transition countries.

This chapter presents empirical evidence on the growth in vertical coordination (VC) in agri-food supply chains in transition countries and its effects. The chapter draws heavily on the findings of a major World Bank study analysing these issues – more detailed findings and case studies can be found in World Bank (2005) and Swinnen (2006).

Various Concepts

Vertical coordination can take various forms, which can be thought of as institutional arrangements varying between the two extremes of spot market exchanges (0) and full ownership integration (1). Within this 0–1 range, there is a large variety of different forms of coordination and an equally vast literature trying to classify these various forms and to explain them.[1] A frequently made distinction, which is useful for our purposes, is between marketing contracts and production contracts. *Marketing contracts* are (verbal or written) agreements between a contractor and a grower that specify some form of a price (system) and outlet *ex ante*. *Production contracts* are more extensive forms of coordination and include detailed production practices, inputs supplied by the contractor and quality and quantity of a commodity and a price (system).

Key factors determining the use of various contract forms or other forms of vertical coordination are the costs and uncertainties involved in the transactions, which themselves are affected by the economic and institutional environment, the need for asset- or transaction-specific investments, the frequency of interacting, commodity characteristics such as perishability, costs of measuring and monitoring product characteristics, uncertainty over product quality or reliability of supplies.

Vertical Coordination in the USA and the EU

There is little systematic empirical evidence, even for developed countries such as the USA and the EU. What is available, shows that vertical coordination is moderately important and that it varies widely between sectors. In the USA and in Germany around one-third of the total value of agricultural production was produced under various types of contracts in the 1990s (Rehber, 2000). Contracts were used mostly by larger commercial farms. Only 11% of US farms used contracts in 2001. However, more than 40% of commercial farms used contracts. In terms of output, 13% of small farm output was under contract, while the commercial farms contracted for more than 40% of their output.

Marketing contracts were more widespread than production contracts: there were almost four times as many farms that used marketing than those using production contracts (twice as many for commercial farms). However, in terms of share of output, production contracts were almost as important as marketing contracts.

The main reason is that different commodities use different contracts. Production contracts are important in some of the livestock sectors and especially in hogs (54%) and poultry and egg production (81%). Marketing contracts are used mostly in crops: more than half of cotton and fruit were produced under marketing contracts. Other studies indicated that in potato and sugar beet marketing contracts, also, were very important. Contracting is not very important in grains – with the exception of malting barley, which is mostly under marketing contracts. The USDA data in Table 5.1 report that more than 52% of dairy production is under marketing contracts. However this probably includes contracts between farmers and their cooperatives as more than 80% of milk was sold to or bargained for by dairy cooperatives in the USA.

Vertical Coordination in Transition

General patterns

The pattern of vertical coordination (VC) in transition countries differs from VC in rich and poor market economies in several aspects. First, there is significant VC in sectors where we do not observe VC in richer countries. Second, in several sectors where important VC exists in other developing and emerging countries,

Table 5.1. Importance of contracting by commodity; USA, 2001 (from USDA, 1997).

Commodity	Marketing or production contract (%)	Marketing contract (%)	Production contract (%)
Maize and soybeans	11.0	10.9	0.1
Wheat	5.6	5.5	0.1
Barley	19.3	–	19.3
Cotton	51.7	51.7	–
Fruit	59.0	56.5	2.5
Vegetables	36.9	30.0	6.9
Cattle	20.9	3.2	17.7
Pigs	60.5	7.1	53.4
Poultry and eggs	88.1	6.8	81.3
Dairy products	53.1	52.2	0.9
All commodities	36.3	20.3	16.0

the forms of VC in transition countries appear to be more extensive and more complex.

At the end of the 1990s in the Czech Republic, Slovakia and Hungary, 80% of the corporate farms, which dominated farm production in these countries, sold crops on contract, and 60–85% sold animal products on contract, numbers which are considerably higher than the shares of even commercial farms in the USA.

A survey of agri-food processors in five CIS countries (Armenia, Georgia, Moldova, Ukraine and Russia) found that food companies which used contracts with suppliers grew from slightly more than one-third in 1997 to almost three-quarters by 2003 (Gorton and White, Chapter 14, this volume). There was also a strong growth in company ownership of farms. Enterprises directly engaged in farming increased from 6% to 26% of all interviewed firms – with most of this vertical ownership integration occurring recently. There is also significant growth of supplier support measures as part of the contracts, and more farms are gaining access to these.

Monetary credit, prompt payments, transportation, physical inputs and quality control are the most commonly offered forms of support. Over 40% of processors in their sample offer credit to at least some of the farms that supply them, and 36% offered inputs in 2003.

Commodity-specific patterns

Dairy

In the dairy sector, we observe extensive production contracts between dairy processors and farms in transition countries (TC), including the provision of credit, investment loans, animal feed, extension services, bank loan guarantees, etc. (World Bank, 2005). This is different from the situation in the West, since there is no production contracting going on in countries like the USA.

Sugar

In the sugar sector we find – as in the developed economies – extensive marketing agreements, but the contracts are much more extensive in TC, including also input provisions, investment loan assistance, etc. (Swinnen et al., 2002).

Cotton

In cotton, the standard model in the USA and Australia, two major cotton producers, is that the cotton (from seed to baled cotton) remains in ownership of the producer and the processing is paid for as a service. In TC, the dominant player in the chain is the gin, who typically contracts farms to supply seed cotton and provides them with a variety of inputs. This model, which has developed in some of the poorer TC countries in Central Asia, resembles that of the gin supply chain structure in developing countries, such as in Africa. However, the extent of contracting and supplier assistance seems to be more extensive in TC, with credit, seeds, irrigation, fertilizer, etc. being provided by the gins (Sadler, 2006).

Cotton producers are generally too small to attract commercial credits directly, as they lack sufficient collateral and present a high default risk. They are mainly financed by gins. Eighty-nine per cent of producer respondents said that they had received financing from a ginner. Gins provide crop finance, as well as supplying inputs and some agricultural services.

Fresh fruit and vegetables

In fresh fruits and vegetables, the rapid growth of modern retail chains with high demands on quality and timeliness of delivery is changing the supply chains. New supplier contracting – which is developing rapidly as part of these retail investments – includes farm assistance programmes, which are more extensive than typically observed in Western markets. They resemble those in emerging economies, but appear more complex in several cases.

Grain

In this commodity VC is also more elaborate and complex. As in Western countries, there is extensive contracting going on for malting barley across the region, but VC is often much more extensive than in the West, with brewing and malting companies vertically coordinating across several stages of the chain. Moreover, there is a remarkable amount of full vertical integration in wheat production in Russia and Kazakhstan, where large agro-holdings and grain trading companies own several large grain farms in some of the best grain-producing regions, sometimes owning 100,000s of hectares (see Box 5.1). For example, large, vertically integrated grain companies are the dominant type of farming in the north of Kazakhstan. In Russia too, VC in grains has grown rapidly since 1998, but in that country it was the state that was the driving force behind the vertical coordination (see Serova, Chapter 15, this volume).

To understand the reasons for these differences, their likely developments and implications, it is crucial to see these developments as an integral part of the process of transition, a process which has involved a major change in the institutions governing exchange and enforcement of contracts.

Exchange and Quality Problems as Drivers of Vertical Coordination

Exchange problems

A major problem has been the breakdown of the relationships of farms with input suppliers and output markets during early transition. The simultaneous privatization and restructuring of the farms and of the up- and downstream companies in the agrifood chain has caused major disruptions. Widespread forms of contracting problems during transition were long payment delays or non-payments for delivered products. Such payment delays caused major drains on much-needed cash flow for suppliers. The result is that many farms faced serious constraints in accessing essential inputs (feed, fertilizer, seeds, capital, etc.) and in selling their products.

This was a major problem for all companies in the food chain. Food processing companies in Eastern Europe in the late 1990s considered late payments one of their most important obstacles to growth (Gorton *et al.*, 2000). It was found to be the single most important obstacle to company growth in Czech Republic and Slovenia and the third most important out of 12 obstacles in Hungary.

These problems have been greatly

> **Box 5.1.** Integrated farm companies in Kazakhstan and Russia.
>
> *Perelyevsky Cooperative Farm (Kazakhstan)*
>
> After bankruptcy, the farm was auctioned in 1997 and now forms a branch of Arai JSC, an integrated complex of companies comprising grain, meat and milk production and the production of alcohol, soft drinks and beer. Conditions improved with an influx of working capital and investment. The full former labour force has been retained on the farm, the cattle herd has been rebuilt to 4200 and the company produces wheat on 4000 ha of land.
>
> *Bisco-Trade (Kazakhstan)*
>
> This is an investment grain company which has taken over several bankrupt farms. The acquisitions followed poor experiences with contract farming as contracts could not be enforced through the courts. The company currently owns 11 farms covering 220,000 ha.
>
> *Ivolga ISC (Kazakhstan)*
>
> This large grain-trading company owns 23 farms, most of them acquired after farm bankruptcies. The company's farms produce grain, vegetables and potatoes. The company owns 12 grain terminals and elevators.
>
> *Orel Niva holding (Russia)*
>
> This enterprise controls 337,000 ha of land and employs 16,000 workers. It processes 200,000–300,000 tons of wheat. Its activities include 102 large farms, 28 processing plants, 100 trade organizations, 32 service enterprises, etc.
>
> *Pshenitsa-2000 Orel holding (Russia)*
>
> This enterprise controls almost 100,000 ha of land and has more than 3000 employees.
>
> *Orel Agro holding (Russia)*
>
> This enterprise employs 12,000 people and controls around 200,000 ha of land. Its activities include – apart from many grain farms – dairy and pig production, animal and dairy processing companies, grain elevators, etc.
>
> From Gray (2000) and Gataulina (2006).

diminished in the most advanced TC countries, often as a result of supply chain restructuring. However, in many countries problems of payment delays and non-payments continue until today, even in some of the European transition countries, as illustrated by the following quote:

> Romanian farmers are holding back supplies of milk as they are experiencing considerable delays in being paid by processors and other buyers. Many farmers have to wait more than two months to be paid for their milk. Some started bringing milk into towns themselves as they will get their money immediately.
>
> (AgraFood East Europe, March 2003, p. 23)

Additionally, farms breached contracts. Guaranteed supplies of quality raw materials are crucial for processors. In transition countries, processors often have severe problems in obtaining sufficient quality supplies. Suppliers may not deliver the quality or quantity of raw materials agreed on. The problems are worsened by the lack of public institutions necessary to support market-based transactions, such as those for enforcing property rights and contracts.

Quality and standards problems

A second reason for VC is the search for supplies with higher safety and quality standards by modern processors and retailers. An increase in public standards and in private standards in TC greatly affects food quality requirements and standards for both domestic consumption and exports (see other chapters in this volume for the motives behind this). The shortage of quality supplies was typical of early transition.

There are several reasons for this. First, farms may not be willing to supply their output to the processor because they fear not being paid once they deliver the product. Secondly, if farms want to supply, they may not be able to because they cannot access basic production factors. Thirdly, if farms want to supply, they may only supply poor-quality supplies because: (i) they lack the necessary inputs to improve the quality; and (ii) they lack expertise and know-how for producing high quality goods.

VC as a private institutional response to market constraints

To overcome these problems of enforcement and constraints on quality supplies, vertical coordination systems were set up by processors, traders, retailers and input suppliers. These companies, often as part of their own restructuring, start contracting with the farms and rural households and provide basic inputs in return for guaranteed supplies. As the evidence in this report shows, these processes of interlinked contracting are growing in importance.

Successful VC has taken many forms, but has typically included conditions for product delivery and payments as well as farm assistance programmes for suppliers. An important component of the contracts is prompt payments. Gorton and White (Chapter 14, this volume) found in their study that 90% of farms get prompt payments in the first year of contracting across five CIS countries. Similarly, other studies on early-stage VC – such as dairy in Romania in 2000 or sugar processors in Slovakia in the mid-1990s – all introduced prompt payments.

Farm assistance has taken many forms including, in some cases, input supply programmes, investment assistance programmes, trade credit, bank loan guarantee programmes, extension and management advisory services, etc.

Once introduced, VC programmes – if sustained – spread to other companies, other suppliers and even to other sectors due to both imitation and competition. Competition for suppliers induces an expansion of VC programmes, sometimes even across sectors.

Sources of finance

VC requires sufficient funds to finance the supplier contracting system, including immediate payments and assistance programmes. Therefore, initiators of contracting with supplier financing include: (i) foreign investors who have access to financial means because of their own resources or because they can access financial markets internationally (e.g. foreign/multinational processing companies active in dairy, sugar, oilseeds, etc.); (ii) companies with financial resources from other sectors investing in the food sector (e.g. financial/industrial groups in Russia); (iii) domestic processors or traders who sell on the international market and have sufficient turnaround to have financial liquidity (e.g. grain traders in Kazakhstan); or (iv) domestic processors who access international finance through contracts with international companies (e.g. cotton gins in Central Asia).

Vertical Coordination Models and Motivations

Empirically successful VC is commodity-specific, transition stage-specific, heterogeneous (varying from rather simple to complex) and often 'non-traditional'. The latter occurs because successful models address specific transition-related problems, some of which are not prevalent in a 'normal market economy environment'. Part of these variations is determined by the same factors which determine variations in contracting in developed market economies, such as transaction cost differences and commodity characteristics (see above), while others are transition-specific.

In the early stages most of the emphasis in VC goes to 'getting the thing going' and on securing supplies. Therefore, most emphasis goes to overcoming basic supply problems, such as input (feed, seeds) and credit (working capital) constraints. This is still the case in some of the cotton supply chains in Central Asia and in emerging dairy and fruit and vegetable supply chains in countries such as Romania and the Caucasus.

In more advanced situations, as is the case in many sectors in Central Europe, there will be more emphasis on product quality. For this, more sophisticated forms of vertical coordination are needed, such as extension services and farm-level investments in technology and equipment, leasing, bank loan guarantees, investment assistance, etc.

Not only may assistance programmes change, but the organization of the supply chain may be entirely restructured. For example, in the case of modern retail investments, important changes in procurement systems occur step-by-step in the supplier–retailer relationship (Dries *et al.*, 2004). These changes include: (i) a shift from local store-by-store procurement to nationally centralized big distribution centres; (ii) an incipient shift to regionalization of procurement over countries; (iii) a shift from the use of traditional brokers to new specialized/dedicated wholesalers; (iv) increasing local use of global multinational logistics firms; (v) a shift to preferred supplier systems; and (vi) a shift to high private standards of quality and safety. These changes dramatically change the contracting relationships between retailers and suppliers.

Motivations and constraints of farmers

The different contract forms also reflect different constraints faced by farms in input and output markets. For example, Table 5.2 shows how the dominant motivation for farms in Central Europe (Hungary, Slovakia and Czech Republic) at the end of the 1990s was guaranteed access to markets (52% of the farms listed this as their primary motive) and, to a lesser extent, guaranteed prices (21%). For very few farms, access to credit or other inputs was the main motive. The farms in this table are mostly large farms as they are the dominant contractors.

However, the motivations for small cotton farmers in southern Kazakhstan to enter into contracts with gins are very different. For them, credit constraints were still by far the most important constraint in 2003, as is clearly reflected in the survey results in Table 5.3.

A different motivation for VC in some countries was the increased bargaining power of the integrated farming companies

Table 5.2. Contract motivations for farms in Central Europe (from Leuven ACE datasets, Belgium).

Most important reason for contracting	Czech Rep. 1999 (%)	Slovakia 1999 (%)	Hungary 1997 (%)	Average (%)
Contract price higher	9	8	10	9
Avoid price uncertainty	7	22	33	21
Guarantee product sales	64	50	43	52
(Part) pre-payment	7	13	3	8
Easier to get credit	0	0	9	3
Contract – inputs and TA	7	6	2	5
Other	6	2	0	3

Table 5.3. Contract motivations for cotton farms in Kazakhstan, 2003.

Reason for contracting	Yes (%)	No (%)	Most important reason (%)
Guaranteed product sales	9	91	8
Guaranteed price	4	96	3
Access to pre-financing	81	19	75
Access to quality inputs	11	89	10
Access to technical assistance	0	100	0
Other	4	96	3

vis-à-vis local and regional authorities which continue to intervene in farming operations (Gray, 2000). These advantages were particularly important in the grain sector in Kazakhstan and Russia, where most farms continued to depend on the local authorities for access to key inputs (such as seed and fuel) and for financing of these inputs, and where the authorities used this dependency to influence farm decision-making.

Vertical Coordination and the Policy Environment

Some of the more sophisticated VC programmes require complex implementation and enforcement systems. Interestingly, these advanced assistance programmes are less widespread in CIS countries than in CEE countries, which are more advanced in the process. These programmes are also apparently not found in developing country VC strategies. Studies on VC in other regions – such as the IFAD (2003) report on East Africa and Key and Runsten (1999) on Latin America – do not mention such sophisticated measures. This may reflect the lower quality standards for supplies in these regions, or larger problems of enforcement for such programmes, or both.

The latter is consistent with observations that both investment in the food industry and the emergence of sophisticated VC programmes are conditional upon the level of reforms in a country. Figure 5.1 illustrates how there is a strong positive correlation between reform progress in transition countries and investments by multinational retailers. (Empirically we observe that FDI has been the most important driving factor behind these programmes. Foreign investment plays an important role as an initiator of change and institutional innovation (Dries and Swinnen, 2004).

In addition, institutional and economic reforms are also essential for the implementation and enforcement of complex VC, such as investment loans, trade credit and bank loan guarantees. Figure 5.2 illustrates a strong positive relationship between the amount (and complexity) of VC in the Eastern European dairy sector and the level of reforms.

Contract Enforcement and Interlinking Markets

Enforcement is crucial in making any of the contracts or supplier assistance programmes sustainable. Enforcement is especially problematic in environments where public enforcement institutions are absent. Evidence suggests that court enforcement of contracts is generally not efficient; even approaches based on collateral are often flawed either because farms cannot provide the necessary collateral or collecting in on the collateral is problematic in many circumstances in transition.

In such environments the best one can do is create 'self-enforcing contracts' by designing the terms of the contracts such that nobody has an incentive to breach the contract (Gow and Swinnen, 2001). This can be done by increasing the costs of breaching the contract or by introducing flexible terms which reduce the chance of breach in case conditions change

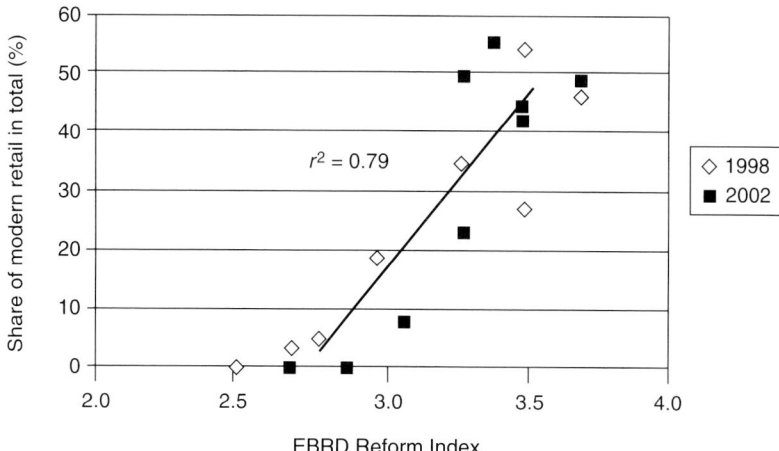

Fig. 5.1. Impact of reforms on modern retail investments in Bulgaria, Croatia, Czech Republic, Hungary, Poland, Romania, Russia, Slovakia and Ukraine (from Dries et al., 2004).

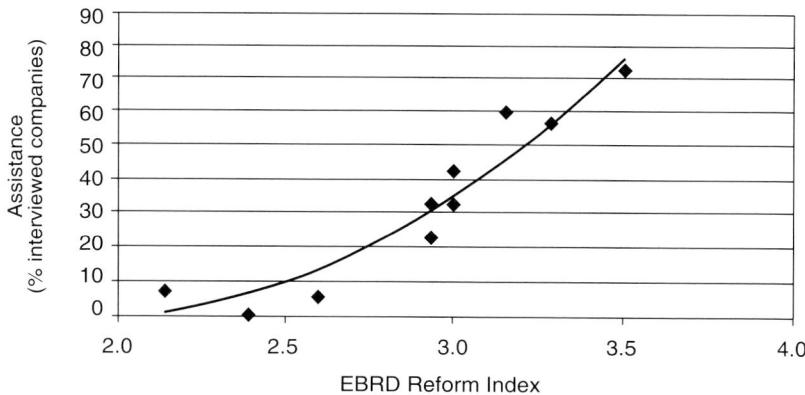

Fig. 5.2. Economic reforms and farm assistance programmes in the dairy sectors of Albania, Bulgaria, Poland and Slovakia (from Swinnen et al., 2006).

unexpectedly. Institutional innovations to ensure supplies for processors or payments for input suppliers help to enforce contracts. Effectively, what companies do is 'interlinking markets'. The enforcement of the credit transaction (loan and repayment) occurs through the output market.[2]

Yet, whether this is sufficient as an enforcement mechanism depends on a variety of factors and, as the evidence shows, it is not always sufficient. An illustration of the problems of setting up self-enforcing contracts is from an FAO project in Macedonia. The project attempted to create markets for vegetable farms by contracting between farms and processors/traders.

A large number of farms and processors joined the project, but many contract breaches occurred, on both sides:

> Quantities and quality of products delivered to the processors did not meet expectations, since contracted farmers sometimes preferred selling on (high-price) fresh markets and supplied processors with products they were not able to sell on the fresh market. In some cases this caused processors, who target quality product

niche markets, to reject the delivered goods. [On the other hand], some processors did not honour the signed contract because they failed in identifying export markets.
(Martinovski, 2004, unpublished report, p. 6)

There are many stories of failed enforcement. In some cases this caused the cancellation of the VC programme, if processors could not enforce their contracts. For example, Gow and Swinnen (2001) reported cases of an international dairy company in Romania and an international brewing/malting investment project in Croatia that ended up cancelling their input pre-finance programme as farms continuously diverted the inputs for other uses.

In other cases, foreign investors left after they failed to obtain sufficient quality of raw materials from their supplying farms despite extension, training and support programmes, as suppliers regularly sold produce to other companies or traders. Again, in the Ukrainian oilseed sector, pre-financing from crushers to farmers has decreased markedly since the late 1990s, after crushers experimented with prepayment for seeds, but many had their fingers burned with significant defaults (EBRD/FAO, 2002).

Another example is from Kazakhstan, where 20 to 30 grain-trading companies were contracting farms in the wheat-growing belt in the late 1990s, together contracting for half of all the cultivated wheat area in Kazakhstan. One company, Agrocenter, in 1998 contracted 11 former state farms totalling about 400,000 ha. The company provided spare parts, chemicals, seeds and paid wages for some employees. However, following a severe drought in 1999, these mechanisms led to large outstanding debts, when farms had accepted inputs on a barter basis but were unable to pay off their input loans. The difficulties experienced with contract and debt management following the 1999 drought caused Agrocenter to withdraw from VC in 1999 (Gray, 2000).

Even in the successful cases it took considerable fine-tuning of the contracts over time to make the contracts self-enforcing. In addition, circumstances change so rapidly in transition that contracts required continuous adjustments as the self-enforcing range itself changes. Creating the right conditions for successful and self-enforcing contracting requires extensive knowledge of the sector and of local conditions and an ability to flexibly adjust the contract terms to circumstances which can change rapidly in transition.

Ultimately, the best way of solving the exchange, contracting and collateral problems in transition countries is to base exchanges and contract enforcement on trust. Unfortunately, due to traumatic experiences during both the communist and the transition periods, trust is generally lacking as a base for business exchanges in many transition countries. However, empirical evidence does suggest that once companies are able successfully to instigate new contractual exchange forms, trust as a basis for business exchanges can develop relatively rapidly.

Efficiency Effects

The impact of these contract innovations is difficult to quantify as several other factors affect output simultaneously and since company level information is difficult to obtain. Still, the evidence suggests that successful private contract enforcement with vertical contracting has important positive effects, both direct and indirect.

The direct impact is on the output and productivity of the processing company that initiates vertical contracting and its suppliers. Supplying enterprises have experienced beneficial effects on output, productivity and product quality through better access to inputs, timely payments and improved productivity with new investments. Case studies indicate that the programmes can lead to double-digit annual growth in output and productivity. For example, a case study of the Slovakian sugar sector showed how new contracts and farm assistance programmes caused output, yields and contracts to grow dramatically (Gow et al., 2000).

Other studies confirm that relatively small changes in the industry's practices can quickly have a major impact at the farm level. For example, Leat and Van Berkum (2003) indicated that dairy farmers, willing to learn, could achieve better performance even when they had access to only modest farm assistance. Another example, from Friesland dairy investments in Romania, is illustrative: in 2001 the company bought a Romanian dairy, utilizing less than 50% of its capacity and with a bad reputation for not paying farmers. Without changing anything but paying-in time, Friesland succeeded in producing 20–30% more milk within a period of 3 months. If farmers were convinced that a processor was reliable in paying, they were generally prepared to deliver their milk (Van Berkum, 2006).

In their survey of TC agri-business enterprise executives, White & Gorton (2006) concluded that various contract support measures had caused (separately) an average increase in yields of around 10%. The measures with the greatest impact on yields were specialist storage (especially cooling equipment in the dairy sector), veterinary support and physical inputs. Specialist storage in the form of on-farm cooling tanks has been particularly important in raising yields and quality in the dairy sector, an effect also found in other countries (Dries and Noev, 2006). Market measures such as prompt payments, guaranteed prices and market access also had large positive effects.

Quality of output also improved due to these measures. In the case of Polish dairy farms, milk quality rose rapidly following contract innovations by dairy processors in the mid-1990s. The share of the market held by highest-quality milk increased from less than 30% on average in 1996 to around 80% on average in 2001 (see Fig. 5.3).

Direct loans and loan guarantee programmes contributed strongly to farm investments. In the Polish study: more than three-quarters (76%) of all farmers in the survey had made investments in previous years, including many small farmers with fewer than ten cows (Dries and Swinnen, 2004). Dairy loans are used for investments in enlarging and upgrading the livestock herd (30%) and cooling tanks (56%). Moreover, dairy assistance in the form of guarantees for bank loans helped farm investments. Also, programmes which assist farms in accessing inputs (mainly feed) enhance investment indirectly by lowering input costs or by reducing

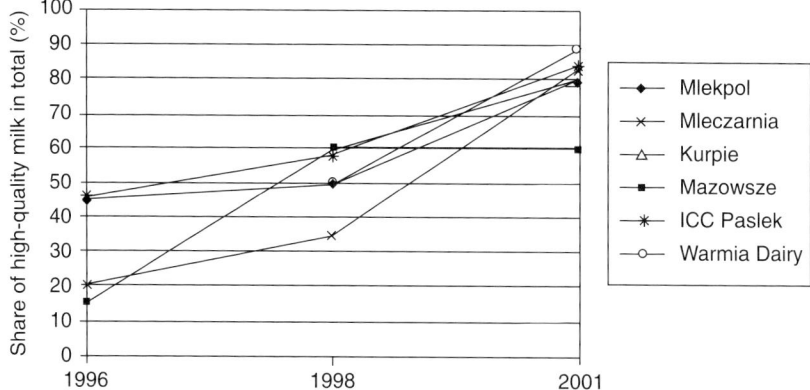

Fig. 5.3. Share of high-quality milk in total deliveries from six selected dairies in the north-east of Poland (from Dries et al., 2004).

transaction costs in accessing inputs and consequently, through improved profitability.

Indirect effects, in particular cross-company spill-overs, occur as firms competing for the same suppliers and their fixed inputs are forced to offer similar contractual arrangements. For example, in the case of the Slovak sugar sector, competition induced other sugar processors to introduce similar contracts. With some delay, this resulted in increases in productivity in the rest of the sugar sector. Other studies confirm the importance of this competition effect. Dries *et al.* (2004) and Noev *et al.* (2004) found that, respectively, in the case of the Bulgarian dairy sector and in contracting by modern retail companies in Croatia, competition for suppliers forces other companies to replicate farm assistance programmes in order to secure supplies.

Impacts on Equity

There are two potential equity problems with the vertical coordination process. The first is the possibility of rent extraction by the dominant company in the chain. The second is exclusion from the vertical coordination process. First, by introducing an interlinked contract, farms can access credit, inputs, etc. which were unavailable beforehand and processing companies can have access to higher quality and timely supplies. Productivity – and therefore income – increases for the chain as a whole.

However, a key question is: who benefits from this increase in efficiency and total income? If the supplier and the processor benefit, both parties share in the gains from the institutional innovation, and everybody is better off. However, if the processing firm can set the terms of the contract such that it captures most or all of the rents, the productivity growth may not benefit the farms, and interlinking may even bestow additional monopoly power upon the processing company. An analysis of this issue and whether competition can prevent companies from exercising monopoly power in the design of the contract conditions and allow farms to share in the benefits can be found in Chapter 7 by Swinnen *et al.* in this volume.

Here, we focus on the second issue, i.e. the problem of potential exclusion of small farms in the VC process. There are three important reasons for this. First, transaction costs favour larger farms in supply chains. Secondly, when some amount of investment is needed in order to contract with or supply to the company, small farms are often more constrained in their financial means for making necessary investments. Thirdly, small farms typically require more assistance from the company per unit of output.

Our studies and interviews with companies generally confirm the main hypotheses coming out of global observations: transaction costs and investment constraints are a serious consideration, and companies express a preference for working with relatively fewer, larger and modern suppliers.

However, empirical observations show a very mixed picture of actual contracting, with many more small farms being contracted than predicted based on the arguments above. In fact, our surveys in Poland, Romania and CIS find no evidence that small farmers have been excluded over the past 6 years in developing supply chains. In the CIS, the vast majority of companies were contracting as many or even more small suppliers in 2003 than in 1997.

More sophisticated supplier assistance programmes tend to be more available for larger farms. Often, supplier programmes differ in addressing the characteristics of the farms. For example, in case studies of dairy processors, investment support for larger farms includes leasing arrangements for on-farm equipment, while assistance programmes for smaller dairy farms include investments in collection units with micro-refrigeration units.

Hence, despite the apparent disadvantages noted earlier, the empirical evidence suggests that vertical coordination with small farmers is widespread. Furthermore, our empirical evidence indicates that companies, in reality, work with surprisingly large numbers of suppliers of surprisingly small size.

Why contracting with small farmers?

There are several reasons. First, the most straightforward reason is that companies have no choice. In some cases, small farmers represent the vast majority of the potential supply base. This is, for example, the case in the dairy sector in Poland and Romania, and in many other sectors in TC.

Second, our case studies suggest also that company preferences for contracting with large farms are not as obvious as one may think. While processors may prefer to deal with large farms because of lower transaction costs in, e.g. collection and administration, contract enforcement may be more problematic – and hence costly – with larger farms. Processors repeatedly emphasized that farms' 'willingness to learn, take on board advice and a professional attitude were more important than size in establishing fruitful farm–processor relationships'.

Third, in some cases small farms may have substantive cost advantages. This is particularly the case in labour-intensive, high maintenance, production activities with relatively small economies of scale.

Fourth, processors may prefer a mix of suppliers in order not to become too dependent on a few large suppliers.

Finally, processing companies also differ in their willingness to work with small farms. Some processing companies continue to work with small local suppliers even when others do not. These companies have been able to design and enforce contracts which both the small firms and the companies find beneficial. This suggests that small-scale farmers may have future perspectives when effectively organized.

Transition countries are a 'supplier market' ... for now

The collapse of farm output and livestock numbers created a gap between processing capacity and supply: hence there is excess demand based on processing capacity. There is even more excess demand for high/better quality supplies because: (i) quality is low due to a history of poor quality in the system; and (ii) reduced access to inputs and finance affects the quality as well.

This renders it a 'suppliers market' in most TC and this, in turn, supports the farms' bargaining position *vis-à-vis* the processing sector in the distribution of supply chain rents. Moreover, in cases where quality supplies are scarce and non-trivial investment is required for quality upgrading, the bargaining power of quality suppliers may increase substantially (post-investment) vis-à-vis the processor or trader.[3]

These arguments are important both for the issue of exclusion and for the rent distribution in the chain because they suggest that the 'power relationship' (and the rent distribution) is endogenous in the development of the supply chain integration.

What will happen when the market turns? If competition among suppliers increases, or if demand falls, pressure on processors may lead to a consolidation of the supplier base. Along the same lines, we find that even companies willing to invest in upgrading small farms only go so far, and tend to have a strategy in the long term to upgrade part of their supply to larger, more efficient and fewer suppliers. In many cases supplier assistance programmes explicitly discriminate between larger and smaller farms, with the focus of upgrading the better farms and ensuring a minimal supply base and quality from the rest as long as it is required.

Hence, in combination, these factors indicate that those who are concerned about the inclusion of small farms in these supply chains should not be complacent despite the observations of significant contracting with small suppliers taking place right now.

Putting the exclusion problem into perspective

Clearly, the equity issues are important challenges. However, several factors suggest that the impact of VC in supply chains will be nuanced. First, the impact of VC is likely to differ significantly between countries and sectors. In some TC countries (for example Slovakia, the Czech Republic, Russia, Ukraine, etc.) a large share of output is produced by corporate farms. In other countries, the importance of farm organizations often differs significantly among sub-sectors (e.g. grains *versus* vegetables), reflecting economies of scale.

Secondly, the impact of VC is likely to be a continuation of important agri-food chain restructuring which started 15 years ago – TC farms have undergone a dramatic restructuring over the past 15 years. In countries such as Estonia, Hungary, the Czech Republic and Slovakia, more than 50% of (officially registered) workers left agriculture early on in transition. This process continued as investments in the food industry and the need to enhance the international competitiveness of the domestic farms have maintained pressure for restructuring. In other countries this adjustment process has been delayed by a variety of problems, but a significant reduction in agricultural employment will be necessary with economic growth, with or without VC.

Thirdly, these VC processes have positive effects by addressing major weaknesses of the TC farm sector. The farm sector is most in need of finance for investments, technology and quality improvements, and access to high-value markets. All these factors contribute to weak competitiveness of TC food supply chains, with negative effects on their trade balances. Investments by modern processing companies and vertical coordination with suppliers can play a significant role in both addressing these weaknesses and improving the global competitiveness of the ECA supply chains.

Fourthly, modern agribusiness and food company investments will not only affect rural suppliers but will have a wider impact on rural development. This includes improved access of better quality and a wider variety of foods and other products for rural households, and the creation of off-farm employment, directly or indirectly, in the supply chain. Investments in packaging, quality control, extension services, etc. are likely to create new jobs in the rural areas, while at the same time the competition from the new chains will cause traditional shops and processors to close. Modern agribusiness and food companies, as motors of market development, will also generate opportunities for differentiation of products and value added.

In summary, these arguments suggest that VC in modern supply chains has the potential for important positive implications for rural households in ECA, despite the challenges that they pose. These investments may bring very significant benefits to the region, but could also pose significant threats where inefficient or undercapitalized farmers cannot 'make the grade'.

The Future of Vertical Coordination in Transition Countries

In this chapter we have demonstrated the growth of VC in supply chains in transition countries, its causes and effects. A key remaining issue is how VC will develop in the future.

VC addresses (transition-specific) problems which traditional financial instruments do not address. This holds also for farm assistance programmes, leasing, warehouse receipt systems, pre-financing in vertical contracts, etc. Hence, when markets start working better, there is less need for VC. An intriguing question is, therefore, to what extent the process as described in this chapter represents a transition-specific phenomenon or not.

The transition from a centrally planned system to a market economy in most of these countries coincided with the break-up of the old state system of strong vertical integration into independent units, as illustrated in Fig. 5.4. However, the transition disruptions of the exchanges in product and factor markets caused independent private companies to take initiatives to vertically integrate to enforce contracts and improve coordination within the supply chain.

In other words, will vertical integration in the supply chain be reinforced (path A), or will it retreat once public institutions are sufficiently strong to enforce contracts, with the development of new public institutions and market actors and once factor markets work better (path C)?

A hybrid path is most likely to develop in the medium term (path B); for some aspects, some forms of VC will remain important – as they are in Western Europe and the USA. However, for other aspects, which are more closely aligned with transition conditions, VC may retreat. For example, recent information suggests that some of the multinational companies, where possible, return to their core business and leave farming to farms, leave lending to financial institutions and leave input supplies to other agribusiness companies, with as little involvement of the company as possible in order to keep the quality and reliability of supplies up to a desirable level.

We already observe these processes taking place in Central Europe where, e.g. international brewing companies have withdrawn from their upstream activities and have simple supply contracts with malting companies, instead of VC through the chain. One should keep in mind that these processing companies have vertically integrated out of necessity rather than intrinsic interest. These companies want to get out of VC if they can, because it is not their core business and because they do not want to carry the risk. These companies' preference is to withdraw from the extensive forms of VC which we observe now, and move towards more 'normal' forms of exchange. Therefore, pattern B appears the most likely to emerge.

Notes

1 There is a significant literature on supply chains and contracting in food chains, some of it on developing and transition countries (see World Bank, 2005 for a survey). There is also a related, mostly theoretical, literature which focuses on optimal contracting and interlinked markets in developing countries (e.g. Bardhan, 1989). The

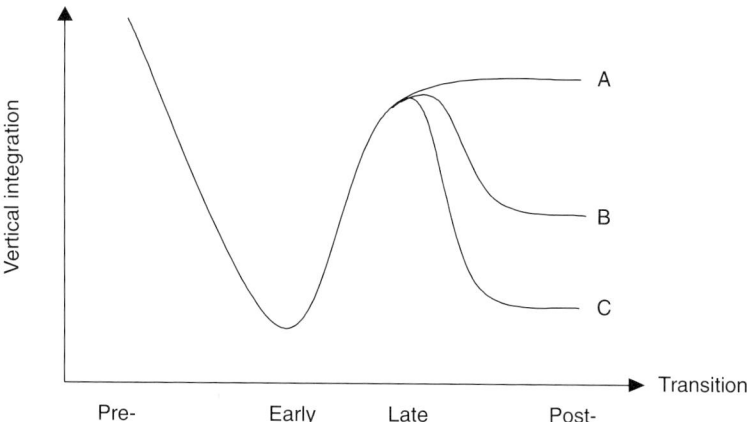

Fig. 5.4. Vertical integration in the agri-food chain during transition.

basic explanations draw often on the seminal work of Ronald Coase and Oliver Williamson. However, in two recent surveys of the literature (Rehber, 2000; Hobbs and Young, 2001), no less than seven different strands of literature are identified as being important in understanding and explaining those differences: (i) transaction costs economics; (ii) agency theory; (iii) competency/capability models; (iv) strategic management theory; (v) convention theory; (vi) life cycle theory; and (vii) contract economics.
2   The issue of interlinking markets has been well analysed in the case of developing countries (see, e.g. Bardhan, 1989; Bell, 1989), but not in transition countries.
3   Studies on international FFV supply chains in East Africa have also found that with increasing demand for traceability, the 'dependency relationship' between suppliers and processors changes, since processors/traders are now more dependent on their suppliers. By working with fewer suppliers, but with higher quality and traceability contracts, the suppliers become more 'powerful' – and tend to get higher prices.

References

AgraFood East Europe, March 2003.
Bardhan, P. (ed.) (1989) *The Economic Theory of Agrarian Institutions*. Clarendon Paperbacks, Oxford, UK.
Bell, C. (1988) Credit markets and interlinked transactions. In: Chenery, H.B. and Srinivasan, T.N. (eds) *Handbook of Development Economics*. North-Holland, Amsterdam, pp. 763–830.
Dries, L. and Noev, N. (2006) A comparative study of vertical coordination in the dairy chains in Bulgaria, Poland, and Slovakia. In: Swinnen, J.F.M. (ed.) *Case Studies on the Dynamics of Vertical Coordination in the agri-food chains of Transition Countries in Eastern Europe and Central Asia*. ECSSD Working Paper No. 42. The World Bank, Washington, DC, Chapter 6.
Dries, L. and Swinnen, J. (2004) Foreign direct investment, vertical integration and local suppliers: evidence from the Polish dairy sector. *World Development* 32 (9), 1525–1544.
Dries, L., Reardon, T. and Swinnen, J. (2004) The rapid rise of supermarkets in Central and Eastern Europe: implications for the agrifood sector and rural development. *Development Policy Review* 22 (5), 525–556.
EBRD/FAO (2002) Ukraine: review of the sunflower oil sector. *EBRD Report No. 2*.
Gataulina, A. (2006) Integration processes in the agriculture-industrial complex: agro-firms and agro-holdings in Russia. In: Swinnen, J.F.M. (ed.) *Case Studies on the Dynamics of Vertical Coordination in the Agri-food Chains of Transition Countries in Eastern Europe and Central Asia*. ECSSD Working Paper No. 42. The World Bank, Washington, DC, Chapter 3.
Gorton, M., Buckwell, A. and Davidova, S. (2000) Transfers and distortions along CEEC food supply chains. In: Tangermann, S. and Banse, M. (eds) *Central and Eastern European Agriculture in an Expanding European Union*. CABI Publishing, Wallingford, UK, pp. 89–112.
Gow, H.R. and Swinnen, J.F.M. (2001) Private enforcement capital and contract enforcement in transition economies. *American Journal of Agricultural Economics* 83 (3), 686–690.
Gow, H.R., Streeter, D.H. and Swinnen, J.F.M. (2000) How private contract enforcement mechanisms can succeed where public institutions fail: the case of Juhocukor a.s. *Agricultural Economics* 23 (3), 253–65.
Gray, J. (2000) Kazakhstan; a review of farm restructuring. *World Bank Technical Paper No. 458*. The World Bank, Washington, DC.
Hobbs, J.E. and Young, L. (2001) *Vertical Linkages in Agri-food Supply Chains in Canada and the USA*. Report. Agriculture and Agri-Food, Canada.
IFAD (2003) *Agricultural Marketing Companies as Sources of Smallholder Credit in Eastern and Southern Africa. Experiences, Insights and Potential Donor Role*. IFAD, Rome.
Key, N. and Runsten, D. (1999) Contract farming, smallholders, and rural development in Latin America: the organization of agroprocessing firms and the scale of outgrower production. *World Development* 27 (2), 381–401.
Leat, P. and van Berkum, S. (2003) Dairy sector analysis. In: van Berkum, S., Davies, S. and Popov, S. (eds) *The Romanian Agrifood Chain: On the Road to Accession*. Ministry of Agriculture, Forests, Water and Environment, Bucharest.
Noev, N., Dries, L. and Swinnen, J. (2004) *Foreign Investment and the Restructuring of the Dairy Supply Chains in Bulgaria*. Working Paper. LICOS-Centre for Transition Economics, KU Leuven, Leuven, Belgium.

Rehber, E. (2000) Vertical coordination in the agri-food industry and contract farming: a comparative study of Turkey and the USA. *Marketing Policy Center Res. Report No. 25*. University of Connecticut.

Sadler, M. (2006) Vertical coordination in the Central Asian cotton supply chains. In: Swinnen, J.F.M. (ed.) *Case Studies on the Dynamics of Vertical Coordination in the Agri-food Chains of Transition Countries in Eastern Europe and Central Asia. ECSSD Working Paper No. 42.* The World Bank, Washington, DC, Chapter 4.

Swinnen, J.F.M. (ed.) (2006) *Case studies on the dynamics of vertical coordination in the agri-food chains of transition countries in Eastern Europe and Central Asia. ECSSD Working Paper No. 42.* The World Bank, Washington, DC.

Swinnen, J.F.M., Gow, H.R. and Maviglia, I. (2002) Modest changes in the West, radical reforms in the East, and government intervention everywhere: European sugar markets at the outset of the 21st Century. In: Schmitz, A., Spreen, T. and Messina, W. (eds) *Sweetener Markets in the 21st Century*. Kluwer Academic Publishers, Netherlands, pp. 215–240.

Swinnen, J.F.M., Dries, L., Germenji, E. and Noev, N. (2006) Foreign investment, supermarkets and the restructuring of supply chains: evidence from Eastern European dairy sectors. *LICOS discussion paper 165/2006*. LICOS, KULeuven. Leuven, Belgium.

Van Berkum, S. (2006) Restructuring and vertical coordination in the dairy sector in Romania. In: Swinnen, J.F.M. (ed.) *Case Studies on the Dynamics of Vertical Coordination in the Agri-food Chains of Transition Countries in Eastern Europe and Central Asia. ECSSD Working Paper No. 42.* The World Bank, Washington, DC, Chapter 7.

White, J. and Gorton, M. (2006) A comparative study of agri-food chains in Moldova, Armenia, Georgia, Russia, Ukraine. In: Swinnen, J.F.M. (ed.) *Case Studies on the Dynamics of Vertical Coordination in the Agri-food Chains of Transition Countries in Eastern Europe and Central Asia. ECSSD Working Paper No. 42.* The World Bank, Washington, DC, Chapter 2.

World Bank (2005) *The Dynamics of Vertical Co-ordination in Agro-food Chains in Europe and Central Asia*. The World Bank, Washington, DC.

6 Trade Liberalization and Rent Distribution in Vertically Related Markets

S. McCorriston and I.M. Sheldon

Introduction

The Doha Round of trade negotiations in the World Trade Organization (WTO) has been labelled the so-called 'development round', a key part of which will be increasing developing countries' access to developed country markets. This process will involve the reduction of tariffs on agricultural goods, given that many developing countries are still major agricultural exporters and that agriculture still accounts for a large share of GDP, particularly in the poorest developing countries.

However, in terms of the potential benefits to developing countries, there are three outstanding issues. First, recognizing the vertically linked nature of the food chain between agriculture, food processing and retailing and the increasing consolidation of the food industry in developed countries, these features of the vertical marketing chain may influence the magnitude of the benefits that developing countries receive from increased market access. In this regard, we show that the impact of trade liberalization may reduce the overall share of value added received by commodity producers.

Secondly, in terms of the total value of the product that reaches consumers, the raw agricultural component typically represents a small share. In this regard, we show that the distribution of vertical rents and the impact of trade liberalization may reduce the overall share of value added received by commodity producers. This has caused many in developing countries – as well as international institutions – to advocate diversification in developing countries, involving the additional processing of and adding value to the raw agricultural commodity. However, developing countries considering this option face the problem of tariff escalation in that tariffs on processed exports from developing countries are often higher than tariffs on raw agricultural commodities.

Thirdly, exporting higher-value products may capture some of the downstream rents, but tariff escalation could become an issue. We also highlight that the stage at which trade liberalization occurs also influences the overall distribution of the impact of trade reform in vertically related markets.

These issues can be related explicitly to the broader popular debate about globalization. First, concerns have been expressed that increasing concentration of the global food system harms producers of those export commodities critical to many developing countries. For example, African countries such as Burundi, Ethiopia, Rwanda and Uganda are highly dependent on exports of coffee, yet all have faced a significant decline in real prices over the past few years.

At the same time, in key export markets such as Europe and the USA, global coffee buyers, roasters and retailers, who in total account for almost 60% of the share of the final sales value of coffee, have benefited from lower coffee bean prices. For example, Nestlé, the second largest coffee roaster in Europe, reported a 20% increase in its profits in 2001, while Starbucks posted a 41% increase in profits (Oxfam, 2001).[1]

While there may be several factors playing a role here, we nevertheless show that the increase in profits for intermediaries, coupled with the decrease in raw commodity prices, is consistent with a vertical market chain characterized by market power.

Secondly, tariff reduction and market access go right to the heart of the debate over whether smallholder farmers in developing countries will truly benefit from globalization. On the one hand, development agencies such as the World Bank (2003) and NGOs such as Oxfam (2003a,b) have argued extensively that removal of trade-distorting agricultural policies in both the developed and developing countries has the 'potential to act as a powerful catalyst for poverty reduction' (Oxfam, 2003b, p. 3) in the developing countries. On the other hand, critics of globalization have argued that it may generate negative effects for developing-country farmers.

However, few studies of the likely outcome from trade liberalization explicitly recognize the potential impact of the structure of the sectors downstream from agriculture that capture the largest share of value added. Given that downstream firms capture most of the vertical rent, clearly the structure of the downstream stages will also influence the distribution of rents following trade liberalization. We show this to be the case and argue that trade liberalization – with respect to tariff reductions on raw commodities – will probably result in an even lower share of total value added being captured by commodity producers.

Finally, analysis of consolidation in the food industry relates more broadly to the unease that has been expressed by various commentators about increased international corporate control over both the food marketing system and the manufacturing sector in general. Importantly, the trend is towards increasing consolidation, both domestically and across borders, suggesting that the issue of downstream market power is likely to increase rather than decrease. In addition, with fewer firms dominating particular commodity sectors, this raises the stakes in accessing downstream food markets, which will not depend solely on tariff concessions.

This chapter is organized as follows: in the first section, we provide a brief overview of the food sector in developed countries that suggests that downstream food markets are more appropriately characterized as successive oligopoly, i.e. where market power exists at each stage of the downstream food sector. We also discuss other aspects relating to vertical market structure and provide evidence of increasing consolidation of the food processing and retailing sectors in developed countries. This forms the background for considering trade liberalization in a vertically related set-up where tariff reductions relate to the raw commodities.

In the second section, we discuss the mechanisms by which price signals are transmitted throughout the vertical chain when the downstream sectors are imperfectly competitive. Drawing on these mechanisms, we outline a simple framework that characterizes the vertically linked nature of developed country food markets and how this may influence the gains from the reduction in tariffs on raw agricultural commodity exports. We also discuss how, in principle, increasing consolidation of the food marketing sector in developed countries may change the impact of increased market access for developing countries.

The issues associated with developing countries increasing their exports of higher-value products are presented in the following section, where we also address the issue of tariff escalation. In the final section we summarize and conclude, and address the three key concerns about globalization laid out above.

Imperfectly Competitive Vertical Commodity Chains

Commodity markets are often perceived as being perfectly competitive, thus perhaps rationalizing why issues relating to market power are inadequately recognized in the literature. Yet, this perception often misses the point that raw commodities are inputs into a vertical commodity chain, such that the raw commodity is only a relatively small proportion of value added, the downstream stages of which may be imperfectly competitive. This is true of both developed and developing countries.

Taking the example of a developed country, farmers account for around 15–20% of total value added in the food chain in the UK. In developing countries, commodity exporters also receive a small proportion of the total value. For example, coffee producers account for 10% of total value added while processors, roasters and retailers receive between 20 and 30%.

In the cocoa market the data are rather similar, with cocoa farmers receiving around 15% of the total value of the finished product. Even where the commodity involved does not require much processing, the shares received by commodity producers can be rather small. For example, in the banana sector, the division of value added is as follows: plantations, 10%; international trading companies, 30%; ripeners, ~15–20%; and retailers as much as 40%.[2]

The key feature of the food/commodity sector is not the producers per se but the nature of market structure that constitutes the downstream sectors. Our key argument is that downstream market structure will have an important influence on determining the total value of vertical rents and how they are distributed, and the distribution of rents following trade liberalization. In this section, we focus on the extent to which food processing and retailing in developed countries is concentrated, with specific focus on these sectors in the USA and the EU. In addition, we also review the nature of vertical contractual relationships in the food system that may impact market access for developing country exporters and increasing consolidation in the food sector.

Food processing

The food processing sector in both the USA and the EU is highly concentrated (Cotterill, 1999). In the USA, a small number of large firms dominate the sector, with the top-20 food and tobacco manufacturing firms accounting for over 52% of the sector's value added in 1995. If food manufacturing is separated from beverage and tobacco manufacturing, the top-20 food manufacturing firms accounted for 37% of value added in 1997, while the top-20 beverage and tobacco manufacturing firms accounted for 79% of value added (US Census Bureau, 2001). The role of a relatively small number of firms is reflected in high concentration in the US processing sector, where the average four-firm concentration ratio is around 76%. Table 6.1 provides evidence of the degree of industry concentration in the US food processing sector.

Food manufacturing in the EU is also highly concentrated, where the average seller concentration is higher than in the USA, ranging from an average three-firm concentration ratio of 55% in Germany to 89% in Ireland, with an average three-firm concentration ratio across nine EU countries of 67%. The data on industry concentration presented in Table 6.2 highlight the high levels of concentration and also the differences across EU states. It should be noted, however, that while seller concentration at the product level is high in many

Table 6.1. Product concentration ratios in US food manufacturing, 1997 (from US Census Bureau, 2001).

Product	CR4[1] (%)
Dog and cat food mfg.	63.4
Malt mfg.	66.5
Wet corn milling	73.7
Soybean processing	73.4
Other oilseed processing	72.7
Breakfast cereal mfg.	86.7
Sugar cane mills	61.8
Cane sugar refining	96.4
Beet sugar mfg.	82.7
Chocolate and confectionary mfg.	86.6
Condensed/evaporated dairy mfg.	68.8
Biscuit/cracker mfg.	64.6
Snack food mfg.	63.0
Brewing	90.7
Distilling	64.8
Cigarettes	98.0
Average	75.9

[1] Share of value added accounted for by the four largest firms.

individual EU country markets, there are few examples of firms that dominate sales across EU countries as a whole (Cotterill, 1999).

Food retailing

In the case of food retailing, there are quite important differences between market structure in the USA and that in the EU. Concentration in food retailing at the national level is much higher in EU countries than it is in the USA, with average five-firm seller concentration in the former being 65%, compared with 35% in the latter. The data for the EU and US food retailing sectors are presented in Table 6.3. However, at the EU-wide level, five-firm seller concentration is much lower, at 26% (Hughes, 2002). In addition, in the USA, it is important to examine concentration in food retailing at the local and regional

Table 6.2. Concentration ratios[1] by product in EU countries (from Cotterill, 1999).

Product	Ireland	Finland	Sweden	Denmark	Italy	France	Spain	UK	Germany	Average
Baby food	98	100	100	99	96	93*	54	78	86	91
Canned soup	100	85	75	91	50	84	–	79	41*	87
Ice cream	–	84	85	90	73*	52	84	45	72	76
Coffee	91	72	71	70	60	100	–	74	67	75
Yoghurt	69	83*	90	99*	36	67	73	50	76	70
Chocolate confectionery	95	74	–	39	93	61	79	74	–	74
Pet food	98	80	84	40	64*	73	53	77	87	79
Breakfast cereals	92	–	52	70	88	70	82	65	67	73
Tea	96	90	63	64	80	82	62	52	55	72
Snack foods	72	70*	80	78	71	50	56	73	48	68
Carbonates	85	50	62	–	60	69	79	55	60*	71
Butter	–	–	–	100	–	32*	–	65	30	65
Pasta	83	97	82	61	51	57	65	37	49	65
Frozen meals	–	–	63	–	90	62	39	39	65	62
Wrapped bread	85	44	47	59	80	70	96	58*	9	59
Biscuits	83	73	51	44	55	61	53	42	50	58
Canned fish	–	70	72	49	68	43*	33	43*	–	55
Mineral water	–	100	74	70	37	–	31	14	22	50
Fruit juice	–	70	50	65*	62	26	38	35	46	48
Canned vegetables	–	68	47	50	36	29	–	–	–	47
Average	89	79	69	69	67	63	61	56	55	68

[1] Three-firm concentration ratios, except *, which are two-firm.

Table 6.3. Seller concentration in US and EU food retailing, 1990s (from Cotterill, 1999; Hughes, 2002; McCorriston, 2002).

Country	CR5[1] (%)
Austria	79
Belgium–Luxembourg	57
Denmark	78
Finland	96
France	67
Germany	75
Greece	59
Ireland	50
Italy	30
Netherlands	79
Portugal	52
Spain	38
Sweden	87
UK	67
USA	35

[1] Five-firm seller concentration.

levels. Cotterill (1999) reports that, in 1998, four-firm seller concentration averaged 74% across the top 100 US cities, while across major US regions, four-firm seller concentration averaged 58%.

As well as the high levels of concentration in US and EU food retailing, it is important to recognize that several firms in this industry, which were previously national in origin, are now becoming international in scope. Hughes (2002) reports that, in the 1980s, food retailers in the EU such as the French firm Carrefour began expanding beyond their national base, while the US-based firm Wal-Mart expanded into Canada and Mexico. This phenomenon continued in the 1990s, with EU-based retailers such as Royal Ahold and Sainsbury expanding into the US market (Cotterill, 1999), Carrefour and Royal Ahold expanding into various developing country markets in Central and Latin America (Chavez, 2002; Farina, 2002; Gutman, 2002) and US-based Wal-Mart expanding into the EU (Hughes, 2002) and into Central and Latin America (Chavez, 2002; Farina, 2002).

As a result, food retailing is becoming increasingly multinational, with three food retailers, Wal-Mart, Carrefour and Royal Ahold appearing in the world's top 100 multinational corporations in 2000 (UNCTAD, 2002a). In summary, the food manufacturing and retailing sectors in the USA and EU are concentrated, so that the vertical structure of the food marketing system in developed countries can best be characterized as one of successive oligopoly.[3]

Vertical contractual relationships

Typically, models of the food marketing system assume that processors and retailers operate at arm's length and, in particular, that food retailers take upstream prices as given, and that neither manufacturers nor retailers attempt to influence contractual terms. Nevertheless, this assumption is perhaps naïve since there are a number of alternative forms of vertical coordination in the food sector that may affect the overall competitiveness of the vertical marketing chain and, hence, the distribution of rents between the vertical stages.

Between retailers and processors there are a wide variety of what are known as vertical restraints, which include practices such as discounts, 'full-line' forcing, exclusive distribution, exclusive territories and 'slotting allowances'. These vertical restraints that characterize the links between retailers and manufacturers are common practice and, as shown by McCorriston and Sheldon (1997), both the USA and UK competition authorities have investigated a wide range of such practices. For example, the UK Competition Commission recently identified 30 different contractual practices between manufacturers and retailers, 27 of which they concluded had the potential for being against the public interest (Competition Commission, 2000).

Moreover, the nature of vertical coordination between downstream food firms and commodity producers also matters where contracts can also take alternative forms, the detail of which will reflect the relative bargaining power of the contracting parties. The key point about these characteristics of vertical coordination throughout the vertical food sector is the extent to which they increase or decrease competitiveness throughout the food chain as a whole. For example, vertical integration (or other vertical contracts that replicate this outcome) may be desirable from the perspective that it ameliorates the double marginalization problem typically associated with successive oligopoly. On the other hand, other forms of vertical coordination may exacerbate the problem of market power by foreclosing competition between downstream stages.

Industry consolidation

One additional feature of the food sector that is not apparent from the one-off look at concentration ratios is how the food sector has changed. Most commentators reflect this change in the rising concentration ratios that have characterized the US and the EU over time (see, for example, Cotterill, 1999). However, since industry consolidation largely occurs via mergers and acquisitions (M&A), a better reflection of consolidation in the food sector is to highlight the extent of this activity directly.

In Fig. 6.1, we record the total number of domestic M&A that have occurred in the food industry from 1986 to 2002. The data cover both the food retailing and food manufacturing activities, though the largest proportion of the merger and acquisition activity is in the food manufacturing sector. In addition, while the definition of domestic M&A activity covers both developed and developing/transition countries, most of this activity takes place (perhaps not surprisingly) in developed country markets.

Nevertheless, the evidence is rather striking in that it shows considerable growth in domestic M&A activity over the last 16 years, though the number of domestic deals increased significantly from 1986 to 1991, then levelled off and subsequently increased again in the late 1990s till 2001. Clearly, while most researchers in the food industry have focussed on 'static' issues associated with the measurement of market power, there has been considerable consolidation in the food industry over the last decade or so that has received comparatively little attention.

An additional feature of corporate change is that a significant proportion of total M&A activity involves cross-border deals. This is related to foreign direct investment (FDI), the main mechanism of FDI occurring

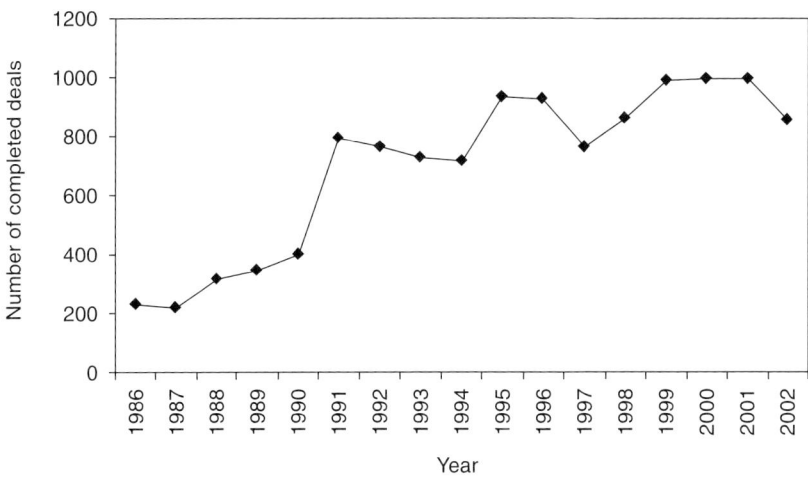

Fig. 6.1. Domestic mergers and acquisitions in the food sector, 1986–2002.

through cross-border M&A deals. McCorriston (2006a) presents the data on cross-border M&A in the food sector, the data again being an aggregate of completed deals in the food manufacturing and retailing sectors. Again, what is striking about the evidence for the food sector has been the significant growth of cross-border deals.

The pattern of FDI/cross-border M&A is also interesting. Reflecting the overall pattern of FDI in the world economy, most of cross-border M&A activity involves the food industry in developed countries. However, there has also been growing cross-border M&A activity involving M&A from developed to developing countries. Farina (2002), for example, noted the nature of industry consolidation in Latin America and how this has involved developed country food retailers acquiring stakes in the food sector in several countries. She noted, for example, that the share of foreign multinationals in the sales of the leading five retailers in Brazil was 84%. The corresponding data for Argentina and Mexico were 91 and 89%, respectively.

Noting also that concentration ratios in the food retailing sector in many Latin American countries has also increased, it is clear that industry consolidation in the food sector has an important international dimension, covering both developed and developing/transition economies.

Trade Liberalization in a Vertically Related Market

Most studies on the effect of liberalization of tariffs for agricultural goods ignore the vertically related structure that characterizes food markets in developed countries. If the processing and retailing sectors were perfectly competitive, this distinction would not matter much. However, as discussed above, these downstream sectors are more typically characterized as being highly concentrated. In this context, the framework set out below highlights two issues of interest to developing countries.

First, the impact of tariff reductions will be contingent on the characteristics of the vertically related food marketing sector as a whole. However, with few exceptions, this issue is largely ignored. Secondly, as the food sector is characterized by increasing concentration, this has an influence on the returns to agricultural exporters as industry consolidation continues.

In this section, we first discuss the mechanisms via which price changes occurring at one stage in the vertical chain are transmitted to other stages. This is key to understanding the outcome of trade reform and the distribution of rents. Drawing on this discussion, we then outline a diagrammatic framework that highlights these mechanisms and the outcome from trade reforms.[4]

Price transmission with imperfect competition

Price transmission relates to how price changes occurring at one (imperfectly competitive) stage are transmitted to other stages in the vertical chain, and ultimately to both commodity producers and final consumers. Focusing on this mechanism has the advantage that it is easy to benchmark against the competitive outcome. This provides insights into the distribution of vertical rents that will probably arise with trade liberalization.

Consider a vertically related food industry where the raw commodity enters at an upstream stage and that the technology linking these stages is fixed proportions and there is arm's length pricing. Suppose initially that the (single stage) downstream food sector is competitive. Tariff liberalization relating to raw commodities will reduce the downstream firms' costs. The effect here would be to reduce the retail price, the extent of this reduction being equivalent to the share of the raw commodity in the food industry cost function, i.e. there would be perfect price transmission.

For example, if the share of the raw

commodity equals 1, then the retail price would decline by the same amount as the raw commodity price. In other words, in a competitive vertical industry, the downstream sector has no role in affecting the outcome from trade liberalization and the standard effects we would get in a textbook competitive model would continue to hold.

If, however, the downstream sector is characterized by oligopoly, the results do differ, as price transmission will not equal one. There are two effects here: (i) there is a direct effect reflecting the change in costs in the downstream industry's cost function since its costs have now changed due to trade liberalization; but also (ii) the change in costs affects the price cost mark-up for the food industry, the magnitude of this second effect being determined by the *change* in the elasticity of demand in the product market (see McCorriston et al., 2001) for a fuller discussion of these issues).

Under reasonable conditions, the change in the retail price will be less than the change in the raw commodity price net of the tariff.[5] This discrepancy in the way in which market power affects the changes in the two prices nevertheless has an important implication: if raw commodity prices fall but retail prices fall by less, then the increase in consumer surplus one would expect from trade liberalization will be diluted. At the producer level, even if commodity prices increase, commodity producers may receive an even smaller share of the overall value added. However, reflecting the discrepancy in these changes relative to the competitive benchmark, the firms that make up the downstream sectors in the food chain will see their rents increase. In sum, imperfect competition will affect who gains, and by how much, from trade liberalization.

There are still further issues to account for. First, tariff reductions may directly affect alternative downstream stages of the food sector, as would be the case where the countries export (semi-) processed commodities but face a tariff on downstream exports and the possibility of tariff escalation. In this case, we may have to consider the 'pass-back' effect, with price signals being passed from retail to processors to farmers rather than (or perhaps in addition to, depending on the characterization of the vertical chain) the 'pass-through' effect, with the transmission of price signals going the other way. If the food sector is competitive, this 'pass-back' effect would be the reciprocal of the 'pass-through' effect, so that they would be observationally equivalent.

However, in the context of imperfect competition, these effects will not be equivalent with the 'pass-through' effect being diluted by market power and the 'pass-back' effect being exacerbated by market power. Again, this will affect the magnitude of the welfare changes arising in the food sector. Secondly, scale effects may also be important. Scale also affects the price transmission effects, though again it affects the 'pass-through' and the 'pass-back' effects differentially.[6]

These effects all relate to the role of oligopoly in the downstream industry. Two further considerations are of concern: first, to the extent there are successive stages in the vertical chain with oligopoly at each, these effects will be exacerbated. For example, suppose we have oligopoly at the processing and retail stages, respectively; the change in the retail price cost mark-up will depend on the elasticity of demand not only at the final stage but also at the intermediate stage, and the change in the elasticity of demand will reflect market power at both the retail and processing stages. Specifically, it will reflect the perceived derived marginal revenue function. In other words, given the inter-linked nature of the vertical market, the price transmission effect (even if focused on a single part of the vertical chain) will reflect market power throughout the vertical chain as a whole.

Secondly, oligopsony power may also be important and, in turn, can affect the price transmission effects. This is an issue that has been largely ignored in the general literature. Nevertheless, the mechanism is similar to that which arises with selling power. With oligopsony, the change in the mark-down following trade liberalization will reflect changes to the elasticity of supply in the raw commodity market (see Weldegebriel, 2004). We explore some of these issues in the discussion below.

Trade liberalization in a vertically related market

In Fig. 6.2, we examine the impact of a tariff reduction on the import of a raw agricultural commodity that enters at the upstream stage of a vertically related food marketing system that is characterized (for ease of exposition) by a technology of one-to-one fixed proportions at each stage, i.e. a unit of the raw commodity is transformed into one unit of the processed product and, in turn, one unit of the final product sold at retail.

We assume that there is no domestic supply of the agricultural commodity and at this point abstract from the problem of vertical restraints by assuming arm's length pricing. The retail demand curve for the final (processed) product that is sold at the retail level is given by D. Assuming neither processing nor retailing costs, if the retailing and processing sectors were perfectly competitive, equilibrium would be where the retail demand and the agricultural commodity supply curves intersect. However, assuming the retailing sector is

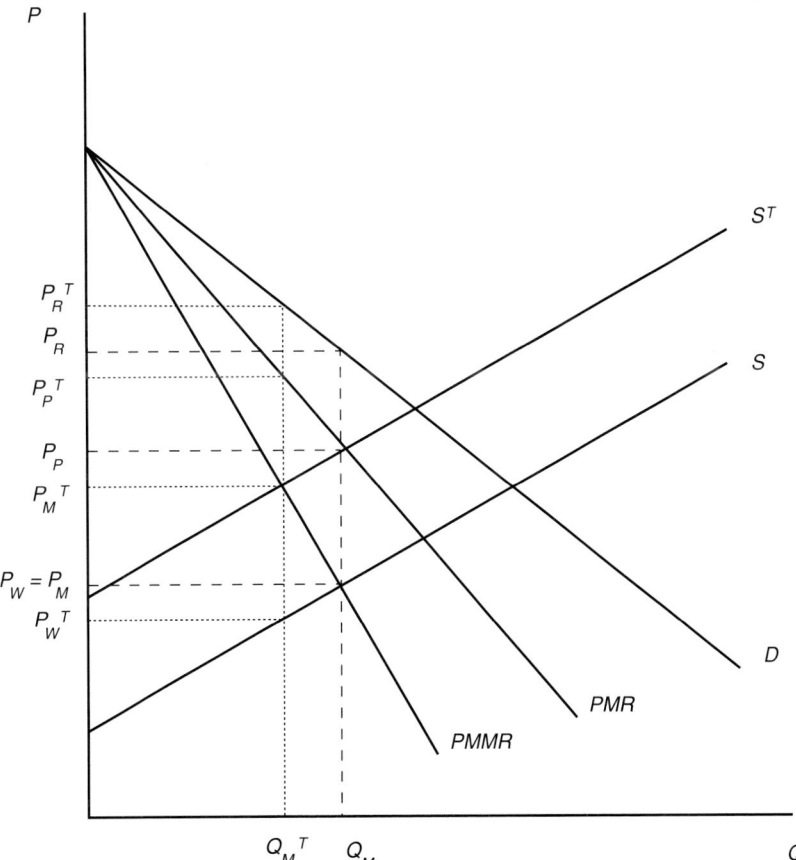

Fig. 6.2. Trade liberalization and the vertical marketing chain.

imperfectly competitive, the marginal revenue curve that corresponds to this retail demand curve is given by *PMR*, the perceived marginal revenue function. Specifically, the slope of *PMR* captures the nature of competition at the retail stage.

At one extreme, if the retailing sector were either a monopoly or group of firms acting as a perfect cartel, the slope of *PMR* would be twice that of the demand curve *D*. As the retail sector becomes more competitive, the slope of *PMR* becomes shallower as it rotates towards the demand curve. Within limits, if the retail sector were perfectly competitive, the marginal revenue curve would coincide with the market demand curve.

In this vertically related set-up, this perceived marginal revenue function is the derived demand curve facing the food processing sector. Again, assuming this sector to be imperfectly competitive, the marginal revenue function corresponding to the processing stage is given by *PMMR*, the slope of the perceived marginal revenue function reflecting competition in both the retail and food processing sectors. In this set-up, the derived demand curve facing the developing agricultural exporter is not the retail demand curve, but is the *PMMR* curve at the food processing stage.

This stylized model characterizes successive oligopoly with imperfect competition at both the processing and retail stages of the food chain. In the context of successive oligopoly, there is the double marginalization problem with mark-ups characterizing the links between the import and food processing sector's output and then the processing and the retail sector's output.[7]

At the first stage, the food processing sector purchases the raw agricultural commodity from the developing country exporter. Assuming that a tariff is applied on the agricultural commodity, the export supply curve is given by S^T. Imports are therefore Q_M^T, giving a margin of $P_P^T - P_M^T$ at the processing stage and $P_R^T - P_P^T$ at the retail stage. Export (world) prices for the agricultural exporter are given by P_W^T, which represents a relatively small share of the final retail price of P_R^T.

Consider now what happens with the trade liberalization through reduction of tariffs. In Fig. 6.2, the export supply function is now *S*. Quantities imported by the developed country increase to Q_M and export (world) market prices rise to P_W from P_W^T, thus increasing export revenues and producer surplus for the exporting country. This is the expected benefit from trade liberalization for developing country exporters. However, it is not as large as it would be if the downstream sectors were competitive. Specifically, mark-ups throughout the vertically related food chain change, with the retail sector mark-up changing to $P_R - P_P$ and the processing margin now being given by $P_P - P_W$.

Importantly, it can be shown under fairly reasonable conditions regarding the shape of the demand function, with incomplete pass-through of the tariff reduction as discussed in the section above, the margins of the food processing and retailing firms both increase as a result of the liberalization of the tariff. Consumers also benefit from trade liberalization, the retail price falling to P_R, but not by as much if the vertically related food marketing system was characterized by perfect competition.

The main point here is that the impact of trade liberalization with industry concentration in a vertically related industry is different – both in terms of magnitude and distributional effects – compared to the case of perfect competition. Specifically, the food processors and retailers are able to absorb some of the benefits from the reduction in the tariff on the imported raw agricultural commodity, and commodity producers receive a lower share of the vertical rents.

Food industry consolidation and developing country exports

We now turn to the impact on developing country exporters of increasing consolidation in the developed country food marketing system. Specifically, assuming with free trade in the agricultural commodity that the food retailing sector becomes more concentrated due, for example, to a merger at the retail stage and, as a result, food retailers act less competitively. The effects of this are shown in Fig. 6.3, where the perceived marginal revenue function rotates to PMR', which in turn rotates the perceived marginal revenue function at the processing stage to $PMMR'$. This reduces market access for the developing country exporter, reducing imports of the agricultural commodity from Q_M to Q_M', with a concomitant reduction in the world price from P_W to P_W'.

Mark-ups at both the food retailing and processing stages also increase as a consequence of the increase in concentration in the retail sector, the retail price increasing to P_R' and the processing price increasing to P_P'. Coupled with reduced market access are the lower export prices that raw commodity suppliers receive. Taken together, increasing concentration of the food sector in developed countries has potentially significant effects on developing country exporters, and this subject has received little attention in the literature.

In conclusion, in this section we have highlighted, with a simple model of the food marketing system in developed countries, three key issues that arise for developing

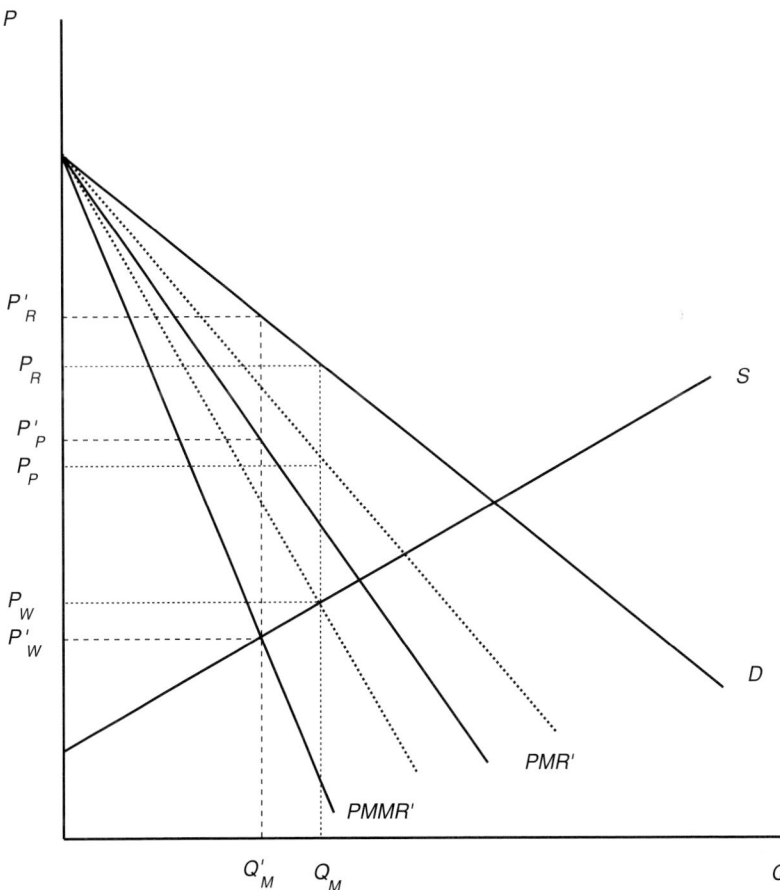

Fig. 6.3. Increased concentration in the vertical marketing chain.

country exporters. First, if exporters of raw agricultural commodities face a marketing system that is characterized by a structure of successive oligopoly and the associated problem of double marginalisation, reduction of import tariffs – while increasing commodity prices – will not necessarily result in exporters obtaining a larger share of the consumer's food 'dollar' in developed countries. In fact, it is more than likely that developed country food processors and retailers will increase their margins due to the fact that they will not fully pass on tariff reductions to consumers. Second, the increase in market access is determined by the degree of market power exerted in the downstream food sectors.

Third, as the food processing and retailing sectors become more concentrated in developed countries – and probably less competitive – this will probably reduce even further the share of commodity exporters in the available rents in the food marketing system. This implies that developing country exporters may benefit as much from focusing on food processing and other value-adding activities further down the vertical marketing chain as from trade liberalization. In other words, even if raw agricultural commodity prices do increase with trade liberalization, over time further consolidation in the food marketing system will simply serve to erode the share of the final retail price earned by developing country exporters.

Developing Country Access to Vertical Chains

In this section, we consider some of the issues involved when developing country exporters are faced with the problem of market access in the context of a vertically related market. Market access at the raw commodity stage – as is presumed by most of the models focusing on trade liberalization – does not give much guidance for developing countries who wish to access markets closer to the consumer stage. We consider two issues: first, the problem of tariff escalation, and second, the issue of governance in global commodity chains and how this may affect the prospects for developing countries in increasing market access through up-grading their food and agricultural exports.

Tariff escalation

For developing countries attempting to diversify and upgrade their exports from raw agricultural commodities to processed food products, one of the most frequently mentioned difficulties is that of tariff escalation. Tariff escalation occurs when tariffs on imports of processed goods are higher than the tariffs on the corresponding raw commodity. UNCTAD (2002b) has recently cited this issue as one of the main problems facing developing country exporters in diversifying their export profile.

Lindland (1998) provides some evidence of tariff escalation in the food sector for the USA, the EU and Japan, a summary of which is provided in Table 6.4. The recent evidence on the extent of tariff escalation is, however, rather mixed since, in many commodity sectors supported by government intervention in the developed countries, the tariff on the raw commodity is often exceptionally high. Nevertheless, for many commodities in which further processing seems possible, tariff escalation continues to be an issue.

The important point about tariff escalation in the context discussed here is twofold. First, the discussion reasonably assumes that the commodity exporting country can process and export the raw commodity and therefore potentially access the downstream rent.[8] Second, the effect on tariff reductions at this stage will depend on the passback effect discussed above. Via this mechanism, commodity prices may fall more so than the intermediate price (and by a greater extent relative to the pass-through effect). Hence, raw commodity producers may receive an even smaller share of the value added. Offsetting this, of

Table 6.4. Levels of tariff escalation by highest group post-Uruguay round (from Lindland, 1998).

Commodity group	Processing stage	Level of tariff escalation (%)
USA		
Dairy and egg products	2nd	39.5
Dairy and egg products	1st	33.6
Sugar products and sweeteners	1st	31.2
Sugar products and sweeteners	2nd	27.7
Dairy and egg products	3rd	15.6
EU		
Fruit products	2nd	84.8
Sugar products and sweeteners	4th	37.2
Dairy and egg products	2nd	34.4
Root and tuber products	1st	19.8
Tobacco and pyrethrum	1st	14.1
Japan		
Dairy and egg products	2nd	160.1
Sugar products and sweeteners	1st	82.2
Root and tuber products	1st	50.3
Hides and skins	3rd	30.0
Dairy and egg products	1st	29.1

course, is a share of the downstream rents which will increase the distribution between the raw and first-stage processing being determined by domestic distributive mechanisms.

Governance in vertical markets

In Figs 6.2 and 6.3, we characterized the vertically linked nature of the food marketing chain, highlighting the role of competition in the downstream stages. As such, market access issues refer not only to the level of tariffs that may be ameliorated by trade liberalization and preferential access agreements but also in terms of the ability of exporters to access the retail stage. This will typically involve some degree of upgrading, either by marketing the product directly or by further processing.

There is a strand in the development literature that deals with these issues, known as 'global commodity chain' or 'value chain' analysis (Kaplinsky, 2000; UNCTAD, 2000). This framework recognizes that market access for developing country exporters is difficult and that successful market access will involve contact with firms throughout the vertically linked chain regarding a broad range of issues including product quality, safety, delivery, packaging and traceability.

As Gereffi (1999) noted, participation in such global commodity chains is a necessary step for upgrading and diversifying developing country exports. By implication, marketing outside these commodity chains would involve considerable search costs, both in terms of finding marketing outlets and in identifying the needs of consumers, barriers that would be formidable given the increasing concentration of the retailing sector in many developed countries.

In contrast, participation in such commodity chains and the establishment of appropriate networks has the potential to play an important role in providing technical assistance, product upgrading, product quality and identifying appropriate marketing opportunities and, more broadly, access to the retail stage of the vertically related food chain.

In this context, this framework serves to highlight that access to developed country markets and capturing some of the downstream rents is more than simply the reduction in tariffs, and that other constraints exist which may also be affected by the existence of non-tariff barriers. Both of these issues and the subsequent distribution of the vertical rent are dependent on the characteritics of market structure in the downstream food sector.

Summary and Conclusions

There are three overall points to be extracted from this chapter. The first is to recognize that, in assessing the impact of trade liberalization, it is necessary to understand fully the vertical linkages that characterize food markets in many developed countries. Given that the food sector is most appropriately characterized by successive oligopoly, with developing country exporters of raw commodities entering at the first stage of the food chain, the implication of reducing tariffs is different in magnitude from that implied by models that assume perfect competition.

Moreover, the distributional effects may also differ relative to the perfectly competitive case and may result, somewhat paradoxically, in developing countries receiving a lower share of the total value added within the food chain as trade reform occurs. This arises since, with incomplete pass-through of the tariff reduction, mark-ups in the downstream sector increase. This issue needs further attention from economists and policy-makers.

Second, consolidation has increased in the food industry in developed (and developing) countries in recent years. This may also have implications for developing country exporters in terms of market access and the prices they receive. In particular, increasing concentration at either the retailing or processing sector (or both), will reduce the share that developing countries receive within the food marketing chain.

Third, there have long been calls for developing countries to diversify the composition of their exports. In recent years, these issues have been reflected in several publications by UNCTAD (2000, 2002b), urging developing countries to reduce their reliance on raw commodities and to export more high-value, processed food products.

As we have argued in this chapter, such a strategy is likely to face obstacles when we account for the highly concentrated nature of the vertical chain that characterizes the food industry in developed countries. This is not just an issue of tariff escalation, but an issue that must also recognize the buyer-driven nature of the food chain.

These issues also have potential consequences for the organization of agricultural production in developing countries, as large farmers may be more capable of meeting the requirements of the food industry in developed countries. Taken together, the vertically related, highly concentrated nature of the food sector in developed countries raises many issues for developing countries attempting to increase market access and the returns from exporting agricultural and food products. These issues have, by and large, been ignored by economists and policy-makers in providing estimates about what further trade reform may bring to developing countries.

Consequently, to understand fully the implications of trade reform for raw commodity exporters and the issues for developing countries attempting to diversify their export profile, further attention needs to be paid to the issue of industry consolidation and market structure in developed country food markets.

Notes

1. All three sectors are dominated by a small number of firms. For example, in 1995, ten firms accounted for 62% of global coffee bean trade while, in 1998, five firms accounted for 58% of sales of roasted coffee in the European market (Fitter and Kaplinsky, 2001).
2. Data are sourced from FAO (2005).
3. It should be noted that numbers do not necessarily equate with behaviour. Nevertheless, empirical methods that have been applied to test for the extent of market power in the food sector confirm the existence of market power. See Sexton and Lavoie (2001) and Sheldon and Sperling (2003).

4   Two related papers also highlight the issues addressed in this section. In Sexton et al. (forthcoming), a theoretical model is calibrated to quantify the distribution of vertical rents following trade reform. In McCorriston (2006b), the comparison between trade reform in the general economics literature and the specific issues that arise with vertical chains are discussed.
5   Specifically, that the retail demand function is not too convex. For example, with a constant elasticity demand function, the pro-competitive effects will not hold as the price cost margin will not change. For demand functions that are sufficiently linear, the pro-competitive effects will hold.
6   For a discussion of the issues of pass-through and pass-back within a unified framework, see McCorriston et al. (2005).
7   This vertically related market structure could easily be changed to one where both food processors and retailers behave competitively in their output markets, but exert oligopsonistic power in the purchase of the raw agricultural commodity and processed food product, respectively. In this case, the perceived marginal resource cost curves at retail and processing would have a steeper slope than the agricultural commodity supply curve, generating oligopsonistic mark-downs at each stage.
8   However, with the increasing role of multinationals in the food sector discussed above, some of this vertical rent may accrue to foreign-owned firms.

References

Chavez, M. (2002) The transformation of Mexican retailing with NAFTA. *Development Policy Review* 20, 503–513.

Competition Commission (2000) *Supermarkets: a Report on the Supply of Groceries from Multiple Stores in the United Kingdom*, Cm 4842. TSO, London.

Cotterill, R.W. (1999) *Continuing Concentration in Food Industries Globally: Strategic Challenges to an Unstable Status Quo. Research Report No. 49.* University of Connecticut, Food Marketing Policy Center, Connecticut, USA.

FAO (2005) *State of Commodity Markets, 2004.* Food and Agriculture Organsiation, Rome.

Farina, E.M.M.Q. (2002) Consolidation, multinationalization, and competition in Brazil: impacts on horticulture and dairy products systems. *Development Policy Review* 20, 441–457.

Fitter, R. and Kaplinsky, R. (2001) *Can an Agricultural 'Commodity' be De-commodified, and if so, Who is to Gain? Discussion Paper 380, 2001.* Institute of Development Studies, University of Sussex, Brighton, UK.

Gereffi, G. (1999) International trade and industrial upgrading in the apparel commodity chain. *Journal of International Economics* 48, 37–70.

Gutman, G.E. (2002) Impact of the rapid rise of supermarkets on dairy products systems in Argentina. *Development Policy Review* 20, 409–427.

Hughes, D. (2002) Grocery retailing in europe and emerging routes to the consumer. *EuroChoices* 1, 12–16.

Kaplinsky, R. (2000) Value chain analysis? *Journal of Development Studies* 37, 117–146.

Lindland, J. (1998) The impact of the Uruguay Round on tariff escalation in agricultural products. *Food Policy* 22, 487–500.

McCorriston, S. (2002) Why should imperfect competition matter to agricultural economists? *European Review of Agricultural Economics* 29, 349–372.

McCorriston, S. (2006a) Imperfect competition and international agricultural commodity markets. In: Sarris, A. and Hallam, D. (eds) *Agricultural Commodity Markets and Trade: New Approaches to Analyzing Market Structure and Instability.* Edward Elgar, Gloucester, UK.

McCorriston, S. (2006b) Trade liberalization in imperfectly competitive commodity markets. Paper given at *Conference on Governance, Coordination and Distribution along Commodity Value Chains.* FAO Rome, April 2006.

McCorriston, S. and Sheldon, I. (1997) Vertical restraints and competition policy in the US and UK food marketing systems. *Agribusiness* 15, 27–38.

McCorriston, S., Morgan, C.W. and Rayner, A.J. (2001) Price transmission: the interaction between market power and returns to scale. *European Review of Agricultural Economics* 28, 143–159.

McCorriston, S., Morgan, C.W. and Rayner, A.J. (2005) Imperfect competition and the shifting of output and input taxes in vertically related markets. *Public Finance* 54 , 73–83.

Oxfam (2001) *Bitter Coffee: how the Poor are paying for the Slump in Coffee Prices*. Oxfam, Oxford, UK.

Oxfam (2003a) *Northern Agricultural Policies and World Poverty: will the Doha 'Development Round' make a difference?* Oxfam, Oxford, UK.

Oxfam (2003b) *Running into the Sand: why Failure at the Cancún Trade Talks Threatens the World's Poorest People*. Oxfam, Oxford, UK.

Sexton, R.J. and Lavoie, N. (2001) Food processing and distribution: an industrial organization approach. In: Gardner, B. and Rausser, G. (eds) *Handbook of Agricultural Economics*, Volume 1B. North-Holland, Amsterdam.

Sexton, R.J., Sheldon, I.M., McCorriston, S. and Wang, H. (forthcoming) Agricultural Trade Liberalization and Economic Development: The Role of Downstream Market Power. Agricultural Economics.

Sheldon, I.M. and Sperling, R. (2003) Estimating the extent of imperfect competition in the food industry: what have we learned? *Journal of Agricultural Economics* 54, 89–110.

UNCTAD (2000) *Strategies for Diversification and Adding Value to Food Exports: a Value Chain Perspective*. UNCTAD/DITC/COM/TM/1; UNCTAD/ITE/MISC.23, United Nations, Geneva.

UNCTAD (2002a) *World Investment Report 2002: Transnational Corporations and Export Competitiveness*. United Nations, Geneva.

UNCTAD (2002b) *Export Diversification, Market Access and Competitiveness*. UNCTAD/TD/B/COM.1/54, United Nations, Geneva.

US Census Bureau (2001) *Concentration Ratios in Manufacturing*. US Department of Commerce, US Census Bureau, Washington, DC.

Weldegebriel, H.T. (2004) Imperfect price transmission: is market power really to blame? *Journal of Agricultural Economics* 55, 101–114.

World Bank (2003) *Global Economic Prospects: Realizing the Development Promise of the Doha Agenda*. World Bank, Washington, DC.

7 Contracting, Competition and Rent Distribution in Supply Chains: Theory and Empirical Evidence from Central Asia

J.F.M. Swinnen, M. Sadler and A. Vandeplas

Introduction

Vertical coordination in agri-food supply chains, often induced by foreign investment, plays an important role in overcoming market imperfections and in creating private contract enforcement mechanisms in transition and developing countries. Contracts between private agents act as substitutes for missing or imperfect public enforcement institutions (McMillan, 1997; Gow and Swinnen, 2001).

Processing, marketing and input-supplying companies have engaged in a variety of, sometimes quite unconventional, forms of contracting with farms (see Swinnen, Chapter 5, Minten *et al.*, Chapter 12 and Maertens *et al.*, Chapter 13, this volume). Processors introduced programmes to improve farms' access to inputs. For example, in the Philippines, Hendriks (1994) noted that wholesale traders provided credit to farmers for fertilizers, pesticides and seeds in order to secure supply. In Kenya, contract farming is widely practised, as input finance is crucial for the production of many high-value and export crops (IFAD, 2003). The same is found in other African countries, e.g. in the cotton sector (Poulton *et al.*, 2004).

Effectively, what the companies do is what is described in the development economics literature as 'interlinking markets' (see e.g. Bardhan and Udry, 1999). In poor country villages that are governed by a dominant landlord, the landlord – because of the size of his assets and urban connections – is able to obtain credit more cheaply than other local agents. Thus the landlord is able to act as a financial intermediary between an outside loan market and his workers or tenants. Enforcement of the loans is secured by the landlord's dominant market position on the land and/or labour market.

An alternative model is of the trader-farmer in distant villages. Here, the farmer is dependent on the trader for access to the output markets while the trader acts as a financial intermediary, which allows the farmer better access to credit. Again, enforcement of the credit transaction (loan and repayment) occurs through the output market.

Interlinking markets can bring farm investment and production closer to optimal levels by circumventing imperfections in credit, input and output markets. In fact, there is substantial empirical evidence that these contracts are having important positive effects on efficiency, productivity and investment (see, e.g. Dries and Swinnen, 2004).

However, in trying to understand the micro-foundations of these new institutions, we should not be blind to their potentially adverse consequences. For example, the very nature of rationale for the emergence of these interlinked transactions may, at the same time, act as an important barrier to entry for other agents and may give the dominant partner in a transaction some additional leverage. As Bardhan and Udry (1999, p. 111) remark, 'the thin line between understanding an institution and justifying it is often blurred, particularly by careless interpreters of the theory'.

The objective of this chapter is therefore to analyse the equity and efficiency effects of interlinking in supply chains and the role of competition therein. The first section presents a conceptual model of interlinking to identify these effects; the second reviews insights from the literature and the third presents new evidence from the Central Asian cotton supply chains. The fourth and final section concludes.

A Conceptual Framework of Efficiency and Equity with Interlinking

To understand the relationship between equity and efficiency with interlinking markets, consider a contract between a supplying farm, with welfare represented by expected utility U^F, and a processing company, with expected utility U^C. Figure 7.1 illustrates the pre- and post-contracting welfare of the agents. Without interlinked contracts, the utility possibility frontier is $U_0 U_0$. Assume that actual pre-contract utility is at (U_0^F, U_0^C), represented by point A.

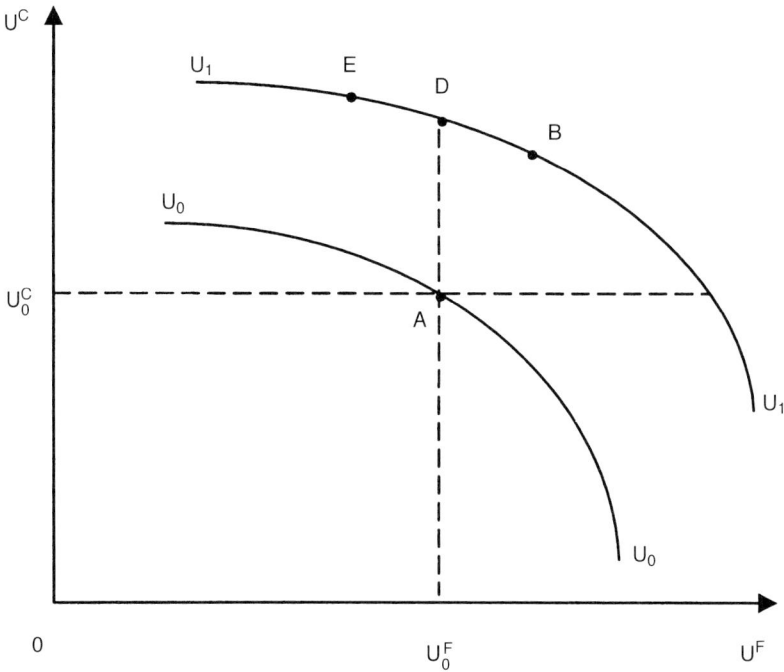

Fig. 7.1. Equity and efficiency effects of interlinking markets.

By introducing an interlinked contract, farms can access credit, inputs, etc. which were unavailable before and companies can have access to higher-quality and timely supplies. Total welfare increases and the utility possibility frontier shifts to U_1U_1. The question is: who benefits from the welfare increase – both agents or only one? In other words, will the new equilibrium be at point B, D, or E? At point B, both parties share in the gains from the institutional innovation, and everybody is better off. At point D, the processing firm extracts all the rents of the innovation.

There are several models in the development economics literature which illustrate how one can arrive at point D. For example, if company C sets the conditions of the contract, supplier F will accept the contract as long as it represents an improvement of its expected utility. Hence, at the margin, it will be optimal for C to present F with a contract with conditions which provide F with an expected utility equal to U_0^F, F's reservation utility. This is the case represented by point D. The development models show how in output–credit market interlinkages (trader-farmer), C typically does this by subsidizing credit (lower interest rates) and taxing output (lower output prices).

However, it can get worse. The interlinking of transactions may actually bestow additional monopoly power upon C. Bell (1988) showed how, in a Nash bargaining framework, a peasant may be worse off in dealing with a landlord with interlinked transactions than with separate bilateral bargains. Personalized and interlinked transactions can weaken the collective bargaining strengths of workers vis-à-vis employers (Bardhan, 1989). In these cases, one may end up at point E, where F's utility is actually lower after the contract innovations, despite the fact that total welfare has improved significantly.

Hence, an important – and very much an outstanding – issue is how to obtain the efficiency gains without negative equity effects from these institutional innovations.

Available empirical evidence indicates that, in many developing and transition countries, positive equity effects seem to have occurred in many cases (Swinnen, Chapter 5, this volume; World Bank, 2006).

In transition countries, the collapse of farm output and livestock numbers created a gap between processing capacity and supply, and an excess demand based on processing capacity, especially for high quality. This makes it a 'suppliers' market' in most of Eastern Europe and Central Asia, and this supports the farms' bargaining position in the supply chain. Similarly, in many developing countries there is a shortage of quality supplies for processing and retail companies in high-value chains (e.g. Codron et al., 2004).

However, an increase in competition between suppliers may lead to a consolidation of the supplier base. Supplier assistance programmes sometimes discriminate between farms with the focus of upgrading the better farms and ensuring a minimal supply base and quality from the rest, as long as it is required. Hence, those who are concerned about the inclusion of small farms should not be complacent, despite the observations of significant contracting with small suppliers nowadays.

The Role of Competition

Intuitively, one would expect that competition among processors and retailers should play an important role in rent distribution. First, excess processing capacity and shortage of quality supplies would increase the incentives for processors to provide farm support, and therefore induce a shift from the $U_0 U_0$ to the U_1U_1 frontier, for example from A to B.

Secondly, competition on the processing side would prevent companies from exercising monopoly power in the setting of the contract conditions and would make it more likely that one would end up somewhere around point B, or even H, rather than at D, or even E. This is illustrated in Fig. 7.2. Companies can either compete on the producer prices offered or on the

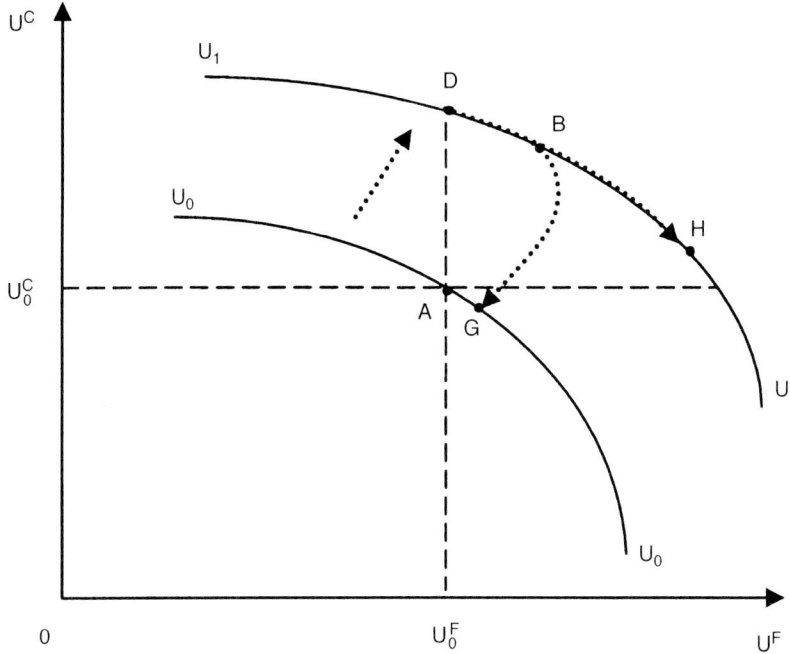

Fig. 7.2. Effects of competition on interlinking markets.

services they provide to their suppliers, including input programmes.

However, thirdly, there may be a problem of sustainability of the new contracts with more competition. For example, with pre-financed feed by dairy companies, or pre-financed seed and fertilizer by crop-processing companies, farms can sell their output to competing processors who can offer higher prices, since these latter do not have to incorporate the costs of the assistance programmes. This may cause the collapse of the contracts, and is more likely to occur with more competition.

Moreover, with more competition, the penalty for opportunistic behaviour becomes lighter: firstly because the threat of cut-off from future credit arrangements is less stringent, as there are other credit providers available (Hoff and Stiglitz, 1998); secondly because reputation effects are less prevalent in a competitive market, where buyers are less likely to coordinate and share information.

In summary, if we consider Fig. 7.2 again, while competition seems important in inducing a desirable distribution of the gains (i.e. being at point B or H instead of D or E), competition could undermine the ability to obtain the gains, i.e. one would fall back to point G.

The two questions of: (i) which of the indicated effects is more important; and (ii) what the resulting welfare effects could be, are essentially an empirical issue. In the rest of this chapter we present two sets of empirical evidence on this issue. In the next section, we review evidence from the literature in developing and transition countries. Afterwards, we present evidence based on a new study of the cotton supply chains in Central Asia.

Empirical Insights from the Literature

The empirical literature reports different, and sometimes even conflicting, effects of competition on interlinking. There is substantial evidence that contract terms improve with more competition, but also that input and credit programmes have collapsed because of (too much) competition and opportunistic behaviour by farmers. More specifically, the literature provides case studies and evidence that support each of the theoretical arguments made above.

First, some studies show that more competition leads to a necessity for support programmes and a concomitant willingness to provide them. Secondly, other studies show that competition increases the suppliers' bargaining position, inducing a shift in producer prices or forcing buyers to provide more extensive farm support. Thirdly, empirical evidence confirms that many input programmes have collapsed due to competition. In the last part of this section we try to provide some general conclusions from this review and to identify institutional mechanisms that can solve the sustainability problems of input programmes in a competitive environment.

Competition improves contract terms for farmers

First, there is considerable evidence that increased competition following price and trade liberalization increased prices for farmers in Asia and Africa. For example, in Tanzania, the parastatal monopoly of the Cotton Board was eliminated in 1994 (Baffes, 2004). As a result of the increasing competition in cotton marketing and ginning, suppliers received an average share of 51% of export prices, compared to 41% before liberalization.

In Zimbabwe, producer prices improved as well, when new companies entered the market: before liberalization, the average producer price was 42% of the world market price (Larsen, 2002). After liberalization, it reached 53% on average. However, there is a huge year-to-year variability in producer prices.

Liberalization also boosted producer incentives in Zambia (Boughton et al., 2003). National cotton production climbed from an average of 20,000 to 80,000 tons. Over the period 1995–2000, Zambia paid the highest average producer price share of Sub-Saharan Africa, amounting to 56% of the export price.

In Pakistan, price liberalization, privatized export trade and the elimination of export restrictions and taxes have all contributed to higher prices and greater production incentives for cotton growers under interlinked arrangements (Smith et al., 1999). Opportunities for rent extraction are minimized as farmers can shift easily between lenders, according to the price and quality of the services offered.

Secondly, several studies report that competition leads to a higher bargaining power of the suppliers, who may threaten to deliver to other buyers if no input or credit is extended to them. This is found to be the case in Africa, Asia and in several transition countries (Fisman and Raturi, 2004; World Bank, 2006). For example, in the Pakistani cotton market, more competition amongst buyers has led to a tighter supply market, and credit was the only way of ensuring availability of supply (Smith et al., 1999).

In Zimbabwe, although price competition among cotton ginners is weak, ginners compete on the services they offer to farmers, more specifically with respect to input and credit provision (Larsen, 2002). In Eastern Europe, competition between dairy and sugar processors contributed to the spreading of farm assistance programmes (Gow et al., 2000; World Bank, 2006).

Competition undermines input and credit programme enforcement

There is also considerable evidence, however, that competition undermines the sustainability of input and credit programmes. For example, in Chile, credit provision programmes from traders in traditional small farmer crops like wheat, maize and beans have been abandoned, because of the numerous alternative marketing channels for these crops and the concomitant frequency of opportunistic sales by suppliers (Conning, 2000).

In Kenya's horticultural sector, companies without a dominant market share are subject to vigorous side-selling (IFAD, 2003). Frigoken, a French bean exporter, loses around 20% of its production to its competitors. Honey Care Africa, a Fair Trade honey exporter and Kenya Nut Ltd., a cashew and macadamia nut processor, closed down their credit provision programmes because of the losses due to 'pirate sales'.

In the Zambian paprika sector, Cheetah Zambia reported that approximately 30–40% of total production ended up with its competitors (IFAD, 2003). Omnia Ltd., a leading fertilizer producer and manufacturer in Zambia, also closed down its credit scheme due to serious credit losses. The main reason for non-repayment appeared to be that smallholders did not expect the company to take serious action against defaulters.

Moreover, while the liberalization process in Asia and Africa has improved prices for farms, it has also undermined some of the traditional input supply systems. For example, in the Tanzanian cotton sector, inputs became more expensive and less available as they were no longer provided by the Cotton Board. In fact, both input and credit provision collapsed. Some authors argue that the main reason why input and credit supply chain programmes are still functioning in some countries is because of the limited competition, due to state intervention. The evidence for this is mostly limited to the cotton sector (Poulton et al., 2004).

For example, in the Zimbabwean cotton sector, input credit provision remains viable. There are only three major players: (i) Cottco, the former parastatal, which continues to assume price leadership; (ii) Cargill, the US multinational; and (iii) Cotpro, in which Cottco has a 60% stake, and the remaining 40% is French. Cottco's loan recovery rate can be up to 98%. Cottco and Cotpro are providing input credit, while Cargill is relying on its competitors' services: suppliers deliver the contracted amounts to Cottco and Cotpro, and the surplus is sold to Cargill at more attractive rates. Up to now, input provision has remained viable, but competition is intensifying in the sector: Cottco's market share decreased from 79% (2000) to 58% (2004). At the same time, the producer share of the export price increased to 78% over the same period (Hanyani-Mlambo et al., 2005).

A large degree of concentration remained after liberalization in the Zambian cotton sector as well; two dominant cotton ginneries, Dunavant and Clark Cotton, together hold a market share of 80–90% in the cotton sector. Dunavant's recovery rate for its input credit programmes was around 85% in 2001.

Mozambican cotton companies work under government-allocated land concessions, forging local monopoly conditions (Boughton et al., 2003; IFAD, 2003). Cotton companies in Mozambique are obliged to provide input credit to all producers. Foreign-owned firms purchasing tobacco and maize from small farmers also benefit from such concessions. Companies without monopolistic concessions do not provide input credit, as this is perceived as being unsustainable. On the other hand, in Mozambique, producer price shares for cotton are the lowest in the region: under 40% of the export price.

Making interlinking sustainable under competition

In summary, farms benefit from price competition between buyers. More competition leads to more equal rent sharing. But if competition becomes too vigorous in the interlinked input and credit market, coordination may break down and farmers may undermine their own productivity through strategic defaulting.

Fortunately, there is evidence that institutional arrangements can prevent, or at least mitigate, these effects. This way, perverse effects of buyer competition are circumvented, such that competition can lead to higher efficiency and more equitable rent sharing.

A first and obvious strategy to avoid side-selling, is to offer reliable and attractive contract terms. In Zimbabwe, incentive premiums are awarded to loyal farmers by Cottco and Cotpro, while defaulting farmers are effectively penalized (Larsen, 2002).

A second strategy is to build an informal, personal relationship between buyer and supplier: frequent monitoring and field contact appears to contribute substantially to the reduction of pirate sales as well. Intensive monitoring is an important element of the high-value interlinked vegetable chains in Madagascar (Minten et al., 2006).

Buyers can coordinate in order to avoid strategic default by suppliers. In Uganda, ginners and exporters have formed an association (UGEA), with compulsory membership of all cotton ginners (Gordon, 2000). Credit is provided by a parastatal, the Cotton Development Organization. Ginners are responsible for credit repayment, based on levies charged to the suppliers. Suppliers are free to sell their cotton to any ginner, as they are all paying the same prices and charging the same levies. Meanwhile, farmers' share in world prices rose from below 50% to 70% in the period 1995/1996– 2003/2004.

A similar strategy is applied in Benin, where the CSPR (Centrale de Sécurisation des Paiements et des Recouvrements) was established in 2000 to insure recovery of input credit and producer payment without delay (Goreux and Macrae, 2003). Since many ginneries are operating below capacity, the CSPR allocates a quota to each ginnery in terms of the maximum amount of seed cotton they are allowed to buy. The system appears to work but, meanwhile, it remains heavily regulated.

However, such coordination may also lead to collusion, with the opposite effects. For example, in Ghana, following liberalization, private cotton companies colluded with respect to prices, such that suppliers were offered relatively low producer prices, but there was no coordination in the interlinked credit market (Poulton, 1998). Incidental side-selling resulted in low credit recovery. To make things worse, the Ministry of Agriculture was then urged to implement a local monopoly system, where each company was allowed the exclusive right of purchasing cotton in a certain zone. Similar developments occurred in Tajikistan (see below). These actions contribute to rent extraction, instead of alleviating it.

Another way of avoiding side-selling to competing buyers is by reinforcing reputation effects. By making information on opportunistic behaviour publicly available, reputation losses can be severe, and violation of agreements is strongly discouraged. This mechanism is not restricted to developing countries: Bernstein (2001) describes the US cotton industry, where buyers' associations are deliberately making reputation-related information available. Members who do not comply with the rules of the association may be suspended or expelled and will have their names publicized. The profitability of their future business will be seriously affected in this way.

In Kenya, side-selling of part of the harvest to competitors at more attractive prices was avoided by conditioning future credit limits on past sales records (Jayne et al., 2003). This system also discourages suppliers from diverting received fertilizer and chemicals to other crops.

A final example is to use alternative, informal mechanisms of contract enforcement. For example, in Zimbabwe, as noted above, input provision by Cottco and Cotpro remains viable, in spite of side-selling to Cargill (Larsen, 2002). Apart from other techniques formerly mentioned, micro-finance group lending techniques are applied, similar to the Grameen banking principle as described by Stiglitz (1990). Interlinked contracts are assigned to groups of 5–30 suppliers. If one of them defaults, the whole group is penalized. In this way, local information is used in the process of self-selection of supplier groups. Other strategies based on peer monitoring were adapted by Pakistani agricultural traders (Smith et al., 1999). New suppliers of cotton need to put forward a 'guarantor' in order to be eligible for input credit provision. In Tanzania (Poulton, 1998), 'local information networks' were addressed to intermediate in supplier selection for input provision programmes. In this way, a supplier's reputation is used as 'social collateral' to obtain a loan: an elegant way of overcoming capital constraints.

Summary

There is substantial empirical evidence not only that contract terms improve with more competition, but also that input and credit programmes have collapsed because of (too much) competition and opportunistic behaviour by farmers. Most empirical evidence presented here comes from developing countries, where contract enforcement institutions are particularly weak and effective sanctions against side-selling are rarely applied. For transition countries, less empirical analysis is available on this topic. Insightful results can be derived from our study of the Central Asian cotton sector, where contract farming is widespread.

Empirical Evidence from the Cotton Chains in Central Asia

Vertical coordination (VC), including contracting and interlinking, is widespread in the cotton supply chains in four Central Asian countries (Uzbekistan, Tajikistan, Kyrgyzstan and Kazakhstan). The reason for VC is to overcome important constraints faced by farms, in particular access to credit, cotton seeds and irrigation. For example, small Kazakh cotton farmers point at access to credit (pre-finance) as their main motivation for entering into contracts with gins (see Table 7.1). The support provided by gins through interlinking arrangements with farmers addresses their primary constraints. For example, a 2003 survey showed that 81% of the Kazakh cotton farmers had received finance from the gins, and more than two-thirds seed and irrigation (water) (see Fig. 7.3).

However, the nature of the contracts and their effects differ dramatically between the countries. The reason is the different policies of the governments concerning privatization and, in particular, competition. In Kyrgyzstan and Kazakhstan farms have benefited from the reforms and from VC, with strong competition, resulting in high prices and strong cotton growth, while in Uzbekistan and Tajikistan VC resulted in major rent extraction of cotton farms due to the absence of competition, resulting in depressed prices and stagnating cotton production (see Table 7.2).

What is remarkable is that in countries where the government has allowed the private gins to develop and to compete, cotton farms are doing much better than elsewhere. In Tajikistan and Uzbekistan, where governments actively control (directly or indirectly) input supplies, production, processing and marketing in the cotton chain, farm prices are considerably lower than in Kyrgyzstan and Kazakhstan, where

Table 7.1. Contract motivations for cotton farms in Kazakhstan, 2003.

Reason for contracting (%)	Yes	No	Most important reason
Guaranteed product sales	9	91	8
Guaranteed price	4	96	3
Access to pre-financing	81	19	75
Access to quality inputs	11	89	10
Access to technical assistance	0	100	0
Other	4	96	3

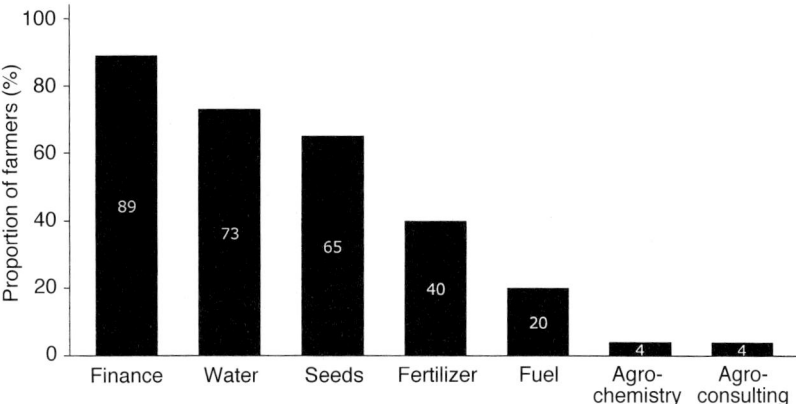

Fig. 7.3. Proportion of farmers receiving specific aspects of farming assistance from cotton gins in Kazakhstan, 2003 (from World Bank survey).

Table 7.2. Variations in Central Asian cotton production, 1992–2003[1] (from Sadler, 2006).

Measure	Kazakhstan	Kyrgyzstan	Uzbekistan	Tajikistan
Annual growth rate of harvested area (ha)				
1993–1998	12.3	6.0	−1.7	−3.7
1993–2003	5.8	7.6	−1.7	−0.1
Seed cotton production (1000 MTs)				
1993–1998	26.7	11.0	−2.3	8.4
1993–2003	8.9	11.5	−2.8	0.1
Baled cotton production (1000 MTs)				
1993–1998	12.6	20.4	−2.7	0.4
1993–2003	5.4	25.9	−2.6	−3.5
Seed cotton price per MT, 2003 (US$)	550.00	450.00	200.00	165.00

[1] There are significant differences in seed cotton production and baled cotton production. The most important reason for these differences is probably smuggling of seed cotton from Uzbekistan and Tajikistan to Kazakhstan and Kyrgyzstan, although there is no hard data to quantify the amounts of smuggled seed cotton.

the private sector has taken on these roles. However, not all is perfect in the latter countries. In Kyrgyzstan, the influx of illegal finance in the cotton chain has caused contract breaches and disruption of pre-finance agreements between gins and international traders, with major negative repercussions throughout the cotton chain. We now present more detailed evidence from each of these Central Asian countries.[1]

Uzbekistan

Cotton exports are a major source of government revenue in Uzbekistan, and the state has continued to impose strict controls on the cotton chain, including those enforced through government-controlled interlinking. Market reform has been slow. Nearly all gins remain under government ownership, and even the privately owned gins are subject to government control.

Cotton farm financing is available through a single form of contracting offered by the state through the two main state banks. These banks provide loans in amounts dictated by the central government. Funds are automatically transferred out of a producer's account to repay these loans as soon as payments are received by the producer. Inputs are provided through a centralized system of state-controlled enterprises. These enterprises give priority to large farms. Small private farmers often obtain access to equipment through unofficial arrangements with equipment operators in these farms. The government re-instituted a state monopoly on the purchase of cotton in 1995, with prices fixed at amounts based on estimated production costs.

With cotton prices set low by the state (see Table 7.2), households tend to sell their inputs for cash or use them on their own private plots for other crops. Officially, producers are required to sell 50% of their cotton production to the state. In practice, they often sell their entire crop to the state because they have no financing options except to use interlinked government financing for cotton.

Tajikistan

In Tajikistan too, the government continues to be heavily involved in the cotton chain, although less transparently. Cotton gins are jointly owned by the government and so-called 'investors', which are financial institutions with (informal) links to the government. There is no competition between the gins. They operate as monopolists in clearly delineated areas and prevent farms from delivering to other gins.

The vast majority of cotton is produced under interlinked finance package schemes, controlled by the 'investors'. They provide crop finance and sales contracts to the farms and also control the processing of the cotton. Their finance comes through pre-finance from the government and from one international cotton trader, Reinhart, which controls the vast majority of Tajik cotton exports. In 1997, this company negotiated a 'financing package' with the government of Tajikistan. Since then, the company, through a local bank (Agroinvest Bank), provides 77% of all agricultural credit in Tajikistan, 90% of which is for cotton (ADB, 2002a, b). Reinhart/Agroinvest Bank provides loans to gins which use these loans to further provide finance to producers through the provision of physical deliveries of fuel, seed and fertilizer.

This monopolized system leads to rent extraction from farmers with low seed cotton prices and inflated input prices (see Table 7.2; Asian Development Bank, 2002a,b). With strict control of cash accounts held by producers and the lack of competition between gins, cotton producers have no alternatives. The situation is worsened by government involvement in farm production plans and farm debts. Producers have no choice in production decisions because they cannot get financing for the production of anything but cotton. Moreover, accumulated debts on their imposed cotton production leave them no choice but to follow local authorities' (who guarantee the debts) production plans.

Kazakhstan

The situation is entirely different in Kazakhstan, where interlinked contracting is also widespread in cotton production, but where both producers and processors have been freed from government control for a few years and where competition between gins has produced much better conditions for cotton farms.

Kazakhstan initially also took a slow approach to the privatization of farms and gins, but much has changed since 1998. Gins were fully privatized by 1998 and, since then, many new gins have been established. Most gins began purchasing or hiring seed cotton delivery points to transport seed cotton from places outside their immediate area. The resulting competition and reduced transport costs have benefited (small) farms.

Cotton producers are generally too small to attract commercial credits directly, as they lack sufficient collateral and present a high default risk. They are mainly financed by gins. Gins provide crop finance, as well as supplying inputs, irrigation (water) and some agricultural services (Fig. 7.3). Large penalties have prevented opportunistic behaviour by farmers, as the perceived loss clearly exceeded the potential gains from side-selling. In case of default, a farmer would have to repay his outstanding debts: he would incur a penalty of 15% of the value of seed cotton not delivered under the contract and an increase in the cost of finance from 18 to 35%.

Gins obtain funds for these financing operations from three sources – trader financing, facilities with domestic banks and from their own cash reserves. Trader financing takes the form of forward sales of cotton, against which the gins receive a percentage of the value of the cotton that is due to be delivered under the contract. Ginners and traders have established good trading relations through this system over the past 10 years.

Kyrgyzstan

The situation in Kyrgyzstan is more complex. Privatization, removal of government control and competition seem to have induced a rapid expansion of the Kyrgyz cotton sector, albeit from a very small base, with similar effects as seen in Kazakhstan for farms. However, a poor supporting infrastructure and contract breaches with international traders a few years ago have negatively affected the growth of the cotton chain and contracting.

That said, cotton production and processing continues to expand strongly, partly based on smuggled Uzbek cotton, induced by the large price gap for seed cotton between Uzbekistan and Kyrgyzstan. Many new gins have been constructed in recent years, often investments by Russian and Turkish textile companies.

Contracts are not needed for the processing of smuggled Uzbek seed cotton, which is bought on a cash basis. However, locally produced cotton is based on prefinance contracts by the gins. This system was functioning well until a few years ago, as gins were themselves financed under pre-finance contracts with international traders. However, ownership and management of several gins changed around 2000 as the cotton sector was a target for money-laundering strategies, and contracts were breached and pre-finance from international traders has largely ceased.

This has strongly affected contracting with farms, as now gins themselves have problems accessing funds to finance the contracts. As a result, ginners have to provide financing out of their own cash reserves and this hampers their ability to finance large amounts of seed cotton. Privatized ginners supply finance under seed cotton 'forward' contracts, with the producer contracting to deliver a predefined quantity of seed cotton to the gin and the ginner agreeing to supply the producer with local currency and inputs at certain times of the season to cover the cost of inputs and labour.

Summary and Conclusions

The evidence presented here indicates that contracting and interlinking is very important in the cotton supply chains in Central Asia, but that the equity and efficiency effects differ strongly between countries. An important reason is the difference in competition between processors.

In fact, this comparative analysis of contracting and interlinking in the cotton sector in Central Asia confirms the importance of competition as an important factor in protecting small farms against rent extraction by large processors. The only places where we find clear evidence that farmers are consistently exploited are in government-controlled monopolized systems, such as the cotton systems in Uzbekistan, Tajikistan and Turkmenistan.

In contrast, in Kazakhstan and Kyrgyzstan, the cotton chain is characterized by strong competition between private gins buying cotton seeds from small farms for processing, with much better conditions for farmers.

While there remain important problems in the Kazakh and Kyrgyz cotton systems, compared to the situation in Uzbekistan and Tajikistan, their situation seems to be considerably more favourable in terms of both equity and efficiency. Hence, competition plays a very important role in the cotton supply chains by inducing both beneficial equity and efficiency effects.

First, competition induces contracting spill-over effects across the sector, as other processors are forced to introduce similar supplier assistance programmes since suppliers may not want to deliver unless they get similar conditions. This finding of our study is a specific case of more general conclusions that competition is a key factor for encouraging innovation and productivity and that technological development is primarily encouraged through the presence of competition.[2]

As a result, farmers get much better prices with competition between processors. Table 7.2 illustrates that prices for Kazakh cotton farmers are two to three times higher than those in Uzbekistan or Tajikistan, where competition does not exist.

For the same reason, competition prevents farmers from being 'exploited' and allows farmers to get better conditions by changing gins. Competition prevents processing companies or input suppliers from exercising monopoly power in the setting of the contract conditions with farms. Almost all (92%) of the interviewed farmers in Kazakhstan said that they had changed ginnery over recent years if they got better prices or conditions, indicating independence and competition. All farmers (97%) said that they would be able to change gins if they wanted to.[3]

This competition process is reinforced by investment by cotton gins in cotton seed collection centres in various places. This means that a farmer now has the option of delivering his seed cotton locally, to a ginner who is not from that area. Competition shifts the cost of the transportation of the seed cotton to the ginner.

Concluding Comments

Vertical coordination in agri-food supply chains plays an important role in overcoming market imperfections and in creating private contract enforcement mechanisms in transition and developing countries. Processing, marketing and input-supplying companies have engaged in different types of contracts with farms. Processors have engaged in input provision in order to secure their supply, while input-supplying firms have engaged in output marketing, in order to increase their sales volume and ensure repayment of provided credit. This system of 'inter-linking markets' has the potential to bring farm investment and production closer to their optimal levels.

This chapter analyses the equity and efficiency effects of interlinking in supply chains and the impact of competition upon those. By introducing an interlinked contract, farms can access credit, inputs, etc. which were unavailable before – and processing companies – have access to higher-quality and timely supplies. Thus total welfare increases. It is not certain, however, that both parties gain from this transaction. That depends, amongst other factors, on the availability of supply, the degree of competition between firms and both parties' relative bargaining strength.

Empirical evidence reveals that competition has positive equity effects, but may have either positive or negative efficiency effects. In general, farmers benefit from competition between processing firms. More competition leads to more equal rent sharing, reflected in higher producer prices. More competition can also lead to competition on the services processing firms provide to farmers. As a result, farm assistance programmes may become widespread, resulting in positive efficiency effects.

But if competition becomes too vigorous in the interlinked input and credit market, coordination may break down. Farmers may undermine their own long-term productivity through strategic defaulting in the short term. Many case studies report input programmes have collapsed due to competition, proving empirical support for the negative efficiency effects of competition. In other cases, input programmes have remained sustainable under competition as a result of special institutional arrangements like frequent monitoring, buyer coordination or local information networks.

Our study of the cotton supply chain in four Central Asian countries indicates that contracting and interlinking is widely applied, but that equity and efficiency effects differ strongly. An important reason is the difference in competition between suppliers. The only places where we find clear evidence that farmers are exploited are in government-controlled, monopolized systems, like the cotton sectors in Uzbekistan and Tajikistan.

In contrast, farmers face much better conditions in Kazakhstan and Kyrgyzstan, where the cotton chain is characterized by strong competition between private gins buying cotton seeds from small farms for processing. In this case, competition has induced both beneficial equity and efficiency effects.

Acknowledgement

Anneleen Vandeplas was supported by the Grant NFWO-Fortis Bank and MeesPierson of the Research Foundation, Flanders, Belgium.

Notes

1 A more detailed and extensive analysis of the Central Asian cotton supply chains can be found in Sadler (2006).
2 These are key conclusions in the World Bank 2005 World Development Report on 'Improving the Investment Climate for Growth and Poverty Reduction'.
3 There appear to be regular contract breakdowns by farmers during the season when another gin offers a higher price. A system exists whereby one can get pre-finance and inputs from one gin and can repay the pre-finance and the inputs to that gin, plus a penalty for non-delivery, and then deliver one's cotton seeds to another gin.

References

Asian Development Bank (2002a) *Report and Recommendation of the President on a Proposed Loan for the Tajikistan Agriculture Rehabilitation Project.*
Asian Development Bank (2002b) *Cotton in Central Asia, a Review of Policy and Technology.*
Baffes, J. (2004) Tanzania's cotton sector: reforms, constraints and challenges. *Development Policy Review* 22, 75–96.
Bardhan, P. (ed.) (1989) *The Economic Theory of Agrarian Institutions.* Clarendon Paperbacks, Oxford, UK.
Bardhan, P. and Udry, C. (1999) *Development Microeconomics.* Oxford University Press, Oxford, UK.
Bell, C. (1988) Credit markets and interlinked transactions. In: Chenery, H.B. and Srinivasan, T.N. (eds) *Handbook of Development Economics.* North-Holland, Amsterdam, pp. 763–830.
Bernstein, L. (2001) *Private Commercial Law in the Cotton Industry: Creating Cooperation through Rules, Norms and Institutions.* John M. Olin Law and Economics Working Paper No. 133. The Law School, University of Chicago, Illinois.
Boughton, D., Tschirley, D., Zulu, B., Ofio, A.O. and Marrule, H. (2003) Cotton sector policies and performance in Sub-Saharan Africa: lessons behind the numbers in Mozambique and Zambia. Paper prepared for presentation at the *25th International Conference of Agricultural Economists,* 16–22 August 2003, Durban, Republic of South Africa.
Codron, J.M., Bouhsina, Z., Fort, F., Coudel, E. and Puech, A. (2004) Supermarkets in low-income Mediterranean countries: impacts on horticulture systems. *Development Policy Review* 22, 587–602.
Conning, J. (2000) *Of Pirates and Moneylenders: Product Market Competition and the Depth of Lending Relationships.* Working Paper. Department of Economics, Williams College, Williamstown.
Fisman, R. and Raturi, M. (2004) Does competition encourage credit provision? Evidence from African trade credit relationships. *The Review of Economics and Statistics* 86, 345–352.

Gordon, A. (2000) *Improving Smallholder Access to Purchased Inputs in Sub-Saharan Africa.* Policy Series 7. Natural Resources Institute, Chatham, UK.

Goreux, L. and Macrae, J. (2003) *Reforming the Cotton Sector in Sub-Saharan Africa.* Africa Region Working Paper Series No. 47. The World Bank, Washington, DC.

Gow, H. and Swinnen, J.F.M. (2001) Private enforcement capital and contract enforcement in transition countries. *American Journal of Agricultural Economics* 83, 686–690.

Gow, H., Streeter, D. and Swinnen, J.F.M. (2000) How private contract enforcement mechanisms can succeed where public institutions fail: the case of Juhocukor as. *Agricultural Economics* 23 (3), 253–265.

Hanyani-Mlambo, B.T., Poulton, C. and Larsen, M.N. (2005) Competition and coordination in the Zimbabwe cotton sector 2001–2004. Presentation at *the Cross-country Workshop,* February 2005, Lusaka, Zimbabwe.

Hendriks, M. (1994) Trade arrangements and interlinked credit in the Philippines. In: Bouman, F.J.A. and Hospes, O. (eds) *Financial Landscapes Reconstructed – the Fine Art of Mapping Development.* Westview Press, Boulder, Colorado, Chapter 13, http://library.wur.nl/way/catalogue/documents/Financial%20Landscapes%20Reconstructed%20TOC.htm (accessed 12 April 2006).

Hoff, K. and Stiglitz, J.E. (1998) Moneylenders and bankers: price increasing subsidies in a monopolistically competitive market. *Journal of Development Economics* 55, 485–518.

IFAD (2003) *Agricultural Marketing Companies as Sources of Smallholder Credit in Eastern and Southern Africa: Experiences, Insights and Potential Donor Role.* IFAD Eastern and Southern Africa Division, Rome, Italy.

Jayne, T.S., Yamano, T. and Nyoro, J. (2003) Interlinked credit and farm intensification: evidence from Kenya. Paper prepared for presentation at the *25th International Conference of Agricultural Economists,* 16–22 August 2003, Durban, Republic of South Africa.

Larsen, M.N. (2002) Is oligopoly a condition of successful privatization? the case of Cotton in Zimbabwe. *Journal of Agrarian Change* 2, 185–205.

McMillan, J. (1997) Markets in transition. In: Kreps, D. and Wallis, K.F. (eds) *Advances in Economics and Econometrics: Theory and Applications.* Cambridge University Press, Cambridge, UK, pp. 210–239.

Minten, B., Randrianarison, L. and Swinnen, J.F.M. (2006) *Global Retail Chains and Poor Farmers: Evidence from Madagascar.* LICOS Discussion Paper 164/2006. K.U.Leuven, Leuven, Belgium.

Poulton, C. (1998) Cotton production and marketing in Northern Ghana: the dynamics of competition in a system of interlocking transactions. In: Dorward, A., Kydd, J. and Poulton, C. (eds) *Smallholder Cash Crop Production under Market Liberalisation: a New Institutional Economics Perspective.* CAB International, Wallingford, UK, pp. 56–112.

Poulton, C., Gibbon, P., Hanyani-Mlambo, B., Kydd, J., Maro, W., Larsen, M.N., Osorio, A. Tschirley, D. and Zulu, B. (2004) Competition and coordination in liberalized African cotton market systems. *World Development* 32, 519–536.

Sadler, M. (2006) *Comparative Analysis of Cotton Supply Chains in Central Asia.* Report. The World Bank, Washington, DC.

Smith, L.E., Stockbridge, M. and Lohano, H.R. (1999) Facilitating the provision of farm credit: the role of interlocking transactions between traders and zamindars in crop marketing systems in Sindh. *World Development* 27, 403–418.

Stiglitz, J. (1990) Peer monitoring and credit markets. *World Bank Economic Review* 4, 351–366.

World Bank (2006) *The Dynamics of Vertical Coordination in Agro-food Chains in Europe and Central Asia.* The World Bank, Washington, DC.

Part II

Empirical Studies on Changes and Effects

Asia

8 Growth in High-value Agriculture in Asia and the Emergence of Vertical Links with Farmers

A. Gulati, N. Minot, C. Delgado and S. Bora

Introduction[1]

Throughout the developing world, the relative importance of grains and other starchy staple crops is declining, while that of high-value agricultural commodities is increasing. This transformation of the agricultural sector has profound effects on the nature of agricultural supply channels, the opportunities for small farmers and the role of public policy and investment. In particular, the growth in high-value agriculture implies a greater need for close linkages between farmers, processors, traders and retailers in coordinating supply and demand.

The growth of high-value agriculture, the development of institutions for vertical coordination and other structural changes in agricultural supply channels present both opportunities and challenges for small farmers in developing countries. They create opportunities for small farmers to raise their income by participating in the growing markets for high-value agricultural commodities. At the same time, the changes pose challenges to small farmers because high-value agricultural commodities often involve higher costs of production and greater production and marketing risk.

Vertical linkages between farmers and buyers can help overcome these obstacles, but in some cases buyers decide that small farmers cannot satisfy new demands from consumers for quality and food safety, leading to the exclusion of these farmers from supply chains. These trends raise new issues for policymakers who wish to promote pro-poor agricultural growth.

The objective of this chapter is to describe the growth of high-value agriculture, its direct implications for the restructuring of the agricultural supply chain and its indirect implications for the role of small farmers. We focus on three countries in South Asia (India, Bangladesh and Pakistan), four countries in South-east Asia (Thailand, Vietnam, Indonesia and the Philippines) and China.

Factors Behind the Growth of High-value Agriculture

What is causing the growth in high-value agriculture in developing countries? On the one hand, there is a growing domestic demand for high-value food commodities, driven by rising incomes, urbanization and perhaps changing preferences. At the same time, trade liberalization has opened export markets in other countries where high-income consumers demand fruit, vegetables, animal products and fish. And, finally, market reforms have (to varying degrees) allowed more foreign direct investment in developing countries, introducing more competition in food processing and retailing sectors, as well as allowing foreign companies to organize production for export.

Income growth

This is a key factor in the rising demand for high-value agricultural goods because, being relatively expensive sources of calories, these products generally have high income elasticities. Thus, rapid economic growth in Asia has stimulated domestic demand for high-value agricultural products. China and Vietnam experienced the most rapid rates of per capita GDP growth over the period 1990–2002, 8.6% and 5.7%, respectively. Bangladesh, India, and Thailand achieved healthy growth rates of more than 3% per year. Average per capita growth rates in Pakistan and the Philippines were the lowest, hovering around 1% per year (World Bank, 2005).

Demographic factors

These also affect the growth of high-value agriculture. The percentage of the population living in urban areas has increased over the period 1980–2002 in all eight of the Asian countries under consideration. Several studies indicate that urban and rural household food consumption habits differ, even after holding income and other household characteristics constant.

Urbanization is associated with lower rice demand in India, Bangladesh, Pakistan, Indonesia and Thailand (Huang and David, 1993). In Vietnam, urban households spend more on meat, fish and sugar and less on rice than rural households, even after controlling for income and household characteristics (Minot et al., 2003). These differences are probably related to three things: (i) in urban areas, the variety of food available is greater; (ii) the opportunity cost of time of household members is higher, and (iii) refrigeration is more widely available.

Outward-looking trade policies

These also contribute to the growth of high-value agriculture. The lowering of import barriers in developed countries has facilitated the growth of high-value exports such as fish and seafood products. Developing countries themselves have reduced import tariffs and moved toward market-oriented exchange rates, which increase the incentives to export.

Since high-value agricultural commodities and processed foods represent a larger share of the food budget of high-income consumers, it is natural that, as farmers in developing countries shift from meeting domestic demand to meeting international demand, they also shift production from staple crops toward high-value agricultural commodities. It should be mentioned, however, that trade liberalization is a two-edged sword when it comes to high-value agriculture. In some cases, trade liberalization makes local farmers more exposed to competition from imported high-value agricultural commodities.

Seven of the eight Asian countries under consideration have reduced the mean import tariff by more than one-half over the 1990s (Vietnam was the exception). The value of agricultural trade as a percentage of agricultural GDP increased significantly between 1990 and 2002 in six of the eight countries (World Bank, 2005).

Foreign direct investment (FDI)

Another factor which has stimulated the transformation of agricultural production toward high-value agriculture is net FDI flows, which have increased dramatically in some countries; however, the trends are erratic due to the 1997/1998 Asian financial crisis. The most dramatic rise in FDI has been in China and India, where it has increased more than tenfold since the early 1990s. Similarly, FDI in Vietnam has grown almost tenfold over this period. FDI inflows in Bangladesh, Pakistan and the Philippines are at least twice as large as in the early 1990s (World Bank 2005).

Foreign investment is usually focused on food processing, animal feed, exporting and (more recently) food retailing. The entrance of foreign companies into the agricultural sector puts competitive pressure on local agribusiness companies, but it has the potential to reduce margins through competition and/or creating new markets, which generally offers new opportunities for farmers (see Gulati et al., 2005 for more details).

Foreign direct investment can promote the growth of high-value agriculture in one of three ways. First, FDI in the export sector may serve to link farmers in developing countries with high-value export markets, particularly those in the home country of the company. This is particularly relevant in the case of the export of fresh produce and fish, where foreign-market expertise is required to meet food safety and quality standards.

Second, FDI in the processing sector may create a new market for high-value agricultural commodities by preserving perishable goods and supplying the processed item to high-income markets. Thirdly, to the extent that foreign companies use their expertise and scale of operations to reduce marketing margins in the processing and/or retail sector, they may reduce the price and increase the domestic demand for high-value agricultural commodities.

Shift in Composition of Food Demand

How are the factors listed above affecting the composition of food demand in Asia? One clear trend is that rising incomes are reducing the share of household budgets allocated to food. Three specific patterns can be observed from household survey data from various countries.[2] First, the food share is substantially higher in rural areas than in urban areas. This is consistent with Engel's Law and the fact that urban incomes are higher than rural incomes.

Second, the food share is declining both in urban and rural areas in each country, the only exception being the urban areas of Indonesia where the food share increased slightly between 1990 and 2002. This is presumably the result of the Asian financial crisis of 1997/1998, which reduced urban incomes more than rural incomes. Third, the decline in food shares was particularly rapid in Vietnam, where it dropped 13 percentage points in 5 years, and in China. This is consistent with the fact that China and Vietnam experienced the fastest economic growth rates among the eight countries under consideration (World Bank, 2005).

At the same time, the composition of food budgets is changing (see Table 8.1). In particular, as incomes rise, there is a shift from grains and other starchy staple crops (such as cassava and sweet potatoes) to meat, milk, eggs, fish, fruit and vegetables. In most of the eight countries considered here, per capita grain consumption increased very slowly (Bangladesh, the Philippines and Thailand) or decreased slightly (China, India and Pakistan).

In contrast, per capita vegetable demand grew fairly quickly (> 2% per year) in five of the eight countries and above 4% in two countries (Vietnam and China). Fruit demand appears to have grown somewhat more slowly, but the growth rate still exceeded that of grains in seven of the eight countries. Milk demand experienced some of the highest annual growth rates: 13% in Vietnam and 5–6% in Indonesia, Thailand, and China. Per capita demand for meat grew very rapidly (> 4% annually) in China, the Philippines and Vietnam, and more modestly in Thailand, Bangladesh and India. Similarly, the growth in demand for fish and seafood was over 3% per year in five of the eight countries under consideration.

Another aspect of the shift toward higher-value food is the growing demand for prepared or semi-prepared foods. Among urban households, particularly higher-income households, there is a trend toward ready-to-cook and ready-to-eat foods, including pre-cut vegetables, de-boned meat and filleted fish. Food consumed outside the household at restaurants, fast-food establishments and street stalls is another trend in urban areas. As income rises and women join the workforce, the opportunity cost of the time spent cooking and shopping rises, making these choices more attractive.

The opportunities faced by farmers in developing countries are increasingly affected not only by the composition of domestic demand but by that of export demand. As shown in Table 8.2, the growth in agricultural and fishery exports in the eight countries has been substantial: 4.8% per year over 1990–2000. But the export demand for high-value agricultural commodities has increased even more rapidly.

By far the largest category of high-value agricultural exports is fishery products.

Table 8.1. Average changes in per capita consumption of selected foods (annual percentage growth rate, 1990–2000) (from FAO Food Balance Database).

	Bangladesh	India	Pakistan	Indonesia	Philippines	Thailand	Vietnam	China
Cereals	0.2	−0.4	0.0	0.9	0.1	0.2	1.2	−1.3
Vegetables	0.1	2.1	2.2	3.3	0.0	0.5	4.9	8.5
Fruit	−1.5	2.9	0.5	1.9	0.2	0.3	1.7	10.0
Milk	0.2	1.9	3.0	5.9	1.5	5.0	13.5	5.0
Meat	1.0	0.9	0.2	0.4	4.7	1.5	4.3	6.8
Eggs	4.6	1.9	1.9	3.7	1.6	−0.4	5.8	9.7
Fish	4.7	2.0	1.6	3.2	−1.4	3.9	3.7	8.4

Table 8.2. Average changes in exports of selected foods[1] (annual percentage growth rate, 1990–2000) (from FAO Agricultural Trade Database).

	Bangladesh	India	Pakistan	Indonesia	Philippines	Thailand	Vietnam	China
Agricultural products (including fishery) (%)	3.7	6.1	1.5	6.8	2.0	4.2	16.2	3.4
Fruit and vegetables (%)	2.3	9.2	7.7	8.1	4.9	4.9	9.8	5.3
Dairy and eggs (%)	–	33.1	–	16.3	46.6	5.9	0.3	4.0
Meat products (%)	−35.2	15.2	23.3	–	6.0	9.5	15.4	−1.6
Fishery products (%)	8.3	12.2	4.8	5.1	1.5	6.8	24.9	5.2
High-value agricultural exports as a percentage of agricultural exports								
1990	56	21	15	41	49	49	30	57
2000	81	36	23	36	56	62	51	61

[1] For the purpose of this table, fruit and vegetables are defined more narrowly than in the FAO category, as we exclude sugar crops, pulses and starch root crops such as cassava and sweet potato. The agricultural exports are defined broadly to include the sum of agricultural exports, as defined by the FAO, and fishery product exports.

Fish and seafood exports from these eight countries grew from US$8.8 to 17.0 billion, representing an annual growth rate of 6.9%. In seven of the eight countries, the growth rate was over 4% per year. Five of these countries (China, Thailand, India, Indonesia and Vietnam) now export more than US$1 billion per year in fish and seafood products. Fruit and vegetables are the second largest category of high-value agricultural exports. The total value of fruit and vegetable exports from the eight countries grew at the rate of 5.6% per year over 1990–2000, surpassing US$5 billion. Furthermore, these exports increased by more than 4.8% per year in every country except Bangladesh. India and Vietnam experienced annual export growth rates of over 9% (FAO 2005).

The share of high-value agricultural exports in total agricultural exports increased substantially over the 1990s in seven of the eight countries. For the eight countries as a whole, high-value agricultural exports increased from 47 to 53% of the total (FAO 2005).

Growth in Production of High-value Agricultural Commodities

In response to the growth in domestic consumption and, to a lesser degree, export opportunities, production of high-value agricultural commodities has grown more quickly than that of traditional grain crops (see Table 8.3). Grain production in the eight countries under consideration grew by about 1.3% per year in volume over the 1990s. This rate is slightly below the annual rate of population growth (1.5%) for the eight countries.

By contrast, the production of high-value agricultural commodities has grown rapidly in many countries. Fruit and vegetable production in the eight countries has grown by 7.7% per year in volume over the 1990s. China represents a large and growing share of the Asian fruit and vegetable output, which grew by over 10% per year over the 1990s, reaching about two-thirds of the output of the eight countries combined. However, fruit and vegetable production growth is not limited to China: it grew at more than 3% per year in India, Pakistan, Indonesia and Vietnam as well.

Milk production has grown at 4.6% annually in the eight countries under consideration. India, Pakistan and China are the dominant producers in the region, and all three have production growth rates above 4% per year. Thailand is a minor producer, but output grew at almost 15% annually over the 1990s. In addition, the production of eggs, meat and fishery products in the eight countries grew by more than 6% per year (FAO, 2005).

In general, the growth in domestic demand for food is much more important than export demand in stimulating the growth in output of high-value agricultural commodities. For example, in China, fishery exports doubled over the 1990s, but this increase represents just 8% of the total increase in production over the decade.

Table 8.3. Growth in production of grains and high-value agricultural commodities (average annual percentage growth, 1990–2000) (from FAO Agricultural Production Database and Fishery Production Database).

	Bangladesh	India	Pakistan	Indonesia	Philippines	Thailand	Vietnam	China
Grains	3.6	1.9	3.8	1.7	1.4	3.7	5.7	0.1
Fruit and vegetables	1.7	4.3	3.8	4.1	2.1	2.1	4.7	10.2
Milk	3.0	4.2	5.7	2.8	−6.5	14.8	3.5	5.8
Eggs	6.4	4.2	4.6	4.9	3.4	1.1	6.7	10.8
Meat	3.4	3.0	2.8	1.6	5.6	3.6	6.3	7.6
Fishery	7.0	4.0	2.7	5.0	0.4	3.0	7.6	11.3

The vast majority of the increase in production was to serve the growing domestic demand.

Consolidation and Vertical Coordination in Food Marketing

Growth in consumption and production of high-value agriculture commodities in Asia has been accompanied by changes in the food supply chains linking the two. Changing consumption patterns towards perishable high-value products imply changes in the characteristics of the products demanded, in addition to increases in quantities demanded. Product attributes such as food safety, convenience and perceived organoleptic qualities become more important and are associated with price premiums.

The new demands require changes in marketing infrastructure such as cold chains, and better management of market information along the chain to deal with the risk of product spoilage before final sale. New forms of retail chain and large-format stores such as supermarkets and their associated procurement and distribution infrastructure have arisen to fill these needs. The entry of private players from outside the traditional food retailing sector and direct foreign investment by existing globalized supermarket chains have also facilitated the consolidation of Asian retail chains in response to new consumer demand.

The changes are most evident for the most perishable commodities with the highest income elasticities, such as fish, meat, eggs and milk, but are also increasingly affecting higher-value fruit and vegetables. These changes have implications – both positive and negative – for the traditional smallholder farmers that still constitute the bulk of Asia's population. Understanding how these changes affect the rural and urban poor requires working backward from changes in urban demand.

Consolidation and growth in the retail food sector

Supermarkets and other modern retail food stores[3] have grown rapidly in Asia. In 1990, China had one supermarket; by 2002, there were 53,000 supermarkets and convenience stores (Hu *et al.*, 2004). In Thailand, annual growth in the number of modern food outlets was 11% in 2001–2002 (USDA, 2002).

In the Philippines, the number of supermarkets has increased from 496 in 1994 to 3989 in 2001, an annual growth rate of 30% (Digal and Concepcion, 2004). In Bangladesh, there are 30 supermarkets today, all of which have opened since 1999 (USDA, 2004). Indonesia has seen the number of supermarkets and hypermarkets grow from 237 in 1989 to 1400 in 2002, though much of this growth occurred before the Asian financial crisis of 1997/1998 (Chowdhury *et al.*, 2004).

The importance of supermarkets and hypermarkets in the total value of retail food sales varies widely across Asian countries. In Thailand and the Philippines, supermarkets and hypermarkets accounted for over half of retail food sales (USDA, 2002; Digal and Concepcion, 2004). This is consistent with the fact that Thailand and the Philippines have the highest income of the eight countries considered here. In Indonesia, these modern retail outlets are estimated to represent 25% of retail food sales. In contrast, the share is about 10% in Pakistan, less than 5% in India and Bangladesh and 30% of *urban* food sales in China (see Table 8.4).

Initially, supermarkets tended to be located only in the largest cities, catering to high-income consumers. This is currently the case in Pakistan, Bangladesh, and Vietnam. As the number of supermarkets and their market share increasesd, they spread to secondary cities and towns, as they have in Thailand and are beginning to do so in China. As part of this process, supermarkets also began to cater to middle- and lower-income urban consumers, although it is likely that supermarket

Table 8.4. Structure of the retail food sector, showing growth in supermarket[1] outlets.

Country	Year	Number of supermarkets[1]	Share of supermarkets[1] in total food sales (%)	Period	Annual growth rate (%)	References
Bangladesh	2004	30	1	1999–2004	97	USDA, 2004
India	2000		2	2003–2008	24–49	Chengappa, 2006{In press}
Pakistan	2000	800	10			SDPI, 2004
Indonesia	2003	1,307	25	1989–2002	15	USDA, 2003; Chowdhury *et al.*, 2004
Philippines	1995	3,989	68	1994–2001	30	Digal and Concepcion, 2004
Thailand	2004	600	54	2001–2002	11	USDA, 2002
Vietnam	2003	< 70	< 2			Tam, 2004
China	2003	37,000	30 (urban)	1995–2002	36	Hu *et al.*, 2004

[1] Supermarkets are defined as including convenience stores, hypermarkets, department stores and large discount stores, though definitions vary from country to country. The India growth rate refers to a projection by EuroMonitor. Growth in supermarket sales is generally greater than growth in the number of outlets since the average size tends to increase over time.

customers still have incomes above the national average (USDA, 2002; Chowdhury *et al.*, 2004).

Causes of retail food restructuring

The rise of supermarkets in Asia (as elsewhere) is partly driven by the rising per capita income. The importance of supermarkets is greater in higher-income countries such as Thailand and the Philippines than in Vietnam or Bangladesh. Additional evidence for this link is found in the fact that the growth in supermarkets seems to be correlated with economic growth, both being highest in China. Supermarket expansion slowed in Indonesia following the Asian financial crisis, as consumers returned to traditional markets during the crisis (USDA, 2002; Chowdhury *et al.*, 2004). Although incomes are lower in the Philippines than in Thailand, the share of supermarkets in retail food sales is similar, perhaps due to the higher level of urbanization in the Philippines.

Liberalization of foreign direct investment has contributed to the growth of supermarkets. The growth of supermarkets in China began in the early 1990s, but took off after 1995 when rules on foreign investment were relaxed. In Thailand, seven of the ten largest chains have foreign investment. In Indonesia, foreign investment regulations were liberalized in 1998, and the share of supermarkets in food retail sales rose from 6% in 1997 to 20% in 2001 (Chowdhury *et al.*, 2004).

India has relatively tight regulations on foreign investment in the retail food sector. Although supermarket chains are growing, particularly in the south, the organized food retail sector still accounts for less than 10% of food sales. In Pakistan, there is no foreign investment in food retailing. In 1998, the sector was dominated by Utility Stores Corporation, a state-owned enterprise with 715 stores. About half have since been closed in an attempt to reduce losses (SDPI, 2004).

Perhaps unique among Asian countries, China is using various policy instruments to accelerate the transition from traditional stores and wet markets to supermarkets, in order to address food safety concerns and enhance tax collection (Bi *et al.*, 2004).

Consequences of retail food consolidation

One consequence of the growth of supermarkets in Asia is increasing competitive pressure on traditional retail outlets. For example, in Thailand, the total number of modern outlets grew at a rate of 10.6% in 2001–2002, while traditional outlets declined by 14.9% in the same period (USDA 2002). In Indonesia, hypermarkets grew at a rate of 20% in 2002, while independent grocers grew at 8.5% (USDA, 2003).

Another consequence of the growth of supermarkets is the change in the procurement channels, especially for fresh high-value products. Small chains and independent supermarkets often procure from wholesalers and wet markets. However, when supermarket chains reach a certain size, they generally establish centralized food distribution centres that supply all stores in the chain. This vertical integration into wholesaling operations allows them to standardize quality, improve bargaining power and achieve economies of scale in distribution. In addition, they usually adopt a list of preferred suppliers who are known to be able to produce consistently the quantity and quality demanded by the supermarket chain.

The need to standardize quality (particularly if the chain offers store brands) leads to the development of detailed private standards, most importantly for fresh fruit and vegetables, meat and fish. The procurement system is more demanding than the ones used traditionally by wholesalers and retailers. Thus, the trend has been to move towards contracts with dedicated suppliers to reduce the transaction costs of bargaining, as well as reducing risks, wastage and guaranteeing food safety and quality control (see Chowdhury et al., 2004; Digal and Concepcion, 2004; Hu et al., 2004).

Supermarkets have started setting food standards, moving away from informal standards to formalized private standards based on quality and food safety. This is partly a response to consumer demand and partly a reaction to the lack of success of public standards. In some countries there are public standards but, where foreign companies have entered the supply chain, the standards become more stringent.

Food processing consolidation

The food processing industry in most countries reflects the changes in income and consumption patterns. As discussed earlier, when income rises, the share of food expenditure declines and consumption patterns change from staples to high-value food commodities. In addition, higher-income households tend to buy more processed food, pay more attention to food safety issues and prefer to buy branded, labelled and packaged products whose quality they can trust.

The development of the food processing sector assumes significant importance due to the growth of high-value products. The seasonality and perishability of high-value products demand that these products be processed as swiftly as possible, since storage for a long period is not possible and processing can avoid wastage and shrinkage. Thus, the emerging trend of demand-driven growth in high-value agriculture has to be accompanied side-by-side by the development of the food processing sector.

Value added in the food processing sector in the selected Asian countries has grown at about 9% per year since 1990[4]. China, India and Bangladesh have smaller food processing sectors (relative to the economy as a whole) than Indonesia, Thailand and the Philippines, as would be expected given the income levels of these countries. At the same time, China, India, and Bangladesh have the fastest growing food processing sectors, a pattern consistent with a shift of food processing capacity from higher-wage economies to lower-wage economies within Asia (World Bank, 2005).

In addition, the economies of China, India and Bangladesh were generally more tightly regulated in the 1990s, and the degree of economic reform – including deregulation of foreign direct investment – may have been greater in these countries since the 1990s.

Furthermore, processed food exports have been growing faster than primary and agricultural product exports in all countries studied. Bangladesh, Indonesia and Thailand have exhibited an annual growth rate of 15% or more. There seems to be a positive correlation between high income growth and exports of processed food. In spite of being the poorest country among the ones studied, Bangladesh has performed better than most countries, largely due to fishery product exports, which are processed (Athukorala and Jayasuriya, 2003).

Emerging Forms of Farmer–Buyer Vertical Coordination

High-value agricultural commodities that are perishable are inherently quality-sensitive and subject to high transactions costs, particularly in the case of smallholder production. These transactions costs arise from asymmetries of information between buyers and sellers, and the nature of the predominant agricultural production systems in Asia. They are difficult to observe, but are quite real. They are in addition to the high marketing costs that arise when infrastructure is poor. Because of high transactions costs in the high-value agriculture sector, institutional forms of vertical coordination are key to giving both buyers and sellers a better deal. The integrating institutions distribute knowledge about the product more evenly between buyers and sellers along the marketing channel.

Both South and South-east Asia have witnessed the rise of arrangements for vertical coordination of primary production of high-value items with input suppliers and processing/exporting firms during the last 20 years. Input suppliers like seed companies and feed millers have typically promoted profit- and risk-sharing relationships with farmers.

Contract farming can be defined as an agreement between a series of farmers and a retailing, processing and/or input supply firm for the production and supply of agricultural products under forward agreements, frequently at a predetermined price, in return for the purchaser providing production support. The latter often includes quality inputs given on credit and technical advice (Eaton and Shepherd, 2001).

Typical contract farming schemes in animal production involve feed millers who supply young animals, feeds, veterinary medicine and extension advice on credit to farmers who provide holding sheds, dispose of waste and provide all required labour, water and electricity. Major production decisions are made by the integrating firm. Processors get involved in contract farming when they need a more reliable supply of raw materials.

Milk is a specialized case of contract farming where dairy coops, processing the milk and facilitating farm access to inputs and extension are often cooperatively owned. Typically, contract farming of high value crops is carried out under the leadership of processing and exporting firms, where quality control throughout the production process is critical. Cut flowers and fruit and vegetables for industrially processed foods are examples. Agri-processors and retail chains that need to be reassured about the quality of their raw materials find it costly to monitor the quality of what they buy, particularly when they are buying from many smallholders.

Agri-processors use a variety of institutional arrangements for obtaining reliable supplies of raw materials of consistent quality for processing. Each form of arrangement embodies a different way of sharing the risks, costs and benefits of high-value commodity supply chains. At one extreme, vertically integrated corporate farming typically involves a processor or exporter who finds it worthwhile to produce the basic raw material itself, without having to deal with independent farmers. Plantation crops such as tea, rubber, coconuts and sweet bananas are typical commodities on such holdings.

On the other hand, contract farming arrangements are typically observed for commodities that require considerable close monitoring in production, have characteristics that are hard to ascertain on an individual basis at sale, require specific quality inputs for quality outputs, have high requirements in terms of producers credits and embody a substantial degree of market risk, defined as a highly fluctuating producer price across time.

Typical contract farming commodities are poultry (broilers in particular), pigs, milk, seed, certain high-quality fruit and vegetables for processors and, to a lesser extent, inputs to industrial processing that require close producer quality supervision such as coffee, tea, cocoa and sugar. In Thailand, for example, virtually all commercially produced broilers are produced under contract, whereas the corresponding figure for the Philippines is 80% (Delgado et al., 2003a). In India, roughly 11% of milk was produced within the public cooperative system in 2001, but a higher share would be correct if contracts with the emerging private sector dairies are included after 1991, and perhaps the majority of production if informal contracts between informal sector milk traders (dudhyas) and producers are included (Sharma et al., 2003).

Under some circumstances, contract farming can represent an attractive short-term opportunity for smallholder producers, and even offer their best chance to remain involved with high-value agricultural production over time.

Vertical Coordination of High-value Agriculture and Smallholders

The analysis above shows that the only part of agriculture in developing countries that will continue to grow significantly faster than population in the next 20 years is the high-value sector. The implications for the vast mass of smallholder farmers in Asia are sobering: to significantly improve their incomes per capita over the next 20 years, they must either be part of the shift to high-value agricultural production or increase the share of income they get from non-agricultural sources.

Furthermore, the analysis in the preceding section suggests that unless smallholders enter vertically coordinated supply chains with processors and retailers, they will increasingly have difficulties in participating in growing, high-value markets. Finally, even if markets worked well in every sense, many poor rural people are faced with such poor infrastructure that they would have trouble taking advantage of new urban and international market opportunities under the best of conditions.

As described by Torero and Gulati (2004), farmers must overcome a 'real access gap' of being able to cost-effectively transport their produce, before being able to address a 'market efficiency gap' that revolves around being competitive with better organized, better informed, better capitalized and larger-scale producers.

Two instruments appear critical to break this deadlock for the smallholders: (i) physical infrastructure (such as information technology, roads and ports) that connects smallholders to markets; and (ii) a set of accompanying institutions that reduce marketing risk and transaction costs in the process of exchange between producers and consumers.

Appropriate policies of investment in infrastructure need to go together with well-functioning market institutions in order to take advantage of market opportunities for sustained increased agricultural output and raising of rural incomes. This is of critical importance for smallholders in countries recently experiencing market liberalization. Even if adequate hard infrastructure exists, farmers capture little of the value that they create when market information and markets themselves are not accessible to the smallholders.

Previous conventional wisdom was that institutions would improve in response to individuals' self interest, and therefore take care of the transaction cost problems arising from information asymmetries (Torero and Gulati, 2004). The reality is that in the presence of coordination failure, innovation failure and authority failure, the necessary institutional solutions to overcome high transaction costs facing smallholders fail to emerge. The high risks of production and cycles of over-supply and price depression create financial risks throughout the distribution chain; these inhibit investment and access to capital.

Monopolistic practices, corruption and excessive regulation also add to the burden of the rural marketplace. The high costs, risks, and 'friction' in high-value agricultural markets prevent these markets from achieving sufficient scale for efficiency and similarly prevent the low-cost and reliable supply of production inputs such as seed, fertilizer and other goods to farmers. Very poor farmers also lack the political empowerment, market knowledge and business knowledge to address these market roadblocks.

Thus, poor rural farmers typically lack the capacity to improve and influence the markets upon which their lives depend. But some of these assets can be developed through effective organization, technical training and means for assembly and communication. Pro-poor market institutions are needed to reduce transaction costs, manage risk, build social capital, enable collective action and redress missing markets.

The necessary institutional infrastructure to facilitate market exchange is a critically important area in countries recently experiencing the shortfalls of market liberalization with regard to smallholder agriculture. When market information and markets themselves are not accessible to the rural poor, farmers capture little of the value that they create, demand and supply are highly unstable and distribution costs for rurally produced goods are very high. Small farmers in Asia in particular tend to be subject to a specific set of marketing problems.

First, traditional smallholder farmers in Asia typically receive relatively low prices for their produce. This stems not only from relatively high margins between the farm gate and retail price but also from low market trust and reputation typically accorded to undifferentiated smallholder output when true quality is not known to the buyer at the time of sale.

With respect to margins, farmers in India receive only 20–30% of the retail price of fruit and vegetables, compared with 50% or more in the USA (US Department of Commerce, 2001). Institutional arrangements such as contract farming can reduce the number of intermediaries, wastage, transaction costs and market risks. With respect to market trust and reputation, which a large firm approaches through branding, smallholders are in a disadvantageous position. They do not have a sufficient sales volume to differentiate the product of individual producers from each other. Sales of sub-standard goods by other smallholders rebound on them.

Even when it is possible for smallholders to band together to give a geographical brand to their product (e.g. Central Gujarat milk), it is not helpful unless a mechanism is in place to credibly ensure that bad product is not included, and to gradually improve the quality of existing product. Performing this market function requires some form of collective action on the part of producers and a form of governance that translates the discipline of the market into enforceable incentives for compliance with norms.

Much of the practical implementation of quality improvement revolves around improving the quality of inputs used and optimizing production and handling practices. In effect, credible certification of output quality revolves around credible certification that only the right inputs and procedures were used in production and handling.

Contract farming is the private-sector solution to accomplishing these functions in a way that distributes costs, benefits and risks in a manner that maintains incentives for all sides to participate. In the animal products sectors, where purchased variable inputs such as young animals and feed are typically 70% of the farm gate price of the output, input supply firms naturally tend to provide the coordination function of contract farming. Transactions costs apply to inputs as well as outputs. Small farmers often are ill-equipped to know the true quality of the animal genetics and feed resources that they buy, compared to larger farmers that either mill their own feed – as most do in countries such as the Philippines (Costales et al., 2003) – or enforce better compliance with standards from suppliers.

Improved inputs are combined with better practices to embody new technology for production. Contract farming schemes are typically associated with significant improvements in productivity of contract farmers compared to otherwise similar independent farmers, particularly in the case of small-scale farming (Delgado et al., 2003a).

This observation is not limited to livestock enterprises. The Pepsi project, a joint venture between Pepsico, Voltas and Punjab Agro Industries Corporation and approved in 1988 by the Government of India in the State of Punjab, set up the biggest tomato paste plant in Asia, with the capacity to process 650 tons of tomato a day. It contracted hundreds of tomato farmers, introduced the technology of deep chiselling and new methods of transplantation – such as shovel techniques and bed-head planting, in addition to the introduction of new seed varieties. The technological innovations introduced in contract farming increased productivity and reduced costs. Within 3 years of operation, tomato yields increased from 7.5 to 20 tons per acre. The harvesting season for tomatoes was extended from 25 to 70 days and the company also successfully initiated the winter cultivation of tomato in Punjab, with the help of greenhouse technology dissemination (Sukhpal, 2004).

Market risk in terms of fluctuating prices is another problem of great concern to smallholders in the high-value area. The short-term price elasticities of demand and supply for perishable products tend to be rather inelastic, leading to considerable day-to-day price instability for these commodities. The daily prices of eggs and broilers in southern India fluctuate by as much as 10%, introducing a large risk – particularly given that the average profit margins are just 4% (Mehta et al., 2003).

Whether on a fee or contract farming basis, the returns to the contract farming enterprise are likely to fluctuate less than for independent farmers. Another factor is that in some localities in Asia inputs such as feed are taxed. Companies working with contract poultry growers escape this tax through accounting transfers of feed to contractors that do not count as sales.

Market risk can be reduced by improved methods of sharing relevant market information in a vertically coordinated framework. One such initiative is the *e-choupal* initiative in India, organized by the Indian Tobacco Company (ITC). *E-choupal* connects 3.1 million farmers from 29,500 villages in six states in India through Internet kiosks running on solar-charged batteries and connected by satellite links.

At the *e-choupal* sites, farmers can: (i) obtain information on commodity prices, weather and news; (ii) search for detailed information on farm and risk management; (iii) purchase inputs and other products; and (iv) sell their crops to ITC centres or the local market.

E-choupal has been used to source a range of agricultural commodities like food grains, oilseeds, coffee and aquaculture, and market a variety of goods and services like agri-inputs, consumer goods, insurance and market research. The new 'e-chain' registered transactions of US$100 million in 2003/2004 and has reduced transaction costs for a typical soybean farmer from Rs 705 to 335 per metric ton. (Sivakumar, 2004).

Farmers selling through *e-choupal* obtain prices for their crops that are 2.5% higher than they would have received through the government auction system because of lower transaction costs. At the same time, procurement costs for ITC are also reduced by 2.5% as they save on the commission paid to traders. The system provides direct market access to farmers and it is estimated that their incremental income is over 20% (World Bank, 2004).

Vertical coordination is also an essential way of lowering the transaction costs of lenders in supplying credit to small rural producers, by helping to ensure that the capital is used as intended by the lender and in a way that ensures repayment. Typical contract farming schemes provide inputs on credit, thus providing the farmer with an important additional resource. Market interest rates for Asian smallholders are typically very high, if they exist at all. In the Philippines, for example, small-scale pig farmers could borrow at private banks for 24% per annum in 2001, whereas large-scale farmers could often borrow at 12%.

Credit provided within a contract farming scheme is more likely to be repaid as the integrator has better control over the final disposition of output. In the animal sectors at least, empirical analysis of field data in Asia consistently points to the role of credit in allowing entry of smallholders to high-value agricultural markets (Delgado et al., 2003a). Since improved production practices are critical to achieving quality, contract farming schemes typically are associated with a much higher incidence of farm visits by technicians than is seen independent smallholder farming. The contract farming scheme basically imposes a package of practices, technology and inputs that it then monitors (Tiongco and Delgado, 2005).

Because they manage the supply chain from the farm to the retailer, contract farming schemes are in a position to credibly certify the quality of output. They can do this by directly marketing items raised by contracting farmers themselves, or else by branding that farmer's output, which is then sold as such on the open market.

Both forms exist in Asia, with Venkateshwara Hatcheries broiler operations being an example of direct marketing (Mehta et al., 2003), and the Soro Soro Ibaba (swine) Cooperative in the Philippines being an example of branding for sale by the farmer on the open market (Costales et al., 2003).

Finally, where direct procurement from the farmer is practised, as is typical for broilers in Thailand, both fee-based and price-guarantee schemes are used for farmer incentives. Fees are a per unit of product return for the farmer's labour, land, buildings, water and electricity. Price guarantees increase the incentive of farmers to cut costs, but greatly increase the burden on the company to monitor production practices and input usage (Poapagsakorn et al., 2003).

A recent study (Birthal et al., 2005) compared contract and non-contract producers of milk, broilers and vegetables in India.[5] Contract farming attained substantially higher net profit than non-contract farming, because both production and marketing costs were lower for contract farming (see Table 8.5). The share of the marketing cost in the total cost for non-contract farmers was 20% for milk and 21% for vegetables, but it was only 2% in

Table 8.5. Production and transaction costs (Rs/ton) of milk, broiler and vegetable production in contract and non-contract farming (from Birthal et al., 2005).

Commodity	Contract farming			Non-contract farming		
	Production cost	Transaction cost	Total cost	Production cost	Transaction cost	Total cost
Milk	5,586	100	5,686	5,728	1,442	7,170
Broiler[1]	808	38	846	27,322	90	27,412
Vegetable[2]	1,485	35	1,520	1,630	437	2,067

[1] For broiler, the firm provides free chicks, feed and medicines to the contract farmers.
[2] Vegetable costs refer to spinach.

both cases for contract farmers.[6] The study also confirms that contract farming leads to a sharing of risks between the producer and firm.

The coefficients of variation (CVs) of profit for contract farmers are much smaller than for non-contract farmers. Price volatility was the main reason for high variability in profits of independents.

Conventional wisdom suggests that, other things being equal, agri-processors will find it more advantageous to deal with a smaller number of larger suppliers of raw materials than with a larger number of smaller suppliers. It is therefore interesting that Birthal et al. (2005) observed that firms were finding it more convenient to contract with smallholders and their associations due to: (i) a lower risk for overall supply in the event of crop failure of one or few farmers; (ii) more flexible production portfolios of smallholders, which would help them to respond to consumers' changing preferences; (iii) higher quality, since smallholders are seemingly more likely to comply strictly with the mandated production practices of firms; and (iv) greater dependency of smallholders on the firm.

Furthermore, apprehensions about contract farming leading to exploitation of farmers were shown to be unfounded, as contract farmers in the year of the survey were offered a higher price than the prevailing market price. Vegetable contract farmers received 8% higher prices on average, and milk producers received 4% more (Birthal et al., 2005).

Impact of Supermarket Growth on Smallholders

The growth of supermarkets – with their heightened concern regarding food quality, consistent volumes and food safety – represents a threat and an opportunity for small farmers. It is a threat in the sense that food safety and quality control are barriers to the entry of smallholders in the supply chain.

For example, in China producers need to have their production environment sampled and checked, and to provide production records and inspection reports in order to be certified as 'green food' growers. Producers of 'green food' can get a margin five times larger selling to supermarkets, so supermarkets signing contracts with large producers with these certifications can not only ensure quality control but also make greater profits (Bi et al., 2004).

In the Philippines, for vegetables, only professional suppliers of small- to medium-scale operations maintain their place in the supply chain. Small producers who have managed to supply hygienic vegetables have found it difficult to maintain this business link and eventually dropped out. The barriers to integration of smallholders in this chain have been countered in some countries by the formation of cooperatives, contract farming and producers' associations which supply directly or through some intermediaries to modern retailers.

However, supermarkets also represent an opportunity for small farmers in that supermarkets know the product requirements of high-income consumers and have the incentive to transmit this information to the farmer through mechanisms of vertical coordination. Thus, potentially, supermarkets offer access to relatively high-income consumers and assistance in meeting their requirements. In practice, supermarkets rarely buy directly from small farmers, with or without contracts, but rather procure goods through commissioned agents or assemblers. Depending on the production characteristics of the crop and the distribution of farmers by size of farm, these assemblers may or may not choose to work with small farmers.

The preponderance of smallholders in many Asian countries makes their inclusion in the changing retail structure especially important. The average size of land holdings is around 1.6 ha in South Asia and South-east Asia. Farms of less than 2 hectares in size account for 88% of the forms in Indonesia and 81% in India. Farms are even smaller in Bangladesh and

Vietnam, where over three-quarters of the farms are less than one hectare in size.[7]

For supermarkets, reducing transaction costs, ensuring quality of output and avoiding supply fluctuations are of utmost significance. Lowering transaction costs requires fewer transactions, thus modern retail chains have started relying on consolidators. This reliance, as well as the practice of passing on any possible costs to consolidators, makes it more difficult for smallholders to penetrate the system. Smallholders who have managed to link up with the chain are either individually equipped or have joined farmer groups or cooperatives.

However, new forms of vertical linkages, especially in South-east Asia, are allowing smallholders to participate in the supply chain. The dominance of smallholders in the regions makes their inclusion necessary, and vertically coordinated supply chains are incorporating smallholders as well as lowering transaction costs and market risks for both small farmers and retail chains. Small and medium enterprises (SMEs) have begun to expand by building production base and contracting farmers as their suppliers, and there are successful cases of producers' associations and farmers' professional associations gaining bargaining power by acting together.

At least three farmers' groups have begun to collectivize efforts and sell directly to retailers in Manila, including fast-food chains (Digal and Concepcion, 2004). Processing enterprises and suppliers are building their own production base or providing technical assistance to contract farmers. Zheijang Plums Association in China is a farmers' professional association comprising big producers, companies, small farmers and research institutes. It set up product standards for all farmers and provided information on variety, production and inputs of members. Technical assistance is provided by universities, extensions services and research institutes, who are also members of this association (Bi *et al.*, 2004).

Summary

There is a strong increase in high-value agriculture and vertical coordination in Asia. The growth of high-value agriculture is caused by a combination of factors, including income growth, demographics and policy changes. The emergence of contract farming and other forms of vertical coordination are a response to: (i) the rising share of perishable high-value foods being marketed; (ii) the increasing scale of processors and retailers, which implies the need for a more organized procurement system; and (iii) the increasing demand by consumers for food safety and very specific quality attributes which are difficult to ensure without some form of vertical coordination.

Contract farming can benefit farmers by providing them with specialized inputs, technical assistance, credit and an assured market, thus solving a number of problems small farmers typically have in producing new high-value commodities. Empirical studies indicate that contract farmers may enjoy higher profits (though the evidence is mixed), greater production efficiency and more stable incomes than independent farmers growing the same crops.

The benefit to buyers is in ensuring a reliable supply of a product that might otherwise not be available on open markets, particularly perishable products, specialized crops or ones that are new to the area. The larger the buyer, the more important it is to establish procurement systems. For example, large supermarket chains generally establish lists of preferred suppliers and set private standards for the products they purchase. The decision whether to source from small farmers or large farmers is based on the nature of the product, the skills and resources of local farmers and the land ownership patterns. In many Asian countries, the overwhelming predominance of smallholders means that supermarkets and other buyers are forced to work with small farmers.

Notes

1 This chapter is a shortened version of Gulati et al. (2005), which contains a more detailed description and documentation of the trends described here.
2 For Bangladesh, see *Report of the Household Income and Expenditure Survey*, 2000; for India, National Sample Survey Organization (NSSO), 1988, 1995, 1998, 2000; for Pakistan, Household Integrated Economic Survey, 1998–1999, 2001–2002; for Indonesia, Central Bureau of Statistics, 1980, 1990, 2002; for Vietnam, the Vietnam Living Standards Survey, 1993, 1998; and for China, National Bureau of Statistics, 1980, 1990, 2000; China Statistical Yearbook, various years.
3 For convenience, we have defined supermarkets broadly to include hypermarkets, convenience stores and other modern retail outlets, although definitions vary from one country to another.
4 These calculations are based on the share of the manufacturing value added in food, beverages and tobacco, as estimated in the World Development Indicators published by the World Bank.
5 A major IFPRI/FAO approach research study comparing the profit efficacy of small *versus* large independent livestock producers and smallholder contract farmers was carried out with national collaborating institutions in Brazil, India, the Philippines and Thailand in 2001–2003 (Delgado *et al.*, 2003). The main empirical findings based on farm surveys of independent and contract farmers of differing scales in the Asian cases provide a mixed set of conclusions (see Gulati *et al.*, 2005 for further details).
6 Note that these estimates include only the transaction costs faced by farmers. To the extent that the buyer undertakes some marketing functions, the transaction costs may be transferred from the farmer to the buyer. This is an advantage to the buyer but does not necessarily imply lower transaction costs for the marketing channel as a whole.
7 For Bangladesh, see Government of Bangladesh, 1997; for India, Government of India, 1995–1996; for Nepal, Government of Nepal, 1991; for Pakistan, Government of Pakistan, 1998–1999, 2001–2002; for Indonesia, the Philippines, Thailand and Vietnam, data taken from the Supplement to the Report on the 1990 World Census of Agriculture, FAO, 2001.

References

Athukorala, P. and Jayasuriya, S. (2003) Food safety issues, Yroude and WTO rules: A developing country perspective. *World Economy*, Vol 26, No. 9.
Bi, X., Dong, X., Huang, J., Hu, D. and Rozelle, S. (2004) Regoverning Markets: Securing Smallholder Producer Participation in Restructured National and Agri-food System. China Country Report. International Institute for Environment and Development. www.regoverningmarkets.org (accessed 15 February 2005).
Birthal, P., Gulati, A. and Joshi, P.K. (2005) *Vertical Coordination in High-value Food Commodities: Implications for Smallholders*. MTID Discussioin Paper No. 85. International Food Policy Research Institute, Washington, DC.
Central Bureau of Statistics, Indonesia (1980, 1990 and 2002).
Chengappa, P.G., Achoth, L., Mukherjee, A., Reddy, B.M. and Ravi, P.C. (2006) *Evolution of Food Retail Chains in India*. International Food Policy Research Institute, Washington, DC {In press}
Chowdhury, S., Gulati, A. and Gumbira Sa'id, E. (2004) *High-value Products, Supermarkets and Vertical Arrangements in Indonesia*. MTID Discussion Paper. International Food Policy Research Institute, Washington, DC.
Costales, A.C., Delgado, C., Catelo, O., Tiongco, M., Chatterjee, A., delos Reyes, A. and Narrod, C. (2003) *Policy, Technical, and Environmental Determinants and Implications of the Scaling-up of Broiler and Swine Production in The Philippines*. Annex I, Final Report of IFPRI–FAO Livestock Industrialization Project: Phase II. International Food Policy Research Institute, Washington, DC.
Delgado, C., Narrod, C. and Tiongco, M. (2003a) *Policy, Technical and Environmental Determinants and Implications of the Scaling-up of Livestock Production in Four Fast-Growing Developing Countries: A Synthesis*. Final Report of IFPRI–FAO Livestock Industrialization Project: Phase II. International Food Policy Research Institute, Washington, DC.
Digal, L. and Concepcion, S. (2004) *Regoverning Markets: Securing Smallholder Producer Participation in*

Restructured National and Agri-food System: the Case of The Philippines. International Institute for Environment and Development. http://www.regoverningmarkets.org (accessed 15 February 2005).

Eaton, C. and Shepherd, A.W. (2001) *Contract Farming: Partnership for Growth*. FAO Agricultural Services Bulletin No. 145. FAO, Rome, Italy.

FAO (Food and Agriculture Organization of the United Nations) (2005) *FAO Statistics Database*. http://www.faostat.fao.org/?language=EN (accessed January and February 2005).

General Statistical Office (GSO) (1998) *Major Social and Economic Information Obtained from the Large-scale Surveys in the Period 1990–1996*. Statistical Publishing House, Hanoi, Vietnam.

General Statistical Office (GSO) (2001) *Vietnam Living Standards Survey 1997–1998*. Statistical Publishing House, Hanoi, Vietnam.

Government of Bangladesh (1997) *Agricultural Sample Survey*. Bangladesh.

Government of India (1995–1996) *Agriculture Census*. Ministry of Agriculture, India.

Government of Nepal (1991) *Agriculture Census*. Nepal.

Government of Pakistan (1998–1999, 2001–2002) *Household Integrated Economic Survey*. Pakistan.

Government of Pakistan (2000) *Pakistan Agricultural Census*. Pakistan.

Gulati, A., Minot, N., Delgado, C. and Bora, S. (2005) Growth in high-value agriculture in Asia and the emergence of vertical links with farmers. Paper presented at the Symposium *Toward High-Value Agriculture and Vertical Coordination: Implications for Agribusiness and Smallholders*. National Agricultural Science Centre, Pusa, New Delhi, India, 7 March 2005.

Hu, D., Reardon, T., Rozelle, S., Timmer, P. and Wang, H. (2004) The emergence of supermarkets with Chinese characteristics: challenges and opportunities for China's agricultural development. *Development Policy Review* 22 (5), 557–586.

Huang, J. and David, C. (1993) Demand for cereal grains in Asia: the effect of urbanization. *Agricultural Economics* 8, 107–124.

Mehta, R., Nambiar, R.G., Delgado, C. and Subrahmanyam, S. (2003) *Policy, Technical, and Environmental Determinants and Implications of the Scaling-up of Broiler and Egg Production in India*. Annex II, Final Report of IFPRI–FAO Livestock Industrialization Project: Phase II. International Food Policy Research Institute, Washington, DC.

Minot, N., Epprecht, M., Anh, T. and Trung, L. (2003) *Income Diversification and Poverty in the Northern Uplands of Vietnam*. Report prepared for the Japan Bank for International Cooperation, Hanoi, Vietnam.

National Bureau of Statistics (1980, 1990, 2000) *China Statistical Yearbook*.

National Sample Survey Organization (NSSO) (1988, 1995, 1998 and 2000) India.

Poapongsakorn, N., NaRanong, V., Delgado, C., Narrod, C., Siriprapanukul, P., Srianant, N., Goolchai, P., Ruangchan, S., Methrsuraruk, S., Jittreekhun, T., Chalermpao, N., Tiongco, M. and Suwankiri, B. (2003) *Policy, Technical, and Environmental Determinants and Implications of the Scaling-up of Swine, Broiler, Layer and Milk Production in Thailand*. Annex IV, Final Report of IFPRI–FAO Livestock Industrialization Project: Phase II. International Food Policy Research Institute, Washington, DC.

Report of the Household Income and Expenditure Survey (2000) Bangladesh.

SDPI (Sustainable Development Policy Institute) (2004) *Regoverning Markets: Securing Smallholder Producer Participation in Restructured National and Agri-food Systems, Pakistan*. http://www.regoverningmarkets.org (accessed 15 February 2005).

Sharma, V.P., Staal, S., Delgado, C. and Singh, R.V. (2003) *Policy, Technical and Environmental Determinants and Implications of the Scaling-up of Milk Production in India*. Annex III, Research Report of IFPRI–FAO Livestock Industrialization Project: Phase II. International Food Policy Research Institute, Washington, DC.

Sivakumar, S. (2004) *Indian Agribusiness and ITC e-choupal*. DuPont NSM

Sukhpal, S. (2004) Crisis and diversification in Punjab agriculture: role of state and agribusiness. *Economic and Political Weekly*, December.

Supplement to the Report on the 1990 World Census of Agriculture (2001) Food and Agriculture Organization, Rome, Italy.

Tam, P. (2004) *Regoverning Markets: Securing Smallholder Producer Participation in Restructured National and Agri-food systems: the Case of Vietnam*. http://www.regoverningmarkets.org (accessed 15 February 2005).

Tiongco, M. and Delgado, C. (2005) *Issues and Pitfalls of Contract Farming for Smallholder Livestock Production*. Working paper. International Food Policy Research Institute, Washington, DC.

Torero, M. and Gulati, A. (2004) *Connecting Smallholders to Markets: Role of Infrastructure and Institutions*. International Food Policy Research Institute, Washington, DC.

US Department of Commerce (2001) *Prospects for Food Processing Industry, India*. International Market Insight, US & Foreign Commercial Service and US Department of State, Washington, DC.

USDA (USA Department of Agriculture) (2002) *Thailand Retail Food Sector Report*. GAIN Report. Foreign Agricultural Service, US Department of Agriculture, Washington, DC.

USDA (2003) *Indonesia Retail Food Sector Report*. GAIN Report. Foreign Agricultural Service, US Department of Agriculture, Washington, DC.

USDA (2004) *Bangladesh Retail Food Sector Report, 2004*. GAIN Report. Foreign Agricultural Service, US. Department of Agriculture, Washington, DC.

Vietnam Living Standards Survey (1993 and 1998) Vietnam.

World Bank (2004) India's e-Choupals: a private sector approach to link farmers to markets. International Finance Corporation, a global learning process and conference, *Reducing Poverty, Sustaining Growth*, 25–27 May 2004, Shanghai, China.

World Bank (2005) *World Development Indicators, 2005*. CD-ROM database. The World Bank, Washington, DC.

9 Small Traders and Small Farmers: the Small Engines Driving China's Giant Boom in Horticulture

X. Dong, H. Wang, S. Rozelle, J. Huang and T. Reardon

Introduction

The supermarket revolution has arrived in China and is spreading as fast as or faster than anywhere else in the world. As the demands for vegetables, fruit, nuts and other high-valued products have risen, urban retailers are finding new venues from which they can sell to the increasingly prosperous city residents. From its start in the early 1990s, supermarkets today take over US$55 billion in sales (Hu *et al.*, 2004). China's supermarkets already sell much higher levels of fresh fruit and vegetables to domestic consumers than exporters sell to overseas markets.

This development has been driven by factors shared by other developing countries – urbanization, income growth and liberalization of foreign direct investment in retailing – as well as a number of policies specific to China (e.g. government investment in the sector and policies promoting conversion of wetmarkets to supermarkets (Bi *et al.*, 2004; Hu *et al.*, 2004)).

Although there has been no systematic study of the penetration of procurement into rural areas, researchers have written about signs that supermarket procurement systems have begun to shift away from the traditional wholesale system toward the use of large, centralized distribution centres, specialized/dedicated wholesalers operating preferred supplier systems and private standards for quality and food safety. Clearly, the spread of supermarkets in particular, and the rise of the demand for horticultural products more generally, present opportunities for China's agricultural producers.

The experience internationally, however, suggests that there could be serious distributional impacts from the rise of supermarkets. For example, there are case studies in Guatemala and Costa Rica that suggest that it is the rich, large farmers that benefit from the rise of demand for fruit and vegetables and the emergence of supermarkets (Alvarado and Charmel, 2002; Berdegué *et al.*, 2005).

Because of the high transaction costs involved with purchasing from millions of small farmers and difficulties in monitoring quality and food safety, it is often assumed that supermarkets and their agents will turn to large and better-off farmers. As a consequence, the rise of demand for horticultural and other high-valued commodities in the consumption basket of consumers, and the concomitant rise in supermarkets, have created concern among the international community about the possible adverse consequences on small, poor farmers (Reardon and Timmer, 2005).

In many respects, the process that will allow China's procurement systems to mature and spread over larger regions faces similar, if not more severe, challenges than those faced by food retailers in other countries. The average farm size in China is small, less than 0.6 ha per household (NBSC, 2005). Farmers are not well organized, since historically cooperatives and associations have not been encouraged. Households which are engaged in mostly farming (that is, full-time farmers) are among the absolute poorest in China and live in relatively poor parts of the nation (Rozelle, 1996; World Bank, 2005).

Hence, the typical farm family faces challenges in meeting the demanding product and transaction attributes that are required by most supermarket retailers. Indeed, the rise of supermarkets, like elsewhere in the world, has also generated a concern among policy-makers about their impact on the small, poor farming sector (Reardon and Swinnen, 2004). In fact, in China this concern has already dampened the enthusiasm of some of those that believed the rise in the demand for high-valued commodities would provide opportunities for farmers to move into the production of goods that could provide them with higher income (Yu, 2003; Yuan, 2004).

Surprisingly, given the importance of this topic, there has been little, if any, systematic empirical analysis of the effect of the rise of demand for high-valued commodities and the rise of supermarkets that are promoting these goods on the welfare of farmers in China.

The work that has been done (e.g. Yu 2003; Hu et al., 2004; Yuan, 2004), while interesting and providing important insights, is unable to answer a few key questions in a systematic way: (i) where are the new high-valued crops being cultivated and who is cultivating them? (ii) are the farmers who are supplying most of the demand rich and large? (iii) are farmers that are poor and small able to benefit? (iv) what is the nature of the supply chains that facilitate the procurement of crops from the farmers? and (v) are these supply chains imposing new quality and food safety standards on farmers?

The main goal of this chapter is limited to one major theme: getting the facts right regarding the emergence of supply chains and the participation of farmers in China's rapidly evolving food economy. We have three main objectives. First, we sketch a picture of who is supplying horticultural products in China. Second, we describe the patterns of marketing chains in China's rural areas, examining who is procuring vegetables, fruit and nuts from farmers, where the transactions are taking place and to whom the first buyer is selling. Finally, we seek to understand how marketing supply chains are affecting the way farmers are producing horticulture crops.

Given such a circumscribed set of objectives, however, we must still further recognize the limitations of our work. First, while our sample is spatially sampled and is able to produce a representative view of China's horticultural economy in rural areas, we are still looking only at one region, the greater Beijing metropolitan region. We also investigate only at the first two links in the marketing chain. Hence, our findings are not able to trace the marketing paths of vegetables, fruit and nuts all the way to the consumer. Hence, while we know from our study that supermarkets are largely absent from rural areas, we can not say anything about how supermarkets procure horticultural goods.

Finally, because exports are such a small part of total horticultural production (only around 2%) and because we are not studying horticultural production in the centres of China's export industry, we are almost exclusively focusing on the domestic side of the industry. Therefore, we are unable to answer many questions about the dynamics of the export segment of the market which, in many cases, may be expected to behave quite differently.

To meet our objectives, the rest of the chapter is organized as follows. The first section describes our data. The following two sections examine the production and procurements sides of the horticultural economy. The next section briefly examines descriptively the way that marketing channels are affecting the way that horticultural crops are being produced. The final two sections use multivariate analysis to try to explain who is benefiting from the rising demand for horticultural goods.

Methods and Data

The data set, collected by ourselves, is comprised of observations on 201 villages in 50 townships in the greater Beijing metropolitan region. In the summer of 2005 enumerators visited each of the villages and interviewed village leaders about the changes in the horticultural economy, from the village's point of view, between 2000 and 2004. Among other things, during several hour-long, sit-down questionnaire sessions with enumerators, village leaders recounted information about production trends of their community's major horticultural commodities.

The leaders also provided information on the most common ways in which horticultural goods had been procured from farmers – including: (i) the type of buyer that had purchased the crop from the farmer (henceforth, the *first-time buyer*); (ii) the location of the first transaction; and (iii) the agent/trading firm to whom the goods were sold by the first-time buyer (henceforth, the *second buyer*).

In total we identified eight main types of first-time buyers and seven main types of second buyers. Finally, we asked leaders to tell us the nature of the contractual arrangement – either explicit or implicit – between the farmer and first-time buyers. Enumerators also asked village leaders about the characteristics of their communities (for example, income per capita, cultivated land per capita, location, etc.).

The main feature by which our study is differentiated from previous research on these issues is in the way that we chose our sample. In simplest terms, we began with detailed administrative maps of Beijing Municipality and Hebei Province. We then used stratified random spatial sampling procedures to choose the townships and villages. In short, this study – unlike most other studies – did not go to where the horticulture suppliers were; instead, we took a random sample, collected data to be able to weight the observations (by the frequency in which we were likely to observe such villages) and, as such, have collected a representative sample of horticulture producers and marketing in one of the nation's important farming regions.

Who are Producing China's Vegetables, Fruit and Nuts?

The rise in demand for horticultural crops (henceforth the term used to describe 'vegetables, fruit and nuts grown in orchards') that has been observed in the demand statistics was beginning to change production patterns of farmers from grain to other crops in the greater Beijing area after 2000 (see Table 9.1). The total sown area of grain between 2000 and 2004 fell from 68 to 58%.

In contrast, cash crops (which include mainly crops such as cotton and peanuts, crops that are *not* the focus of our study) rose by four percentage points. During the same period, the area sown to horticultural crops also rose by seven percentage points (from 22% in 2000 to 29% in 2004). Vegetables rose by two percentage points; fruit – the crop category with the largest share of horticultural crops – rose by three

Table 9.1. Cropping patterns and the role of horticultural crops in greater Beijing, 2000 and 2004.

Crop	Greater Beijing (total, %)		40 km concentric circle sample region (%)		60 km concentric circle sample region (%)		80 km concentric circle sample region (%)		100 km concentric circle sample region (%)		140 km concentric circle sample region (%)	
	2000	2004	2000	2004	2000	2004	2000	2004	2000	2004	2000	2004
Grain	68	58	64	52	63	47	68	62	72	64	72	62
Cash crop	10	14	9	12	9	13	9	11	9	14	12	17
Horticultural crops[1]	22	29	27	36	28	39	23	27	18	22	16	21
Vegetables	4	6	4	4	4	9	6	7	2	3	4	6
Fruit	13	16	19	26	13	13	12	16	13	16	10	11
Nuts	5	7	4	6	11	17	5	5	3	3	2	5

[1] Sown area for horticultural crops includes area sown to vegetable, fruit and nut orchards.

percentage points; and nuts rose by two percentage points.

While the production trends for the Beijing area match fairly closely the rise in horticulture demand in China's urban areas, we are most interested in the types of farmers that are participating in supplying horticulture crops. In fact, when information on the typical farmer who is engaged in farming inside each of the concentric circles is compared (i.e. information on those farmers close to Beijing is compared to those far from Beijing), it can be seen that farmers in all areas are adjusting their production.

In particular, while the average farmers in all areas reduced the share of their area sown to grain by 10% (from 68 to 58%), as might be expected (Fafchamps and Shilpi, 2003), farmers in the first two circles (40 km and 60 km circles) reduced the share of area sown to grain (12 to 16%) more than did farmers in the other three circles (6 to 10%) that are far away from Beijing. Although the production of horticultural crops rises everywhere, the largest rise in terms of the share that a village's land is allocated to horticulture crops is found in the 40 and 60 km circles. While the rising share of horticultural crops in 40 km circles came mainly from fruit (19 to 26%), the rise in 60 km circles came from vegetables and nuts (vegetables, 4 to 9%; nuts, 11 to 17%).

Participation by the Poor

While the relatively smaller rise of horticultural area share in remote area is what one may expect, the most significant finding, based on our data, is that poor farmers are increasing their share of the production of horticulture crops (see Table 9.2). To demonstrate this, we divided the villages into four quartiles, according to each village's reported income per capita.

Between 2000 and 2004 we found that farmers in the very poor and poor categories (those farmers living in villages with incomes below the median income level) had increased their share of total sown area of horticultural crops, in general (top row). In fact, by 2004 farmers in the poor and very poor villages were producing more than half (55%) of horticultural crops in greater Beijing. Even more significantly, farmers in the very poor villages had increased their share of vegetables, fruit and nuts between 2000 and 2004.

A similar picture emerges when examining different types of horticultural crops (see Table 9.2). For example, in the case of fruit, production was dominated by the farmers in the poor and very poor villages. In contrast, farmers in above-average income villages produced most of the vegetables. Of course, one of the most interesting findings of Table 9.2 is that the richest farmers are not the driving force (or beneficiary) of vegetables, fruit or nuts.

Hence, according to our data, we have strong evidence that the rise of horticultural production in the greater Beijing area was not following the trends that had been observed in other developing countries (e.g. Farina and Machado 1999). Clearly, our data show that farmers in poor and

Table 9.2. Contribution of sampling areas by income category (quartiles) to horticultural production in greater Beijing, 2000 and 2004 (from authors' survey).

Crop	Very poor (first quartile, 1–25, %)		Poor (second quartile, 26–50, %)		Above average (third quartile, 51–75, %)		Rich (fourth quartile, 76–100, %)	
	2000	2004	2000	2004	2000	2004	2000	2004
Horticultural crops	15	23	31	32	33	25	20	19
Vegetables	9	12	25	29	53	47	12	12
Fruit	16	25	37	37	34	24	14	14
Nuts	21	30	17	19	8	9	54	42

very poor villages are not being left out. In fact, especially in the case of the very poor, they are the driving force behind the rise in the supply of fruit and nuts. Moreover, there is no evidence – even for vegetable crops – that richer farmers are dominating production. Indeed, farmers that live in the richer villages (above average and rich) have lost their share in all categories of horticultural crops (e.g. 65 to 59% for vegetables, 48 to 38% for fruit and 62 to 51% for nuts). In 2004 the richest 25% of farmers cultivated only 19% of the region's horticultural area.

Where are the Supermarkets?

The unexpected findings on the supply side, if anything, are matched by those on the procurement side. Although there has been a lot of discussion about the potential implications of the rise of modern supply chains and the effect of their procurement agents on welfare in rural areas, according to our data supermarkets are completely absent. Indeed, not one of the 201 village leaders that we interviewed reported the presence of supermarkets for the procurement of any horticultural goods (see Table 9.3).

Likewise, village leaders reported that only 2% of procurement from farmers was from specialized suppliers and only 2% from processing firms. Hence, in the greater Beijing area in 2004, only 4% of all horticultural goods were procured by those operating in firms that could be described as part of the modern supply chain.

Even when we look at data on the second buyer in the supply chain, the modern supply chain plays a fairly minor role (see Table 9.3). When asked to whom the first buyer sells, supermarkets only are involved in 3% of the volume. Specialized supply firms also account for only 3%. Processing firms are the second buyer for 10% of the volume of horticultural crops. Hence, in total, even by the second link of the marketing chain, modern supply chains are playing a relatively minor role, accounting for only 16% of the volume. Therefore, in summary, it is safe to say that in the greater Beijing sample villages, despite the rise in demand for high-valued horticultural products, and despite the rapid emergence of supermarkets in urban areas, modern supply chains in 2004 were almost non-existent at the producer end of the marketing chain.

Small Traders and Their Domination of Traditional Supply Chains

Instead, the main theme of horticultural marketing in China in 2004 is the domination of traditional supply channels, mostly by small traders. According to our data, fully 79 of the first-time buyers of

Table 9.3. Supply and marketing channels of horticultural markets in greater Beijing area, first-time buyers, 2004.

	Modern supply chains			Traditional supply chains		Other supply chains		
	Super-markets (%)	Specialized suppliers (%)	Processing firms (%)	Small traders (%)	Farmers selling in local periodic markets (%)	Coopera-tives (%)	Consumers purchase direct from farmers (%)	Others[1] (%)
Horticultural crops	0	2	2	79	8	0	7	2
Vegetables	0	3	5	82	5	0	1	3
Fruit	0	1	1	75	11	0	9	3
Nuts	0	6	0	88	3	0	3	0

[1] 'Others' (first-time buyers) includes purchases by agents of hotels or restaurants, gifts to other farmers or procurement by organized groups (such as enterprises for distribution to their workers).

horticultural goods were small traders (see Table 9.3). These small traders, who during harvest season can be seen virtually everywhere in areas that are producing horticultural crops, enter the village itself and buy directly from farmers. Almost all transactions are spot market transactions, exchanging the commodity for cash. In addition, in another 8% of the cases, farmers take their crop – as they have done for hundreds of years – to local period markets to sell to local consumers and traders (Rozelle and Huang, 2001).

Almost certainly due in part to the domination of traditional small traders, it can be seen from our data that the supply chain penetrates far into the village (see Table 9.4). While some of the traders bought from farmers in local periodic markets (~6%), most of them came direct to the farmer. In fact, when aggregating procurement by traders in the farmer's own fields (65%), at some spot in the village centre (9%) or at the side of the road near the village (3%), more than 75% of all procurement took place inside or immediately next to the boundary of the village. Only 15% of first-time sales take place in formal wholesale markets (11%) or in urban wet-markets (4%).

Finally, small traders not only make up the first link in the marketing chain; in fact, 49% of second buyers also were small traders (see Table 9.5). In other words, in nearly half of all cases, small traders bought from farmers and sold their goods to a second small trader. In addition, 13% of small traders took their goods to a nearby retail market and sold their goods to consumers.

While a comprehensive study of traders is still needed, given their primary role in the rural segment of the marketing chain in the horticultural economy, from interviews and from another data set collected by the authors in 2000 we can sketch a simple profile of small traders.[1] To a great extent, from discussions with village leaders and farmers, most small traders in the greater Beijing area are from three poor provinces, Hebei, Henan and Anhui. On average, small traders worked in small groups (henceforth, trading firms) of three to four people. On average, they had received only 7 years of education and their average age was over 30 years (older and less well-educated than the average migrant to China's largest cities).

In almost all cases, the employees/partners working in the same small trading firm were either relatives or fellow villagers, people who could be relied upon to work hard and trusted to work for the good of the firm. Moreover, despite the long hours of work (on average, for 8 months per year), the average income of traders was only about 3200 yuan per person.

If this was their only source of income and if we assume each small trader has to support, on average, one single dependent, this would put them right at the height of the international poverty line (about US$2 per day in purchasing power parity terms). Hence, these small traders can be thought of as poor themselves and willing to engage in labour-intensive economic activities, including travelling long distances to procure horticultural crops from farmers.

Table 9.4. Supply and marketing channels of horticultural markets in greater Beijing area, location of first transaction, 2004.

	Farm fields (%)	Village centre (%)	Roadside (%)	Periodic markets (%)	Wholesale markets (%)	Urban wetmarkets (%)	Others[1] (%)
Horticultural crops	65	9	3	6	11	4	2
Vegetables	64	0	3	6	18	9	0
Fruit	60	12	3	9	12	3	2
Nuts	86	11	0	0	0	0	4

[1] 'Others' (second-time buyers) includes sales to other villages and sales to market sites that supply processing and other food firms.

Table 9.5. Supply and marketing channels of horticultural markets in greater Beijing, second-time buyers, 2004.

	Modern supply chains			Traditional supply chains		Other supply chains	
	Super-markets (%)	Specialized suppliers (%)	Processing firms (%)	Small traders (%)	Traders sell to consumers in periodic markets (%)	Cooperatives (%)	Others (%)
Horticultural crops	3	3	10	49	13	0	22
Vegetables	6	0	6	57	11	0	20
Fruit	1	2	9	46	16	0	26
Nuts	3	10	19	50	6	0	12

Marketing Supply Chains and their Impact on the Quality of the Supply

In this section we examine the data that we collected about technology used by farmers in our sample. Our main purpose is to examine the effect that marketing supply chains have on the use of technology. Although in this chapter we examine questions that will allow us to see how those at the village level perceived marketing supply chains effects, a more definitive answer, based in rigorous multivariate analysis, awaits further research.

On the one hand, there may be reasons to believe that the rise of the horticultural economy has spawned linkages between markets and production choices in the village. In the sample farmers frequently changed technologies – either the crop they were producing or the type of variety they were planting. For example, for the 201 villages in our sample, the main vegetable, fruit or nut crop that was planted in the village in 2000 had, in 2004, been replaced by another crop in 14% of these villages. When discussing their main vegetable, fruit or nut crop, farmers reported that they had switched varieties on average about once every 3–5 years. Clearly, farmers in the horticultural economy in the greater Beijing area are actively searching for new technologies.

These descriptive statistics, however, do not really answer our question about the impact of modern supply chains. There are many other reasons why farmers may switch technologies beyond the marketing supply chain. In other words, counts of technology turnover can be deceiving. In fact, during the 1980s – a time when there were clearly no modern supply chains in the grain sector (Sicular, 1988) – farmers changed their grain varieties up to once every 3 years (Jin et al., 2002). Moreover, during the 1990s, when the market clearly played a larger role in grain marketing, farmers slowed their turnover of varieties to once every 5 years. Hence, the observed turnover in varieties/crop types may be due to other factors.

In fact, when we asked village leaders directly about whether or not their farmers were being required by the procurement agent (including small traders) to change the way in which they were producing their horticultural crop, the answer was nearly zero. In only three of 201 villages (or 0.9% of villages when weighting is used) was it reported that trading firms had influenced the timing, quantity or brand of the fertilizer that farmers used on their crop. In only six of 201 villages (or only 1.5%) was it reported that trading firms had influenced the timing, quantity or brand of the pesticide that farmers used on their crops. Hence, in our sample – at least from the viewpoint of the producer in 2004 – there is little *direct* link between the demands of the trader and the farming practices of the producer.

The Poor are Enjoying the Fruits of the Horticulture Boom

Since descriptive statistics may not be able to gauge accurately the net impact of any single factor on horticultural production or marketing, in Wang *et al.* (2006) we estimate econometrically the determinants of horticultural production. Although our original intention was to analyse the determinants of participation in modern marketing channels and the effect of modern marketing channels on the way farmers produce and market their horticultural crops, because there are so few villages that had any direct interaction with modern supply chains it was not possible to conduct the analysis on modern supply chain participation or its impacts.

In fact, since traditional, small trader channels are so pervasive, and farmers are mainly interacting with buyers in their villages; the real question of importance is: what are the determinants of participation in the horticultural sector? In addition, an important objective of this analysis is to ascertain whether poor people are benefiting from the boom in the horticultural economy (that is, holding all other factors constant, are those that are poor able to participate in the production of horticultural crops?).

Our multivariate analysis yields several interesting findings. First, our results demonstrate that villages that are in mountainous areas are relatively more likely to enter the horticulture economy. This may be a sign that the economy is reacting to market signals, since farmers in mountainous areas may have a comparative advantage (though not necessarily an absolute advantage) in the production of fruit and nuts in their villages.

Secondly, our results show that over time the poor are benefiting increasingly more from the rise in China's horticultural economy. Specifically, we find that when looking at the *income quartile dummies* in the year 2000, those villages in the very poor category, *ceteris paribus*, were not participating as much as villages in the other income quartiles. Farmers in very poor villages allocated less of their land to horticultural crops in the year 2000 (the base year), but between 2000 and 2004 many of these farmers were able to expand their cultivated area significantly. Hence, since 2000 – a time when the horticultural economy has booming – we see that, all other things being equal – the farmers in the poorest villages have expanded their area relatively more than the others.

Discussion and Conclusions

In this chapter we set out to assess the effect that modern supply chains and the rise of the horticultural economy in China has had on the farming sector in China. Although we have data only for a single area of China, greater Beijing, our sample is spatially sampled and so we are able to produce regionally representative figures on the rise of opportunities for planting horticultural crops and the penetrations of modern marketing supply chains into rural areas. These questions have worried policy officials not only in China, but are of concern to leaders around the world.

Interestingly, although we showed that the rise of horticultural crops was paralleled by a surge in the emergence of supermarkets in urban areas, there has been almost no penetration by modern wholesalers or retailers into rural communities. Less than 6% of first-time buyers and less than 16% of second buyers could be identified as being from modern supply chains – either supermarkets, professional suppliers or processing firms.

Instead, China's horticultural economy is dominated by small traders who are themselves poor and small, operating in firms of around four people and are themselves earning low wages. Moreover, unlike the evidence found in other countries, it appears as if in China, far from being damaged by the rise of supermarkets and the horticulture boom that has come with it, poor, small farmers in our sample appear to have gained. The richest farmers, in contrast, were playing a smaller role in 2004 than in 2000. Clearly, it appears as if this is a special case of 'Producing Horticultural Crops with Chinese Characteristics'.

So what makes China special? While a full analysis and more definitive conclusions require more research, it is our opinion that there are seven characteristics about China's horticultural economy that produce these surprising results. First, China's land holdings (and those in our sample – see Table 9.6) are relatively equal in size (characteristic 1). In essence, there are no large farmers in China; indeed in our sample, the average farm size of the biggest 20% of farmers is only 0.36 ha per capita.

Second, there also are almost no farmer cooperatives that could allow farmers to act in concert with one another (characteristic 2). In our sample, only 11.4% of the villages reported that they had a horticultural or general farm cooperative. Only

Table 9.6. Summary statistics for sample households and villages, 2004.

Variable	Total concentric circle sample region	40 km concentric circle sample region	60 km concentric circle sample region	80 km concentric circle sample region	100 km concentric circle sample region	140 km concentric circle sample region
Household level						
Sample households (n)	494	143	60	111	90	90
Cultivated land per capita (ha)[1]	0.14	0.09	0.07	0.16	0.13	0.17
Share of households belonging to a cooperative (%)	1.05	2.68	0.00	3.58	0.59	0.00
Proportion of labourers having off-farm job (%)[2]	35	42	53	24	43	31
Average time per labourer of those having off-farm job (days p.a.)	96	111	125	67	122	82
Proportion of off-farm income in net income (%)[3]	40	44	61	25	50	34
Average household size (persons)	3.98	4.06	4.19	3.70	4.46	3.77
Average size of household labour force (persons)	2.82	2.75	2.89	2.72	3.09	2.72
Average income per capita (yuan)	2913	3881	2974	2299	3085	2752
Village level						
Sample villages (n)	201	40	40	41	40	40
Average distance from village to nearest county road (km)	4.95	2.46	3.51	6.09	6.30	4.65
Proportion of villages within 5 km of paved road (%)	79	86	76	77	80	78
Proportion of households having cell phone	48	66	53	42	50	43

[1] Cultivated land includes all farmer-managed land, including contracted land and land rented in, but excluding land rented out.
[2] Labour includes all able-bodied persons 16–65 years old and excludes persons within this age bracket that are at school.
[3] 'Net income' includes cropping net income, off-farm net income and other sources of net income.

1.05% of farmers said that they belonged to a cooperative (see Table 9.6). These numbers, as it turns out, are remarkably similar to the figures for the whole of China reported by Shen et al. (2004), using data from a national representative sample of more than 2000 villages. Because of characteristics 1 and 2, it is easy to see why it could be so difficult for supermarkets and other modern supply firms to deal with farmers, given their miniscule size and the absence of organization. Clearly, the transaction costs of contracting or direct procurement would be high.

The third characteristic that may be relevant in explaining the role of small, poor farmers in the rise of China's horticultural economy is that although land is relatively equally allocated across all communities in China, there are still differences (characteristic 3). In the case of horticultural producers, farm households in poorer, more remote areas have relatively more land (0.17 ha per capita) than those in areas nearer to the richer, urban centres (0.09 ha per capita).

In addition, there are also differences in the access that these households have to labour for working on the farm (characteristic 4). Although horticultural farmers have the same family size as those not engaged in horticultural farming, the main differences are due to differential access to off-farm jobs (see Table 9.6). Farm households that are nearest to Beijing have a higher percentage of their labour force in off-farm employment (42 for those nearest; 31 for those furthest) and they work a greater number of days per year (111 for those nearest; 82 for those furthest).

The same is true when dividing the sample between better-off and poorer households. Poorer households have more land and labour available for use in producing horticultural crops (see Table 9.7). Hence, when considering characteristics 3 and 4 together, it is easy to see why poor farmers have increased their share of land area in many of the horticultural crops – they are relatively land- and labour-rich, the two factors that are key factors in the production of horticultural crops.

Two additional characteristics help reinforce the propensity for poorer farmers to increase their participation in the horticultural economy, while the supermarkets are almost completely absent from

Table 9.7. Summary statistics by asset wealth categories, 2004 (data from authors' survey).[1]

Variable[2]	Total sample	Poor (percentile range: 1–25)	Average (percentile range: 26–75)	Rich (percentile range: 76–100)
Sample households (n)	494	124	247	123
Cultivated land per capita (ha)	0.14	0.14	0.16	0.08
Proportion of able-bodied labourers having off-farm job (%)	35	24	35	50
Time worked off-farm by those with off-farm jobs (days)	96	90	87	128
Proportion of off-farm income in net income (%)	40	34	37	53
Average household size (persons)	3.98	3.54	4.16	3.98
Average size of household labour force (persons)	2.82	2.72	2.86	2.83
Average net income per capita (yuan)	2,950	1,870	2,795	4,971
Average asset wealth per capita (yuan)	10,485	1,064	6,143	35,525

[1] Wealth categories were developed from household level data on total household assets including housing, own business, farm tools and consumer durable assets.
[2] See Table 9.6 for categorization of variables studied.

the production areas. Since China's horticultural economy is almost completely unregulated (characteristic 5) and since China's road and communication networks have improved remarkably over the past 10 years (characteristic 6, see Table 9.6), small traders working with a limited amount of capital and using extremely large amounts of low-cost labour (while utilizing the relatively efficient road and communication infrastructure) appear to be outcompeting all other types of would-be procurement agents.

According to our interviews with the small traders and producers, the competition between small traders is fierce and profit margins on traders are almost always wafer-thin. There are few above-normal profits available to attract new, more innovative entrants. Interestingly, in this type of small trader-dominated system, there is little or no effort being made to monitor quality or impose safety standards directly on producers.

Finally, one of the main characteristics of China's economy that creates the *status quo* is that China is still a relatively poor nation and its consumers, so far, may not be placing a very high premium on food safety or obtaining a standard product (characteristic 7). Although there is a rising middle class, most urban consumers still live in households earning ~US$1000 per capita annual disposable income (NBSC, 2005). Many of them are becoming increasingly stressed with rising payments in other expenditure categories – housing, automobile ownership, education and health care (among other expenditure categories).

Combined with the absence of an active pro-consumer lobby (which may be limiting the information consumers have on the quality of their food), it is almost certain that the premium the average urban consumer is willing to pay is still relatively small. When this low premium is combined with the high transaction costs that would have to be born should the supermarket want to maintain tight control over its horticultural supply, along with the thriving, deep, extremely competitive wholesale markets, it may be (although further research is required to confirm this) that, at least now and in the immediate future, China will still be relying mostly on traditional wholesale channels.

If this is true, food safety in China's food system may suffer. However, it is good news for small, poor farmers. Nevertheless, it should be realized how fast China is changing in so many areas and, if any one (or perhaps several) of these characteristics change, we should expect to see China's horticultural economy – from both the supply and procurement side – change. This change, like so many other things in China, could be very rapid.

Note

1   We thank Jian Zhang, a PhD student in the Department of Agricultural and Resource Economics, University of California, Davis, California, USA, for these statistics. The data are from a 2000 household data set collected by the Center for Chinese Agricultural Policy and the University of California, Davis. Among other sections of the survey, one part focused in family-run businesses and carefully enumerated the income and expenses, assets and liabilities and working hours of more than 350 small micro-enterprises, including more than 50 small trading firms.

References

Alvarado, I. and Charmel, K. (2002) The rapid rise of supermarkets in Costa Rica: impact on horticultural markets. *Development Policy Review* 20 (4), 473–485.

Berdegué, J.A., Balsevich, F., Flores, L. and Reardon, T. (2005) Central American supermarkets' private standards of quality and safety in procurement of fresh fruits and vegetables. *Food Policy* 30 (3), 254–269.

Bi, X., Dong, X., Huang, J., Hu, D. and Rozelle, S. (2004) *Securing Small Producer Participation in Restructured National and Regional Agri-food Systems*. China Country Project Report on 'Regoverning Markets'. Center for Chinese Agricultural Policy, Chinese Academy of Sciences, Beijing.

Fafchamps, M. and Shilpi, F. (2003) The spatial division of labour in Nepal. *Journal of Development Studies* 39 (6), 23–66.

Farina, E.M.M.Q. and Machado, E.L. (1999) Government regulation and business strategies in the Brazilian fresh fruit and vegetable market. Presented at the *International Food and Agribusiness Management Association (IAMA) Congress*, Florence, Italy.

Hu, D.H., Reardon, T., Rozelle, S., Timmer, P. and Wang, H.L. (2004) The emergence of supermarkets with Chinese characteristics: challenges and opportunities for China's agricultural development. *Development Policy Review* 22 (5), 557–586.

Jin, S., Huang, J., Hu, R. and Rozelle, S. (2002) The creation and spread of technology and total factor productivity in China's agriculture. *American Journal of Agricultural Economics* 84 (4), 916–930.

National Bureau of Statistics of China (NBSC) (2005) *China Statistics Yearbook*. China Statistics Press, Beijing.

Reardon, T. and Swinnen, J.F.M. (2004) Agrifood sector liberalization and the rise of supermarkets in former state-controlled economies: comparison with other developing countries. *Development Policy Review* 22 (4), 515–524.

Reardon, T. and Timmer, C.P. (2005) Transformation of markets for agricultural output in developing countries since 1950: how has thinking changed? In: Evenson, R., Pingali, P. and Schultz, T.P. (eds) *Handbook of Agricultural Economics: Agricultural Development: Farmers, Farm Production, and Farm Markets*. Volume III, Elsevier, Netherlands, Chapter 13.

Rozelle, S. (1996) Stagnation without equity: changing patterns of income and inequality in China's post-reform rural economy. *The China Journal* 42 (1), 63–96.

Rozelle, S., Huang, J. and Benziger, V. (2002) Continuity and change in China's rural periodic markets. *China Journal* 49, 89–115.

Shen, M. (2004) Farmers professional associations and the supermarket development: a double win institutional arrangement. Paper Presented at the *International Conference 'Supermarket and Agricultural Development – Challenges and Opportunities'*, May 2004, Shanghai, China.

Sicular, J. (1988) Plan and market in China's agricultural commerce. *Journal of Political Economy* 96 (2), 283–305.

Wang, H., Dong, X., Rozelle, S., Huang, J. and Reardon, T. (2006) *Producing and Procuring Horticultural Crops with Chinese Characteristics: a Case Study in the Greater Beijing Area*. Working Paper. Center for Chinese Agricultural Policy, Chinese Academy of Science, Beijing, China.

World Bank (2005) *China – Compliance with Food safety requirements for Fruits and Vegetables. Promoting Food Safety, Competitiveness and Poverty Reduction*. World Bank, Washington, DC.

Yu, H.F. (2003) Research on management of fresh food in supermarket in China. PhD Thesis. Beijing, China.

Yuan, Y.X. (2004) Supermarket – an effective main body agri-food entered market. Paper presented at *Shanghai International Forum – 'Supermarket and Agriculture Development – Challenges and Opportunities'*, May 2004, Beijing, China.

10 Quality Control and the Marketing of Non-staple Crops in India

M. Fafchamps, R. Vargas-Hill and B. Minten

Introduction

The objective of our study is to assess how the market for non-staple crops currently functions in India and how existing agricultural marketing institutions can be improved. India is rapidly changing. Over the years, Indian governments have put in place institutions for dealing with agricultural marketing. These institutions focus primarily on staple crops such as rice, wheat, pulses and oilseeds. There is a growing suspicion that these institutions are no longer adapting to current trends, and this suspicion is based on two observations.

First, the pattern of domestic demand for agricultural products is evolving. As India gets richer, many consumers become relatively less interested in staple foods and more interested in fruit and vegetables. Rising incomes favour a growing demand for meat – particularly chicken. This generates an expansion in the market for feed crops such as maize. Increased incomes also fuel concerns about food safety and are expected to generate a demand for better food quality among high-income Indian consumers.

Until now, Indian markets for agricultural products have focused primarily on quantity. Today, many consumers in the upper tier of income distribution are probably prepared to pay extra for food quality and safety. Satisfying the demand for better and safer fruit and vegetables by the richer segments of the population can thus be a way of increasing farmers' income. The question is whether the market for non-staple foods is organized in such a way as to enable growers to capitalize on the rising demand for quality.

Secondly, India has come to realize that it can take advantage of international trade liberalization to export agricultural products. India's confidence in its capacity to take on international markets has risen markedly. If India can compete on international manufacturing and service markets, then it should be able to compete on agricultural markets as well. India is already the world leader in turmeric exports, capturing the lion's share of the international market. Within policy circles there is growing interest in exploring the possibility of breaking into new agricultural export markets, particularly those for processed food products such as mango chutney. As recent history has demonstrated, the keys to these markets are food quality and safety.

While agricultural markets in India have been extensively studied (e.g. Acharya,

2001; Umali-Deininger and Deininger, 2001; Ramaswami and Balakrishnan, 2002; Deshingkar et al., 2003; Banerji and Meenakski, 2004), little specific information seems to be available about the value chain for non-staple crops. This study seeks to fill this lacuna.

We conducted a combined survey of growers, traders and processors of five selected non-staple crops in four states. Data were also collected at the market and village levels. Information was collected on the production and marketing practices of 400 growers and on the trading practices of 400 traders in each state. Interviews were conducted with 300 processors across all four states (for more detailed information, see Fafchamps et al., 2006).

The four states covered by this study are Maharashtra, Orissa, Tamil Nadu and Uttar Pradesh. They were chosen because they represent the diversity of agricultural marketing institutions and agro-climatic zones that is characteristic of India today. The five crops are maize, mango, potato, tomato and turmeric. These crops were chosen because they are cultivated and consumed throughout the country and are representative of the diversity of non-staple crops in terms of perishability and end-uses.[1]

The chapter is structured as follows: (i) we summarize our main findings on crop production, market infrastructure and organization, quality control and equal access; (ii) we discuss these results; and finally (iii) make some suggestions regarding possible policy improvements.[2]

Production of Non-staple Crops in India

Before discussing the market infrastructure in India we briefly provide some descriptive statistics on the production of turmeric, mango, potato, tomato and maize. The farmers that produce and sell these crops devote a significant proportion of their land to the production of these crops – at least one-third when the crops are in season. The majority of farmers use bought inputs in crop production: three-quarters of farmers use chemical fertilizers, over half use pesticides and one-quarter use fungicides. The most commonly used chemical fertilizers are urea, nitrogen, phosphate and potash. The majority of farmers also use non-traditional seeds: 71% of maize farmers, 59% of tomato farmers, 59% of potato farmers and 55% of turmeric farmers.

Producers of non-staple crops appear to have unencumbered access to agricultural inputs, but when we compared the welfare characteristics (land holding, education, caste) of farmers of non-staple crops with the average farmer in each state we found a positive relationship between land ownership and the propensity to grow non-staple crops for sale (Fafchamps et al., 2006). However, it is unclear whether this relationship exists because land-rich farmers are more likely to grow non-staple crops or because farmers who grow non-staple crops can afford to purchase more land.

Market infrastructure and organization

The most common form of sale for non-staple crops is through the nearest wholesale market: 80% of farmers in the study reported selling one of the five study crops at the nearest wholesale market in the 12 months prior to the survey, compared with only 11% of farmers who reporting selling at the nearest retail market.[3] Sales at the farm gate were also observed for some crops.

Cooperatives play a role in marketing of maize and turmeric in some of the states visited, but are largely absent in the marketing of other crops. Using regression analysis we investigated whether farmers have equal access to wholesale markets. Our findings indicate that, within a given area, there is little difference across wealth levels but that farmers with larger quantities for sale seem to be courted by traders for farm-gate sales (Fafchamps et al., 2006).

The survey shows unambiguously that the wholesale market infrastructure for non-staple crops is not very well developed (see Table 10.1). The majority of wholesale markets are not paved, many do not have dedicated stalls for non-staple traders and there are few grading or cold storage facilities. Sanitation facilities are largely deficient, with few public toilets, inadequate drainage and little or no coordinated pest control.

As anticipated, postharvest losses are rather large in this trading environment: 3% of tomato and potato and 10% of mango is lost at each trading level. This is probably due both to the perishable nature of the crop and to the handling practices.

Survey results indicate that states with more markets regulated through the State Agricultural Produce Market Act (Maharashtra and Uttar Pradesh) tend to have better market infrastructure. These differences are driven not so much by regulation itself but rather by differences across states in the level of their involvement in agricultural markets. Farmers do not appear to be more satisfied with regulated markets and there is, in fact, some evidence of lower satisfaction.

Auctions are conducted in half of the markets visited (55%). In most cases they are conducted in an informal manner, with little information explicitly conveyed to buyers, who have to inspect each consign-

Table 10.1. Infrastructure, drainage and pest control in agricultural markets (unweighted average over the four states of Maharashtra, Orissa, Tamil Nadu and Uttar Pradesh).

Market infrastructure	
Proportion (%) of markets with	
Paved road inside market yard	12
Cold storage facilities	7
Grading machine[1]	16
Authorities that offer grading services, e.g. visual inspection/certification	21
Drying machine	1
Area to dry crops	16
Crop fumigation equipment	5
Public toilets	50
Proportion (%) of stalls that have	
Electricity	61
Piped water	25
Telephone (land line)	40
Grading equipment	3
Packing equipment	1
Fumigation machine	4
Drainage and pest control in markets	
Proportion of markets with no drainage (%)	32
Proportion of markets with drainage provided by open sewer (%)	46
Proportion of markets where drainage is adequate (%)	56
Measures taken against rats (% of markets)	
Employees of market/association in charge	5
Pest control contracted to outside firm	3
Individuals take care of rats in their store	32
No particular measure taken	59
Measures taken against insects damaging crops (% of markets)	
Employees of market/association in charge	7
Pest control contracted to outside firm	3
Individuals fumigate in their store	27
No particular measure taken	59
Other	4

[1] In the case of grading machines are available, this is mostly for rice/other cereals (40%) and potato (30%).

ment personally. The grade or size of the crop is reported in less than two-thirds of the auctions and in only half is the place of origin or the name of the buyers and sellers reported. Information about quality is rarely conveyed and in only 12% of auctions is information supplied about how the crop was produced.

State regulations require farmers to sell through 'commission agents' in Uttar Pradesh and Maharashtra, on the premise that doing so will help farmers receive a higher price for their product. In principle, a commission agent is a broker who matches buyers and sellers in exchange for a commission. A commission agent is not supposed to purchase the crop he has been asked to sell because doing so creates a conflict of interest: the commission agent is supposed to help the farmer get the highest price, but if he is planning to purchase the crop for himself, what incentive does he have to raise the price?

However in wholesale markets in India, commission agents were nearly all found operating as wholesalers for the crops for which they were brokers. An analysis of the prices received by farmers suggests that farmers who sell through a commission agent do not receive a significantly higher price (for details of regression analysis see Fafchamps et al., 2006). These findings seriously put into question the merit of forcing farmers to sell through commission agents.

We started the study concerned that the State Agricultural Produce Market Act may serve as a barrier to entry to trading and, hence, might increase transaction costs for non-staple crops. This is difficult to test formally given the lack of variation across space within each state. But the somewhat obscure way in which auctions are held, the dual role of commission agents and the implicit transfers embedded in stall rental contracts suggest that the Produce Market Act generates rents that are captured by a few traders. Whether these rents are sufficiently large to reduce farmer prices and increase consumer prices significantly remains unclear.

When we initiated this study, we also expected interlinked arrangements (e.g. credit and inputs supplied by the buyer) to be frequent for high-value crops. Given the high cash requirements to purchase all the inputs, we indeed thought that farmers would be unable or unwilling to make these investments without financial help from buyers – or at least without a guaranteed outlet for their production, but we did not find this to be the case. There was very little evidence of interlinked arrangements: only 9% of farmers reported receiving an advance from the buyer of their produce, and only 5% of farmers reported engaging in contract farming.

More than half the contracts observed in the survey were simple forward sales of mangoes, in which the mangoes are sold while on the tree and the buyer usually provided labour to harvest the mangoes. Such contracts involve no input supply, and the buyer does not provide any guidance or quality control. A handful of contracts were observed for potato, and were a broadly similarly means for traders to guarantee supply rather than a means by which inputs or advice are provided to farmers.

A suspicion exists that farmers under interlinked marketing arrangements receive lower returns. The reason for this suspicion is that farmers who sell forward sometimes do so because they are in need of cash. Survey results show that a number of farmers point out that forward sales yield a lower price but also reduce risk. Most surveyed contract farmers say that the price is fixed in the contract. Consequently, the price at harvest can be higher or lower than the contract price, depending on the evolution of demand and supply conditions in that year.

Regression analysis shows that contract farming has a significant negative effect on the average price received by the farmer only for tomato. We found no significant effect in the four other crops. It appears there is a substantial demand for contract farming among farmers: 47% of farmers not in a contract said they would like to be. Of course, the absence of contract farming may simply be due to the fact that it is illegal in many states – although, as the example of Orissa illustrates, laws are not always enforced.

Turning to processors, we found most of them to be very small enterprises. They perform very basic transformation, often of damaged or inferior-quality produce. This is completely ill-adapted to the evolution of the Indian market today. We examined whether the State Agricultural Produce Market Act makes it more difficult for processors and exporters to source inputs, particularly for spices, fruit and vegetables. As we have already pointed out, vertical coordination arrangements (contract farming, backward and forward arrangements) are rare and we found that very few – if any – processors and exporters in our survey source produce directly from farmers. We suspect that the current market structure does not hinder the activities of the overwhelming majority of small processors serving poorer consumers.

The handling losses that are pervasive in the marketing chain may even benefit them, as damaged fruit and vegetables are probably recycled into processed products. The big losers are absent from our survey: these are the processors and exporters who need to guarantee quality and consistency in order to access high-value markets. Given that the current system makes it illegal for them to approach farmers directly, they simply cannot operate within the current marketing arrangement. For them, liberalization is essential.

We encountered difficulties in identifying and meeting processors and exporters in spite of numerous attempts to work through agro-processing and exporter associations. From these difficulties, we gather that these associations are not very active since they were, in many cases, unable to provide an up-to-date list of agro-processors and had little useful information to share about their members. This is yet another sign of the poor state in which the agro-business industry currently operates in India.

Quality control

Much emphasis was built into the study on how quality control takes place in the value chain. In agreement with theoretical predictions (Fafchamps et al., 2006), we found that market participants are largely unaware of food safety risk. This is particularly true of farmers and small traders. As an example of this, only 2% of farmers reported that, in the previous 5 years, a buyer had indicated they should not use certain inputs or required a change of postharvest production practices. Large wholesalers and exporters appear slightly more concerned about food safety, but food safety goes basically unrewarded in the value chain.

We also found no evidence that growers or traders alter production and postharvest practices to comply with newer specifications or requirements of buyers, as would be the case if a new breed of wholesalers and exporters were trying to improve quality in order to break into new markets (see Table 10.2).

We found that information about the type of irrigation crops received or the application of pesticide and chemical fertilizer is not passed along the value chain (Table 10.2). In contrast, growers appear quite interested in agricultural practices that raise the quantity sold or improve observable characteristics of the crop, such as grading, packaging or drying. The same is true for postharvest treatment such as fumigation, which is undertaken by few traders and seldom reported to buyers (see Table 10.2).

Sellers, in general, reported only observable attributes to potential buyers. This is consistent with the absence of trust: if the buyer does not trust the seller, there is no point making unverifiable claims about items for sale. Further confirmation of this interpretation is found in the observation that buyers always the check observable attributes of what they purchase – they do not rely on seller's report.

An analysis of the prices received by growers shows that a significant price premium is paid to growers for drying, grading and packaging the crops they sell.

Table 10.2. Information transmission and requirements for buyers.

	Crop				
	Maize	Potato	Tomato	Mango	Turmeric
Information available to buyers					
Proportion of crop grown by farmer who reports buyer can tell practice has been undertaken: (% of those that have undertaken practice)					
Choose particular seeds/variety	62	85	58	81	78
Plant at a specific time	23	65	48	–	44
Apply pesticides	11	33	20	7	21
Apply fertilizer	9	63	21	5	16
Irrigate	23	56	32	7	11
Dry after harvest	84	–	–	–	91
Clean after harvest	75	77	54	62	77
Grade	39	80	62	69	54
Fumigate/treat after harvest	10	14	9	27	30
Proportion of crop grown by farmer who tells buyer practice has been undertaken: (% of those that have undertaken practice)					
Choose particular seeds/variety	2	6	16	6	6
Plant at a specific time	1	5	7	–	6
Apply pesticides	1	10	10	6	7
Apply fertilizer	1	6	9	2	5
Irrigate	1	4	12	2	1
Dry after harvest	1	–	–	–	0
Clean after harvest	3	10	7	3	0
Grade	1	6	13	3	0
Fumigate/treat after harvest	0	25	8	2	4
Package/crate	13	65	10	3	7
Mill/grind	3	10	3	1	15
Requests on production, postharvest and phytosanitary practices by buyers					
Proportion of crop sold for whom buyers have (in last 5 years, %):					
Changed specifications regarding product quality	1	15	8	1	0
Indicated they should not use certain chemicals/inputs	5	4	4	0	1
Requested/required change of postharvest practices	3	9	6	0	2
Paid more if farmer complies with new specs/reqs	2	2	3	0	0
Proportion of crop grown by farmers who have changed to comply	2	0	2	0	1
Buyers of agricultural products in this village pay attention to (% of villages):*					
What type of seed has been used	32	40	38	13	33
What kind of pesticides has been used	17	22	22	6	14
When pesticides have been applied	13	17	17	6	12
What kind of irrigation water has been used	10	8	14	2	12
Buyers of agricultural products in this village refuse Produce affected by pests/fungus (% of villages)*	54	54	63	35	52

* Source is village survey; for other variables source is farmer survey.

These attributes of the consignment serve to reduce transactions costs to traders. Consequently, they are only valued by traders and do not translate into a price premium further down the value chain. This is consistent with the view that packaging only serves to facilitate the work of wholesalers, but carries no useful information further down the value chain. The data also suggest that many processors purchase low-quality fruit and vegetables and care little about quality.

By vertically integrating the value chain and by creating a long-term trust relationship between grower and buyer, contract farming can in principle provide a commitment mechanism capable of overcoming the information transfer problem but, as detailed in the previous section, few contracts were observed for the non-staple crops studied. When they are observed they do not seem to be used to ensure quality of produce. It is possible that more sophisticated contract farming practices exist in India, but given survey findings it appears they account for only a small proportion of traded quantities of the five non-staple crops studied.

These findings suggest that the value chain for non-staple crops in India remains fairly undeveloped. It is conceivable that, given the level of development of the country, many Indian consumers are unwilling to pay a large price premium for higher-quality fruit and vegetables. We also suspect that few consumers would value organically grown produce. Given the cost of upgrading existing market infrastructure and the difficulty inherent in enforcing contracts about unobservable crop attributes, our findings are probably not surprising. However, rapid growth and the rapid rise in incomes are likely to result in a dramatic rise in the demand for safe, high-quality food. The current value chain is unable to satisfy this demand.

Discussion

The unprecedented increase in standards of living that many countries have enjoyed since the beginning of the Industrial Revolution can ultimately be explained only by the increased productivity that results from the application of science to technology. Technological innovation can take many forms: some are embedded in equipment and infrastructure, while others are embedded in new industrial inputs and consumer products. Yet others are embedded in new organizational forms – new contracts, new institutions, new ways of organizing the factory floor, new ways of doing business, etc.

Many factors play a role in how technological innovation is generated and how it permeates through the world economy, and it is beyond the scope of this analysis to discuss them here. In particular, it is no secret that more technologically advanced ways of doing things do not always spread naturally to all sectors of the economy. There is room for a lot of variation. But what is important to observe is that the degree of sophistication of an industry can be judged by examining its technology level – in terms of equipment, infrastructure, products and organization. Higher productivity can ultimately be achieved only by upgrading technology. Sometimes this means bringing in new capital, sometimes it means reforming organizational forms.

In this chapter we have examined the value chain for non-staple crops. Perhaps the most striking feature that comes out of our analysis is the stark contrast between the high level of technological sophistication achieved in the production of fruit and vegetables and the rather primitive state of the marketing chain. As highlighted, nearly all the growers of non-staple crops that we interviewed use modern techniques of agricultural production, but the marketing chain appears quite backward by comparison.

In fact, the forms of market organization that we described here resemble those described by Greif (1993) for Medieval Europe and by Fafchamps (2004) for sub-Saharan Africa. The limited use of modern equipment and infrastructure in the non-staple value chain in India results in large crop losses and makes sanitation problematic, with inadequate drainage and sewers and improper pest control.

Forms of organization also appear rather primitive. Although in many states the law requires that the sale of agricultural products be performed in auctions, for non-staple crops these auctions appear problematic. Farmers are supposed to sell their produce through commission agents, but in nearly all cases these commission agents are also wholesalers who buy and sell the same products, thus creating a conflict of interest.

We found little contracting among traders or between traders and farmers. Quality control is limited to observable attributes and crop certification is absent. Processors are predominantly small and uninvolved in improving quality and, in fact, we suspect that in many cases it is the low-quality fruit and vegetables that are used for processing.

These findings are surprising. India has done extremely well in improving agricultural productivity through agricultural research, dam construction and green revolution-type innovation. But, for the non-staple crops we have studied, it seems to have missed the boat entirely on agricultural marketing. This is probably because the emphasis so far has been on quantity: India needed to feed its growing population, and to do this it had to increase staple production. It is likely that, in the eyes of policy-makers, the role of the marketing chain has historically been viewed as no more than a transmission mechanism to take the pulses and grain to the consumer, with little or no value added and at the lowest cost possible.

With the growing importance of non-staple crops, this emphasis on quantity alone is no longer sufficient. For these crops, raising productivity takes the form not only of increased quantity but also of improved quality. What ultimately matters is the revenue growers receive. If certain consumers abroad and in India are willing to pay more for high-quality agricultural produce, then raising rural income requires that farmers be incited to produce those quality fruit and vegetables and that the value chain be in a position to guarantee quality to potential consumers.

This study has shown that this cannot be accomplished with the current market organization, because many quality attributes are not immediately observable, or are only observable at a cost. Furthermore, even if a given attribute is conferred to a crop by farmers – e.g. safe and healthy food – this attribute must be preserved through the value chain for it to be rewarded by customers.

Policy Recommendations

Several institutional solutions can be envisaged for improving the non-staple value chain. We have discussed one of them – contract farming. As far as we can judge from the results of our study, contract farming does not, for the moment, contribute to enhancing product quality. But it could potentially be used by exporters and by processors aiming at the higher end of the market, provided the law is changed to allow direct purchases from farmers.

In other parts of the world where retail trade has been liberalized, supermarkets (often run by multinationals such as Carrefour or Tesco) have rapidly taken a major share of grocery retail trade. So doing, they have revolutionized the value chain for fruit and vegetables (Reardon et al., 2001). In India, current laws and regulations hinder market development in this direction. Indeed, many states require most crops to be traded through regulated wholesale markets. As we have seen, however, this is not true in all states. In Tamil Nadu, for instance, regulated markets are few while in Orissa they are largely ignored by traders. In more advanced states such as Maharashtra, further development of the fruit and vegetable value chain most probably requires a change in the law.

We are aware of the fact that the liberalization of retail trade is on the political agenda in India. We realize that many issues are involved and that the decision whether to liberalize or not has many more ramifications than its effect on fruit and vegetable markets. It is neither our role nor our intention to tell the Indian government how to resolve this issue, but we can inform the policy debate.

Based on evidence from other Asian countries, there is no doubt in our minds that the non-staple crop value chain would be revolutionized by a liberalization of retail trade, coupled with a revision of the State Agricultural Produce Market Act to allow supermarkets and wholesalers to buy directly from farmers. This would lead to more vertical integration of the fruit and vegetable value chain, thereby enabling information about quality and food safety to travel through the chain.

Even without a change in the law, we expect supermarkets to take a more active role in fruit and vegetable marketing, simply because the rapid expansion of the Indian middle class makes the transformation of consumption habits inexorable. But without liberalization the role of supermarkets will remain stunted and it will fail to reach its full potential, which is to raise the price of non-staple crops paid to the majority of farmers.

As the evidence from Tamil Nadu and Orissa suggests, deregulation will not answer all problems, however. Agricultural markets have deficient infrastructure, irrespective of whether they are publicly regulated or not. We are particularly concerned about the poor sanitation that characterizes most non-staple markets. Although the Indian poor may not have the money to pay for more sanitary food, we suspect that poor sanitation in fruit and vegetables is responsible for non-negligible morbidity and mortality in the Indian population, particularly because of poor drainage, absence of toilets and contact between food and rats or other pests.

We also worry about poor sanitation in the food processing industry and the possible accumulation of unsanitary elements in processed food (e.g. *Escherichia coli* and other bacteria, pesticide residues, extraneous materials, etc.). The findings reported here suggest that, because of credibility issues, the market cannot deliver sanitary food in a decentralized manner. There is therefore room for coordinated action to improve the infrastructure and pest control practices of existing markets.

Based on these observations, a two-pronged approach may be best suited to the enablement of Indian farmers to capture gains from quality upgrading while, at the same time, ensuring that small farmers and poor consumers are not sacrificed. Ultimately, the objective is to raise farmers' incomes by making it possible for them to tap into new, more remunerative markets. This can only be accomplished by raising quality and food safety and this, in turn, requires a different organization of the value chain.

Subject to the caveats we raised earlier, we therefore propose to liberalize retail and agro-processing while at the same time reinforcing existing wholesale market infrastructure – particular sewers, drainage and pest control. The rationale behind this approach is that, as has taken place in South-east Asia and Latin America, liberalization will foster entry by large, experienced processors and supermarket chains. These new entrants will, in all likelihood, set up dedicated sourcing arrangements with modern wholesalers, large farmers and farmer cooperatives.

The liberalization of retail trade can take agricultural marketing a long way forward, but it tends to favour larger farmers. The experience from these other countries indeed suggests that large processors and supermarkets are uninterested in sourcing produce directly from a myriad of very small producers who find it difficult to follow strict quality norms. This raises equity concerns. Indeed, while many farmers will be able to sell their produce at a premium to new processors and supermarkets – either directly or through cooperatives – some will be too small to produce the quantities large firms need.

It is, of course, possible to compensate

the natural propensity of supermarket chains to deal with large farmers by helping small farmers meet their stringent quality requirements and delivery schedules. A recently completed case study, for instance, shows how this was accomplished in Madagascar, where European supermarkets now procure French beans from small farmers in the highlands. Success stories like this one should not, however, obscure the fact that support systems of this kind cannot be put in place for all small farmers in the country. Fortunately, this probably does not matter too much.

India's demand for fruit and vegetables will continue to rise. While the upper end of the market will progressively put more emphasis on quality and food safety, we expect that, as more and more people move above the poverty line, they will demand more fruit and vegetables, focusing initially on quantity rather than quality. This segment of the market, which is growing, will continue to be served by the existing market chain. Poor and middle-income consumers will continue to be served by the current value chain, where quality is not much rewarded and where direct observation of product attributes is central.

We also expect many small-scale processors to remain in existence to serve poorer consumers who are less willing to pay for quality and food safety. We therefore do not expect liberalization to result in the collapse and abandonment of the current marketing institutions. Quite the contrary: it will probably become stronger. The study has shown that small farmers currently have equal access to wholesale markets. We do not see a reason for this to change.

In practice, our two-pronged approach requires that the market for non-staple food be 'deregulated' in the following sense. We see no reason for states and local government to divest from wholesale markets. In fact, if anything they should invest more. Even in Tamil Nadu, where agricultural markets are – for the most – unregulated, more markets are the property of local government.

There is thus an important role for local government to play. What needs to change is the prohibition that precludes traders and processors from buying directly from farmers and from setting up long-term contracts with growers. Unless these restrictions are lifted, the sector will not reach its full potential and will remain stuck with a set of institutions that may have been justified at a certain stage of Indian development but that are no longer adapted to current needs and opportunities.

With respect to the upgrading of existing wholesale markets, it is our opinion that much can be accomplished by using the fees currently raised by market authorities. Based on the information we gathered, it is our impression that these revenues are implicitly used by local authorities as a form of tax revenue. They are not sufficiently used to improve market infrastructure, especially simple improvements such as better drainage, public latrines and pest control.

With an audit from central government, many wholesale markets may turn out to have sufficient funding to pay for their own improvement. More expensive improvements such as cold storage may not be self-funding, but they are not needed everywhere. Actual market management could be sub-contracted to a private provider who can then be held accountable for insufficient maintenance and sanitation.

The self-funding approach will not work in all states, however. In Orissa, for instance, regulated markets exist on paper but are not used in practice. In Tamil Nadu many markets are run by the local municipality but generate few revenues. In these cases, upgrading wholesale markets will require an infusion of funds from elsewhere in government.

We would also like to suggest ways of improving the current auction system. The work of Banerji and Meenaski (2004) indeed suggests that, even in some of the most sophisticated auctions in the country – rice auctions in Delhi, for instance – there is evidence of manipulation. Unfortunately, it has proved difficult to elicit information on the way auctions are conducted in practice. We even suspect that, in a number of cases, market authorities have reported auctions taking place when, from other sources, we found little evidence that auctions were occurring for the five studied crops. This is particularly true in Orissa, where auctions of non-staple crops are close to non-existent.

One could hope to increase market efficiency by decoupling the movement of physical quantities from trade itself, which could in principle take place in another location (e.g. in a commodity exchange) in a more transparent manner. For this to be feasible, however, one must unambiguously describe the physical attributes of each lot offered for sale. As we have seen, many auctions do not report detailed information about consignments; buyers are supposed to observe the produce in person.

The current role of commission agents also needs to be revisited. As detailed, survey results show that this separation of roles, which is present, for instance, among brokers in the cereal market in Ethiopia (Gabre-Madhin, 1997, unpublished PhD thesis), is not practiced in India. The phrase 'commission agent' seems to be used only as a title conferred by market authorities. Our suspicion is that commission fees are a way for large wholesalers to restrict competition by guaranteeing themselves a minimum margin. But without detailed price data – that market authorities do not collect – it is difficult to prove this statistically.

Notes

1. Maize is a feed crop. Turmeric is a spice also used as a dye. Tomato, potato and mango differ in terms of perishability and ease of transportation.
2. This chapter is a brief summary of the results of a larger report (Fafchamps et al., 2006) and the reader is referred to this report for more details.
3. Although variation was observed across states. For example, in Maharashtra 96% sell at the wholesale market, whilst in Orissa 59% sell at the retail market. See Fafchamps et al. (2006) for more details.

References

Acharya, S.S. (2001) *Agricultural Marketing in India*, Part of the Millennium Study of Indian Farmers (mimeo).
Banerji, A. and Meenakski, J.V. (2004) Buyer collusion and efficiency of government intervention in wheat Markets in northern India: an asymmetrical structural auction analysis. *American Journal of Agricultural Economics* 86, 236–253.
Deshingkar, P., Kulharni, U., Rao, L. and Rao, S. (2003) Changing food systems in India: resource Sharing and marketing arrangements for vegetable production in Andra Pradesh. *Development Policy Review* 21, 627–639.
Fafchamps, M. (2004) *Market Institutions in Sub-Saharan Africa*. MIT Press, Cambridge, Massachusetts.
Fafchamps, M., Vargas-Hill, R. and Minten, B. (2006) *The Marketing of Non-Staple Crops in India*. Report submitted to the World Bank, Washington, DC.
Greif, A. (1993) Contract enforceability and economic institutions in early trade: the Maghribi Traders' Coalition. *American Economic Review* 83 (3), 525–548.
Ramaswami, B. and Balakrishnan, P. (2002) Food prices and the efficiency of public intervention: the case of public distribution system in India. *Food Policy* 27, 419–436.
Reardon, T., Codron, J.-M., Busch, L., Bingen, J. and Harris, C. (2001) Global change in agrifood grades and standards: agribusiness strategic responses in developing countries. *International Food and Agribusiness Management Review* 2, 421–435.
Umali-Deininger, D.L. and Deininger, K. (2001) Towards greater food security for India's poor: balancing government intervention and private competition *Agricultural Economics* 25, 321–335.

Latin America

11 Supermarkets and Small Horticultural Product Farmers in Central America

J. Berdegué, T. Reardon, F. Balsevich, L. Flores and R. Hernández

Introduction

Driven by rising incomes and urbanization, as well as by foreign investment and procurement technology change, the share of supermarkets in food retail in Latin America rose from a mere 10–20% in 1990 to 50–60% by the early 2000s, displacing small shops and open-air markets (Reardon and Berdegué, 2002). That trend started somewhat later in Central America and has made slower progress (reaching 30–40% of food retail by the early 2000s), but is also developing quickly. One of the poorest countries in the region, Nicaragua, has shared that trend, with the its share reaching 20% by 2005 (Berdegué et al., 2005).

Such change downstream in the agri-food system can be hypothesized to be changing market conditions facing farmers. Generally, compared to traditional retailers, supermarkets have different and more demanding product and transaction requirements. However, despite the increasing importance of the rise of supermarkets, there has been little empirical research on supermarket procurement systems and, in particular, supply chains from farmers and the interface between farmers and supermarkets – including the determinants of channel choice of farmers (between supermarket and traditional market channels) and the effects of those choices (on net incomes and technologies).

This chapter synthesizes new research on these topics from fieldwork carried out by the authors, spanning 2002–2005. The second part synthesizes findings concerning the retail sector in the horticultural product market, both as a marketer and as a procurer of produce from wholesalers and farmers. This work took place in all the Central American countries apart from Panama and Belize. It is based on Berdegué et al. (2005).

The concluding section synthesizes findings from studies that built on the first study, and investigates the issue of the determinants and effects of grower participation. It is based on Balsevich et al. (2006) on tomato farmers and supermarkets in Nicaragua, Hernández et al. (2006) on tomatoes in Guatemala and Flores and Reardon (2006) on lettuce producers and supermarkets in Guatemala. These countries were chosen for variation in degree of supermarket-sector development, and the products were chosen to contrast a bulk basic commodity (Roma tomatoes) with a niche product (lettuce).

Retail Sector Changes in Central America

The findings in this section are a synthesis from Berdegué et al. (2005) of case studies from Costa Rica, Guatemala, El Salvador, Honduras, and Nicaragua – the range being in decreasing order of household income, share of supermarkets in overall food retail and from strongest to weakest domestic public health standards. The research is based on fieldwork by a team of researchers over the periods November 2002 to May 2003 and March and July 2004, including rapid reconnaissance surveys of supermarket chains, wholesalers and producers. The questions focused on procurement practices and application of standards, including private enforcement of public standards and application of private standards.

Diffusion of supermarkets in Central America and penetration of produce markets

Supermarkets have risen very quickly from a negligible niche to a major force in Central American food markets in only a decade. In 2002, supermarkets had a 36% share in the overall food retail in the region, with a high of 50% in Costa Rica and a low of 19% in Nicaragua. There are 600 supermarkets today in the five countries on which we focus here, up from at most a hundred or so in the early 1990s.

Even more relevant to our discussion is the fact that supermarket purchases and sales of local horticultural products are now approaching the importance of the non-traditional exports from the region. FAOSTAT data for 2001 for fresh produce exports (excluding bananas) from these five countries give a figure of around US$600 million,[1] while a rough estimate of local supermarket sales of fresh produce is US$180 million.

After removing export-powerhouse Costa Rica (349 of 599) from the set, the comparison shows that exports are double supermarket sales (horticultural products exports are US$260 million and supermarkets sales are US$116 million). The gap is closing quickly because supermarket sales are growing much faster (36% between 1997 and 2002) than exports (15% between 1997 and 2001).

Changes in procurement systems

Supermarket procurement officers have a dual objective of minimizing cost (both product costs and diverse transaction costs) and maximizing quality and product differentiation (SKUs, or stock-keeping units). To meet that dual objective, supermarket chains in Central America have been shifting over the past few years away from the old procurement model – based on sourcing horticulture products from the traditional wholesalers and the wholesale markets – toward the use of four key pillars of a new kind of procurement system: (i) specialized procurement agents we call 'specialized wholesalers' instead of traditional wholesalers; (ii) centralized procurement through Distribution Centres (DCs); (iii) assured and consistent supply through 'preferred suppliers'; and (iv) high-quality and increasingly safe product through private standards imposed on suppliers.

The first three pillars (organizational change in procurement) together make possible the fourth (institutional change in procurement – that is, the rise of private standards first for quality and increasingly for safety of produce). Below, we detail each of these four pillars.

First, there has been a substantial shift by supermarkets in the study countries away from reliance on traditional wholesale markets for procurement of produce. The shift is away from traditional wholesalers toward the use of specialized wholesalers who classify product collected from suppliers, sometimes have their own production and often have semi-contractual relations with 'lead suppliers', discussed further below.

This shift has occurred partly because the traditional wholesalers lack quality standards and, in particular, lack consistency in standards. The traditional wholesalers who used to supply most supermarkets did serve these demanding clients with the best horticultural products they could find on a given date; such 'best' was too often of 'below acceptable' quality, according to the procurement officers of the leading supermarket chains that we interviewed.

Since traditional wholesalers normally do not get involved in any sort of production support programmes, do not enter into long-term commercial relationships with selected producers (out-grower schemes) and, in general, buy and sell on a day-to-day basis (spot market), they often lack the capacity to define, monitor or enforce a quality or safety standard which goes beyond the norm for the wholesale market (e.g. no rotten horticultural products, basic grading of horticultural products according to size and appearance, weights and measures).

Since the vast majority of their sales are with clients who, in turn, have no particular quality demands, traditional wholesalers also lack the incentive to develop, monitor and enforce standards from which they will gain little benefit, if at all. An objective of supermarkets' horticultural products procurement officers is to not find themselves as the weak party in the negotiation process. This is more difficult to achieve with wholesalers than with individual producers, as wholesaling is usually quite concentrated per product rubric.

Second, as an alternative to traditional wholesale markets, supermarket chains in Central America are setting up their own Distribution Centres (DCs) to maintain centralized procurement of horticultural products. Of course, this is implemented only when the chain has passed a certain size in terms of number of stores or throughput to justify this shift. La Fragua in Guatemala has risen from 32% centralized (2001) to 78% (2003) and then to 98% by the end of 2004. CSU is almost 100% centralized in Costa Rica.

The main reasons for this procurement centralization are as follows:

1. There are major cost savings from reduced coordination costs and from spending less time ordering and tracking.
2. There are inventory management cost savings, as chains can implement best-practice logistics; centralization creates economies of scale and so justifies investments too expensive for small chains with decentralized distribution.
3. There are supervision cost savings as it is cheaper and more effective for the chain to monitor deliveries at only one point rather than per store.[2]
4. There are savings in transport and other transaction costs for suppliers who formerly had to make the rounds of widely dispersed stores on deliveries. Centralization also allows suppliers to adjust rapidly to the results of the quality control.
5. Centralization helps chains by upgrading their supplier base, as being able to deal in larger volumes without the bother of delivering to many stores makes it more attractive (in sales, less transaction costs) for bigger suppliers to sell to the chain.
6. Centralization can bring substantial product cost savings: buying in one place in bulk can mean economies of scale and better bargaining with suppliers. These savings can be substantial.

Third, in Central America the main supermarket chains and/or their dedicated, specialized wholesalers (which we have termed 'new-generation wholesalers' as being analogous to 'new-generation cooperatives' in many ways) are switching to lists of preferred suppliers. In the relationships with these suppliers they use new commercial practices vis-à-vis suppliers that reward consistently high performance in delivery.

The reasons for shifting to preferred suppliers are as follows.

1. Supermarket chains need to reduce the risk of shortages on a given item and want to minimize the costs of putting in place a procurement system that reduces that risk. Having a list of preferred suppliers falls short of issuing formal contracts, but is not so 'loose' as to merely engage in spot markets and find whatever is on offer and whoever is selling on a given day. These can, in fact, be considered 'contracts' in the broad sense that includes informal and implicit relationships in which there is some cost (tangible or intangible) to not performing.

2. Constituting the list of preferred suppliers requires an initial act of selection, and that selection screens farmers who cannot meet supermarket requirements (cost, volume, consistency, safety, quality, ease of transaction), and thus reduces search costs.

3. The information exchange linked to a preferred supplier relationship means that the suppliers can 'internalize' the requirements and so supervision costs and the counterpart – costs of product rejection – can be minimized.

4. In what we call in the next section 'active relationships' with preferred suppliers, supermarket chains can resolve problems of generalized or idiosyncratic market failure in factor markets for their suppliers; for example, it can help with credit and agronomic advice. The chain can also resolve the problem of the missing market for management services by helping the supplier establish crop calendars and undertake commercial planning, even planning for income diversification.

Fourth, via the above 'procurement system' or combination of the first three pillars, leading Central American supermarket chains have very recently started to apply tougher and effectively enforced quality standards.

These quality standards, plus the transaction attribute requirements (timing, consistency, volume) imply – at least in theory – a set of specific practices and investments by farmers. That in turn suggests that, according to their assets and other contextual variables, farmers will differ in their capacity and incentive to participate in the supermarket channel (*versus* alternative traditional channels) and will condition the impacts of such participation on farmers. We explore that below, but first note some differential application of the above trends as between broad, mass-market commodities (in our case here, Roma tomatoes present in most Guatemalan and Nicaraguan lunches and/or dinners) and lettuce (a niche product reserved for some meals and some dishes and with a tendency to be consumed regularly only by the middle class).

Berdegué *et al.* (2005) give an illustration of differences in procurement practices, and the reasons for them, over the full spectrum of produce, by La Fragua, the main retailer in Guatemala (and El Salvador). We focus on the difference between (Roma) tomatoes and lettuce as most germane to our comparison of commodities *versus* niche products in this chapter.

La Fragua stores sourced only 20% 'centrally', via its DC, in 1999, but by 2004 that figure was 98%. The category 'large-volume products' constitute 30% of their produce and includes mainly Roma tomatoes, potatoes, bell peppers, melons and watermelons. In 1999, only 40% were procured via the DC, while by 2004 that figure was 100%. The chain sources these commodities from six large wholesalers who, in turn, source them from thousands of tiny farms scattered over Guatemala.

These wholesalers are, in many ways, fully 'new-generation wholesalers', as they select the commercial-grade product for La Fragua. The latter does not, however, have any direct sourcing from producers as it does from banana producers or lettuce producers, because tomatoes are not produced in greenhouses and thus can be sourced from a given zone all year, are quite cheap per unit and yet come from dispersed production, small farmers and with high transaction and sorting costs, and La Fragua wants large volumes in large lots delivered fresh daily. This spells the need for specialized wholesalers to be intermediaries.

Another category, 'medium-volume bulk products' – consisting of lettuce, carrots, limes, etc., only 15% of produce sales – also moved from being nearly all locally delivered, store by store, in 1999 (when only 20% of lettuce passed through the DC) to 100% centralization by 2004. In 1999, 70% of the total volume of these products was sourced via large and small intermediaries in the traditional wholesale market – while only 30% today are sourced thus; now 70% come from preferred suppliers, some of whom are fully new-generation wholesalers and the others are small, own-production companies (basically a handful of medium commercial farmers) and cooperatives and companies with contract schemes.

Both of these categories, one starting on the road to modernization and the other well along the pathway of modernization of the procurement structure, are sharply in contrast to the category, for example, of fresh herbs, which are still sourced locally or through the traditional wholesale market. These distinctions are important in terms of expected impacts on farmers, in the sense that one expects the rewards to be higher for quality, the signals more direct and clear and the involvement of intermediaries in the sourcing process more developed in the case of products like lettuce, where the supermarket and direct agents are closely involved. In contrast, products such as Roma tomatoes, where the supermarket has agents but agents that are only roughly and incipiently differentiated from the traditional spot market wholesaler, have added selection, boxing and client-specific services.

Impacts on Farmers

Data and methods

The surveys took place in 2004, roughly from June to September, in Guatemala and Nicaragua and, in all, involved about 600 farmers. Details of sampling are found in the source papers. The farmers were divided between those selling both to the supermarket and the traditional channel and those selling only to the traditional channel. The questionnaire asked detailed questions about household and farm characteristics, marketing, production and participation in associations. Supply chain contextual analysis was performed in each country, as were several case studies of firms and associations.

Key findings by country and product context

The relations of the Nicaraguan and Guatemalan tomato-growers with the supermarket chains differ.

Nicaragua

The CSU chain in Nicaragua is a Costa Rican subsidiary and uses the same procurement method the mother company uses in Costa Rica, as they procure tomatoes via their own (own in the sense that it is literally part of the same holding company) procurement company, Hortifruti. They have direct relations with all the tomato suppliers. Moreover, as we will show, there is a certain bimodality in the preferred supplier set, with a number of very small farmers working in groups who participate in the assistance (credit, technical assistance) of NGOs dedicated to helping 'business linkages', as such projects are called in current parlance.

The other farmers are not assisted by NGOs and, as we show, are still officially small farmers but at the upper end of that stratum, and more capitalized. So, in the Nicaraguan case there is an interesting four-way stratification by both market channel and NGO-assisted *versus* unassisted. Moreover, the directness of the relation with the chain makes for a more proximate and direct signalling of the latter requirement.

Guatemala

In contrast, the La Fragua chain, although in the same regional joint venture (previously with global chain Ahold, now with Wal-mart), has a different procurement method, working through specialized wholesalers in an approach pitched between fully spot market and fully internalized. While tomato growers may be in associations, they are not grouped for group marketing of tomatoes and are not assisted by NGOs, at least to the degree of the latter being involved in promoting 'business linkages' with supermarkets. Moreover, while the chain signals requirements to the few large specialized wholesalers it uses, the latter use those signals to sort product to suit the chains, and signal only indirectly the requirements to the farmers.

The Guatemalan lettuce growers are again in a different configuration relative to the supermarket channel (while the traditional market-channel growers of lettuce are much like, in marketing terms, their counterparts in tomatoes). Supermarkets have essentially ceased sourcing lettuce in the spot market, finding the quality inconsistent and coordination costs high, and having then to source directly from: (i) own-production medium farmers or small companies; (ii) contract-farming small companies (who contract small farmers); (iii) farmers' associations (who started supplying the spot market, then entered regional trade and finally became suppliers to supermarkets in Guatemala and regionally); or (iv) specialized tomato wholesalers.

Hence, there is a unique plethora of sourcing channels, spurred by the high value and quality requirement of lettuce, and that lettuce became part of the 'one-stop shopping' package that various groups began offering, only a few years ago, to supermarket chains to solve their sourcing transaction cost and uncertainty problems.

The following findings concerning differences in characteristics of farmers selling to the supermarket *versus* traditional channels are summarized in Table 11.1 and discussed below.

Asset correlates

In all three of the above cases, while still in the small-farmer category (in fact, if one excludes scrubby pastureland, the arable farmland is 1–2 ha per farm for lettuce and 2–4 ha per farm for tomato farms), the supermarket-channel growers – relative to the traditional channel growers – have larger farm sizes, roughly twice the size in the case of lettuce farms in Guatemala, about half as large again as tomato farms in Guatemala. In Nicaragua, a mixed case, the leading chain actually has smaller farmers (both assisted and non-assisted) than do either the traditional channel or the secondary chain channel.

In every case, the supermarket channel growers tend to be considerably more specialized in the particular product. The size and specialization points, taken together, mean that the supermarket channel prefers sufficient volume per producer from farmers more dedicated to the product, and hence presumably less risk for the buyer in terms of finding the needed volumes and quality.

In all three of these cases, the supermarket-channel growers are more 'capitalized' than the traditional-channel growers. Irrigation and vehicle ownership are of great importance. Supermarket-channel growers have twice the share of irrigated land in the case of lettuce, threefold in the case of tomatoes in Guatemala and one-quarter more in the case of tomatoes in Nicaragua. Supermarket-channel growers have a greater probability of having a vehicle, or are closer to road access, or both. Both these assets reduce transaction costs for the buyers, and increase quality and freshness.

While we did not go into detail with the farmers in terms of how they spent their credit, it is very clear that, in general, the supermarket channel farmers received more credit; again, for the smallest farmers associated with NGOs, and this is influenced by the NGOs; for the other 'independent' farmers working with supermarkets, this is probably associated with their being larger, more commercialized and more specialized, normal factors influencing local informal creditors, the main source of credit.

Moreover, receipt of technical assistance

Table 11.1. Characteristics of growers marketing to supermarkets *versus* traditional channels.

Variable	Lettuce growers, Guatemala		Tomato growers, Guatemala		Tomato growers, Nicaragua	
	Supermarket channel	Traditional channel	Supermarket channel	Traditional channel	Supermarket channel	Traditional channel
Total land per farm (ha, average)	2.5	1.2	9.3	7.8	7.7	9.8
Cropping land per farm (ha, average)	1.7	0.9	4.6	2.5	3.5	3.5
Lettuce/tomato area per farm (ha, average)	0.86	0.21	4.2	1.7	1.6	1.4
Proportion of farms having irrigation (%)	67	46	80	35	97	94
Proportion of lettuce/tomato land irrigated (%)	63	37	49	16	72	84
Yield (1000 kg /ha)	37.3	33.7	44.0	37.0	32.4	23.8
Proportion of farms receiving credit (%)	78	49	83	71	83	68
Proportion of farms receiving technical assistance (%)	48	42	81	62	71	49
Gross income/ha (US$ thousand)	8.9	6.8	12.5	10.1	7.7	5.2
Total cost/ha (excluding family labour, US$ thousand)	5.4	4.8	9.1	6.7	3.1	2.4
Hired labour (subset of total cost, US$ thousand)	1.0	1.4	2.2	2.1	0.522	0.541
Chemicals and fertilizers (subset of total cost, US$ thousand)	3.3	2.2	4.9	3.5	1.43	1.04
Net income/ha (excluding own labour, US$ thousand)	3.6	2.0	3.4	3.4	4.6	2.8
Cost of own labour/ha (imputed at wage rate, US$ thousand)	0.4	0.5	0.6	0.6	0.237	0.164
Net income/ha (including own labour, US$ thousand)	3.4	1.7	2.8	2.8	4.3	2.6

is broadly greater for the supermarket-channel producers, but not uniformly so: for example, in Nicaragua tomatoes, while the suppliers to the lead chain (CSU) tend to receive much more technical assistance (whether they are assisted by NGOs or not), the farmers selling to the second chain are in the same situation (of less technical assistance) as the traditional growers, reinforcing the image that those selling to the second chain are in more of the traditional situation of selling to brokers rather than in tight, preferred-supplier, 'two-way' relationships.

In contrast, several assets that are important in more 'technified' agricultural systems are not significant or have mixed results in the case of this essentially smallholder, domestic market-oriented horticulture: tractor or animal traction equipment access (with the exception of the somewhat larger small farms in Nicaragua), education and greenhouses do not play a clear differentiating role.

Interestingly, while much is made of the need for small farmers to be in associations, this was a significant factor in only two cases: (i) the lettuce producers in

Guatemalan (who use the association to market and enforce standards among themselves for a quality-demanding, high-value product); and (ii) the smallest farmers, who sell tomatoes to the supermarkets in Nicaragua and who belong to marketing cooperatives that were organized – or at least helped – by the NGOs.

But, in all the other cases, the associability rate is low or no different from that of the traditional channels. This suggests that the collection arrangements used by the wholesalers are at least minimally sufficient to permit small farmers, especially if they have trucks and are relatively specialized, to deliver their produce or have it collected.

Technology correlates

The technology story is strikingly consistent across these cases, and is predictable due to the quality and transaction attributes required by the supermarket channel relative to the traditional channel.

In general, supermarket growers use much more non-labour-variable inputs (chemicals, fertilizers) than do the traditional growers: for lettuce in Guatemala, 50% more; for tomatoes in Guatemala, 40% more; and for tomatoes in Nicaragua, 35% more. This is correlated with the higher credit and technical assistance (some of the latter is from the input suppliers).

An aside, but one of interest, is to think of these results in light of the debate on chemical use in horticulture. This is a very important issue for Central America as it has a very chemical-intensive horticulture, and Costa Rica is known to have one of the highest rates of stomach cancer in the world, believed to be attributed to the use of lots of pesticides. Thrupp (1995) noted that this heavy chemical use was driven by the need for produce quality for export.

It is ironic that, some years later, international public and private standards are tending to push down the use of chemicals on produce for export to demanding markets such as Europe (Reardon *et al.*, 2001), while the demanding quality (but not yet safety standards, which are only in their incipience for a few products for supermarkets; see Berdegué *et al.*, 2005) of supermarkets – plus perhaps overuse by farmers – is resurrecting the situation of a new market driving heavy chemical use in Central America, but this time it is the modern, urban market locally rather than the export market.

Moreover, the supermarket channel producers, as we noted above, use more physical capital (in particular, irrigation, but also other items) and more non-labour-variable inputs, but in general somewhat less labour on average, compared to the traditional-channel producers; in the case of lettuce, it is considerably less; for Guatemalan tomatoes, similar; and for Nicaraguan tomatoes, slightly more. This substitution of capital for labour among the more demanding channel producers thus makes sense and emerges as a clear image.

The exception, interestingly, is the smallest farmers (NGO-assisted) in Nicaragua, who use 15% more, presumably substituting labour for their very limited land. Abstracting from the consideration that the latter group is getting so much (implicitly subsidized) help from NGOs, it is good news that smaller farmers have some 'wiggle room' in the technology needed to meet the requirements of the new market channel, using 'sweat equity' to make up for their tiny parcels.

Income correlates

In Nicaragua, supermarkets pay about 10% more per kg, but remember that input costs are 35% more and labour costs are similar; however, yields are roughly 40% higher (so the capital and non-labour-variable inputs, plus presumably some unobservables in terms of management) compensate for higher costs, thus arriving at net income/ha 1.75 times higher. Similar patterns give rise to that differential being near twofold for

Guatemalan lettuce. However, there is no difference between net income/ha for Guatemalan tomato producers in the two channels. Producers informed us that they were compensated by the transactional ease and lower risk of the supermarket channel.

The upshot is that, on average, the quality-niche product, lettuce, shows a much clearer advantage in the supermarket *versus* the traditional channel. This advantage is less in the early supermarketization situation of Nicaragua, and disappears in the more advanced supermarketization stage situation (Guatemala), combined with a procurement system that is still largely intermediated.

Conclusions and Implications

Supermarkets are spreading in Central America, but with a lag compared to processed foods, penetrating progressively the fruit and vegetable markets. The farmers who sell to the supermarkets, relative to traditional-channel farmers, tend to earn higher profits, with the effect much sharper for the niche-quality-differentiated products than for the mass market commodities. This mirrors a similar trend in the USA.

The lead chains are following trends observed elsewhere of modernizing their procurement systems in terms of organization and standards. These together imply challenges to farmers. The farmers who can meet those challenges are of two types.

1. The 'unassisted' type, the farmer that one would probably observe ubiquitously should donors, governments and NGOs not intervene with implicit subsidies and projects, is the upper-tier small farmer. The latter has more capital in the form of irrigation, vehicles and other equipment. This farmer tends to have a bit more land than the traditional farmer but still be in the 'small' category, tends to use considerable chemical input but not as much labour as the traditional farmer. This type tends to receive more credit and technical assistance, but not to be significantly more organized than others.

2. In contrast, there is the 'assisted' type of farmer, who appears more like a traditional farmer – a smaller small farmer, substituting labour for land, but using somewhat more chemicals than traditional. It is good to see the smallest farmers having access to these opportunities.

Nevertheless, the dilemma facing policy-makers, donors and researchers – as well as farmers – is that, in Nicaragua, we calculated that this latter type of farmer receives (in terms of NGO project budget per farmer) about eight times more than the Ministry of Agriculture in Nicaragua spends per farmer. In other words, to include the smallest farmers, hyper-subsidization is used. That is very probably not an approach that can be directly scaled up to serve the majority of farmers as market modernization progresses in the retail and wholesale sectors.

In the decade ahead, the challenge will be to help farmers upgrade to meet the needs of the supermarket channels now taking over the market, where the farmers have that potential, and to work to create alternative markets or strengthen traditional wholesale markets to provide alternatives for the smallest producers who are too-undercapitalized to make the modern market but want to diversify their crops and markets and not fade away as impoverished grain farmers.

Acknowledgements

This chapter is an outcome of and the authors are thankful to a set of donors and projects supporting the collaborative work, citing in no particular order: (i) 'Assistance for Trade Capacity Building in Relation to the Application of Sanitary and Phytosanitary Measures' (RAISE-SPS), funded by USAID, primed by DAI and implemented for this project by Michigan State University, USA; (ii) 'Regoverning Markets, Phase 1', a project coordinated by the

International Institute for Environment and Development (IIED), the Royal Tropical Institute (KIT) and Rimisp-Centro Latinoamericano para el Desarrollo Rural, and funded by the Department for International Development (DFID) of the UK; (iii) 'Partnerships for Food Industry Development – Fruits and Vegetables' (PFID-FFV), funded by USAID and implemented by Michigan State University, USA; (iv) The Agribusiness Development Project of the Centro Internacional de Agricultura Tropical (CIAT); and (v) The International Livestock Institute (ILRI), funded by the Common Fund for Commodities.

Notes

1. Note that this figure includes intra-regional exports, and many of the latter go to supermarkets, and thus from the point of view of comparison of exports with supermarket sales, this export figure is overstated.
2. Interviewees familiar with the traditional procurement systems of supermarkets noted that per-store deliveries subjected suppliers to arbitrary and inconsistent monitoring, and even the need for payments to product receivers. These damage both the supermarket and supplier, reduce product quality and ability to enforce standards and raise costs.

References

Balsevich, F., Berdegué, J. and Reardon, T. (2006) *Supermarkets, New-generation Wholesalers, Tomato Farmers, and NGOs in Nicaragua.* Agricultural Economics Staff Paper 2006-03. Michigan State University, East Lansing, Michigan.

Berdegué, J.A., Balsevich, F., Flores, L. and Reardon, T. (2005) Central American supermarkets' private standards of quality and safety in procurement of fresh fruits and vegetables. *Food Policy* 30 (3), 254–269.

Flores, L. and Reardon, T. (2006) *Supermarkets, New-generation wholesalers, Farmers' Organizations, Contract Farming, and Lettuce in Guatemala: Participation by and Effects on Small Farmers.* Agricultural Economics Staff Paper 2006-07. Michigan State University, East Lansing, Michigan.

Hernández, R., Reardon, T. and Berdegué, J.A. (2006) *Tomato Farmer Participation in Supermarket Market Channels in Guatemala: Determinants and Technology and Income Effects.* Agricultural Economics Staff Paper 2006-04. Michigan State University, East Lansing, Michigan.

Reardon, T. and Berdegué, J.A. (2002) The rapid rise of supermarkets in Latin America: challenges and opportunities for development. *Development Policy Review* 20 (4), 317–334.

Reardon, T., Codron, J.M., Busch, L., Bingen, J. and Harris, C. (2001) Global change in agrifood grades and standards: agribusiness strategic responses in developing countries. *International Food and Agribusiness Management Review* 2 (3), 195–205.

Thrupp, L.A. (1995) *Bittersweet Harvest for Global Supermarkets: Challenges in Latin America's Agricultural Export Boom.* World Resources Institute, Washington, DC.

Africa

12 Global Supply Chains, Poverty and the Environment: Evidence from Madagascar

B. Minten, L. Randrianarison and J.F.M. Swinnen

Introduction

Globalization, trade liberalization and the lowering of barriers to trade has generally led to an increased inflow of foreign investments, the establishment of multinationals in developing countries and to their integration in global supply chains. There has been a lively debate on how these developments affect poverty and the environment in developing countries. Critics argue that these types of investment cause more harm than good, because they: (i) contribute to poverty by, among other means, exploiting the workers in developing countries; and (ii) might contribute to permanent environmental damage.

On poverty, the critics argue that countries eager to attract multinationals offer tax concessions and let poor countries compete between themselves such that the countries that allow those firms in end up losing out financially. However, other studies show that there are significant beneficial effects, i.e. the learning of productivity-enhancing techniques from foreign firms with better technology and management practices (Bhagwati, 2004; Dries and Swinnen, 2004).

On the environment, it is argued that globalization contributes to degradation through two factors. First, the increase in trade might lead to higher incomes that would alter demand for environmental goods and services. Researchers thus looked at the linkages between income and environmental indicators and have found the evidence to be mixed (Chichilnisky, 1994; Cropper and Griffith, 1994; Grossman and Krueger, 1995; Cavendish, 2000; Foster and Rosenzweig, 2003). Second, globalization might also lead to increasing investments in countries with lower environmental standards and the global natural resource base might end up irreversibly depleted or damaged (Reed, 2001). While these arguments are potentially valid, they ultimately have to be tested and verified by empirical evidence.

A particularly interesting area for the study of the effects of these developments is in the agricultural and food sector and, more specifically, the production, marketing and trade of fresh and processed fruit and vegetables, one of the most dynamic segments of developing-country participation in world markets (Diop and Jaffee, 2005).[1] Given the high labour requirements in this sector, the low land costs and longer cultivation periods in developing countries as well as the trade incentives given by some developed countries, developing countries have been able to capture a significantly increased share of world trade (Diop and Jaffee, 2005).[2] However, modern retailing companies increasingly dominate international and local markets in fruit and vegetables and set the standards for food quality and safety in this sector (Reardon and Barrett, 2000; Reardon and Berdegué, 2002; Reardon et al., 2003).

There is very little rigorous evidence on the impacts of global supply chains on the environment. There is more evidence on its impact on poverty and small farmers' incomes. Available evidence on Africa points mostly at negative implications for small farmers. Several studies indicate that small farmers are left behind in the supermarket-driven horticultural marketing and trade (Delgado, 1999; Key and Runsten, 1999; Reardon and Barrett, 2000; Weatherspoon et al., 2001; Kirsten and Sartorius, 2002; Reardon et al., 2003).

For example, UK supermarkets have been buying increasingly from estates instead of smallholders in Kenya (Kherallah, 2000; Dolan and Humphrey, 2001; Gibbon, 2003; Humphrey et al., 2004). While Minot and Ngigi (2004) confirm this decline in the importance of smallholders for exports, they, however, still estimate that half of Kenya's fruit and vegetable exports are grown by smallholders. This is in contrast with Côte d'Ivoire, where most of the fruit and vegetable exports are grown on large industrial estates.

Weatherspoon et al. (2001) find that the rise of supermarkets in Southern Africa is hardest for the small producers, who are excluded from dynamic urban markets due to the tough quality and safety standards. Our findings on small farmers in Madagascar producing for EU supermarkets, as presented in this chapter, are very different.

Madagascar is a particularly interesting country in which to study the effects of these global supply chains on poverty and the environment. First, poverty is very high in Madagascar, and especially so in rural areas: the poverty headcount ratio was estimated in 2001 at 77% in rural areas. Education levels are low and it is estimated that only about half of the population are able to read and write. Malnutrition levels are equally high and 45% of the children under 3 years are growth retarded (INSTAT, 2005).

Second, Madagascar is largely an agricultural economy: agriculture counted for about one-quarter of GDP and 80% of employment in 2002. However, agricultural performance has been sluggish over the years.[3] Third, while being one of the poorest countries in the world, Madagascar has very important environmental resources, such as the unique biodiversity of its forests. However, these environmental resources are under threat from land extensification and deforestation to feed the rapidly growing – and impoverished – population.

This chapter summarizes the findings of two studies which analyse the effects of contracting of 10,000 small poor farmers in the highlands of Madagascar for the production of vegetables for supermarkets in the EU (Minten et al., 2005a, b). The production and marketing of these vegetables have grown rapidly over the last 15 years despite the imposition of more stringent public and private safety and quality requirements over time. The number of farmers of vegetables for export has grown in Madagascar, despite major disadvantages of geography, bad local infrastructure, low rural education levels and high compliance and transaction costs.

We document contracts in the supply chains that have been used sustainably and flexibly adopted to new niche markets over the last 15 years and we analyse the effects of these contracts on farming practices, on the welfare of the local farmers and on the environment. The analysis of the supply chain and its effects is based on a series of interviews at various levels of the supply chain and a representative survey of 200 supplier (farm) households in the summer of 2004. We refer to Minten et al. (2005a, b) for more details on this survey.

We find that, given the right incentives and contracting systems, small farmers in developing countries – and in Africa in particular – can participate successfully in these emerging value chains. Thousands of small farmers benefit because of a combination of effects such as improved access to inputs, credit, extension services, technology adoption and also from productivity spillover effects on other crops and enhanced income stability. Moreover, we find important positive environmental effects, resulting from spillover effects on land use and land intensification, reducing the pressure on valuable forest land.

The Global Supply Chain

High-quality vegetables from Madagascar are exported to Western Europe. The main vegetable exports are hand-picked and hand-handled fine French beans. Exports from Madagascar currently account for around 10% of the processed French bean market in Europe.[4]

The vast majority of high-value vegetable exports from Madagascar go through a local company, Lecofruit. Currently, the company processes mostly French beans: in the 2004/2005 season, the firm exported 3000 tons of produce, of which 70% were French beans. Ninety percent of this tonnage was processed and put into jars in its plant in Antananarivo and was shipped to Europe by boat. The other 10% were fresh French beans and peas (*pois mangetout*) shipped by plane.

Two-thirds of the vegetables are sold in European supermarkets. Half of this is sold directly to seven main supermarket chains in France, Belgium and the Netherlands. The company has regular contracts with five of these chains. The other half is sold through industrial distributors which then organize the sales to supermarkets. One-third of the produce is sold directly to retail outlets and restaurants – mostly in the neighbourhood of Paris – through European wholesalers. Sales and distribution within Europe are organized by an independent firm that is paid a margin of the final price for these services.

Production

Lecofruit itself buys vegetables from more than 9000 small farmers based on contracts. The total household area cultivated by contracted farmers is, on average, a little below 1 ha in the survey, about the national average farm size in Madagascar (Minten et al., 2003). One-third of the total household area is in the more valuable lowland used for rice cultivation. On average, households own three rice plots of which 1.3 lowland plots are under contract with the firm while 1.7 lowland plots are not under contract.

The contracting farm households in the survey have, on average, six members. Half of the members are less than 15 years old. Seven percent of the households are female-headed. The average age of the household head is 37 years. The households that have contracts with the firm are considerably better educated than the average Malagasy household: 64% of them had finished primary schools and only 1% of them did no studies at all. This compares with almost half of the national population that is analphabetic (Razafindravonona et al., 2001).[5] About 27% of the contractors are members of a farmers' organization. The selected household has, on average, 8 years of experience with contract farming.

The company rule is that an area under contract should be approximately one *are* (0.01 hectare, or 100 m^2). Different contracts can be applied to the same plot over the year, given the relatively short production cycle. In general, there is only one contractor in the household but households sometimes subcontract land to people outside the households. A contracting agent can only have one contract at a time. However, different members of the same household are allowed to take on and bear responsibility for a contract.

During the agricultural season 2003/2004, farmers in the survey had, on average, five ares (0.05 hectares) under contract in total over the whole year. This was equal to about the same number of contracts and indicates that the rule of the firm – that an area under contract should be about one are – is respected. The contracted crop was, in most cases, French beans. Ninety-seven per cent of the farmers declared to having grown this crop over the previous agricultural season. To a lesser extent, the contract involved gherkins (86%). Leek, peas and other crops were relatively less important.

Standards and contracts

Lecofruit signs a yearly contract in advance with most clients in Europe, in which the delivery conditions and product standards are specified for the year as a whole (minimum quantity, prices, time of delivery and payment dates). As is increasingly common in international trade (Jaffee and Henson, 2004), the firm is obliged to stick to the requirements of the clients through private protocols ('*cahier de charges*'). The requirements in these protocols differ by client but concern demands related to the quality of the product (length of the beans, colour, etc.), ethical standards (no use of child labour, for example), employment practices as well as hygiene instructions in the processing plant.

Controlling and enforcing of the food safety and agricultural health standards imposed in the protocols is done at several levels. First, the firm itself carries out regular controls of its produce to ensure that the norms on phytosanitary conditions, the absence of foreign objects, etc. are met. Secondly, each European client also hires private auditors which come to Madagascar for follow-up on these conditions and for inspection at least once a year. These auditing controls have become more frequent and more stringent in the previous 5 years, due to the food chain problems related to the dioxin crisis and BSE (mad cow disease) in Europe.

In addition, Lecofruit has set up an elaborate system of contracting and on-farm monitoring of the vegetable production. With a vegetable supplier base of more than 9000 small farmers, the imposition of the product and process standards and requirements requires a major organization in terms of monitoring and control. The institutional arrangements between the firm and the farmers are set up as micro-contracts. The written contracts are standardized with identical inputs, credit conditions and prices by product. Once a contract is signed, the farmer is then required to follow the rigid instructions of the firm. They have to labour the land in good time and have to apply two card-loads of compost to the plot before planting. As part of the contract, seeds, fertilizer and pesticides are distributed by the firm and have to be paid back in kind. Farmers might also receive, under conditions of good performance, other material that has not to be paid back.

Monitoring and supervision

To monitor the correct implementation of the supplier contracts, the firm has put in place a strict hierarchical system of around 300 extension agents who are permanently on the payroll of the company. Every extension agent, the *chef de culture*, is responsible for about 30 farmers. To supervise these, (s)he coordinates five or six extension assistants (*assistants de culture*) that live in the village itself. The chef de culture has a permanent salary paid by the firm.[6] As well as these personnel in the field, another 200 people are employed at the processing plant located in Antananarivo, the capital of Madagascar.

During the cultivation period of the vegetables under contract, the contractor is visited, on average, more than once (1.3 times) per week. This intensive monitoring is to ensure correct production management as well as to avoid 'side-selling'.[7] The vegetable production management is particularly important with regard to pesticide use. For example, to export to Europe, the produce has to fulfil the norms on MRL (Maximum Residue Levels) of the country to which it is exported. The firm adheres to the most stringent requirements,[8] which have become stricter over time. The pesticide application is monitored very closely and is, in several cases, applied by representatives of the firm to ensure that it is correctly done.

Supervision of the management of the production process also has a significant impact on compost application (Minten et al., 2005b). Supervision is important in assuring that the right procedures are followed, even for those farmers that have worked for a lengthy period for the firm. The firm will pay for only those products that fulfil the quality norms on size and length set by the firm. This control is applied by the assistants de culture in the field as well as in the plant itself. The produce that is not bought by the firm is sold on the local market, used for own consumption or given as feed to animals. The prices that the firm offers are most often significantly higher than those in local markets.

Supplier assistance packages and contract enforcement

As in other modern supply chains where the processor or trader provides inputs to farms which are constrained in their access to these essential inputs (see Swinnen, Chapter 5, this volume), Lecofruit distributes seeds, fertilizer and pesticides as part of the contract. The value of these pre-financed inputs has to be paid back in kind. The average input value per contract is estimated at about 10,000 Ariary (US$5). This compares to an average value of produce sold under each contract of US$20. The first harvests that come in are used for reimbursements of these inputs.

While there is a written agreement, these contracts are seldom legally enforceable in practice, as is often the case in other developing and transition countries (Gow and Swinnen, 2001; Kirsten and Sartorius, 2002). The poorly developed legal institutions, the small amount involved and potentially souring relationships between agri-business and farming communities ensure that the only threat at the disposal of the firm is to discontinue the contract with the farmers.

Yet, the firm has high pay-back rates and, during the year of the survey, about 98% of the farmers expected to pay the full credit back to the firm.[9] To be able to follow-up farmers on their performance and payment ratings, the firm keeps a meticulous database of all the farmers that it works and has worked with – in addition to its intensive monitoring system in the field.

The impact on technology adoption and land use

One of the benefits of contracting with Lecofruit is that it teaches farmers how to make compost. The compost consists of a mixture of manure and vegetable matter. Its main benefits on the fields are in: (i) maintaining the soil structure; (ii) providing nitrogen and other minerals that promote healthy crop growth; and (iii) allowing the soil to retain moisture (Jacoby and Mancuri, 2004). The use of compost is long-lasting and can have an effect on the fertility of the soil for some years, and might therefore be the cause of spillover effects. The compost that the farmer makes is then combined with chemical fertilizer.

Farmers were asked to what extent the requirements on the making of compost and the use of chemical fertilizer had changed the way they were farming and would be farming in the future. The majority of the farmers stated that they were using compost on their plots and that they had not done so before the contract with the firm started (see Table 12.1). They also report that they were currently using compost on plots other than those that were under contract.[10] In the event that the firm would stop their contract, they reported they would continue to produce compost and apply it to their fields.[11]

It was then asked to what extent the contract with the processing firm had changed their agricultural practices: 93%

Table 12.1. Impact of contracts on technology adoption (from farmer survey, 2004).

Farmers in agreement (%)	
Use of compost	
Are you obliged to produce compost and use it on your plots?	93
Before your first contract with the firm, did you already use compost?	12
Are you now using compost on plots other than those under contract?	87
If the contract were terminated for one reason or another, will you continue using compost?	95
Suppose that there were no contract, would you use more compost than before?	66
Changes in agricultural practices	
Did you change the way you perform other off-season crop cultivation because of the contract?	93
Use of compost	96
More maintenance (weeding, watering)	72
Did you change the way you perform other rice cultivation because of the contract?	6
Use of compost	50
More maintenance (weeding, watering)	50

of the farmers reported that they had changed the way they cultivated their other off-season crops. More than 90% of the farmers reported using compost and inputs on these plots. About 70% of the farmers stated that they also carried out more weeding.

It thus seems that the contracts with the firm have led to significant changes in the way farmers grow off-season crops and it seems to be having a lasting impact. However, when asked about changes in the cultivation of rice, only 6% of the farmers reported to having changed the way they cultivated rice since the start of the contract. This is not surprising, given the stark differences in the cultivation of rice and off-season crops.

Spillover effects on food production and the environment

Madagascar is a rice economy *par excellence*. Per capita rice consumption is always at or near the top of world tables, a majority of cultivable land in the nation is sown in rice and Malagasy culture and politics are symbolically structured around rice. It makes up around 50% of the value added in agriculture and represents 45% of the calories consumed for an average Malagasy person (Dorosh *et al.*, 2003).

Nevertheless, median rice yields in Madagascar are among the world's lowest, roughly 2 t/ha consistently over the last 40 years (Dorosh *et al.*, 2003). This low level has often much to do with the lack of the replenishment of nutrients, bad water management and the low adoption rate of improved agricultural technologies (de Laulanié, 2003; World Bank, 2003; Minten and Barrett, 2005). It should come as no surprise that the use of chemical fertilizer is one of the lowest in the world. For example, it is estimated – based on data from the national household survey – that chemical fertilizers were applied on only 4% of the plots in the agricultural season of 2000/2001 (Minten *et al.*, 2003).

A very important effect of the contracts was the spillover on rice productivity. Our estimations are that rice productivity increased dramatically: it is 64% higher on the plots with a contract compared to those plots without a contract and off-season crops: yields increased from 4200 to 6500 kg/ha (see Fig. 12.1). There are thus significant spillovers from contract farming on the production of rice, Madagascar's major staple, probably due to organic and chemical fertilizer use in the off-season.

Besides the obvious welfare effects (see next section), these spillover effects are also very important for the environment. Land extensification and deforestation has been the norm in Madagascar in order to feed the rapidly growing population. It is estimated that, over the last 40 years, about 80% of the increase in agricultural production has

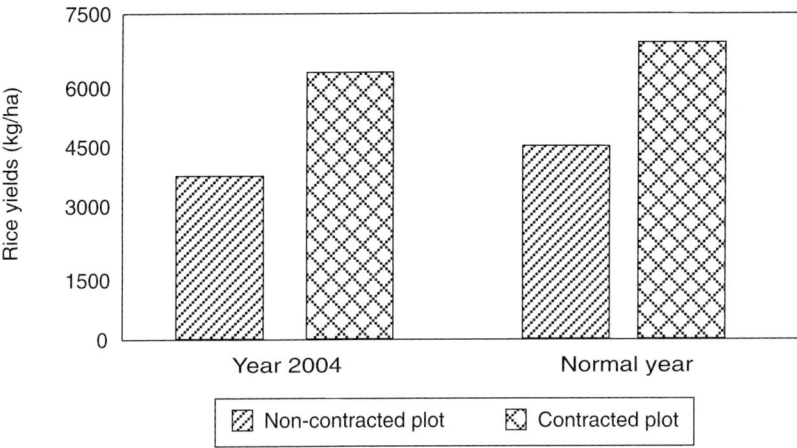

Fig. 12.1. Comparison of rice yields for contract and non-contract plots, Madagascar.

been achieved through land extensification – often at the expense of forested land – and only 20% through intensification of the existing land (Green and Sussman, 1990; Jarosz, 1993; Keck *et al.*, 1994; World Bank, 2003; Moser, 2004).

This is even more dramatic given the unique biodiversity that is found in the forests in Madagascar (Kull, 2000; McConnell, 2002; Goodman and Benstead, 2003). The government and the donors alike have therefore been trying to devise schemes, but mostly unsuccessful or unsustainable, to increase productivity on the existing land in cultivation.

Our findings indicate that there are potentially great beneficial environmental spillovers from contract farming for exports. First, the existing agricultural land is more intensively used as land is cultivated in the off-season. Secondly, land productivity is higher in the main season. As we have explained, participation in these high-value supply chains also eases crucial production constraints in rice productivity, as access to inputs is mentioned by the majority of the farmers as the main constraint to higher rice productivity (see Fig. 12.2). Participation in these supply chains can therefore contribute to land intensification in Madagascar and, thereby, potentially reduce the pressure on valuable forest resources. Under these conditions, increasing globalization might lead to the much sought-after land intensification.[12]

The impact on welfare

First, higher rice productivity has strong welfare effects in Madagascar, especially for the poor, as improved productivity would lead to relatively lower food prices and higher real wages for unskilled wage labourers (Goletti and Rich, 1998; Dorosh *et al.*, 2003; Minten and Barrett, 2005). Second, although the areas that are cultivated are small, the income that contract farmers receive out of the contract is important. For the average household, the contract income represents almost 50% of their monetary income. As expected, French beans are the most important, representing 66% of the total contract income. The total average contract income the contractors earned during the season 2003/2004 amounted to about 87,000 Ariary (US$45).[13]

Contract farmers perceive the contracts to be good for their welfare, especially for seasonality smoothing. High seasonality in production and consumption is a major characteristic in rural areas in Madagascar (Minten and Zeller, 2000). As a significant

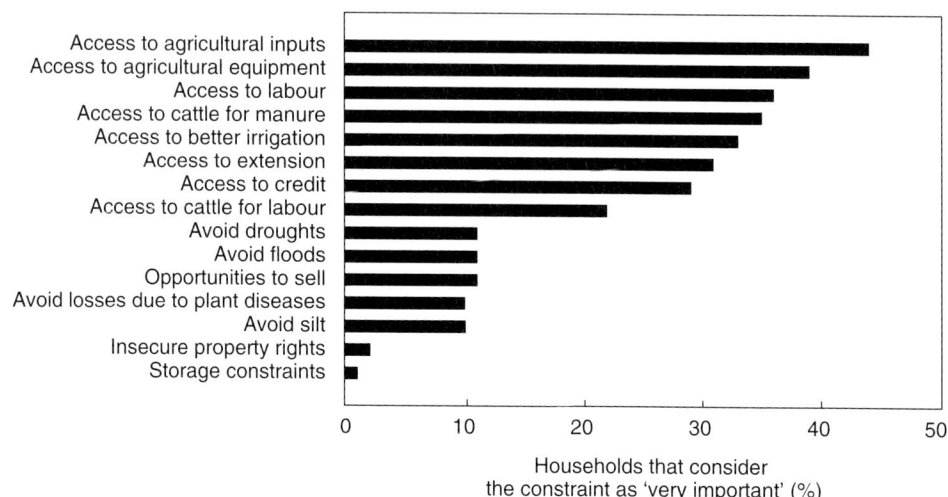

Fig. 12.2. Ranking of importance of specific constraints on rice productivity, Madagascar.

number of households are constrained to reduce consumption during the lean period, it is characterized by higher incidences of disease and mortality (Waltisberger et al., 1998). The length of this lean period varies between regions and by household, but is estimated in the province of Antananarivo, where the contract farmers are mostly situated, to be around 4.4 months (Minten et al., 2003). The estimated length of the lean period of the contract farmers is 1.7 months.

The farmers were also asked about the length of the lean period before they started contracts with the firm and to compare the lean period to households similar to theirs but who had no contract. In both cases the household believed it is better off, as lean periods are estimated to be, respectively, 3.7 and 4.3 months.

The importance of the reduction in risk and variability is also reflected in the reasons given by the farmers themselves as to why they had signed a contact with the firm. About three-quarters stated that access to a source of income during the lean period was, for them, a major reason for the signing of the contract; 66% of the farmers found it very important that they received a stable income during the year.

Other major reasons that were mentioned were access to inputs on credit and the learning of new technologies. Surprisingly, few people mentioned a higher income as their reason for contracting. In fact, our analysis shows little price elasticity and high loyalty of the producers towards the firm.

Conclusions and Policy Implications

Global retail companies ('supermarkets') have an increasing influence on developing countries, through foreign investments and/or through the imposition of their private standards. The impact on poverty and the environment in developing countries is often assessed as negative. In this chapter we show the opposite, based on an analysis of primary data collected to measure the impact of supermarkets on small contract farmers in Madagascar, one of the poorest countries in the world. Almost 10,000 farmers in the highlands of Madagascar produce vegetables for supermarkets in Europe. In this global supply chain, small farmers' micro-contracts are combined with extensive farm assistance and supervision programmes to fulfil the complex quality requirements and phytosanitary standards of supermarkets.

Small farmers that participate in these

contracts have higher welfare, more income stability and shorter lean periods. We also find significant effects on improved technology adoption, better resource management and spillovers on the productivity of the staple crop, rice. There are also important benefits for the environment through more intensive land use and higher productivity, both of which reduce the pressure on valuable forest resources.

These findings raise several issues for further analysis and have important implications. An important issue is whether the benefits of this model can be extended to allow a larger proportion of poor farmers in Madagascar to benefit. It seems that the major constraints are the high transport and transaction costs in Madagascar. Transaction costs are even higher than in competing developing countries, seemingly contributing to lower producer prices than in competing countries.

A first constraint for expansion for this type of activity in Madagascar is the bad road infrastructure. The firm thus only has contracts with farmers in a 120 km radius around the capital, Antananarivo, where its processing plant and export units are situated, but the recent rural road improvements – the priority of the government in its Poverty Reduction Strategy Paper (PRSP) – have allowed the firm to expand the number of contracting farmers by almost 1000 in just 1 year. However, in order to allow the trucks to pass, the firm itself is continuously obliged to organize road maintenance.

The second constraint is low human capital, causing high training costs and long duration required for training of the assistants de culture who organize and supervise the contracting farmers in the field. It is estimated that it takes, on average, 2–3 years' training till the firm can give him/her full responsibility in the field. This slows down growth and expansion.

Third, transaction costs are large because of individual contracts. If farmers were able to constitute farmers' groups, internalize the verification system and provide as great economies of scale, more firms might be attracted to invest in Madagascar. This type of group has been shown to be successful in other countries (Kirsten and Sartorius, 2002; Winters et al., 2005). However, while there are significant interventions of donors and the government for initiating such groups, these generally have a weak track record in Madagascar, especially relating to export agriculture, given the difficulty in overcoming moral hazard and asymmetric information problems.

Another important implication from the study is the importance of trade agreements and export zones. The results indicate that the tax incentives make a difference for enterprise development in the poorest countries. The preferential access in European and American markets is an important determinant for firms to initiate activities in countries such as Madagascar. Given the temporary nature of these interventions (AGOA), as well as the broadening of these measures (WTO), it remains to be seen, however, whether countries such as Madagascar will still be able to continue to compete in these markets in the near future.

Finally, the study suggests that effects on farmers from investments by global retailers in supermarkets in Madagascar have not yet materialized. The expectation was that this would create a domestic demand for high-quality, high-value vegetable production. However, local supermarkets seem to purchase mostly from local, informal suppliers rather than from companies selling high-quality vegetables. Local supermarkets do not value quality and standards sufficiently and are hesitant to engage in the contracts that are needed for producing such standards.

These results seem to contrast with other studies which argue that the emerging modern supermarket sector has difficulties finding local supplies which fulfil their high standards: we find that the suppliers of high standards find the modern retail chains in Madagascar not (yet ?) interested in their products.

Notes

1 World trade reached US$71.6 billion in 2001, an increase of 30% compared with 1990.
2 While fresh and processed fruit and vegetable products accounted for 17% of total exports from developing countries in 1980/1981, this share increased to 22% in 2000/2001, and this despite a significant price decrease over the same period (Diop and Jaffee, 2005).
3 For example, the yields of its main staple (rice) are about 2 t/ha and have been at this level for the last 40 years. This low level often has to do with the lack of replenishment of nutrients, bad water management and the low adoption of improved technologies (World Bank, 2003; Minten and Barrett, 2005).
4 The other major exporters to the Western European market – most importantly France, Belgium, the UK and the Netherlands – are Kenya, China and Morocco; the last of these countries entered this market more recently, but very quickly became an important player.
5 However, analysis of national census data of 1993 of the fivondronana – where the contracting farmers are located – indicates that 'only' 39% of the people did not finish primary school, similar to the numbers in our survey. This illustrates the long-standing, well-known bias in education investments towards the highlands.
6 It is interesting to note that export farmers in Kenya developed to a similar model, but in this case driven by demands of small farmers rather than by the firm. Minot and Ngigi (2005) tell the story of a horticultural farmers' group in Kenya that were formed in part by a desire to eliminate brokers and to deal directly with exporters. The group employed a field supervisor charged with the responsibility of supervising and monitoring production practices to ensure that the farmer members followed the prescribed methods. The supervisor was trained by the exporter.
7 See Minten et al. (2005a) for a discussion and analysis of side-selling problems.
8 The European Union pesticide legislation is under review and various countries have different standards. Lecofruit uses the most stringent one. The setting of MRL is based on the work done by Codex Alimentarius, an international standards-setting group based in Rome.
9 This coincides with the declaration of the manager who said that, every year, only 0.5–1.0% of the peasants did not manage to reimburse the inputs advanced by the firm.
10 We tested this statement for the one rice plot that was not under contract and about which we asked detailed information. Compost was used to a large extent – 60% of the plots where off-season crops were grown.
11 While the teaching of the use of compost might seem to be a small contribution, this is a clear illustration of technology improvement in rural areas of a country where the state had never succeeded in providing decent agricultural extension services and where most of the agriculture is still carried out as it was centuries ago.
12 However, this does not need to be the case in general. Minten and Méral (2005) show that an increase in trade has also led to increased deforestation, especially in the south-west of the country.
13 While this might be low at first sight, one must remember that the average agricultural household income (including auto-consumption) in Madagascar was estimated in 2001 at US$315 (Randrianarison, 2003). Given that the largest part of agricultural production is auto-consumed, this comprises an important part of *monetary* income, as stated by these farmers.

References

Bhagwati, J. (2004) *In Defense of Globalization*. Oxford University Press, Oxford, UK.
Cavendish, W. (2000) Empirical regularities in the poverty-environment relationships of rural households: evidence from Zimbabwe. *World Development* 28 (11), 1979–2003.
Chichilnisky, G. (1994) North–south trade and the global environment. *American Economic Review* 84 (4), 851–974.
Cropper, M. and Griffith, C. (1994) The interaction of population growth and environmental quality. *American Economic Review* 84 (2), 250–254.
De Laulanié, H. (2003) *Le Riz à Madagascar: un Développement en Dialogue avec les Paysans*. Éditions Karthala, Antananarivo, Madagascar.
Delgado, C. (1999) Sources of growth in smallholder agriculture in sub-Saharan Africa: the role of vertical integration of smallholders with processors and marketers of high value-added items. *Agrekon* 38, 165–189.

Diop, N. and Jaffee, S.M. (2005) Fruits and vegetables: global trade and competition in fresh and processed product markets. In: Aksoy, M.A. and Beghin, J.C. (eds) *Global Agricultural Trade and Developing Countries*. World Bank, Washington, DC, pp. 237–257.

Dolan, C. and Humphrey, J. (2000) Governance and trade in fresh vegetables: the impact of UK supermarkets on the African horticulture industry. *Journal of Development Studies* 37 (2), 147–176.

Dorosh, P., Haggblade, S., Lungren, C., Razafimanantena, T. and Randriamiarana, Z. (2003) *Moteurs Economiques pour la Réduction de la Pauvreté à Madagascar*. INSTAT, Antananarivo, Madagascar.

Dries, L. and Swinnen, J. (2004) Foreign direct investment, vertical integration and local suppliers: evidence from the Polish dairy sector. *World Development* 32 (9), 1525–1544.

Foster, A. and Rosenzweig, M. (2003) Economic growth and the rise of forests. *Quarterly Journal of Economics* 118 (2), 601–637.

Gibbon, P. (2003) Value-chain governance, public regulation and entry barriers in the global fresh fruit and vegetable chain in the EU. *Development Policy Review* 21 (5/6), 615–625.

Goletti, F. and Rich, F. (1998) Analysis of policy options for income growth and poverty alleviation. In: IFPRI/FOFIFA, *Structure and Conduct of Major Agricultural Input and Output Markets and Response to Reforms by Rural Households in Madagascar*. IFPRI, Washington, DC and Antananarivo, Madagascar, Part 5.

Goodman, S.M. and Benstead, J.P. (2003) *The Natural History of Madagascar*. University of Chicago Press, Chicago, Illinois.

Gow, H. and Swinnen, J. (2001) Private enforcement capital and contract enforcement in transition countries. *American Journal of Agricultural Economics* 83 (3), 686–690.

Green, G. and Sussman, R. (1990) Deforestation history of the eastern rain forests of Madagascar from satellite images. *Science* 248, 212–215.

Grossman, G. and Krueger, A. (1995) Economic growth and the environment. *Quarterly Journal of Economics* 110, 353–377.

Humphrey, J., McCulloch, N. and Ota, M. (2004) The impact of European market changes on employment in the Kenyan horticulture sector. *Journal of International Development* 16 (1), 63–80.

INSTAT (2005) *Enquête Démographique et de Santé: 2003–2004*. Institut National de la Statistique, Antananarivo, Madagascar.

Jacoby, H.G. and Mancuri, G. (2004) *The (In)efficiency of Share Tenancy Revisited: Evidence from Pakistan*. World Bank, Washington, DC (mimeo).

Jaffee, S.M. and Henson, S. (2004) Standards and agri-food exports from developing countries: rebalancing the debate. *World Bank Policy Research Working Paper* 3348, Washington, DC.

Jarosz, L. (1993) Defining and explaining tropical deforestation: shifting cultivation and population growth in colonial Madagascar (1896–1940). *Economic Geography* 69, 366–379.

Keck, A., Sharma, N.P. and Feder, G. (1994) *Population Growth, Shifting Cultivation and Unsustainable Agricultural Development: a Case Study in Madagascar*. World Bank Discussion Papers, Africa Technical Department Series 234, World Bank, Washington, DC.

Key, N. and Runsten, D. (1999) Contract farming, smallholders, and rural development in Latin America: the organization of agroprocessing firms and the scale of outgrower production. *World Development* 27 (2), 381–401.

Kherallah, M. (2000) *Access of Smallholder Farmers to the Fruits and Vegetables market in Kenya*. International Food Policy Research Institute (IFPRI), Washington, DC.

Kirsten, J. and Sartorius, K. (2002) Linking agribusiness and small-scale farmers in developing countries: is there a new role for contract farming? *Development Southern Africa* 19 (4), 503–529.

Kull, C. (2000) Deforestation, erosion, and fire: degradation myths in the environmental history of Madagascar. *Environment and History* 6, 423–450.

McConnell, W. (2002) Emerald isle or paradise lost? *Environment* (October), 12–21.

Minot, N. and Ngigi, M. (2004) *Are Horticultural Exports a Replicable Success Story? Evidence from Kenya and Côte d'Ivoire*. EPTD/MTID discussion paper, International Food Policy Research Institute.

Minten, B. and Barrett, C. (2005) *Agricultural Technology, Productivity, Poverty and Food Security in Madagascar*. Cornell University, New York/World Bank, Washington, DC.

Minten, B. and Méral, P. (2005) *International Trade and Environmental Degradation: a Case Study of the Loss of Spiny Forest in Madagascar*. WWF, Madagascar (mimeo).

Minten, B. and Zeller, M. (2000) *Beyond Market Liberalization: Welfare, Income Generation and Environmental Sustainability in Rural Madagascar*. Ashgate, Vermont.

Minten, B., Randrianarison, L. and Randrianarisoa, C. (2003) *Agriculture, Pauvreté Rurale et Politiques Économiques à Madagascar.* Cornell University/FOFIFA/INSTAT, Antananarivo, Madagascar.

Minten, B., Randrianarison, L. and Swinnen, J. (2005a) *Spillovers from globalization on land use: Evidence from Madagascar.*

Minten, B., Randrianarison, L. and Swinnen, J. (2005b) *Supermarkets, international trade and farmers in developing countries: Evidence from Madagascar.*

Moser, C. (2004) *Causes and Misconceptions: Population, Roads, Poverty, and Deforestation in Madagascar.* Cornell University, New York.

Randrianarison, L. (2003) Les revenus extra-agricoles. In: Minten, B., Randrianarison, C. and Randrianarison, L. (eds) *Agriculture, Pauvreté Rurale et Politiques Économiques à Madagascar.* Cornell University/FOFIFA/INSTAT, Antananarivo, Madagascar.

Razafindravonona, J., Stifel, D. and Paternostro, S. (2001) *Changes in Poverty in Madagascar: 1993–1999.* World Bank Africa Region Working Paper Series 19, Washington, DC.

Reardon, T. and Barrett, C.B. (2000) Agroindustrialisation, globalization and international development: an overview of issues, patterns and determinants. *Agricultural Economics* 23, 195–205.

Reardon, T. and Berdegué, J. (2002) The rapid rise of supermarkets in Latin America: challenges and opportunities for development. *Development Policy Review* 20 (4), 371–388.

Reardon, T., Timmer, C.P., Barrett, C. and Berdegué, J. (2003) The rise of supermarkets in Africa, Asia, and Latin America. *American Journal Agricultural Economics* 85 (5), 1140–1146.

Reed, D. (2001) *Poverty is not a Number, the Environment is not a Butterfly.* WWF-MPO, Washington, DC.

Waltisberger, D., Cantrelle, P. and Ralijaona, O. (1998) *La mortalité à Antananarivo de 1984 à 1995.* Document et Manuel du CEPED No. 7, Paris.

Weatherspoon, D., Cacho, J. and Christy, R. (2001) Linking globalization, economic growth and poverty: impacts of agribusiness strategies on sub-Saharan Africa. *American Journal of Agricultural Economics* 83 (3), 722–729.

Winters, P., Simmons, P. and Patrick, I. (2005) Evaluation of a hybrid seed contract between smallholders and a multinational company in East Java, Indonesia. *The Journal of Development Studies* 41 (1), 62–89.

World Bank (2003) *Review of Agricultural and Environmental Sector.* World Bank, Washington, DC.

13 High-value Supply Chains, Food Standards and Rural Households in Senegal

M. Maertens, L. Dries, F.A. Dedehouanou and J.F.M. Swinnen

Introduction

Trade liberalization and the integration of developing countries in global trade, and in particular in high-value supply chains, is advocated as a major potential engine for global poverty reduction (Aksoy and Beghin, 2005). At the same time it is argued that new product and process standards of rich countries are offsetting the gains from trade liberalization as they introduce new barriers for developing country exports (Unnevehr, 2000; Brenton and Manchin, 2002; Augier et al., 2005).

Moreover, some studies argue that the benefits from new high-value and high-standards global supply chains will go to multinational investors and developing country elites, and may do little for the fate of poor farmers as they are likely to be excluded from these supply chains (Reardon et al., 1999; Dolan and Humphrey, 2000; Farina and Reardon, 2000).

The agricultural and food sector, and more specifically the export of fresh and processed fruit and vegetables (FFV) from Africa to the EU, is a particularly interesting area to study these developments and their effects. First, Africa is the region generally considered most lagging in global market integration and poverty reduction.

Second, developing countries are increasingly participating in international FFV trade (Diop and Jaffee, 2005).[1] Given the high labour requirements in this sector, the low land costs and longer cultivation periods in developing countries, as well as the trade incentives given by some developed countries, developing countries have been able to capture a significantly increased share of world FFV trade (Diop and Jaffee, 2005).[2]

Third, the high – and tightening – EU standards on FFV are providing important constraints on developing country imports. Fourthly, large trading and retailing companies play a very important role in international markets in FFV and have an additional impact on standards and requirements on FFV (Reardon and Berdegué, 2002; Reardon and Swinnen, 2004).

There is considerable debate and

© CAB International 2007. *Global Supply Chains, Standards and the Poor* (ed J.F.M. Swinnen) uncertainty on the impacts of these developments for farmers and poverty in developing countries. Available evidence presents a mixed picture. Several studies indicate that small farmers are excluded from supermarket-driven horticultural marketing and trade (Delgado, 1999; Key and Runsten, 1999; Reardon and Barrett, 2000; Weatherspoon et al., 2001; Kirsten and Sartorius, 2002; Reardon et al., 2003).

For example, UK supermarkets have been buying increasingly from estates instead of from smallholders in Kenya. Also, in Côte d'Ivoire, most of the fruit and vegetable exports are grown on large industrial estates, and in southern Africa the rise of supermarkets is said to be hardest for the small producers, who are excluded from dynamic urban markets due to the tough quality and safety standards (Dolan and Humphrey, 2000; Kherallah, 2000; Gibbon, 2003; Weatherspoon and Reardon, 2003; Humphrey et al., 2004).

Very different findings come from a study by Minten et al. (2006) on Madagascar. They find that, given the right incentives and contracting systems, thousands of small farmers in one of the poorest countries in Africa participate successfully in these emerging value chains, with major benefits to them. Also Minot and Ngigi (2004), while observing a decline in the importance of smallholders for exports, still estimate that half of Kenya's fruit and vegetable exports are grown by small farmers.

Our analysis studies the impact of the export supply chain of FFV from Senegal to the EU on small farmers in Senegal. We analyse how the structure of the export supply chain in Senegal has changed in response to tightening food standards and changing coordination in global FFV value chains, and investigate the impact for the local population.

The study yields four important findings. First, we find that FFV exports from Senegal to the EU have grown steadily over the past decade. Second, we find that participation in high-value export production through contract farming has major benefits for small farmers, both directly in terms of enhanced income and indirectly by improving access to credit and modern inputs.

Third, we find that tightening food standards are causing structural changes in the export supply chain and a shift from smallholder contract farming to agri-industrial production. Fourth, we find nuanced welfare effects of these changes. The gains from high-value export production for local farmers have diminished with the shift to agri-industrial production; however, there are also positive distributional consequences as the poorest benefit more from increased employment on agri-industrial farms.

The structure of the chapter is as follows. In a next section we describe the data and the methodology used. In section three, the global supply chain for FFV and the importance of public and private food standards in that chain are discussed. Section four deals with the structural changes in the export supply chain of FFV in Senegal. We investigate the welfare effects of these changes for the local population in section five. Finally, we present the main conclusions and implications from our study.

Data and Methodology

This study is based on primary data collected at different levels of the horticulture export supply chain in Les Niayes, Senegal. The research region is the main horticulture region of the country from which the majority (over 90%) of exported green beans originate. Les Niayes stretches over a width of some tens of kilometres along the coast north of Dakar. It is a fairly densely populated region where agricultural land is becoming scarce. Due to salinity problems, access to water forms an important constraint for agricultural production. Next to green bean production for export, the majority of households in this region are horticultural farmers producing a large variety of vegetables for the local market.

We use a unique dataset derived from surveys and interviews at the level of both horticulture agri-exporting companies and individual farm households. In April 2005, we conducted interviews with nine of the 20 exporting companies in the research region. This sample constitutes a mixture of smaller exporters (organized in the association SEPAS[3]) and larger exporting companies (members of ONAPES[4]), which jointly represent 38% of the exported volume of horticultural products and 44% of the exported volume of green beans.

Among the selected firms, the exported volume (t) for the last season ranges from 30 to more than 2000 (see Table 13.1). Some smaller firms specialize in green beans while larger firms also export other products, mainly mango, melon and cherry tomatoes. Some of the selected firms entered the market only recently, while others have been exporting green beans for a decade or more. Two selected firms have a majority share of foreign ownership, while the others are domestic firms. From this sample of agri-exporting companies we gathered qualitative information on the developments in the export supply chain and some quantitative firm-level information.

In August/September 2005, we implemented a quantitative survey that covered 300 households in 25 randomly selected villages in the research region. In the sample, households who produced green beans on contract with an agri-exporting company are overrepresented and constitute 59 of the 300 sampled households (see Table 13.2). To take into account this oversampling and draw correct inferences we used sampling weights in all subsequent analyses. These were calculated with information gathered at the village level as the inverse of the probability that an observation is included in the sample due to the sampling design.

For the 59 households who produce green

Table 13.1. Characteristics of selected agri-exporting companies (from company-level interviews).

| Company name | Exported volume in 2004 (t) | | Year starting export of green beans | Membership of an exporters' organization | Share of foreign ownership (%) |
	Green beans	Other horticultural products			
Soleil Vert	800	1100	2000	ONAPES	80
Sepam	883	1410	1992	ONAPES	0
Master	68	0	1989	ONAPES	0
Baniang	80	150	1999	ONAPES	51
Agriconcept	100	80	2002	SEPAS	0
ANS Interexport	64	0	2001	SEPAS	0
Pasen	30	0	2000	SEPAS	0
Agral Export	180	0	1992	SEPAS	0
PDG	173	239	1993	SEPAS	0

Table 13.2. Characteristics of the sample of contracted and non-contracted households (calculated from survey data).

	Number of households	Frequency in the sample (%)	Frequency in the population (%)	Sampling weight
Households which had a contract for the cultivation of green beans at the time of the survey	59	20	8	5,745
Households which did not have a contract for the cultivation of green beans at the time of the survey	241	80	92	14,784
Total sample	300			

beans on contract, the sampling weight is 5.75, as these 59 observations are drawn from a population-stratum of 339 contracted households in the 25 selected villages. For the other households the sampling weight is 14.78, as these are drawn from a population-stratum of 3563 non-contracted households. The 59 contractor-households thus represent 20% of the sample but only 8% of the population (see Table 13.2).

We obtained additional qualitative information on the horticultural sector in Senegal from representatives of SEPAS and ONAPES – two professional organizations of horticultural exporters and from CDH – a horticultural research centre that is part of ISRA.[5] Secondary statistics on horticultural production and exports were obtained from the *Direction de l'Horticulture*.

High-value Exports and Food Standards

Horticultural exports to the EU

Exports of FFV from Senegal have been increasing sharply since the devaluation of the FCFA[6] in 1994. The exported volume has more than tripled during the past decade from 4500 t in 1994 to almost 16,000 t in 2005 (see Fig. 13.1). The export of green beans, in particular, has slowed down after a period of rapid growth during the second half of the 1990s, but still represents 42% of the total volume of horticultural exports.

Apart from green beans, other major export crops include cherry tomatoes (23% of the volume) and mangoes (16%). Also some melon, hibiscus, onions, asparagus, eggplant and potatoes are exported, but only to a minor extent. FFV are the fifth most important export commodity for Senegal. The horticultural sector is important as a foreign exchange earner and also plays a central role in Senegal's export diversification strategy towards high-value export commodities.

Apart from some small volumes exported to neighbouring countries, FFV are exported to the EU under preferential trade agreements, such as the Everything But Arms Agreement and the Cotonou Agreement. They are especially destined for France (40%), the Netherlands (35%) and Belgium

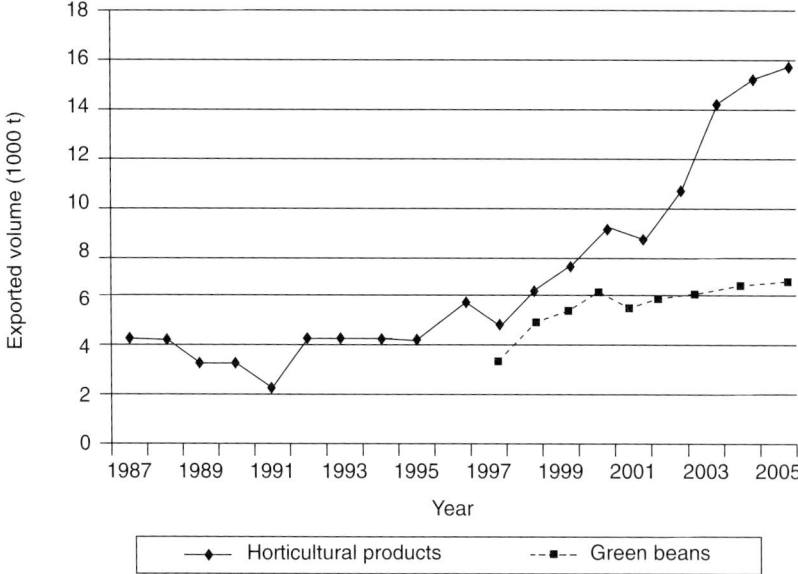

Fig. 13.1. Exported volume of horticultural goods from Senegal, 1987–2005. Data calculated from DH (Direction de l'Horticulture, 2005).

(16%). Senegal ranks fourth as an external supplier of green beans to the EU, after Morocco, Egypt and Kenya.

Competition in the EU market is increasing, especially from Morocco,[7] and Senegal's market share for green beans has decreased from 6.9% in 2000 to 3.5% in 2004 (see Fig. 13.2). Due to increased competition in the EU market, timely delivery becomes an important issue. At the end of the growing season in Senegal, EU importers can easily shift to buying from Morocco, where the harvest has then just started.

To compete in the EU market Senegal has opted for a strategy of quality upgrading. The value of exports to the EU has increased more than the quantity. The average value of green beans imported from Senegal in the EU increased from 1752 Euro/ton in 2000 to 1952 Euro/t in 2004 (Eurostat, 2005). For Morocco and Egypt this figure is decreasing and was 1121 and 1163 Euro/ton, respectively, in 2004 (Eurostat, 2005). This indicates that there is a quality premium for green beans imported from Senegal.[8] The Senegalese government has played a role in this quality upgrading through the validation of the label *Origine Sénégal*[9] as a tool to promote Senegal's horticulture exports as a high-quality produce.

EU food standards

EU legislation puts forward specific public standards concerning food quality and food safety for FFV. First, quality requirements are laid down in the common marketing standards for FFV. For example, the Commission Regulation (EC) No. 912/2001, an amendment of EC No. 2000/96, specifies a classification for green beans based on quality and size, and stipulates provisions concerning the presentation and marketing of the beans.

Second, food safety standards include phytosanitary measures such as maximum residue levels (MRL) for FFV. These have been laid down since 1976 and have become stricter in 1986 and again in 1990.[10] Also, new regulations concerning the treatment of wooden packaging material and maximum levels of contamination by heavy metals for FFV have applied since 2005 and 2002, respectively.

Third, the General Food Law of 2002 – that resulted from the restructuring of EU food legislation after the food crises of the 1990s – specifies general hygiene rules based on HACCP control mechanisms.[11] These measures are legally binding for food produced in and outside the EU except for primary producers, who are not obliged to be certified or to implement HACCP controls themselves.

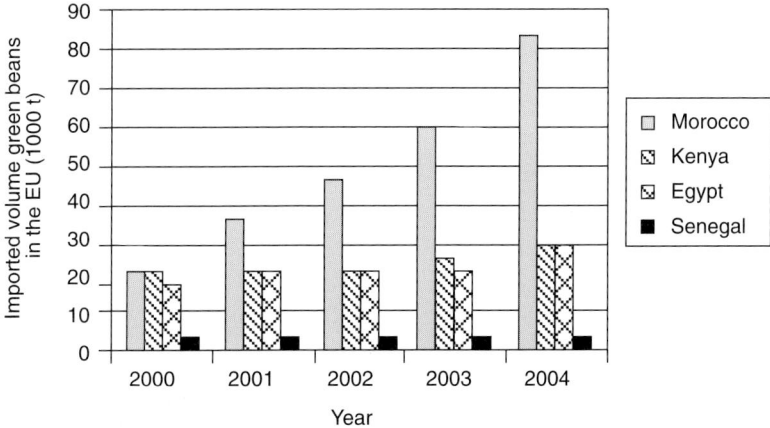

Fig. 13.2. Imported volume of green beans in the EU from the four largest suppliers, 2000–2004. Data calculated from EUROSTAT, 2005).

Fourth, traceability requirements have come into force since 2005 as part of the General Food Law. This involves agri-food businesses documenting from/to whom they are buying/selling produce such that products can be traced back to their origin in case of food safety problems. These public traceability standards apply only to agri-food businesses located in the EU.

Next to these public food standards, many large trading and retailing companies have engaged in establishing private standards for food quality and safety that are even stricter. Many importers in the EU request complete traceability throughout the chain for products supplied to them. For example, the Euro-Retailer Produce Working Group (Eurep) has engaged in adapting traceability (and other) standards into the EurepGAP certification protocols. The Eurep members – among them many food retailers and supermarket chains and various other importers – require complete traceability and EurepGAP certification from their overseas suppliers. Hence, traceability requirements are a mixture of public and private standards.

Compliance with food standards

The increasingly stringent public and private food standards in the EU have consequences for the FFV agri-industry in Senegal. Exporters are forced to keep up to date with the changing legislation and make additional investments in order to comply with food standards. Among the nine selected FFV exporting firms in our sample, only one – Sepam – has been EurepGAP- and HACCP-certified since 2004. Three other firms – Soleil Vert, Baniang and *Agriconcept* – are in the process of certification and this is expected to be completed by 2006.

In order to obtain a certificate, these firms have made substantial investments in the past couple of years, including cold storage and transport capacity, facilities for selection and packaging, control mechanisms, improvements in sanitary conditions at conditioning stations, etc. The two firms with foreign capital – Soleil Vert and Baniang – were able to finance these investments mainly from own resources, while the other firms relied heavily on credit and assistance programs from different institutions.

The other firms in the sample are not certified, not in the process of becoming certified and are not undertaking particular investments in the scope of certification. These smaller exporters face constraints because of the high cost related to complying with food standards.

In 1999, the seven largest FFV exporters in Senegal founded the organization ONAPES[12] to comply with traceability standards – which were then still private standards, imposed by a number of importers in the EU – and to become EurepGAP-certified. They agreed that each member should seek to be present in the market every season with a volume of at least 200 t FFV and that at least 50% of that volume should originate from the companies' own production – a measure that is having a profound impact on the structure of the export supply chain. The organization also coordinates the transport of FFV by air or sea, provides market information – including information on food standards – and assists its members in contacting overseas buyers.

Structural Changes in the Export Supply Chain

Public food quality and safety standards and the increasing importance of private standards from large trading and retail companies are increasing the need for tighter coordination in high-value global food chains. This has led to important structural changes in the export supply chain for FFV in Senegal.

Changes in the industry

Increased coordination with EU importers

The exporting horticulture industry in Senegal, especially for larger firms, is increasingly engaging in tighter coordination with downstream importers and wholesalers in the EU market. Four of the smaller exporters in our sample deal with importers through indicative agreements on the supplied quantity. These are oral or written agreements in which no prices or delivery dates are specified and which are not binding for either of the parties.

However, larger exporters recently changed from such a coordination system with indicative agreements to more binding contracts with overseas buyers. Four selected companies – including three ONAPES members – signed contracts with wholesalers in the EU – one since 1996, the other two since 2002. Within these contracts a fixed (minimum) price and the quantity of green beans to be delivered are specified. Also, the timing of delivery is important and indicated by week. Contracts are usually renewed every season. In addition, three firms receive pre-financing from their buyers – one as recently as last season, two for a couple of years.

Thus, during recent years the degree of vertical coordination at the export–import node of the supply chain has increased, with more binding contracts and pre-financing. Among the reasons mentioned by exporting companies for engaging in such tighter coordination are the volatility of prices in the EU market and the incidence of produce refusal by importers.

In the green beans sector, there are no cases yet of complete vertical integration with export from Senegal and distribution in the EU market organized within subsidiaries of multinational companies. There is some foreign ownership in the agri-export sector (see Table 13.1), but this concerns investments by individual foreign entrepreneurs rather than by subsidiaries of multinational companies. Yet, the degree of vertical coordination has increased, with larger exporters especially engaging in binding contracts with overseas wholesalers.

Consolidation since 2000

The number of horticultural exporters in Senegal is shifting every season, as smaller firms, in particular, can easily enter and exit the market – either permanently or temporarily for one or more seasons. Yet, consolidation has been ongoing since 2000. The number of exporters is steadily decreasing while the market share of the three largest firms is increasing.

In 2002, green beans were exported through 27 companies. This number decreased to 24 in 2004 and by 2005 only 20 firms remained. During the last season (2005), the three largest companies exported two-thirds of the total volume of green beans, while in 2002 their market share was slightly less than half. This consolidation might result from the constraints smaller firms face in complying with food standards.

Changes in the farming system

Increasing vertical coordination with farms

Upstream in the supply chain, the degree of vertical coordination is increasing. For the supply of primary produce, exporting firms rely on contract farming and on integrated production on bought or rented land. Among the sampled companies, the share of produce supplied through contracts ranges from 20 to 100% (see Table 13.3). Most contracts are specified, with small family farms who usually allocate 0.5 ha or 1 ha to the production of green beans on contract. Only two companies in the sample have contracts with one or two large commercial farms. One firm deals with up to 50 small contract farmers.

The contracts that exporting firms offer to farmers are usually specified for one season and indicate the area to be planted, the technical itinerary to follow – including the variety to plant, the type and quantity of fertilizers and pesticides to use and the timing of planting and/or harvesting – and the price. All firms provide inputs, especially seeds and chemicals, on credit and give technical assistance during the growing season.

Certain contract specifications and the way contracts are coordinated differ by

Table 13.3. Changes in procurement system of selected agri-exporting firms (calculated from survey data).

Company name	Proportion of supply from contract-farming (%)		Number of contracted farms	
	First year of operation	Previous season	Household farms (< 10 ha)	Commercial farms (> 50 ha)
Soleil Vert	100	20	40	1
Sepam	100	60	50	2
Master	50	40	na	na
Baniang	85	85	na	na
Agriconcept	30	30	na	na
ANS Interexport	100	100	50	0
Pasen	100	60	8	0
Agral Export	100	100	30	0
PDG	100	100	45	0

na, data not available.

firm. Some firms go as far in their technical assistance as the complete management of fertilizer and pesticide application and daily or weekly inspection of the farmers' fields. Other firms leave management decisions to the farmers and provide technical field assistance only a couple of times during the season. Also field preparation, planting and/or harvesting can be organized and financed completely by the exporting firm.

Apart from in-kind credit in the form of inputs, some firms also give cash credit to their contractors. Larger exporting firms, in particular, provide pre-financing and apply tighter coordination within the contracts for smallholders. The most extreme case is Sepam, which manages the whole production on smallholders' land except for irrigation and harvesting. The reason why firms apply such tight contract coordination is to assure quality and accurate timing of production and harvesting.

However, rather than relying on contract farming, larger exporters are increasingly engaging in their own production on bought or rented land. The two largest exporters in the sample (Soleil Vert and Sepam) depended completely on contract farming in their first year of operation, while for the last season (2005) they procured 80 and 40%, respectively, of produce from their own production (see Table 13.3). Also, some smaller exporters and recent entrants into the market, e.g. Pasen and Agriconcept, rely heavily on their own production.

The causes of these changes relate to quality issues and food standards. Exporting firms who became members of ONAPES specifically agreed to reduce contract farming and increase their own production on account of compliance with food standards. Interviewed firms cited quality rather than quantity as being the reason for changes in their procurement system. Even firms that still rely fully on contract farming mentioned vertically integrated production to be an important strategy for compliance with food standards in the future, and hence for the survival and growth of the firm.

However, the access to land and water in the region is a limiting factor. Some agri-exporting firms think about expanding and/or starting production activities in other areas where land and water are less scarce. The shift from contract farming towards vertically integrated production translates into a decreasing volume of green beans that is procured from small farmers through contract farming, and hence a consolidation in the supply chain at the level of the primary production.

The changing role of household participation

There has been a dramatic increase in the participation of local households in the export supply chain for green beans, from less than 10% in 1992 to about 40% in 2005 (see Fig. 13.3). During the second half of the 1990s – when the export of green beans was growing rapidly – households increasingly participated in export production through contract farming (Fig. 13.3).

In 2000, an estimated 24% of local households produced green beans on contract with an exporting firm. From 2000 onwards, household participation grew further – despite a slowdown in export growth – through wage employment in the agri-industry while contract farming was decreasing (see Fig. 13.3). Food standards induced changes in the procurement system of exporting firms, which resulted in a decreasing share of households participating in contract farming; from 24% in 2000 to 8.5% in 2005 (see Fig. 13.3).

However, as a result of increasing vertically integrated production in agri-exporting companies, employment in the agri-industry has increased from less than 10% of local households in 2000 to 35% in 2005. Participation of rural farm households in green bean export production has increased substantially, but their role has shifted from contract farmers to employees.

Summary

The structural changes in the export supply chain for green beans from Senegal can be summarized in four points: (i) private and public food standards are increasingly important and only larger exporters can make the necessary investments to comply with these standards and obtain certificates; (ii) as a result, the export sector is increasingly concentrated, with smaller exporters dropping out; (iii) to guarantee food quality and safety throughout the supply chain, exporting firms – especially larger firms – increasingly rely

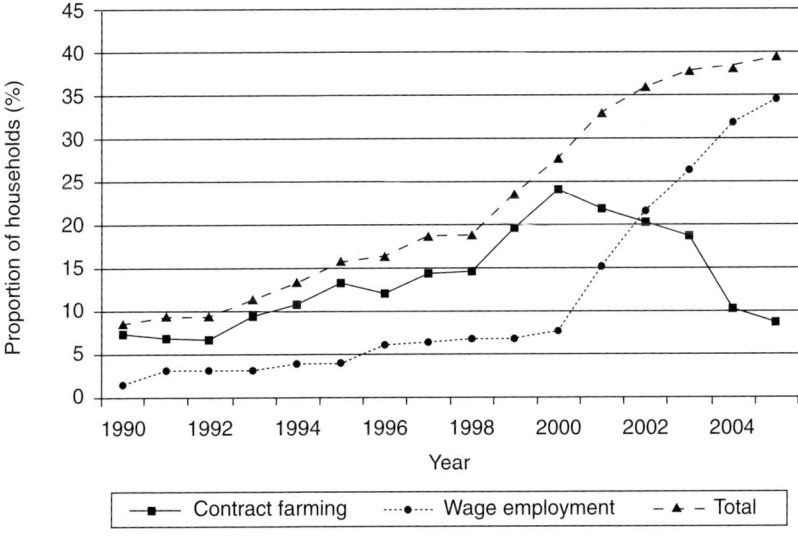

Fig. 13.3. Proportion of Senegal households involved in the green bean export sector through contract farming and wage employment (from Maertens and Swinnen, 2006). This figure is based on recall data from a sample of 300 households in 2005. To account for demographic effects, households for which the head of household did not reach the age of 25 in a particular year – and households which migrated to the area only after a particular year – were excluded from the data for that year. To account for biases due to sampling design, sampling weights were used in the calculations.

on tighter vertical coordination with downstream buyers in the EU, as well as with upstream suppliers of primary produce; and (iv) this results in a sharp decrease in the volume that is sourced from small farmers through contracts and an increase in employment in agri-industrial estates.

In what follows we investigate the general welfare effects of these changes. More details on the efficiency and equity effects of these changes can be found in Maertens and Swinnen (2006).

Welfare Effects

Participation of small farmers in high-value export production

Participation of local households in green bean export production has increased substantially during the past decade, even after 2000 when export growth slowed down and food standards had become more stringent. Our survey data reveal that, in the period 2000–2005, 80 farmers in the sample (or 27% of the population) started wage employment in the agri-exporting industry. In addition, 26 farmers (or 3.5% of the population) were able to obtain a contract with an agri-exporting firm in that period.

However, between 2000 and 2005, 80% of the farmers who were cultivating green beans on contract lost that that contract without being able to sign a new contract. Most of them had contracts with firms which had started their own primary production (e.g. Sepam and Soleil Vert) or firms which have exited the market. Among the reasons these farmers mention for the interruption of their contract, 24% indicated they had ended the contract themselves – either because they didn't want to engage in contract farming any more or because of difficulties with access to land and water.

The other farmers (76%) said that the exporting firm had ended the contract and did not always know the reasons why. In addition, the majority (90%) of farmers who had never cultivated green beans on contract with an exporting firm indicated that they would like to do so if they could have the opportunity. Many farmers are excluded from contract farming.

To draw correct inferences on the welfare effects of the structural changes in the FFV export sector, it is imperative to know whether participation in export production – through either contract farming or wage employment – is biased towards certain households. The survey data reveal that farmers who were able to continue or start contract farming with an exporting firm after 2000 had more land, more livestock, more productive assets and more labour endowments (see Fig. 13.4). Farmers whose contract ended after 2000 had considerably smaller amounts of these endowments, and farmers who had never had access to a contract even less.

Comparing households which had engaged in wage employment in the FFV agri-export industry with those who hadn't; only the difference in labour endowments remained (see Fig. 13.4). These results imply that contract farming is biased towards richer households with more productive assets, while wage employment in the agri-industry is biased towards larger households.

Farmers' benefits from export production

To investigate the impact of the above described changes in the sector on the well-being of households in the region, we looked at how contract farming and wage employment in the green bean export industry had contributed to household income. We compared income for four groups of households: (i) households which did not participate in green bean export production (159); (ii) households which were employed in the green bean agri-industry (82); (iii) households which currently cultivated green beans on contract with an exporting firm (35); and (iv) households which participated through both contract farming and wage employment (24).

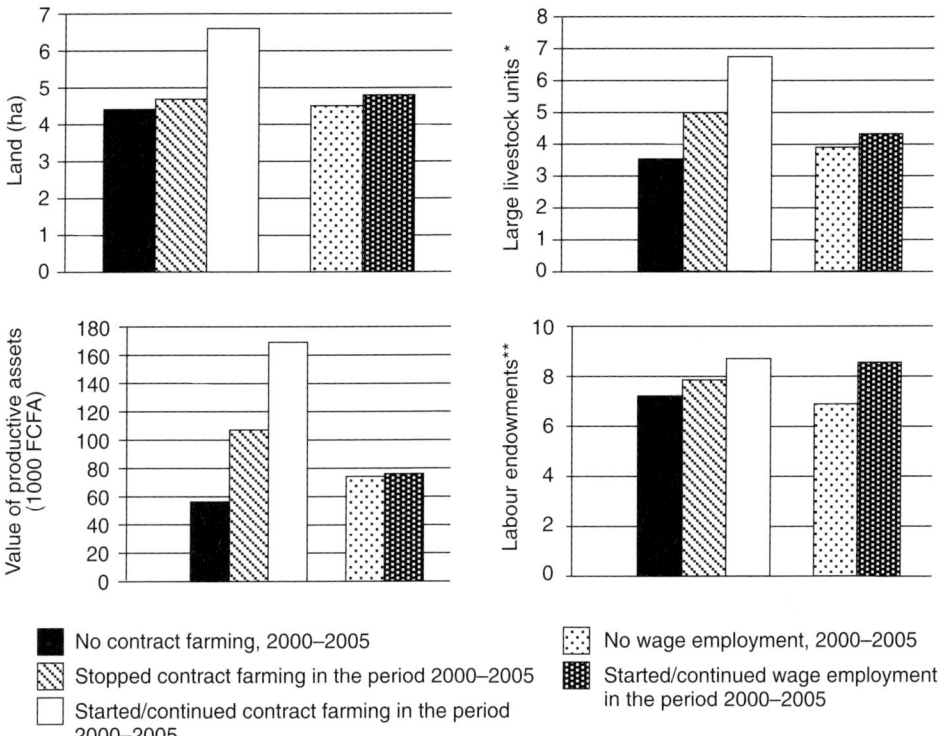

Fig. 13.4. Asset position in 2000 for households which stopped, started or continued contract farming and households which started wage employment in the agri-industry in the period 2000–2005 (calculated from survey data). * 1 large livestock unit = 1 cow or horse, 0.8 donkey and 0.2 sheep or goat. ** Labour endowments are all household members between the ages of 12 and 60 years who are physically able to work.

The figures in Table 13.4 indicate that household income is almost twice as high for households which engage in wage employment in the green bean sector compared to that of households which do not participate in export production: 3.4 million FCFA compared with 1.7 million FCFA. Moreover, households producing green beans on contract have an income that is more than three times higher: 5.9 million FCFA.

These differences remain when we correct for the size of a household and look at per capita income. In addition, these results are corroborated by findings from regression models in which the differences in asset position between households are corrected for (see Maertens and Swinnen, 2006). So, high-value export production significantly contributes to household income, but significantly more so if households are involved through contract-farming in comparison with wage employment.

One of the main reasons farmers mention engaging in contract farming is the access to modern inputs and credit. Contracted farmers receive credit from the exporting firms – mainly in the form of seeds and other inputs, but sometimes also in cash. This in-kind and cash credit – with an average value of 293 thousand FCFA – is quite important. It compares to the average value of credit that contracted households are able to obtain from other sources – 333 thousand FCFA – and is much higher than the credit non-contracted households are able to obtain – 108 thousand FCFA on average.

Contract farmers not only receive credit from the companies they work with, they also have a better access to credit from other sources. Credit is an important constraint in the region. Thirty-two per cent of the farmers in the sample mentioned that access to credit is the main limitation they face in horticultural production for which input requirements at the beginning of the season are quite high. Hence, contract farming does not only contribute directly to income growth through participation in high-value export production; it also contributes indirectly through alleviating credit constraints for farmers.

The figures in Table 13.4 show that agriculture is by far the most important source of income for all types of households. Even for households working for a wage in the agri-exporting industry, agriculture remains the main source of income. It is striking that those households not only have a higher income from wage employment but also a higher agricultural income than households which do not participate in export production, despite the fact that they did not have significantly larger asset holdings. This indicates that wage employment in the agri-exporting industry has spillover effects on households' farm businesses, which could arise from technical and managerial spillovers as well as from earned wages in the agri-industry alleviating capital and credit constraints.

Summary

The survey data reveal that the benefits from contract farming in terms of higher income are substantial. Also, wage employment in the agri-exporting industry contributes to household income but to a lesser extent. Hence, the shift from procurement through contract farming towards vertically integrated production in agri-industrial estates has diminished the gains local farmers receive from export production. Yet, this shift has positive distributional consequences since poorer households – who face constraints to engage in contract farming – are involved in agri-industrial wage employment.

Conclusion

The export of FFV from Senegal to the EU has grown considerably during the past decade and has created opportunities for local farm households to engage in this high-value export production through contract farming with exporting companies or through agri-industrial wage employment. Our study shows that, in the region we

Table 13.4. Average total and per capita household income in from different sources (calculated from survey data). Italicized figures are an index, with households not participating in export production as the reference group.

Household category	Average household income (FCFA 1000)	Average per capita income income (FCFA 1000)	Sources of household income			
			Agri-culture (%)	Wage employ-ment (%)	Self-employ-ment (%)	Other sources (%)
Not participating in export production	1,716 *100*	132 *100*	76	4	14	6
Participating through wage employment	3,385 *197*	215 *163*	78	12	7	3
Participating through contract farming	5,794 *338*	595 *452*	84	2	9	5
Participating through contract farming and wage employment	5,303 *309*	425 *322*	81	10	5	5

investigated, a large share of rural households have become involved in this high-value production. Moreover, we find large benefits for farmers as contract production significantly contributes to higher incomes both directly and indirectly, through increasing access to modern inputs and credit.

During the past 5 years, tightening EU food standards and the increasing importance of private standards from large trading and retail companies have led to important structural changes in the export supply chain for FFV in Senegal. The sector had become increasingly concentrated, with smaller exporters – who face constraints in making the necessary investments for compliance with food standards – exiting the market.

In addition, the volume of FFV that is sourced from small farmers through contract farming has decreased enormously in favour of vertically integrated production in agri-industrial estates, which has substantially increased employment opportunities. The income effects are nuanced. Households whose contract had ended lost income. However, these losses are partially offset by income from employment in agri-industrial farms. Moreover, wage employment in the agri-industry is not biased towards richer households with more land, livestock and other assets while contract farming is. Hence, the overall welfare effects are complex and nuanced. The benefits from high-value export production for the local farmer population have decreased but are more equally distributed.

Our study empirically confirms the beneficial effect of vertical coordination in high-value supply chains, but it also provides evidence for the pertinent argument in the literature that the poorest farmers are excluded. Another insight is that the poorest may benefit more from employment on large industrial farms then from household contract farming. A mixed strategy of vertical coordination and estate farming (vertical integration) in high-value supply chains seems to be the most beneficial from a distributional point of view.

Notes

1. World FFV trade reached US$71.6 billion in 2001, an increase of 30% over 1990.
2. While fresh and processed fruit and vegetable products accounted for 17% of the total exports from developing countries in 1980/1981, this share increased to 22% in 2000/2001 despite a significant price decrease over the same period (Diop and Jaffee, 2005).
3. SEPAS: Syndicat des Exportateurs des Produits Agricoles.
4. ONAPES: Organisation National des Producteurs Exportateurs de Fruits et Légumes de Sénégal.
5. CDH: Centre pour le Développement de l'Horticulture; ISRA: Institut Sénégalais de Recherche Agricoles.
6. FCFA: Franc de la Communauté Française d'Afrique; the currency of the West African Economic and Monetary Union, pegged to the Euro at an exchange rate of 655.49 FCFA/Euro.
7. The EU has preferential trade agreements with Morocco under the Euro-Mediterranean Partnership.
8. It is very unlikely that the increasing price for green beans from Senegal indicates a cost disadvantage, as transport costs are substantially reduced with the shift from air cargo to maritime transport.
9. The label for Senegalese horticultural exports was validated within the project PPEA – Projet de Promotion des Exportations Agricoles, which was jointly financed by the government of Senegal and the World Bank.
10. The EU has started a procedure for the harmonization of the current legislation with respect to MRL in its member states, but this was not expected to be finalized before July 2006.
11. HACCP: Hazard Analysis and Critical Control Points.
12. In addition, smaller exporters have been included in the organization SEPAS since 1994.

References

Aksoy, M.A. and Beghin, J.C. (2005) *Global Agricultural Trade and Developing Countries*. World Bank, Washington, DC.

Augier, P., Gasiorek, M. and Lai Tong, C. (2005) The impact of rules of origin on trade flows. *Economic Policy* 20 (43), 567–623.

Brenton, P. and Manchin, M. (2002) *Making the EU Trade Agreements Work. The Role of Rules of Origin*. CEPS working document 183, Centre for European Policy Studies, Brussels.

Delgado, C. (1999) Sources of growth in smallholder agriculture in sub-Saharan Africa: the role of vertical integration of smallholders with processors and marketers of high-value-added items. *Agrekon* 38, 165–189.

Diop, N. and Jaffee, S.M. (2005) Fruits and vegetables: global trade and competition in fresh and processed product markets. In: Aksoy, M.A. and Beghin, J.C. (eds) *Global Agricultural Trade and Developing Countries*. World Bank, Washington, DC, pp. 237–257.

Dolan, C. and Humphrey, J. (2000) Governance and trade in fresh vegetables: the impact of UK supermarkets on the African horticulture industry. *Journal of Development Studies* 37 (2), 147–176.

Eurostat (2005) Statistical web site, http://epp.eurostat.cec.eu.int/portal/ (accessed 15 December 2005).

Farina, E.M.M.Q. and Reardon, T. (2000) Agrifood grades and standards in the extended Mercosur: their role in the changing agrifood system. *American Journal of Agricultural Economics* 82 (5) 1170–1176.

Gibbon, P. (2003) Value-chain governance, public regulation and entry barriers in the global fresh fruit and vegetable chain into the EU. *Development Policy Review* 21 (5/6), 615–625.

Humphrey, J., McCulloch, N. and Ota, M. (2004) The impact of European market changes on employment in the Kenyan horticulture sector. *Journal of International Development* 16 (1), 63–80.

Key, N. and Runsten, D. (1999) Contract farming, smallholders, and rural development in Latin America: the organization of agroprocessing firms and the scale of outgrower production. *World Development* 27 (2), 381–401.

Kherralah, M. (2000) Access of smallholder farmers to the fruits and vegetables market in Kenya, IFPRI, Washington, DC, mimeo.

Kirsten, J. and Sartorius, K. (2002) Linking agribusiness and small-scale farmers in developing countries: is there a new role for contract farming? *Development Southern Africa* 19 (4), 503–529.

Maertens, M. and Swinnen, J.F.M. (2006) Trade, Standards and Poverty: Evidence from Senegal. LICOS Discussion Paper, Centre for Transition Economics, Leuven, Belgium.

Minot, N. and Ngigi, M. (2004) *Are Horticultural Exports a Replicable Success Story? Evidence from Kenya and Côte d'Ivoire*. EPTD/MTID discussion paper, IFPRI, Washington, DC.

Minten, B., Randrianarison, L. and Swinnen, J. (2006) *Global Retail Chains and Poor Farmers: Evidence from Madagascar*. LICOS Discussion Papers 164/2006, Leuven, Belgium (http://www.econ.kuleuven.be/LICOS/DP/dp.htm).

Reardon, T. and Barrett, C.B. (2000) Agroindustrialisation, globalization and international development: an overview of issues, patterns and determinants. *Agricultural Economics* 23, 195–205.

Reardon, T. and Berdegué, J. (2002) The rapid rise of supermarkets in Latin America: challenges and opportunities for development. *Development Policy Review* 20 (4), 371–388.

Reardon, T. and Swinnen, J.F.M. (2004) Agrifood sector liberalization and the rise of supermarkets in former state-controlled economies: a comparative overview. *Development Policy Review* 22 (5), 515–523.

Reardon, T., Codron, J.M., Busch, L., Bingen, J. and Harris, C. (1999) Global change in agrifood grades and standards: agribusiness strategic responses in developing countries. *International Food and Agribusiness Management Review* 2 (3), 421–435.

Reardon, T., Timmer, C.P., Barrett, C. and Berdegué, J. (2003) The rise of supermarkets in Africa, Asia, and Latin America. *American Journal Agricultural Economics* 85 (5), 1140–1146.

Unnevehr, L.J. (2000) Food safety issues and fresh food product exports from LDCs. *Agricultural Economics* 23 (3), 231–240.

Weatherspoon, D.D. and Reardon, T. (2003) The rise of supermarkets in Africa: implications for agrifood systems and the rural poor. *Development Policy Review* 21 (3), 333–356.

Weatherspoon, D., Cacho, J. and Christy R. (2001) Linking globalization, economic growth and poverty: impacts of agribusiness strategies on Sub-Saharan Africa. *American Journal of Agricultural Economics* 83 (3), 722–729.

The Former Soviet Union

14 Transformation and Contracting in the Supply Chains of the former Soviet Union: Evidence from Armenia, Georgia, Moldova, Russia and Ukraine

M. Gorton and J. White

Introduction

Restructuring and privatization in the Commonwealth of Independent States (CIS) has led to the separation of many previously horizontally and vertically integrated enterprises, together with the emergence of *de novo* businesses. Enterprises have had to forge their own relationships with buyers and suppliers in an environment of both: (i) weak public institutions for enforcing contractual obligations and property rights; and (ii) a high level of macroeconomic instability.

These problems have been identified as being impediments to growth with the dislocation to, and failure of, inter-enterprise relationships being a causal factor in the falls in the quantity and quality of output witnessed in the early years of transition (Blanchard and Kremer, 1997; Gow and Swinnen, 2001).

With the break-up of former state and collective farms, established food processors in the CIS lost guaranteed, state-directed supplies and demand. Food processors have had to institute their own relationships to effectively procure agricultural raw materials. In meeting this challenge processing enterprises can source farm level output through three main mechanisms: spot markets, vertical ownership integration or contracting. Spot markets, such as livestock auctions and commodity exchanges, are governed by immediate market transactions with no pre- or post-purchase commitments held by buyers or suppliers. Buyers have no prior involvement in terms of what is produced, when it is available for sale or the means of production.

Vertical ownership integration refers to arrangements where at least two stages of the same supply chain are owned by the same actor, e.g. a milk processor that also owns a dairy farm. In between these two extremes are various forms of vertical coordination, of which contracting is the most common, where buyers and suppliers remain as distinct, separate actors but agricultural production is supervised to meet pre-arranged terms.

Contracting is therefore an intermediate institutional arrangement which gives buyers the ability to influence and partially control the production process without owning or managing farms directly (Key and Runsten, 1999). It seeks to solve the problem of securing more reliable supplies at a level of quality that is acceptable to the processor without resorting to ownership integration, which may place too high a demand on the firm's capital and management capabilities.

Contracts may take a number of forms, ranging from solely *market specification* (an agreement by a buyer to purchase a seller's output) to more complex arrangements which are *resource providing*. In the latter case, the buyer provides goods and/or services to the farmer: for example, credit, physical inputs and technical advice. These goods and services can be collectively termed *contract support measures* and, in return for their provision, buyers typically specify tighter quality thresholds.

Contracting appears to be the favoured mechanism of many large food and agribusiness companies in the region and the introduction of contracting has been linked to significant improvements in productivity (Gow *et al.*, 2000). However, while case study evidence points to the potential role of contracting as an engine for growth in agri-food supply chains (Gow *et al.*, 2000; Gorton *et al.*, 2006), there is a lack of systematic evidence on its impact.

Notwithstanding some notable exceptions (Dries and Swinnen, 2004), scant attention has been paid to the impact of contracting and contract support measures on product quality, despite the latter being widely seen as a major barrier inhibiting international competitiveness in the region (Strokov and Meyers, 1996; Keyser, 2004). In fact, as Ioffe and Nefedova (2001) note for Russia, there is a dearth of information on how processors are reconfiguring their relationships with farmers. This chapter analyses the use and determinants of contracting and contract support measures, and changes in the quality of raw materials procured, over a 6-year time period (1997–2003) for a sample of food processing enterprises in the CIS.

The chapter is divided into five sections. The next section outlines the dataset used in the analysis and discusses how companies were selected. Section 3 presents descriptive statistics on the use of contracting and contract support measures, relationships with small farms and product quality. Determinants of the use of contracting and contract support measures are explored in 4. Conclusions are presented in the final section.

Methodology

To analyse the use and determinants of contracting and contract support measures, data was collected from food processing enterprises using a standardized survey instrument. As the survey was concerned with the impact of contracting and contract support measures, which are not common to all enterprises, purposive sampling was employed. Purposive sampling can be defined as the selection of cases 'from which the most can be learned' (Merriam, 1998, p. 61). Respondents that are best able to offer insight into the factors of interest are chosen (Churchill, 1999). In this case, only respondents that met three criteria were selected:

- Senior executives of agri-food industry enterprises (excluding micro-enterprises and those that had just been established);
- Enterprises that had made recent capital investments in the agri-food sector; and
- Enterprises that had contracted with farmers for some part of the period 1997–2003.

These criteria were designed to ensure that the sample contained companies that were engaged in activities that the study sought to understand and evaluate. Local researchers, who checked that potential respondents met the criteria listed above, drew up a quota of 12 companies per country.

For each country a target of four milk

processors, four plant-based enterprises (sugar, milling, fruit, etc.) and four value-added companies (reflecting products of national importance that varied between states such as wine, brandy and speciality cheeses) was set. This division was designed to pick up on sub-sector differences and reflect the broad balance of the agri-food sectors in the countries studied. In subsequent analysis, companies were divided into six sub-sectors: liquid milk dairies, speciality dairies, fruit and vegetables, sugar, wine and brandy, and other. Data were collected through face-to-face interviews.

The survey instrument contained both open and closed questions. Numerical data were obtained on company performance and background characteristics, the value of capital investments, contract relationships with farmers, the impact of contracting, quality standards and contract breaches. To analyse dynamics, data were collected for 4 years over a 6-year time period (1997, 1999, 2001 and 2003). The year 1997 was chosen as the starting point, as the privatization of major food processing plants began in most CIS states in the mid-1990s. The last year for which data were collected (2003) represented the final year for which full financial data were available at the time of the study (2004).

The sample of 60 enterprises, in 2003, collectively accounted for 18,556 employees and had a combined turnover of US$215.6 million. The mean level of employment and turnover for the sample was 309 full-time equivalents and US$3.6 million per annum, respectively (see Table 14.1).

While it is recognized, therefore, that the sample is relatively small and excludes micro-businesses and very recent start-ups, it does capture some of the largest food processors in the region, which are major players in the markets in which they operate. What these companies are doing matters greatly for understanding industry dynamics, and our knowledge of how agriculture-food processor relationships are evolving in the CIS has, to date, been severely limited.

Descriptive Statistics on Sourcing Strategies, Contract Support Measures, Procurement from Small Farms and Product Quality

Sources of supply

Table 14.2 details the different sources of supply utilized by processors in the four years 1997, 1999, 2001 and 2003. The number of enterprises using a particular potential relationship to source farm-level output is reported and the valid percentage figure corrects for missing data for earlier years in a small number of cases. Small farms are distinguished and are defined as producers with less than 1 ha of land or, for the dairy sector, less than five cows.

Table 14.2 reveals that the use of all potential channels for sourcing agricultural raw materials increased over the period 1997–2003. This reflects the impact of macroeconomic recovery and the overall growth in demand during this period and the consequent requirement to source more raw materials.

The greatest growth has been recorded for contracting with larger farmers (from 42.3

Table 14.1. Sample characteristics by country.

Country	Sample size	Mean employment (2003)	Mean turnover (US$, 2003)
Armenia	12	134	3,305,602
Georgia	12	527	1,460,057
Moldova	12	259	3,678,057
Russia	12	218	1,808,042
Ukraine	12	409	7,712,667
Total	60	309	3,592,885

Table 14.2. Use of potential supply relationships in sourcing agricultural raw materials (1997–2003).

	1997		1999		2001		2003	
	n	Valid (%)	n	Valid (%)	n	Valid (%)	n	Valid (%)
Spot markets								
All	22	44.0	24	46.2	28	48.2	31	52.5
With small farmers	23	44.2	23	44.2	27	45.8	30	50.0
With larger farmers	10	19.6	15	28.3	16	27.6	15	25.4
Contracts								
All	24	46.2	35	66.0	44	74.6	47	78.4
With small farmers	19	35.8	22	40.7	25	42.4	27	45.0
With larger farmers	22	42.3	34	63.0	42	71.2	45	75.0
Own farms	4	7.5	5	9.3	10	17.2	15	25.0
Other agents	10	18.5	18	32.7	29	49.2	30	50.0

to 75% of the sample), using other agents and own farms, albeit the last is from a low base. More enterprises have contracts with larger farms than with small farms, but the reverse is true for sourcing from spot markets, where relationships with small farms are more prevalent. Between 1999 and 2003 there was relatively little change in the number of enterprises using spot markets as a source of supply, with a slight decline in the number of processors using spot markets with larger farms in 2003 compared to 2001.

These figures would suggest significant reforms are occurring in farmer–processor relationships: contracting is becoming more prevalent, especially with larger farmers; the use of spot markets as a source of supply is stagnating and the use of other agents such as intermediaries and traders increasing. One-quarter of the sample was also engaged in farming in 2003 and most of this vertical ownership integration occurred recently: in 1997 only four respondents reported that their enterprise also had farming operations.

Contract support measures

In agriculture, commonly found contract support measures include credit, technical assistance and the provision of physical inputs (Goodhue et al., 2003). Table 14.3 details the distribution and mean impact of contract support measures on farm performance. Measures are listed in descending order of frequency, with the most popular measures applied being prompt payments, transportation and monetary credit.[1] One-third of the sample also provided physical inputs to at least some of the farms that supplied them. Investment loans from processors to farmers were provided infrequently.

The vast majority of the contract support measures have been introduced for proactive reasons, to improve processors' control over the quality and quantity of raw materials available for procurement. Contracting and contract support measures have therefore attempted to deal with the transition-specific problems related to the dislocation of food supply chains in an environment of, post-1999, rising demand within the CIS.

Regarding those firms that apply a specific measure, the mean percentage of farms that received that measure in the first year of its operation, and the mean percentage of farms that had access to the measure at the time of the study, are detailed in the fourth and fifth columns of Table 14.3, respectively. The sixth column of Table 14.3 presents the percentage of processors that operate a minimum farm size policy in offering a particular measure. These figures give an insight into the diffusion of measures and whether small farms are being excluded. Measures such

Table 14.3. Distribution and impact of contract support measures.

Measure	Distribution of support measures to farms				Impacts of specific contract support measures on farms			
	Firms offering support measure (n)	Proportion of sample offering support (%)	Mean of farms offered support to in 1st year (%)	Mean of farms offered support at time of study (2004, (%))	Firms operating minimum farm size for measure (%)	Mean change in farm yields due to measures (%)	Change in farm output reaching higher standard (%)	Change in farm output reaching basic standard (%)
Prompt payments	28	46.7	88.0	84.5	3.7	11.4	12.0	2.1
Transportation	27	45.0	64.2	69.6	46.2	6.8	5.7	3.5
Credit	23	38.3	39.8	50.9	60.8	9.3	8.8	3.0
Physical inputs	20	33.3	48.2	51.2	57.9	12.4	14.2	3.5
Quality control	19	31.7	76.8	79.4	15.8	7.6	17.2	5.6
Guaranteed prices	14	23.3	86.7	91.7	14.3	11.1	8.9	1.1
Agronomic support	13	21.7	82.0	84.5	8.3	6.5	5.0	1.4
Farm loan guarantees	11	18.3	7.0	15.1	27.3	6.8	6.0	0.0
Machinery	10	16.7	19.4	30.5	60.0	5.0	4.0	5.2
Specialist storage	9	15.0	32.8	32.9	33.0	10.0	8.3	4.4
Harvest/handling	7	11.8	30.6	18.6	71.4	9.3	5.4	2.6
Market access	6	10.0	68.3	69.7	0.0	11.2	14.2	2.0
Business/financial management	6	10.0	45.8	47.5	50.0	6.2	4.2	2.5
Veterinary support	5	8.3	58.0	66.0	40.0	17.0	17.0	0.0
Investment loans	4	6.7	4.0	0.3	75.0	5.5	5.0	2.5
Average						9.1	9.5	2.9

as agronomic support, guaranteed prices and prompt payments are typically applied to the vast majority of farms with which a processor deals. Support measures such as investment loans and the provision of machinery are more selectively applied. Around 60% of processors that offer credit and physical inputs had a minimum farm size below which they did not offer these supports.

Regarding diffusion, of the 15 possible support measures listed in Table 14.3, in only three cases is the mean percentage of farms to which the measure is currently offered lower than in the first year that the measure was introduced.[2] This suggests that measures tend to be offered to more farms over time rather than assistance becoming more selective.

The last three columns of Table 14.3 report the mean percentage change in farm level yields, percentage of output that reaches higher standards and the percentage change in the amount of output meeting basic standards attributable to each support measure as judged by respondents.

The support measures with the largest impact on yields are the provision of specialist storage, veterinary support and physical inputs, followed by a set of market measures (prompt payments, guaranteed prices and market access). Each of these measures is credited with increasing yields by over 10%. Specialist storage in the form of on-farm cooling tanks has been particularly important in raising yields and quality in the dairy sector, a trend also noted in Poland by Dries and Swinnen (2004).

In raising standards, a major challenge in the region is to preserve better the quality of what is already produced. In the dairy sector the lack of effective cooling facilities rapidly decreases the value of milk produced and, in the arable sector, post-harvest losses through inappropriate storage have eroded competitiveness (Striewe, 1999). Investment in farm-level production will generate poor returns if the effective means to store output prior to processing are absent.

The impact of investment loans has been modest and this may explain why the number of farms to which this support is offered has been falling. The provision of physical inputs has had an above-average impact on yields and quality and has been more successful in inducing improvements than credit. This may reflect how credit can more easily be diverted to other, non-farm activities and be difficult to monitor (Gow and Swinnen, 2001). Both public and private sector support in the region has suffered from credit being diverted from the intended uses. Programmes that improve market access and the dissemination of veterinary and quality control advice appear to have more beneficial effects on yields and quality and are easier to monitor.

In terms of raising the quality of output, particularly the percentage of output reaching higher standards, the most beneficial measures have been quality control, veterinary support, physical inputs, market access and prompt payments. Premiums, which are linked to access to higher-value-added markets, are an important element in stimulating improvements in quality at the farm level.

Access to value-added markets depends on both demand on the domestic market and export opportunities. In countries with restricted local purchasing power, such as Moldova, access to higher-value-added markets will principally depend on international trade. Quality improvements are also linked to a set of market measures – in particular, prompt payments and guaranteed prices.

Cash flow is a major concern and some of the implications of delayed payments on the viability of agri-food supply chains in the CIS have been discussed elsewhere (Swinnen, 2005). Support measures have had less impact on the amount of farm-level output that reaches basic standards, as most farm output already passes this threshold.

Procurement from small farms

To investigate whether small farms are being excluded from food supply chains, the survey solicited information on the share of agricultural raw materials procured from small farms by each processor during the period 1997–2003. Similar data were collected regarding the total number of small farms that each processor dealt with during this era. Small farms, as discussed above, were defined as producers with less than 1 ha of land or, for the dairy sector, less than five milking cows.

From these questions it is possible to analyse how the share of total agricultural raw materials sourced by processors from small farms has changed since 1997, together with an assessment of the number of small farms with which they have a relationship (see Table 14.4).[3] A comparison is also drawn for the years 2001–2003 only, to identify the most recent trends.

For the period 1997–2003, Table 14.4 indicates that for just over one-third of enterprises, the share of agricultural raw materials sourced from small farms declined, with an increase registered in about one-quarter of respondents' businesses. Twelve firms reported no change and 11 have never dealt with small farmers. In terms of the number of small farms dealt with, however, the majority reported an increase. This increase in most cases was due to political reforms (land reform and decollectivization) rather than to processors' strategies.

For example, ten out of the 12 companies surveyed in Moldova reported an increase in the number of small farms they dealt with over the period 1997–2003. During this period, Moldova implemented a radical National Land Programme that saw the break-up of former state and collective farms, with distribution of land and physical assets to members (Csaki and Lerman, 2002).

Only 13 of the enterprises reported that they dealt with fewer small farms in 2003 than in 1997, and three indicated no change over this time period. This implies that there are a number of processors that, while the share of agricultural raw materials sourced from small farms is declining, are none the less dealing with more small farms. For the 2001–2003 period, slightly fewer processors recorded a growth in the number of small farm suppliers and this may reflect some consolidation. Overall, there is a lack of evidence of small farms being formally excluded but, as demonstrated in Table 14.3, they do have poorer access to some contract support measures such as credit and physical inputs.

Product quality

For the years 1997, 1999, 2001 and 2003, dairies were asked to indicate the percentage of milk delivered to them that was extra class, first class, second class and rejected/unusable. Enterprises without dairy operations were asked, for the same years, to indicate the percentage of agricultural raw materials supplied to them that was of premium quality, acceptable quality and rejected/unusable.

From these figures it is possible to assess broad changes in the quality of farm produce supplied to processors. An improvement

Table 14.4. Change in share of agricultural raw materials sourced from small farms and number of small farms dealt with by processors.

	Change in share of agricultural raw material sourced from small farms				Change in number of small farms dealt with			
	1997–2003		2001–2003		1997–2003		2001–2003	
	n	%	n	%	n	%	n	%
Decrease	22	36.7	18	30.0	13	21.7	11	18.3
No change	12	20.0	20	33.3	3	5.0	8	13.3
Increase	15	25.0	9	15.0	33	55.0	28	46.7
Never deal with small farmers	11	18.3	13	21.7	11	18.3	13	21.7
Total	60	100.0	60	100.0	60	100.0	60	100.0

indicates that a greater proportion of produce fell into premium/extra class categories with less being deemed unusable or rejected.[4] Table 14.5 reveals that the majority of firms reported an improvement in the quality of farm-level produce supplied to them; 16 reported that quality worsened, with seven enterprises indicating no change.

It is possible to look at the linkage between product quality data and contracting in two ways. First, are there significant differences between the firms that report improved, unchanged and worsened product quality and the percentage of agricultural raw materials procured using contracts? Secondly, one would expect an improvement in product quality to be associated with the use of the contract assistance measures detailed in Table 14.3.

The last two columns of Table 14.5 reveal that there are significant differences between firms that report improved, unchanged and worsened product quality on both these measures. Processors that reported an improvement in the quality of agricultural raw materials supplied to them procure a greater proportion using contracts.

On average, those that have witnessed an improvement in farm-level product quality procure 56.5% of agricultural raw materials using contracts, compared to only 30.3% for those that have suffered from worsening product quality. A significant difference is also apparent regarding the mean number of contract assistance measures employed (based on the 15 possible assistance measures listed in Table 14.3) and product quality. The mean number of contract assistance measures employed by firms that have witnessed improved product quality is 4.24, compared to 2.00 and 1.86, respectively, for those that recorded a decline and no change.

Econometric Analysis

Models

Given that processors that have witnessed improvements in the quality of farm-level raw materials that they procure source significantly more using contracts and use a greater number of contract support measures, the determinants of the use of contracting and contract support measures have been assessed in further detail. Two models were investigated, with the dependent variable for the first (Model 2.1) being $CONTSH_{it}$ – the percentage of total supply procured via contracts with farmers for firm i in year t ($t = 1997, \ldots 2003$).

This percentage has been employed elsewhere (Katchova and Miranda, 2004; Morrison Paul et al., 2004) as a measure of the intensity of contracting. As this variable is not continuous but censored at the lower and upper limits (values can take any value within a range from 0 to 100), a censored (Tobit) regression was applied (Greene, 2000). The two-limit Tobit model assumes that a latent variable y^* can be expressed as:

$$y^* = \beta'x + \varepsilon, \varepsilon \sim N(\mu, \sigma^2) \qquad (2.1)$$

where

Table 14.5. Relationship between contracting and product quality.

Change in product quality supplied	n	%	Raw material bought using contracts in 2003 (%)	Mean number of contract support measures used
Worse	16	26.7	30.3	2.00
No change	7	11.7	37.9	1.86
Improvement	37	61.7	56.5	4.24
Total	60	100.0	47.4	3.37
F-test (ANOVA comparison of means)			3.014*	6.195**

* 10% level of significance; ** 1% level of significance.

$$y = L_1 \text{ if } y^* \leq L_1, y = y^*$$
$$\text{if } L_1 \leq y^* \leq L_2, y = L_2 \text{ if } y^* \geq L_2. \quad (2.2)$$

In our case, y^* represents the censored dependent variable (contract intensity), x is a vector of independent explanatory variables, $L_1 = 0$ is the lower limit (no farm-level input bought on contract), $L_2 = 100$ the upper limit (all supplies from farmers sourced via contracts), and ϵ the error term with mean μ and constant variance σ^2. The likelihood function for the model (Greene, 2000; Kosarek et al., 2001) is:

$$L(\beta, \sigma, y, x, L_1, L_2) = \prod_{y=L_1} \Phi\left(\frac{L_1 - \beta'x}{\sigma}\right)$$
$$\prod_{y=y^*} \frac{1}{\sigma} \phi\left(\frac{y - \beta'x}{\sigma}\right) \quad (2.3)$$
$$\prod_{y=L_2} \left[1 - \Phi\left(\frac{L_2 - \beta'x}{\sigma}\right)\right]$$

The parameter estimates β and σ, which are derived from maximizing the logarithm of Equation 2.2, characterize the variability of the dependent variable.

Five independent variables were included in the model. *SIZE* is the annual turnover of the food processing enterprise, expressed in US$1000, and was expected to have a positive sign, as contracting has been associated with larger firms in Western markets (Katchova and Miranda, 2004). *FDI* is the percentage of the firm's equity owned by foreign investors and was expected to have a positive sign.

Case study evidence from Central and Eastern Europe (Gow and Swinnen, 2001) and developing countries (Singh, 2002) has highlighted that foreign investors often act as catalysts for the introduction of contracting. A dummy variable was included for each *country*, with Russia the reference category. Russia was selected as the reference country as it is supposed that contracting is less prominent in this particular state due to the slowness of land reform and rural privatization, and the constraints that remain on transactions (Lerman and Shagaida, 2005).

Dummies were also included for *subsector* (liquid milk, speciality dairy, fruit and vegetables, wine and brandy, other products, with sugar set as the reference category) and *year* (1999–2003). A distinction was made between those dairies specializing in pasteurizing liquid milk and speciality dairies (ice cream, cheese, etc.), as it was expected that they would have different supply relationships. Sugar was chosen as a reference category to test the hypothesis that contracting is more developed in that industry (Gow et al., 2000).

To evaluate the determinants of the use of contract support measures a second regression model (2.2) was estimated, with the dependent variable being $CONTSUP_{it}$ – the number of contract support measures offered to farmers by firm i in year t (t = 1997 ... 2003). As the lower tail of the number of contract support measures employed is bounded by 0, Tobit was also applied in this case. The same independent variables were included in the model as in the case of $CONTSH_{it}$.

Given a total of 60 firms with data for 4 years, 240 data points were potentially available for analysis. However, due to missing data, there were 196 useable observations.

The software package LIMDEP was employed in undertaking the analysis. The Tobit maximum likelihood estimates and their corresponding marginal effects are presented in Table 14.6 for both models. The marginal effects measure the effects of a one-unit change in the independent variables on the dependent (i.e. the percentage of farm level input bought on contract), given the censoring of the dependent variable.

Results

Reviewing the regression results presented in Table 14.6, *SIZE* has a positive effect on both contract intensity (the percentage of supply secured via contracts) and the number of contract support measures

Table 14.6. Tobit analysis of contracting intensity and number of contract support measures employed (data from authors' calculations).

Variable	Model 2.1 (Contract intensity)			Model 2.2 (No. of contract support measures)		
	B	Standard error	Marginal effects	β	Standard error	Marginal effects
Intercept	24.6165	12.2954		−0.23785	0.1149	
SIZE	0.0035***	0.0012	0.0018	0.0002***	0.0000	0.0001
FDI	0.2072	0.2020	0.1060	0.3412***	0.0087	0.0227
Armenia	19.4066	16.1051	9.9315	2.4709***	0.6642	1.6413
Georgia	−11.3680	15.5834	−5.8177	3.3581***	0.6902	2.2306
Moldova	13.0318	15.1995	6.6691	3.7876***	0.6547	2.5159
Ukraine	−65.7150***	16.3210	−33.6303	−2.4294***	0.6828	−1.6137
Liquid milk	25.1111**	12.2396	12.8509	−1.4799**	0.5372	−0.9830
Speciality dairy	−11.9081	18.1559	−6.0941	−1.7632*	0.7743	−1.1712
Wine and brandy	−18.9095	17.4844	−9.6771	−3.4165***	0.7598	−2.2694
Fruit and vegetables	−33.6616*	18.1862	−17.2267	−3.2211***	0.7822	−2.1396
Other sub-sector	−31.8120*	12.3710	−16.2801	−6.5632***	0.9616	−4.3595
Year99	28.7244**	13.4275	14.7000	2.1758***	0.5862	1.4453
Year01	43.4155***	13.6624	20.2889	3.4097***	0.5912	2.2649
Year03	49.2256***	13.8940	25.1917	4.0034***	0.6014	2.6592
Log-likelihood	−725.52			−408.36		

* 10% significance level; ** 5% significance level; *** 1% significance level.

employed. The positive relationship between SIZE and contract intensity is in line with expectations based on studies of Western agri-food markets (Katchova and Miranda, 2004). FDI is positively related to the number of contract support measures employed but has no significant effect on contract intensity.

The level of contracting is significantly lower in the Ukraine. The dummies for Armenia, Georgia and Moldova for the contract intensity model are not significant. However, the dummies for the latter three countries are significant and positive for the model of the number of contract support measures employed. In contrast, the dummy for the Ukraine is significantly negative.

In other words, the use of contract support measures is significantly more developed in Armenia, Georgia and Moldova as compared to the situation in Russia and Ukraine. The former group of countries has seen a greater penetration of FDI (Krkoska, 2001) and, if foreign investors often act as catalysts for the introduction of contracting (Gow and Swinnen, 2001) and use significantly more contract support measures, domestic firms wishing to protect their supply base have to respond by improving the terms that they offer farmers. This represents an important spillover effect of FDI and it is noticeable that the worst deal for farmers, with endemic late payment and minimal contract support – as in provincial Russia – is where FDI in the agri-food sector has been absent.[5]

Regarding the sub-sectors, contract intensity is significantly higher for liquid milk. This may be as expected given that regular deliveries of milk on a daily basis are critical for these companies. Differences between the coefficients for liquid milk and speciality dairies, regarding contract intensity, justify their separation in the analysis. Contract intensity is significantly lower, albeit at a 10% level of significance, in the fruit and vegetables and other sub-sectors.

The use of contract support measures is most developed in the sugar industry and, as with contract intensity, least used in the other sub-sector. The use of contract support measures is also relatively low in the wine and brandy and fruit and vegetables sub-sectors. The latter reflects how much of the fruit and vegetable processing in the CIS is low-value added, often accepting produce that is unsuitable for, or left over from, fresh sales (IFC, 2003).

Analysing the year coefficients, it is evident that both contract intensity and the number of contract enforcement measures employed grew strongly during the period 1997–2003. All bar one of the year coefficients are significant at the 1% level. This provides clear evidence that contract intensity and the use of contract support measures have grown significantly.

Conclusions

Based on the survey findings of key food processors in the FSU, both farm-processor contracting and the use of contract support measures have become more prevalent in the CIS since the mid-1990s. These private sector-led reforms have been implemented to deal with dysfunctional supply chains that operated in an environment of protected domestic markets and rising local demand. The implementation of contracting and contract support measures has, overall, had a significant and positive impact on the twin problems of poor product quality and low yields.

This is an important finding because of the role these factors have played in inhibiting the international competitiveness of CIS agriculture (Strokov and Meyers, 1996; Keyser, 2004). However, while support from processors for farmers has become more prevalent, it may not always be so in future, particularly if output rises appreciably, quality problems are rectified and agricultural markets become saturated.

The degree to which contract support measures have stimulated improvements in yields and the quality of output has been far from uniform. Of particular importance for support agencies is how investment loans and machinery grants, while being the mainstays of many private and public sector development projects, have had only a modest impact on yields and product quality. The provision of specialist storage (especially cooling tanks in the dairy sector), veterinary support, prompt payments, guaranteed prices and physical inputs have all had a greater impact on yields and product quality.

The Tobit analysis reveals that foreign investors use significantly more contract support measures than their domestic counterparts and this relationship holds even when size and sub-sector are accounted for. In this regard, foreign investors are important catalysts and it is noticeable that contracting is more developed in the three states with the highest level of foreign penetration.

An important spillover effect of FDI has been that domestically owned firms, to protect their supply base, have had to improve the terms and conditions they offer farmers. While this may not always be the case, particularly if one foreign investor gains a monopoly position, it is noticeable that farmers currently receiving the worst terms from buyers are located in areas where FDI has been entirely absent.

One often-expressed concern of contracting is that it can lead to the marginalization of small farms (Escobal et al., 2000). The marginalization of small farms can be considered in two main ways. First, marginalization can be defined in terms of an exclusion of small farms from formal food supply chains and, secondly, small farms may, although not formally excluded, receive significantly worse terms and conditions. In terms of the former, there is little evidence that small farms are being excluded but there is some evidence regarding the latter, particularly concerning access to contract support measures such as credit and physical inputs. However, contract support measures have, overall, become available to an increasing number of farmers after their introduction rather than support becoming progressively more selective.

To date, there is thus little indication that the introduction of contract support measures per se reduces overall farm access to inputs and technical advice. Taken together, therefore, the evidence presented here suggests that the growth of contracting and employment of contracting support measures has, to date, been beneficial in tackling the twin problems of poor yields and quality. These impacts on yields and quality are of particular importance, as they are the two most commonly cited barriers to improving the international competitiveness of the CIS agri-food sector.

Acknowledgements

The research undertaken for this chapter was funded by the World Bank as part of a wider study on vertical coordination in ECA agri-food chains as an Engine of Private Sector Development: Implications for Policy and Bank Operations (Contract Nos 7615040/7620016). Data were collected by: Naira Mkrtchyan and Vahe Heboyan (Armenia), Alexander Didebulidze (Georgia), Mikhail Dumitrashko and Anatolie Ignat (Moldova), Alexander Yermolov (Russia) and Alexander Skripnik (Ukraine). Their assistance is gratefully acknowledged.

Notes

1 While it may be expected that all processors say that they offer prompt payments to farmers, none of the Russian firms included in the study reported that they apply this measure.
2 The three cases where the mean has fallen are: investment loans, harvesting and handling support and prompt payments. The first two are capital-intensive measures and the fall in the percentage of farms to which prompt payments are offered is slight.
3 If data were not available for 1997, the assessment was made on the difference between the least recent year for which information was available and the figures for 2003.
4 The comparison was made for 1997–2003. If data for 1997 were not available, the comparison was made for 1999 with 2003.
5 For example, none of the Russian food processors in the sample said that they offered prompt payments to any of the farms which supplied them.

References

Blanchard, O. and Kremer, M. (1997) Disorganization. *Quarterly Journal of Economics* 112 (4), 1091–1126.
Churchill, G.A. (1999) *Marketing Research: Methodological foundations.* Dryden Press, Orlando, California.
Csaki, C. and Lerman, Z. (2002) Land reform and farm restructuring in Moldova: a real breakthrough? *Problems of Post-Communism* 49 (1), 42–52.
Dries, L. and Swinnen, J.F.M. (2004) Foreign direct investment, vertical integration and local suppliers: evidence from the Polish dairy sector. *World Development* 32 (9), 1525–1544.
Escobal, J., Agreda, V. and Reardon, T. (2000) Endogenous institutional innovation and agroindustrialization on the Peruvian coast. *Agricultural Economics* 23 (3), 267–277.
Goodhue, R.E., Heien, D.M., Lee, H. and Sumner, D.A. (2003) Contracts and quality in the California winegrape industry. *Review of Industrial Organization* 23 (3/4), 267–282.
Gorton, M., Dumitrashko, M. and White, J. (2006) Overcoming supply chain failure in the agri-food sector: a case study from Moldova. *Food Policy* 31 (1), 90–103.
Gow, H.R. and Swinnen, J.F.M. (2001) Private enforcement capital and contract enforcement in transitional economies. *American Journal of Agricultural Economics* 83 (3), 686–690.
Gow, H.R., Streeter, D.H. and Swinnen, J.F.M. (2000) How private contract enforcement mechanisms can succeed where public institutions fail: the case of Juhocukor a.s. *Agricultural Economics* 23 (3), 253–265.
Greene, W.H. (2000) *Econometric Analysis*, 4th edn., Prentice Hall, London.
IFC (2003) *Summary of the Russian Agribusiness Sector.* IFC, Moscow.
Ioffe, G. and Nefedova, T. (2001) Russian agriculture and food processing: vertical cooperation and spatial dynamics. *Europe–Asia Studies* 53 (3), 389–418.
Katchova, A.I. and Miranda, M.J. (2004) Two-step econometric estimation of farm characteristics affecting marketing contract decisions. *American Journal of Agricultural Economics* 86 (1), 88–102.

Key, N. and Runsten, D. (1999) Contract farming, smallholders, and rural development in Latin America: the organization of agroprocessing firms and the scale of outgrower production. *World Development* 27 (2), 381–401.

Keyser, J.C. (2004) *Thematic Study on Comparative Advantage and Agricultural Marketing: Phase 1 Synthesis Report*. The International Fund for Agriculture Development (IFAD), Rome.

Kosarek, J.L., Garcia, P. and Morris, M.L. (2001) Factors explaining the diffusion of hybrid maize in Latin America and the Caribbean region. *Agricultural Economics* 26 (3), 267–280.

Krkoska, L. (2001) *Foreign Direct Investment Financing of Capital Formation in Central and Aastern Europe*. Working paper No. 67. EBRD, London.

Lerman, Z. and Shagaida, N. (2005) *Land Reform and Development of Agricultural Land Markets in Russia*. Discussion Paper No. 2.05. Center for Agricultural Economic Research, Hebrew University of Jerusalem.

Merriam, S. (1998) *Qualitative Research and Case Study Applications in Education*. Jossey-Bass, San Francisco, California.

Morrison Paul, C., Nehring, R. and Banker, D. (2004) Productivity, economies and efficiency in U.S. agriculture: a look at contracts. *American Journal of Agricultural Economics* 86 (5), 1308–1314.

Singh, S. (2002) Contracting out solutions: political economy of contract farming in the Indian Punjab. *World Development* 30 (9), 1621–1638.

Striewe, L. (1999) *Grain and Oilseed Marketing in Ukraine*. Iowa State University Ukraine Agricultural Policy Project (UAPP), Kiev, Russia.

Strokov, S. and Meyers, W.H. (1996) *Producer Subsidy Equivalents and Evaluation of Support to Russian Agricultural* Producers. Center for Agricultural and Rural Development, Iowa State University, Ames, Ohio, mimeo.

Swinnen, J.F.M. (2005) *When the Market Comes to You – or Not: the Dynamics of Vertical Coordination in Agri-food Chains in Transition*. World Bank, Washington, DC, mimeo.

15 Agro-holdings: Vertical Integration in Agri-food Supply Chains in Russia

E. Serova

Background

In the middle of the 1990s, various analysts of Russian agriculture noticed the emergence of a new organizational form of farming which was quite different from the main type of agricultural producers in all post-Soviet economies (Serova and Khramova, 2000; Uzun, 2001; Koester, 2003; Serova and Khramova, 2003; Rylko and Jolly, 2005). This process has become especially evident since the crisis of 1998, after which a recovery of growth in the agri-food sector has started.

There is no common name for this new type of farming in the literature: Rylko and Jolly (2005) call them New Agricultural Operators (NAO); Khramova (2003) vertically integrated companies; in official Russian practice the name of agro-holdings has already been assigned. Regardless of the name one uses to identify this phenomenon, it unites a number of quite different types of agricultural companies, established in different ways and motivated by different incentives. Moreover, the structure of these forms can differ dramatically. They are not necessarily organized as holding companies or with vertical integration along the supply chain. In this respect the term 'new operators' reflects the essence of this phenomenon most accurately.

These are much larger than the traditional Soviet farm enterprises or the existing large farms, and are established with capital from outside the primary sector. Sometimes capital comes from the downstream sector when processors invest into supplying farms, sometimes it comes from the upstream sector when suppliers tend to control buyers of inputs; very often, capital originates from entirely outside the agri-food sector – mainly from the most profitable sectors of the Russian economy such as energy, finance or metallurgy.

In some cases several farm enterprises are under one holding company, but it can also be in the form of one huge farm enterprise. Sometimes such companies are organized under the control – and with participation of – the regional and/or local administrations. However, in the majority of cases it is a purely private initiative. The management structure also differs tremendously from company to company. Land tenure issues can be arranged in different ways: huge areas can be in ownership of one company, but most often they rent land shares.

What distinguishes these new operators from the traditional farm enterprises is not only, or predominantly, the scale of operation but the investment inflow to the primary sector, the new type of management, new technologies, the commercial orientation of the business and aggressive behaviour in markets.

There is still no clear understanding and definition of this new phenomenon in Russian agriculture, but it has grown rapidly in the last decade and plays a significant role in the agri-food sector. This is quite a different direction for Russia's agricultural development than was expected after the collapse of the Soviet system: the former collective and state farms are not being split into individual farms but are becoming united into even bigger aricultural companies. This paper discusses the preconditions of their emergence and the motivations, scope and possible consequences of their functioning.

In order to understand how the farmland and business are accumulated in these new operators we should recall the way Russia's agrarian reform was implemented in the early 1990s. As it is broadly known the Russian land reform and farm restructuring was based on the procedure of so-called land sharing. Workers from the *kolkhozes* and *sovkhozes* – as well as pensioners and social service officers – received equal (conditional) shares in the land operation of the parent farms. The conditional shares were not marked on the ground and can be considered as a type of options: they gave the right for the holder to withdraw with a physical plot any time without the permission of the other land shareholders.

These land shares were transferable in all types of legal transactions. In the reform of 1992–1994, around 12 million such shares were allotted to the rural dwellers. About 300,000 households utilized their right to withdraw from the farm enterprises and set up their own family farms. The rest of the rural dwellers preferred to maintain their existing status. In the majority of cases these rural dwellers leased their land shares to the farm enterprises.

The current structure of agricultural production in Russia has an ambivalent nature. On the one hand, farm enterprises dominate the area of farmland (see Fig. 15.1). On the other, since 1991 the area in farm enterprises has been reduced by almost 20%. The share of gross agricultural output originating from farm enterprises is now less than half (see Fig. 15.2). At the deepest point of recession in Russia's agriculture (1998) output fell to 56% of the 1991 output, and the gross output on the farm enterprises was at the level of just 35% of the pre-reform level.

At first glance, this means that farm enterprises maintain the major part of their lands, while actual production is concentrated in the individual farms. However, the data on household production (see Fig. 15.3) show that this sector has not extended its output significantly, except in

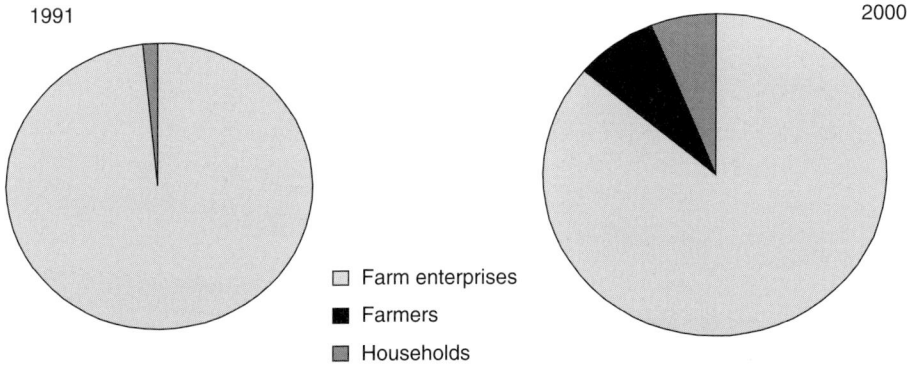

Fig. 15.1. Land use by farm category (figures calculated from Russian Cadastre Service data).

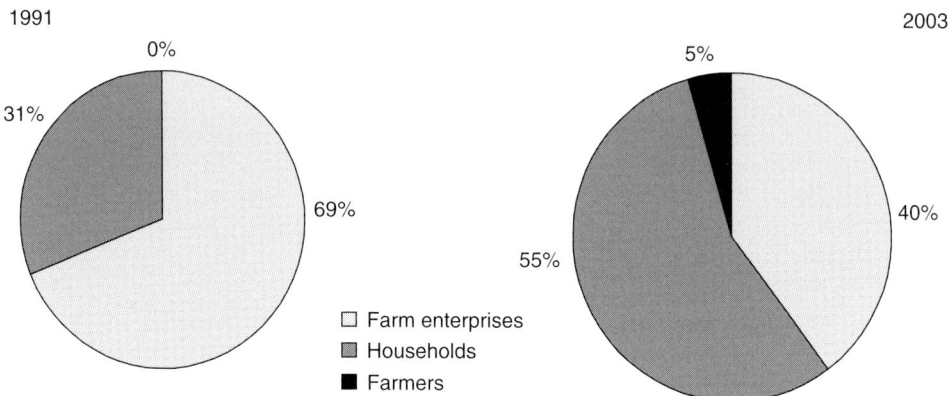

Fig. 15.2. Gross agricultural output by farm category (figures calculated from Russian Cadastre Service data).

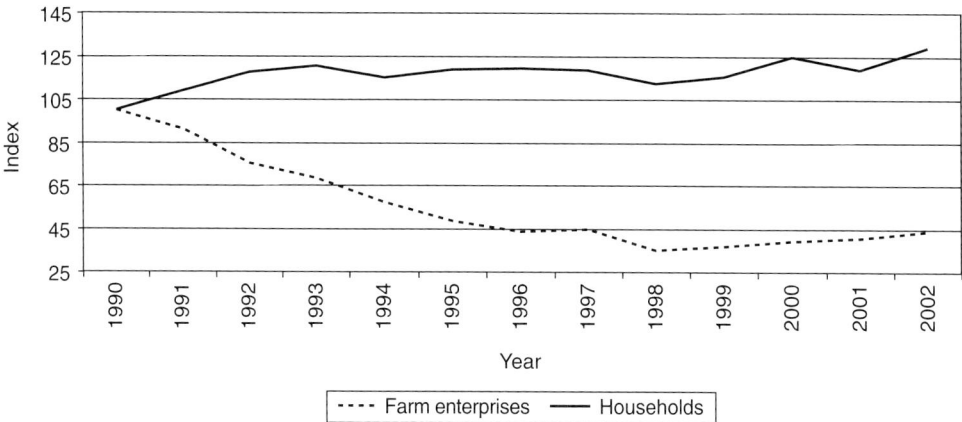

Fig. 15.3. Index of gross agricultural output originating from farm enterprises and households (figures calculated from Russian Statistics Service data).

potatoes, vegetables and fruit. In the pre-reform period, household plots mainly produced for self-consumption: only 13% of total output went for sale (Serova, 1999).

Therefore, the remarkable fall in the proportion of farm enterprises in the total output reflects the same remarkable fall in food consumption in the Russian Federation with the start of the reforms. Demand for agri-food products fell due to the drop in purchasing power of the population, and output of the commercial (market-oriented) farm enterprises was reduced by the same amount; the household carried on producing for self-sufficiency puposes at the same level as pre-reform. Arithmetically, the share of individual farms increased.

So, the reform process created a special agrarian structure in Russia characterized by a large-scale farm structure domination. In 1992–1994, the millions of rural dwellers had received conditional shares. The customary law of turnover of these shares was formed during last decade. Moreover, in the last 3–4 years, the land market has developed mostly in the form of land share transactions. More than half of farmland belongs to land sharholders, the majority of whom do not work on farm enterprises (they are mainly pensioners). The land shares were rented for life-long support: the aged rural dwellers passed their shares to the new owners who, in return, provided some lifelong services and payments to these people. It was a social guarantee for rural aged people, who have far fewer social security services than do urban dwellers.

This system of agriculture provided a base for the integration that we explore in this chapter. Large-scale business made the process of merging easier than with the system of dispersed farming. The land shares market and the willingness of rural people to rent their shares created a base for land accumulation by outside investors. However, before 1998 these options were not utilized because agriculture was a loss-making sector, and financial markets provided much better alternatives for investors in Russia than the real sector, and farming in particular.

The situation changed radically in 1998 (see Fig. 15.4). The fourfold rouble devaluation in August 1998 was a trigger for agri-food import substitution, which started in Russia almost immediately after the default. Already by September agri-food imports had been reduced drastically, creating market opportunities for domestic producers.

The financial crisis of 1998 also implied a significant reduction in financial speculative markets. The post-crisis government imposed more severe controls on capital exports, and therefore domestic capital-holders were looking for the real sector for investments. The projects with a short investment cycle and small initial level of investment were the most attractive in this crisis environment. Food, and later light industry, were such sectors to meet these two requirements. So, even by the autumn of 1998 there was a clear flow of domestic investments toward the food industries.

The boom in the food industry faced a limited supply of raw material due to a fall in the imports. The domestic primary sector demonstrated very high transaction costs. This inspired a vertical integration process and a corresponding downward investment flow to the farming sector.

At the same time, Russia's huge businesses (mostly mineral oil holdings, some financial holdings, etc.) had to look for options for business diversification in order to avert financial risks. Agriculture appeared to be one of the most attractive industries for such diversification: grain and oil net returns were strongly negatively correlated at that time. In addition, some agricultural sectors were very profitable by then. For example, the grain capital return peaked at 400% in a number of regions. Together with considerable tax concessions for agriculture, this caused investment attractiveness and capital inflows to the sector.

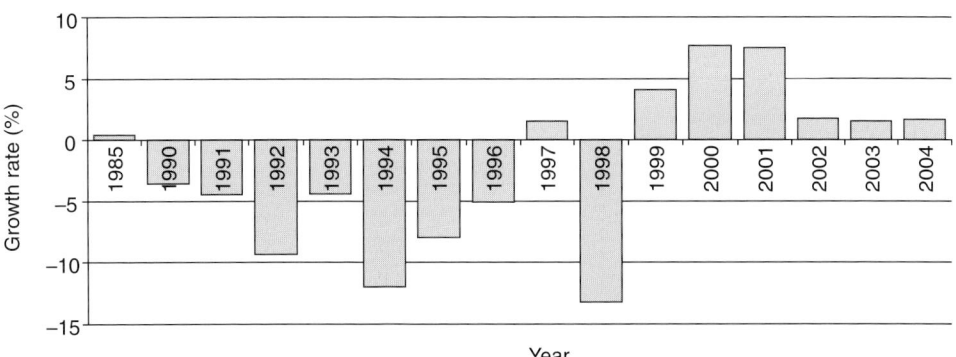

Fig. 15.4. Rate of growth in gross agricultural output (figures calculated from Russian Statistics Service data).

So, as a result of these factors, there was considerable investment growth in the agri-food sector (see Figs 15.5 and 15.6) in the post-crisis years, stronger than that in the economy as a whole. Large companies from various sectors of the economy acquired agricultural assets and farmland, established the agricultural companies, invested quite significantly and became important players on the agricultural markets.

Incentives for Establishment of Agro-holdings

There are two major types of 'new' investors. First, there are a large variety of downstream companies – traders, processors, storehouses, etc., and those upstream ones operating for agriculture – feeds, fertilizer suppliers, for example. With a severe fall in imports after the 1998 crisis many of these agribusiness companies searched for domestic supplies of primary agricultural products. However, they found that domestic markets were severely underdeveloped; and the collection of domestic raw materials was costly and involved considerable business risks. Therefore, many of these companies started to expand their control over farming.

Secondly, those with a stake in banking, oil and gas, metallurgy, etc. also started to invest in primary agriculture. They were attracted by the extremely low initial investment rates, high net value returns

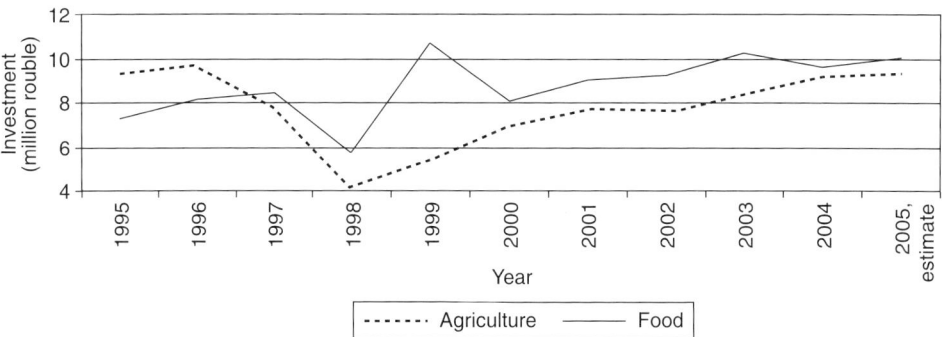

Fig. 15.5. Investment in food industry and agriculture (figures calculated from Russian Statistics Service data).

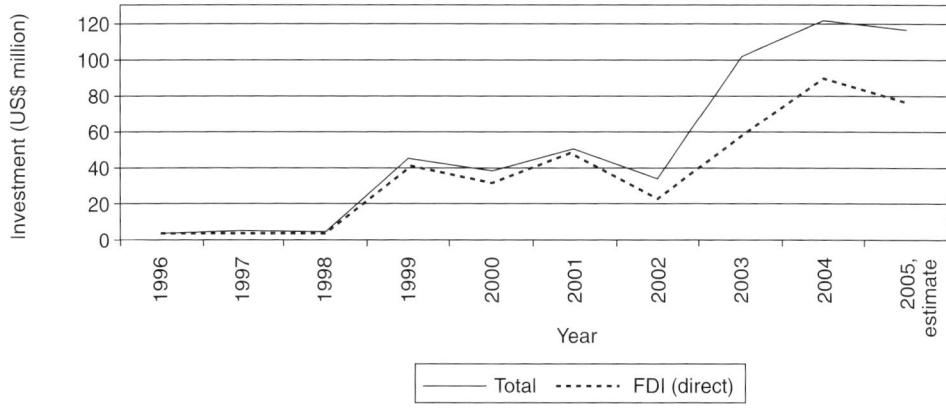

Fig. 15.6. Foreign investment in agriculture sector (figures calculated from Russian Statistics Service data).

and specific tax concessions for agriculture. In addition, primary agriculture was one of the last sectors of the economy where secondary privatization had not yet taken place.

One more motivating factor for entering agriculture by non-agricultural businesses was the extreme low liquidity of farms at that time. More than half of farm enterprises were insolvent. It was easy to acquire farms by purchasing their debts through the formal bankruptcy process. Low profitability of agriculture had reduced the value of assets tremendously and it was easy to buy mills, elevators, storehouses, etc. at ridiculously low prices. In the transition environment this temporary cheapness of these assets was an important motivation for their acquisition. And once they had acquired some agricultural assets, the companies started to expand their activity into this area (see Box 15.1).

Box 15.1. Vertical integration in the grain company OGO (from Nichols *et al.*, 2002).

The evolution of the private grain company, OGO, was typical for a Russian business that emerged in the years of perestroyka and was activated by the economic reforms of the 1990s. By 1994, the company became interested in privatization, suddenly realizing that 'privatization is passing us by'. Since the company had free capital, it had started to purchase grain storage and processing facilities.

Knowledge of European and American grain markets led them to estimate that the sale prices of the Russian elevators were fantastically low. Thus, the purchase price of an elevator with a storage capacity of 100,000 t at the moment of actual purchase was US$100–700 thousand in Russia and US$3–10 million in the USA.

At that time the company had no strategy targeted at food manufacturing; it understood only that the enterprises should be acquired because of the company's interest in the grain sector. Initially, the company intended to resell the purchased enterprise, which was more often than not in a dilapidated state from a managerial point of view. However, replacement of managers and technological changes (even without related replacement of the equipment) transformed a loss-making enterprise into a profitable one. Through this experience, awareness that food manufacturing could be profitable was gained. The company started to expand its purchases of storage and processing capacities.

OGO was buying so-called grain products combines. In the Soviet Union a grain products combine was an enterprise that included elevators, milling facilities and plant for the production of compound feeds. Once the feed capacities had been acquired, the company faced a series of problems. The feed producing plant, which OGO bought in 1994, had an unfavorable geographical allocation. The competitors of the company were assigned territories closer to the main regional feed consumers. To create competitive advantages, OGO decided to direct its production toward high-quality feeds. It was decided that the production of high-quality feeds would significantly increase the effect of their application and, thus, attract more customers.

The company shifted to the production of feeds primarily for poultry. High-quality feeds, however, did not meet market demand. The high quality of feeds and additional services with which the company supplied the customers led to a growth in individual costs of the feeds. These were 15–20% higher compared to those of the national average. In other words, the company did not take into consideration the restrictions of the feed consumers. The poultry-producing agricultural enterprises faced significant budget constraints. They were also unsure of the return from using new feeds, so they preferred not to buy the higher-price formulations.

Thus, the company faced a problem. It had spent capital to invest in acquisition of the feed-producing facilities, in overseeing their modernization, in elaboration of new technologies and in generating new balanced rations for feeding; finally it invested in training skilled personnel and in improving the managerial structure of the company. Everything proved to be for naught.

A strategic solution was chosen which comprised the stimulation of vertical integration towards the poultry sector. For OGO, this choice was linked with answering the question: 'What is more profitable, production of cheap feeds or cheap meat?' They concluded that sales of feeds as a final product was not profitable and that the company would produce a final product, i.e. poultry meat.

Continued

Box 15.1. *Continued*

A psychological factor, which had pushed the company toward vertical integration, also existed. The integration processes began in the domestic poultry sector. The fear of remaining outside the integration wave, in a situation where the feed consumers were vertically linked with the competitors, also affected the company's choice.

OGO initiated the vertical integration processes in the poultry sector by leasing two large-scale broiler farms in 1997. The company tried to organize demonstrations featuring the advantages of using its own feeds. It used its own broilers and feeds at these two broiler farms in order to demonstrate to the local poultry producers all the advantages of using high-quality feeds and new technologies. Because broiler feeding was ex-tremely sensitive to technologies, it was necessary to observe all stages of the technological cycle; results of the usage of high-productive feeds fell immediately if one was late with distributing the grain or water to the poultry. However, the poultry farms, which were leased by OGO, failed to follow rigorously enough the new technologies. As a result this market strategy failed.

Even the application of a highly sophisticated ration of broiler feeding when the industrial – as well as the managerial – culture proved to be poor at the agricultural enterprise level (which at that moment was not available within the company) often caused serious distortions in the technological cycle. It led the company management to conclude that leasing of the farms was too ineffective a form of investment in general and of vertical integration in particular.

Step by step, the company concluded that it was necessary to acquire the poultry farms. In 2000, OGO became the owner of two broiler farms and susequently acquired two more. Thus, in 2000 the company became the owner of four large-scale broiler farms in the Smolensk, Tula, Kaluga and Astrakhan regions. This vertical integration under full ownership permitted the company to realize completely the advantages of putting together an application of their own feeds and the use of sophisticated technologies and management.

As a result, in a short period of time, the company had managed to increase significantly both the productivity and the profitability of its broiler farms.

In order to understand better the processes in the agri-food sector one should be aware that such vertical integration is not a peculiarity of this sector: it is now widespread throughout the economy. Such a system of business is part of a tax optimization policy of companies, and it helps also to establish regional monopolies. Moreover, the creation of vertical holdings is often urged by local administrations.

This process is not all positive: its consequences can be negative both for the business involved and for the entire society. However, it is a reality and the agri-food sector was just lagging behind in this general trend of Russia's economy.

Apart from these general incentives for vertical integration and holdings setting in Russia's economy there were two major incentives for this process in agriculture, briefly mentioned above. One of them was real vertical integration along supply chains as a reaction to the high transaction costs in the food chain.

Prior to the 1998 crisis, those downstream of food companies sourced major raw materials from abroad with quite low transaction costs, but the rouble devaluation rendered these deliveries extremely expensive. In this circumstance downstream companies were forced to turn to local suppliers. However, local suppliers demonstrated very opportunistic behaviour, which raised transaction costs dramatically. Vertical coordination with regular contracts did not work due to: (i) poor law enforcement; and (ii) low legal and business culture in the economy in general – and in the agricultural sector in particular.

Thus, the downstream companies had to expand their business to the primary sector to maintain their main business: this is a textbook situation of vertical integration when high transaction costs cause vertical integration along the food chain (Williamson, 1996; Coase, 2001).

Naturally, in a vertically integrated company, outsourcing should not be allowed to a large extent: if the deliveries from (or supplies to) the agents outside the integrated company are with low transaction costs than there is no need to expand business to that stage of the food chain. However our case study showed that such outsourcing is still widespread in these agro-holdings. Thus, as mentioned in Box 15.1, the company OGO did not insist that its poultry factories purchase compound feed necessarily from its feed plant. Profits of these poultry factories – as well as those of all other divisions of the company – were centralized and redistributed from the parent company (holding company).

Therefore, it was more like risk aversion activity than real vertical integration. Theory says that risk aversion induces the firm to diversify its activities so that those activities have independently – or better, negatively – correlated net returns (Lee et al., 1988). Thus, in the OGO example, this was exactly the case. The company bought its poultry factories in 1997. In 1996–1999 net returns in the grain and meat poultry sectors correlated with coefficient −0.997 (calculated from Russian Statistic Service data). So, although feed production and poultry production are stages of the same supply chain, their unification within one company was not motivated by vertical integration but was the result of risk aversion.

This conclusion was even truer for cases where mineral oil companies invested in grain production. In Russia at that time 40% of grain production costs were fuel costs. Therefore, a raise in fuel prices reduces, ceteris paribus, the profitability of grain but, on the other hand, increases profitability of fuel, and vice versa. In such a way a firm diversifying its business portfolio with fuel and grain interests has a high probability of having stable net returns regardless of changes in grain and fuel prices.

The motivation for establishing these new agricultural operators has long-term consequences for corporate behaviour. Those that were established following the vertical integration pattern would be more stable, the integration between company divisions would be closer and more sustainable and would be supported by long-term investment and technological linkages. Those that were driven by risk aversion portfolio diversification would tend to be more flexible in their reactions on economic situation. The main emphasis in the future will be on financial control of the divisions and on centralization of profits. As happened in other sectors of Russia's economy during previous stages of development, they would tend to get rid of 'non-specialized assets'.

Data on Agro-holdings

The official statistics do not distinguish these new forms of farming which are discussed in this chapter. In fact, all farm enterprises in Russia are still the subject of obligatory reporting. These data are aggregated by regions and nationally. Therefore, those farm enterprises that have been merged into bigger companies are also reported but not identified by statistics. Hence, from the official data it is not possible to identify agro-holdings, their land use, sales, profitability or other parameters of functioning. Only surveys maintained by various groups of researchers provide more useful information for analysis.

At present we are familiar with three major sources of data on agro-holdings. One is a dataset of the 300 biggest farm enterprises maintained by the Agrarian Institute (Moscow) which, since 2001 also includes data of 33 agro-holdings. Data on these agro-holdings are collected by postal survey and include a very limited number of indicators. Around 130 agro-holdings are described by the analytical centre IKAR (Moscow), which holds a much bigger set of indicators. In 2002, we carried out our own survey in one of the major agricultural areas of Russia – Rostov. This survey included 14 agro-holdings and consisted of more than 20 questions, both quantitative and qualitative.

These 14 companies comprise around

7–8% of total farmland and 21% of wheat area and 38% of gross wheat output of the region (see Table 15.1). The average agro-holding operation is more than five times bigger than the average farm enterprise of the area (though the Rostov area is known for relatively big farms) and is mostly specialized in grain production.

Among the 14 surveyed agro-holdings nine were established after the 1998 crisis. However, those which were established pre-1998 acquired the majority of their land post-1998. The average size of operation is 32,000 ha (standard deviation 39,000) (see Table 15.2). These 14 companies make up around 7–8% of total farmland of the region and close to 10% in terms of sales.

The IKAR database demonstrated the same distribution of agro-holdings by period of establishment (see Fig. 15.7). So, the major proportion of agro-holdings was established post-1998, as stated at the beginning of the chapter.

According to the IKAR data, in 2001 the average parcel of land in use for the 115 surveyed agro-holdings was 55,000 ha and, in 2003, 54,000 (Rylko and Jolly, 2005). So the results of the two surveys are very similar.

The surveyed Rostov agro-holdings were asked about the motivation for expanding their business to primary agriculture. Of course, the responses cannot be considered as being the real explanation of the companies' incentives, but they allow some understanding of the thinking of the top management regarding this process. Table 15.3 shows that the two major incentives were: (i) the securing of raw materials; and (ii) some input by the regional authorities. Risk aversion was the least-mentioned motivation in the opinion of the managers.

Table 15.1. Comparison of operation of average surveyed agro-holdings and average area farm enterprise, Rostov (from AFE Centre survey, 2002).

	Agro-holdings	Farm enterprises
Per one farm operation, average (n)	14	949
Land in use (1000 ha)	31.6	6.0
Wheat area (1000 ha)	18.2	1.3
Wheat output (1000 t)	98.6	3.8
Wheat yield (kg/ha)	29.4	29.9
Wheat production cost (rouble/t)	1.2	1.1

Table 15.2. Surveyed sample of 14 agro-holdings, Rostov area (from AFE Centre survey, 2002).

Number of agro-holding	Year of establishment	Land in use (ha)
1	1998	0
2	2000	2,021
3	2000	4,600
4	2000	6,000
5	1995	7,500
6	1997	14,000
7	1992	15,853
8	2000	25,000
9	1999	26,000
10	2000	36,000
11	1998	45,000
12	2000	53,000
13	1992	58,000
14	1993	150,000

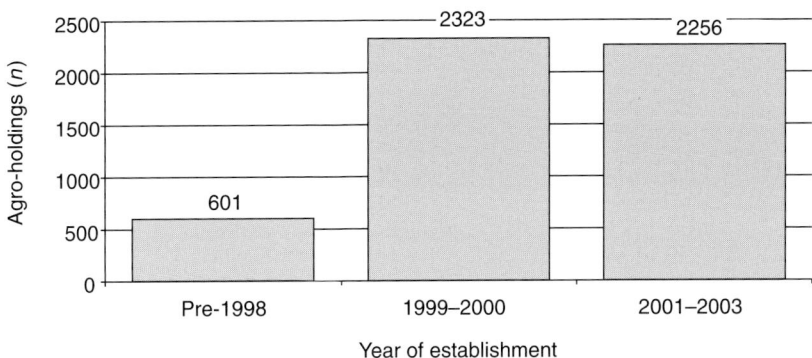

Fig. 15.7. Distribution of agro-holdings by year of establishment (from Rylko and Jolly, 2005).

Table 15.3. Incentives for expanding the original business towards primary agriculture in 14 surveyed agro-holdings, Rostov area (from AFE Centre survey, 2002).

Incentive	Positive replies (n)*
Secure raw material deliveries	8
Expand market for manufactured inputs	5
Ensure collection of outstanding debt	6
Profitable business	5
Risk aversion by portfolio diversification	3
Enforcement/recommendation by regional authorities	8

* Multiple answers allowed.

These results are partially determined by the bias of the sample. Among 14 questioned agro-holdings there was none established by a non-agri-food company. Rostov is a huge grain and sunflower seed-producing area of Russia, and both of these crops are export-oriented cash crops. Agro-holdings were mostly established by exporters and/or processors, for which access to raw materials was the main motivation for organizing their own farming business, thus securing regular supplies.

The role of authorities in establishing agro-holdings as a motivation is frequently mentioned in the literature (for instance, Gataulina *et al.*). However, it was not one of the original reasons for establishing such companies. On the contrary, the authorities at the federal and regional levels have started talking about agro-holdings when they noticed their emergence in the economy post-1998.

They grasped the advantages of this form of investment attraction for a severely under-invested sector. Also, it was a good means of relieving the chronic insolvency of the farm enterprises in that region. Thus, the administration had begun to press local business – especially agri-business – to affiliate farm enterprises; sometimes it is demanded as a precondition for acquiring other assets the company requires (a type of additional charge for desired assets).

Sometimes regional authorities can recommend (indeed, insist upon) particular farm enterprises joining in case an investor is looking for such farms. This process can be implemented with a degree of administrative pressure, but it is always a hidden process that is difficult to record in surveys. However, even in the Rostov area – known for its more *laissez-faire* policy among agricultural areas – our survey shows that eight agro-holdings of the surveyed 14 faced government involvement in expanding the business towards farming (see Table 15.3).

In such areas as Belgorod and Oryel which, like the Rostov area, are characterized by the prevalence of agro-holdings but known for a considerable degree of government intervention in the economy, the degree of such involvement could be much higher still (see Box 15.2). However, IKAR data show that only 5% of the 133 surveyed agro-holdings belong to the state.

In some cases, state-owned agri-business companies were transformed into private agro-holdings (see Box 15.3).

Access to Land

Most land that new operators use for cultivation is acquired through land share transactions (see Table 15.4). In the majority of cases the new operators cannot transfer land into private ownership because ownership of large areas creates a barrier for exit from the business. In the event of a company wishing to exit from farming it would be very difficult to recoup the capital invested in land by selling – land prices would fall due to the huge surplus of land in one region. In this situation rent of land shares is appropriate for both sides: on the one hand it allows

Table 15.4. Means of land acquisition by agro-holdings, Rostov area (from AFE Centre survey, 2002).

	Positive replies (n)*
Joint venture with farm enterprise	1
Investment in farm enterprise equity	1
Land share purchase	1
Land purchase	1
Land use right from federal authorities	2
Renting of land	2
Renting of land share	8

* Multiple answers allowed.

Box 15.2. Oryel Niva: an agro-holding set up by regional administration from Gataulina *et al.*, AFE Centre data).

Currently, Oryel Niva controls 337,000 ha of land and employs 16,000 workers. It processes 200,000–300,000 tons of wheat annually. Its activities include 102 large farms, 28 processing plants, 100 trade organizations, 32 service enterprises, etc. The company was established and is run by the regional ministry of agriculture. The main idea underlying its creation was the late-Soviet pattern of agribusiness administration, when all regional farm enterprises, processors and service enterprises were merged into one administrative unit. The official target for such administrative mergers in the late 1990s was control over the administration of value-added distribution among value chains, since at that time they were operating under the poor market scenario of farms *versus* processors and traders.

As a result, Oryel Niva acquired a tremendous monopoly power, along with regional policy instruments. Thus, local farms could not deliver their output to any other than Niva purchasers, even in the event of better terms, because of the threat that they would be deprived of their regional subsidies and privileges. Later, several parallel agro-holdings (Oryel agro-holding, Pshenitsa-2000) were set up in order to eliminate this monopoly. However, all these new establishments are under all-embracing control of the administration and do not assist much in this respect.

Box 15.3. Tyumen Grain Company: a state-owned agro-holding preparing to be privatized (from AFE Centre data).

Tyumen Grain Company was set up in 1999 as a state-owned machinery service company. With regional budget provisions, a number of high-quality harvesters were acquired that were supposed to serve local farm enterprises. However, farms did not pay properly for services and the company went bankrupt.

In 2004 a crisis manager was appointed, who re-established the company as a joint stock company with 100% state ownership. This new company affiliated two farm enterprises with grain and poultry production (via land shares' rent from holders). Today, its portfolio consists of three kinds of business: machinery services for regional farms, grain trade and poultry production. The current aims of the company are to acquire grain storage facilities and grain processing (mainly for compound feed) assets, thus establishing a trading division. The company is now preparing for privatization.

quick and cheap access to land for new operators and on the other it provides a subsistence for rural dwellers, a mostly aged and low-income population.

The new land legislation introduced since 2001[1] has dramatically increased transaction costs on the land-share market (Shagaida, 2005). Prior to this, a land shareholder could rent out their share individually, and it was the tenant's business to consolidate rented shares into one land plot. A tenant wishing to cultivate a certain land area could sign individual agreements with every shareholder and then would have to parcel out the corresponding physical plot (or several large plots).

Each owner in this case received rentals individually (in theory, the rentals could differ but in practice it happens rather infrequently). Under the new law, shareholders have first to come to an agreement on joint renting out of a common land holding, to parcel it out and only then to rent it out on behalf of the whole collective. The latter becomes the recipient of rental payments.

First of all, collective rent raises rentals, i.e. the cost of gaining access to land for outsiders: reaching an agreement with each individual shareholder is, *ceteris paribus*, less expensive than that for the entire collective. This, in turn, results in smaller outside investments in farming: external investors have to pay more for accessing land and hence have less funds for investing in production. Besides, collective rent is most likely to fall under the control of large farm management, thus enhancing their power to dispose of land that they do not own. Also, the procedure of transaction registering and plot mapping is legally conditioned with a lot of administration steps and fees, which sometimes make the transaction unfeasible.

The process of land privatization and farm restructuring in the early 1990s led to the situation where the land was owned by certain people but farms, generally speaking, by others. Therefore, new operators need not only to access land but also to acquire the businesses per se. Our small survey in the Rostov area showed that bankruptcy procedures were the most common way of purchasing farming businesses, at least in this particular area (see Table 15.5).

This fact also explains why the percentage of agro-holdings established with government involvement was rather high in our survey: the investors preferred farm enterprises with a better financial status but, due to administrative pressure, they were forced to buy the insolvent farms with which the regional government did not know what to do.

Management Structure

Table 15.6 gives an impression of internal management processes in the agro-holdings. All holdings set the intra-firm transfer prices to optimize the tax burden. Russian legislation releases farms from profit tax. Therefore, with well-designed transfer prices, companies can redistribute value added from other levels of the supply chain towards farming divisions. Almost all agro-holdings have centralized the profits from farming divisions for tax reduction. Centralized profits from the farming sector are mostly used for investment in farming but not used for other purposes.

Almost all sampled agro-holdings control sales of output and supply of inputs. This latter phrase means the control over technological policy throughout the entire company. The central holding company appoints managers to the farms, who are

Table 15.5. Means of farm enterprise acquisition by agro-holdings, Rostov area (from AFE Centre survey, 2002).

	Positive replies (n)*
Initial privatization	2
Purchase in bankruptcy procedure	7
Joint venture with existing farm enterprise(s)	1
New enterprise	4

* Multiple answers allowed.

Table 15.6. Management and control within agro-holdings, Rostov area (from AFE Centre survey, 2002).

Centralized functions	Positive replies (n)*
Redistribution of farm profits by holding company	13
For farm uses	13
For other uses	5
Centralized product sales	11
Control of selling prices within the group	14
Obligation of intra-firm transactions	12
Centralized input purchasing	11
Inputs supplied by holding company at transfer prices	7
Inputs purchased at market prices with intermediation of holding company	4
Appointment of farm managers	12
Intervention in labour hiring	4

* Multiple answers allowed.

frequently not locally domiciled (which is important, as we shall see below). The farm enterprise managers are responsible for only a set of negligible issues: labour relations, minor technological decision-making, etc.

The structure of the biggest agro-holdings can be very diversified and agriculture comprises only a small part of the portfolio (see Box 15.4). On the other hand, there are many companies that are not organized as holdings and operate solely in farming, but they are similar to the diversified companies: they have huge farmland areas in operation, they brought initial capital from outside the sector and they are commercially oriented (e.g. the company Grain Industry in Saratov region, cultivating around 35,000 ha for grain in crop rotation).

Agro-holdings' Impact on Input Markets

The emergence of the agro-holdings has significantly changed the demand for farm inputs in Russia in recent years (Serova and Shick, 2005), being the largest purchasers of farm inputs. Vertically inte-

---

Box 15.4. Business structure of some agro-holdings (from AFE Centre data).

Company OGO

Nowadays, the company OGO is one of the biggest Russian grain market operators. It is a large-scale, diversified company, involved not only in trade, handling and transportation of grain but also in food and feed processing. OGO produces a vast range of processed commodities, like flour, groats,[1] vegetable oil, beer and feeds. Vertical integration, started by the company a few years ago, turned it into one of the biggest poultry market operators (see Box 15.1). OGO controls the whole vertical poultry chain from grain production and feed production up to the wholesale and retail marketing of poultry meat (see Figs 15.8 and 15.9).

Company Agrico (2003)

This company was established as an affiliated division of one of the biggest mineral oil companies of Russia, but was later separated and now operates as an independent agro-holding. It farms more than 50,000 ha, has around ten farms, several grain elevators and processing facilities, a sugar refinery, assets in poultry and swine sectors, transport divisions, guard services, construction divisions, investment division and others. The key crop production of the company is grain and oil seeds.

[1] Hulled or crushed grain, especially oats.

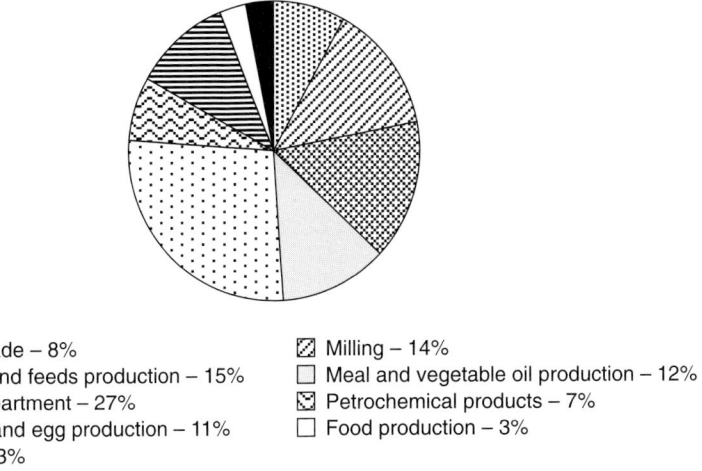

- Grain trade – 8%
- Compound feeds production – 15%
- Fuel department – 27%
- Poultry and egg production – 11%
- Other – 3%
- Milling – 14%
- Meal and vegetable oil production – 12%
- Petrochemical products – 7%
- Food production – 3%

Fig. 15.8. Distribution of single product segments in total turnover of OGO, 2000 (from Nichols et al., 2002).

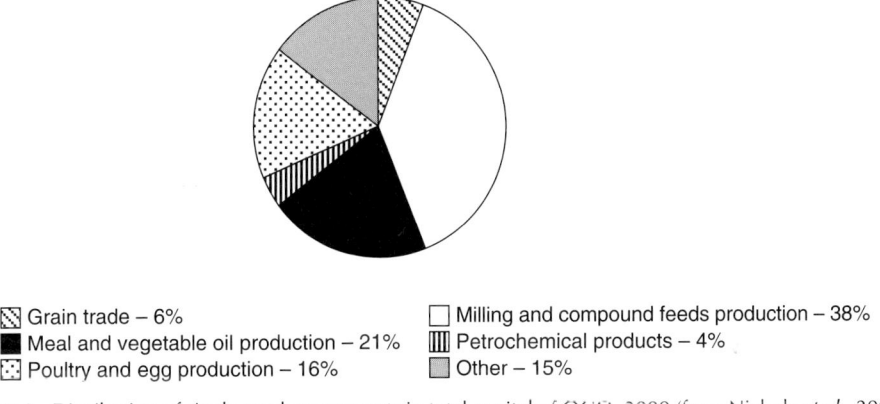

- Grain trade – 6%
- Meal and vegetable oil production – 21%
- Poultry and egg production – 16%
- Milling and compound feeds production – 38%
- Petrochemical products – 4%
- Other – 15%

Fig. 15.9. Distribution of single product segments in total capital of OGO, 2000 (from Nichols et al., 2002).

grated companies purchase inputs directly from the manufacturers, but most often from dealers. They use financial leasing, although according to experts it is not profitable under the current conditions. These holdings are the major importers of agricultural machinery. This group is the mostly rapidly growing and largest player in the demand for inputs.

Another specific feature of farm input demand in Russia today is the development of custom farming. Contrary to the Soviet era, when farms possessed all necessary machinery – that could be utilized only during a very limited seasonal period, today, machinery services are rapidly emerging (see Box 15.2).

Thus, the demand for farm inputs is not only reduced due to the fall in output, but also due to a change of input use, due to an emergence of the new purchasers in the downstream sector, in addition to the conventional farms.

In recent years there has been remarkable growth in the use of vertical contracting schemes in deliveries of inputs to farms. There are two types of the vertical coordination contracts: production contracts and vertical integration. In the former case buyers of the agricultural raw material (traders, but more often processors) supply inputs to the contracted farms, which must grow and deliver agreed volumes of agreed-quality agricultural product. Quite often the technology of growing and the use of delivered inputs use are also under agreement.

However, under these contracts farms remain legally independent and often behave opportunistically, using delivered inputs for non-contracted crops and breaking the obligations of contract. Therefore, the second type of vertical contracts is becoming more widespread, with downstream companies acquiring full control over the farming process. Thereby, input deliveries to the farm (branches of the big agri-business holdings) are conducted as internal transactions of the vertically integrated company.

In the 3-year Russo-American research project BASIS (Lerman, 2005), 144 farm enterprises were surveyed in three Russian regions. The sampled farms acquired the significant part of their inputs under such vertical contracts. In the Rostov region vertical integration in agriculture is especially widespread and, correspondingly, the share of vertical contracts creates a bigger share in the total-input purchasing contracts of the farms than in the entire sample (see Figs 15.10 and 15.11).

Conclusion

Agro-holdings have brought a lot of changes to Russia's agriculture and agribusiness, yet the consequences of their emergence and functioning are still not clear. Below, we discuss some of the positive and negative sides of that process that are already evident.

First, let us dwell on a positive influence of agro-holdings. Without doubts, their emergence and development has brought a flow of capital investment to the sector, which was lacking for almost a decade. This investment has allowed the modernization of primary agriculture, as well as that of the downstream sector and market infrastructure.

Our small survey in the Rostov area showed that the profits are not extracted from agribusiness but re-invested in farming. The agro-holdings are the major purchasers of the modern machinery and equipment for farms; they introduce the most advanced technology. Moreover, extending farm operations from the south to the north allows increased utilization of agricultural machinery: the companies move the tractors and harvesters from their

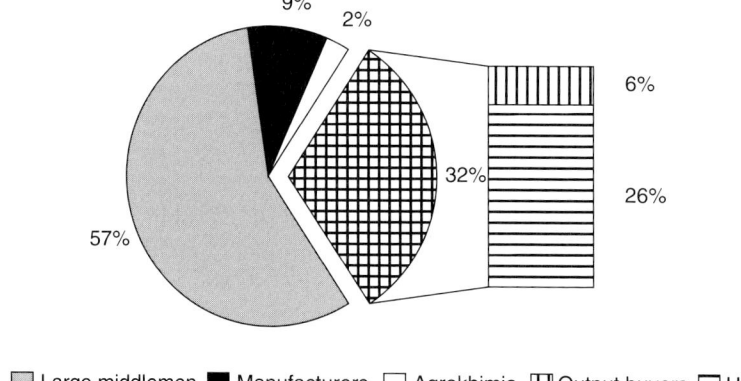

Fig. 15.10. Vertically coordinated contracts for purchases of mineral fertilizers, Rostov area (from BASIS survey data, 2002). Agrokhimia is a former state-owned, currently privatized, monopoly for supply and application of farm chemicals.

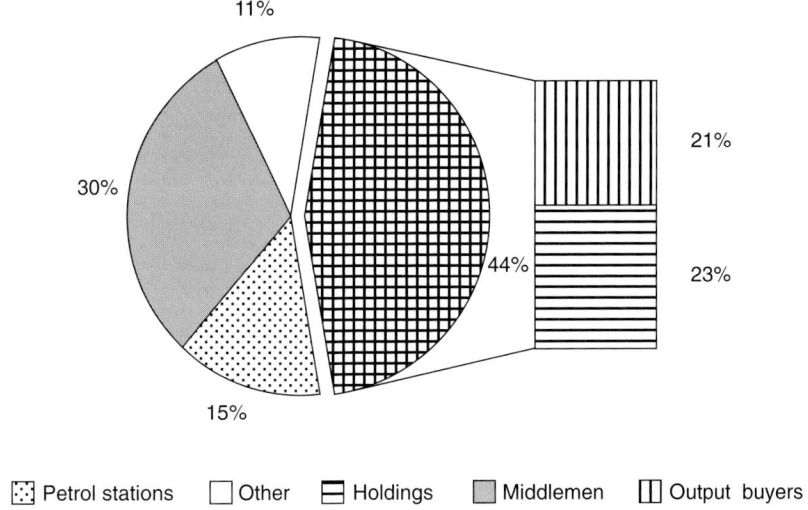

Fig. 15.11. Vertically coordinated contracts for purchases of petrol, Rostov area (from BASIS survey data, 2002).

southern farms to the north, as the seasons change. That decreases production costs *ceteris paribus*.

Agro-holdings bring to the farming sector new management skills; they train farm personnel and send people for training to the main educational centres in Russia and abroad (see Box 15.5). Six of the 14 sampled agro-holdings in Rostov area sent their labourers for short-term training courses; one paid for university education while five provided housing in rural areas in order to attract more skilled labourers to their farms.

The agro-holdings have enough means at their disposal to maintain quality and control standards and to comply with international standards.

These strengths, coupled with the huge scale of production, allow them to collect more commercially competitive commodities. The agro-holdings have stronger market power both within the country and abroad and they have better access to financial resources because of better collaterals.

So, from one aspect their development has inserted energy and quality into the growth of Russia's agriculture over recent years; notably increased its competitiveness and productivity. However, there are a number of disquieting aspects of this process.

The agro-holdings follow a labour-extensive pattern of development. Modernization of the farming business increases labour productivity and correspondingly decreases the demand for a labour force in rural areas. Moreover, with the costly control of workers in large-scale farm enterprises, agro-holdings tend to substitute labour with machinery (wide-cut machinery, automatic equipment, space technology, etc). This tactic leads to increasing unemployment in rural areas.

The Soviet epoch left the heavy burden of a severe shortage of non-agricultural jobs in rural areas. Therefore, redundant workers from the farms have no jobs in the villages and the geographical size of most Russian regions is not conducive to commuting for employment in townships. As a result, the more agro-holdings develop their business the more unemployed people appear in the rural areas where they operate. This causes social tensions, which are only aggravated by the growing inequality in the incomes of the village dwellers. Half of surveyed agro-holdings complain about pilfering and vandalism on

> **Box 15.5.** Introduction of new technologies and training of personnel (from Nichols et al., 2002).
>
> The company OGO bought a compound feed plant in the Vologda area, together with a grain storage facility, and developed its own feed business. Two employees of the company then studied (mainly in the USA) technology in feed production. After this, the company started to produce high-quality feeds ready for consumption by poultry; these feeds did not need any additional processing at the place of consumption (i.e. at the poultry farms). This was an unprecedented step for Russia at that time.
>
> The technicians of OGO evolved balanced rations of feeding for each customer (which are mostly large-scale agricultural enterprises), taking into account the genetical potential of particular poultry crosses or livestock breeds, the geographical location of the agricultural enterprises and the level of their production. They also provided livestock producers with assistance in feeding programmes and management aspects.

their farms. Many of them run their own guard services, some pay external guards. Some companies have developed social programmes in the villages they operate in order to maintain the social *status quo* there.

Irrespective of the way in which the companies try to solve this problem, our estimate shows that the corresponding spending accounts for around 10% of total production costs, what means 10% loss in competitiveness.

Another visible problem of the agro-holdings is over-investment. Investors from outside the agri-food sector normally follow worldwide best practice for the technological development of their farming business. However, these technologies are being introduced into an economic environment, where labour and land are extremely cheap. The marginal product of these technologies is below their marginal costs. Therefore, the allocative efficiency of the farms belonging to the agro-holdings is low. Of course, this can be a short-term effect while a longer-term investment in high technology will eventually bear fruit.

However, agro-holdings face strong competition for the best traditional farms. Although the Rostov survey dealt with a small sample, it indicates this outcome to a certain extent. Table 15.1 shows that, on average, agro-holdings had worse yield and higher production costs for wheat compared to traditional farm enterprises.

In the BASIS project (Lerman, 2005), the allocative efficiency for 144 farm enterprises were estimated (by the production function method). For nine farm enterprises, belonging to agro-holdings, the allocative efficiency was lower than for the traditional farm enterprises for the same region.[2]

If one recalls that agro-holdings are usually established by huge national capital owners with great lobbying power, it will be clear that in this situation the agro-holdings began requesting protectionist measures from Russia's government. This is one of the reasons for the growth in protectionism in Russia's agri-food sector in the last 3–4 years (IET, 2005).

Traditional agricultural economics start from the axiom that the farming sector is non-monopolistic in principle. The practice of agro-holding operations is inconsistent with this postulate. In particular, at the regional level, the biggest agro-holdings monopolize the main agri-food markets with all the negative effects of monopolies.

Notes

1. At the end of 2001 a new Russian Land Code was adopted. The issues of agricultural land turnover were excluded from this code in order to make its adoption easier politically. In spring 2002 a special law, 'On Agricultural Land Turnover', was adopted.
2. The results are not yet published.

References

Coase, R. (2001) *The Nature of the Firm*. Delo, Moscow (in Russian).

Gataulina, E., Petrikov, A., Uzun, V. and Yanbykh, R. (2005) Vertical integration in an agroindustrial complex: agrofirms and agroholdings in Russia. In: Swinnen, J.F.M. (ed.) *The Dynamics of Vertical Coordination in Agrifood Chains in Eastern Europe and Central Asia*. Working Paper No. 42. World Bank, Washington, DC, pp. 45–73.

IET (2005) *Russian Economy in 2004*. http://iet.ru (accessed 15 December 2005).

Koester, U. (2003) A revival of large farms in Eastern Europe? How important are institutions? Paper delivered at the *25th Conference of IAAE*, Durban, Republic of South Africa, 16–22 August 2003. http://www.iaae-agecon.org/conf/durban_papers/papers/Koester.pdf (accessed 15 December 2005).

Khramova, I. (2003) Agroholdings operations in Russia's food sector: case study. In: Gaidar, E. (ed.) *Economy in Transition: Selected Works, 1999–2002*. Djelo, Moscow.

Lee, W.F., Boehlje, V.D., Nelson, A.G. and Murray, W.G. (1988) *Agricultural Finance*. Iowa State University Press, Ames, Iowa.

Lerman, Z. (2005) Factor market constraints on economic growth in Russian agriculture: Golitzino Papers: an introduction to special issue. *Comparative Economic Studies* 47 (1), 80–84.

Nichols, J., Serova, E. and Khramova, I. (2002) Case study of grain company OGO. Taxes A&M (accessed on worldwide web).

Rylko, D. and Jolly, R.M. (2005) Development of agroholdings in Russian agriculture. *Comparative Economic Studies* 47 (1), 115–126.

Serova, E. (1999) *Agrarian Economics*. Higher School of Economics, Moscow (in Russian).

Serova, E. and Khramova, I. (2000) Emerging supply chain management in Russia's agri-food sector. Discussion papers. Series: *Russian Agri-Food Sector in Transition*. Bonn, Germany, 14.

Serova, E. and Khramova, I. (2003) Farms and factors markets in Russia's agriculture. In: Spoor, M. (ed.) *Transition, Institutions and the Rural Sector*. Lexington Books, Lanham, Maryland, pp. 61–80.

Serova, E. and Shick, O. (2005) Markets for purchased farm inputs in Russia. *Comparative Economic Studies* 47 (1), 154–166.

Shagaida, N. (2005) Agricultural land market in Russia: living with constraints. *Comparative Economic Studies* 47 (1), 127–140.

Uzun, V.Y. (2001) Organizational types of the agricultural production in Russia. In: Serova, E. (ed.) *The Markets of Production Factor in Russia's Agriculture*. AFE, Moscow.

Williamson, O. (1996) *Economic Institutes of Capitalism: Firms, Markets, Relational Contracting* (in Russian). The Free Press, New York.

Central and Eastern Europe

16 Restructuring Market Relations in Food and Agriculture of Central Eastern Europe: Impacts upon Small Farmers

C. Csáki and C. Forgacs

Introduction

The overall transition to market economies and changes in the political system have made significant impacts upon the various components of the food chain and related market relations in the region. Privatization in agriculture and food processing in the first half of 1990s has been followed by a revolution in the retail sector created by the entry of multinational trading companies and the opening of super- and hypermarkets in the late 1990s and in more recent years. Markets and market relations have been in constant change and the process is still continuing, but developments have not been uniform across the region.

The new EU member states are far more advanced than Eastern Europe and the Balkan States – and more so especially than some segments of the CIS. There is, however, a uniform concern about how these changes impact upon the small farmers and what kind of measures can be recommended to facilitate the adjustment of these farms to the evolving new market relations. There is a limited source of information available on these changes in the region. (Reardon and Swinnen, 2004) and a recent World Bank study (2005) have provided the first assessments in the international literature.

This chapter intends to provide an analysis of the evolving relations in the food chain and impacts upon small farmers based on case studies conducted in three countries (Hungary, Poland and Romania) within the framework of an international project organized and coordinated by the International Institute for Environment and Development (IIED, UK).[1] Each country represents a specific path and level of development. Both Hungary and Poland are quite advanced in concentration of the retail and food processing sectors while Romania is less advanced in changes of the vertical structure of food production. In each country, two specific vertical product chains were analysed in detail.

The conclusions in the summary reflect mainly the information gathered in these three countries but must be treated with caution regarding the rest of the region, especially for countries located further east.

Evolving Components of Vertical Relations in Food and Agriculture

The reforms of the past 15 years and the transition from a centrally planned to a market economy have resulted in significant changes in the individual components of the supply chains and upon the relations between the individual components.

Primary agriculture

The current state of primary agriculture in the region is a result of a relatively complex reform process including: (i) land privatization/restitution; (ii) decollectivization; (iii) emergence of new, private ownership-based farming organizations; (iv) market and price liberalization; and (v) the introduction of a market conform support and incentive framework.

These reforms are more or less complete but the transformation is, however, not fully finished and the results have, so far, only partially met initial expectations. Reforms in agriculture have been overpoliticized and have often included economically questionable decisions. The level of production is 20–30% below pre-reform levels in most countries and many of the farms exhibit limited competitiveness, though agricultural productivity has increased significantly in recent years.

Table 16.1 gives an overview of the farming structure in the region. CEECs have a dual farming structure, including relatively large farms but also a considerable number of smaller farms. The agricultural structure in the three countries mirrors the overall situation in the region, Hungary providing one of the best examples of this dual structure in the region. Poland maintained small-scale private agriculture during the Communist period. Another example of dual-farming structure can be found in Romania, with a very large (> 4 million) number of holdings.

The food processing industry

Privatization of the food processing industry has been part of the national privatization process. However, in the countries concerned it started at different times and has reached various levels. The privatization of food processing has attracted significant FDI, first in Poland, Hungary and the Czech Republic, later in Slovakia and the Baltic countries and, very recently, in Romania and Bulgaria. For example, in Poland FDI in food processing increased from US$1886 million in 1994 to US$6402 million by 2002.

Table 16.1. Farm structure by farmland use in CEECs, 2000 (from Forgacs, 2004).

	Proportion of land area (%)					Average land area (ha)		
			Individual farms					
	Family farms (> 1 ha)	Household farms (< 1 ha)	1995–1998	2000	Large farms	Large farms	Family farms (> 1 ha)	Household farms (< 1 ha)
Slovakia[a]	8.9	2.5	5 (96/97)	11	77	1,360	10.6	0.21
Bulgaria[c]	5.7	17.3	52 (95/96)	23	77	535	6.2	0.9[b]
Czech Rep.	25.7	0.7	24 (1998)	26	74	998	27.4	1.5[b]
Hungary	53.2	3.8	60 (1998)	57	43	960	8.6	0.26
Estonia	68.9	10.4	63 (1997)	79	21	470	20.8	0.5
Romania	81.8[d]		65 (1998)	82	18	212	2.36	
Poland	84[d]		82 (1996)	84	16	440	7.2	0.38
Lithuania[d]	71.0	22.0[b]	67 (1996)	93	7	223	4.8	
Slovenia	93.9	–	96 (1997)	94	6	288	5.3	–
Latvia[e]	57.5	37.5	95 (1997)	95	5	1,135	13.7	4.9[b]

[a] 11.3% of farm is not classified; [b] defined as household farms; [c] cultivated agricultural land out of total 5,582,100 ha; [d] family and household farms together; [e] 1997 data. Some 10% of agricultural land is not classified. Lithuania: household farms: 22% of total farmland with an average of 2.2 ha.

Foreign capital first appeared in the tobacco, beverage and confectionery industries but now it has become widespread across the whole industry. Privatization and FDI had resulted in significantly improved production technologies and product quality and enlarged access to lucrative foreign markets. A large proportion of food processing is now under foreign ownership.

For example, in Hungary two-thirds of the capital in food processing is foreign owned. Countries such as Romania, which started later with privatization, have lost the early momentum and have attracted less FDI. In 2002, FDI in Romanian food processing amounted to only US$46 million and the restructuring of food processing is less advanced.

Companies owned by multinationals have become integrated into the enterprise business strategy and are part of regional specialization and concentration programmes. This is not always welcome by some countries, especially by workers and suppliers, and has thus negatively impacted. This foreign presence and growing concentration process are well illustrated by the example of concentration in the Hungarian dairy industry (see Fig. 16.1).

Foreign capital-driven restructuring and privatization of food processing have changed the behaviour of the industry in the raw materials market. Methods common in Western market economies became widespread, replacing delivery based on plan targets. The relation of industries to small farmers has entered to a new phase, as we describe it later.

The retail sector

The retail sector has gone through revolutionary changes. Similarly to the food processing sector, this change, however, was sequenced in various phases. The privatization of the inherited retail system and the emergence of small, private food and vegetable shops were the first steps in all featured countries. The real revolution in retail – the emergence of a highly concentrated and largely foreign-owned retail system – started later, first in Central Europe during the second half of 1990s and subsequently, with great rapidity, across the whole region. Hungary, the Czech Republic and Poland have the most modern retail systems, while the rest of the region is fast catching up but still lagging behind. Table 16.2 provides an overview of the results of changes in the three case study countries.

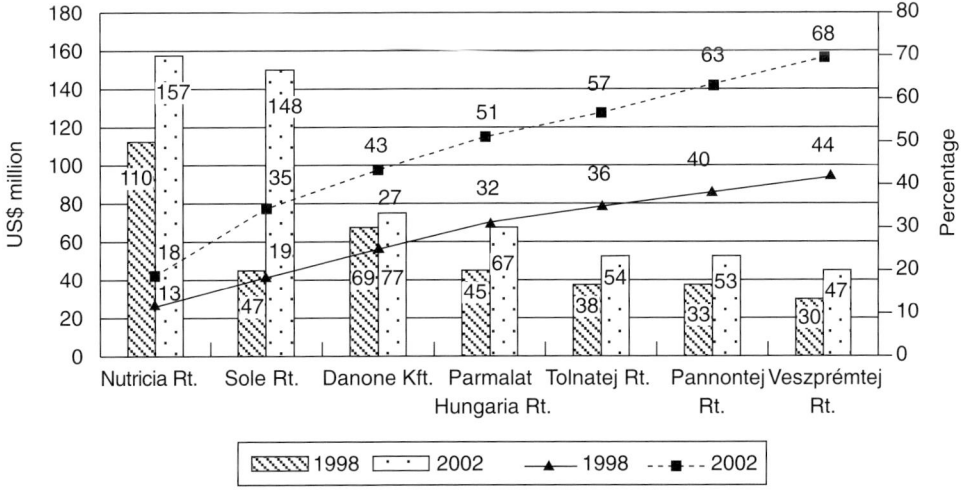

Fig. 16.1. Concentration in the Hungarian dairy industry, 1998 and 2002 (from Fertö et al., 2004).

Table 16.2. Key characteristics of the retail transformation in CEECs (from Csáki et al., 2004).

Characteristic	Political era											
	Communism			1990–1995			1995–2003			2003/2004		
	Hu	Po	Ro	Hu	Po	Ro	Hu	Po	Ro	Hu	Po	Ro
Concentration in retail sector	H	H	H	L	L	L	LH	LH	L	H	LH	L
Dominant source of capital	D	D	D	D	D	D	DF	DF	D	F	DF	D
Share of modern retail	L	L	L	L	L	L	LH	LH	L	H	LH	L
Share of large multinationals	L	L	L	L	L	L	LH	LH	L	H	H	L

Hu, Hungary; Po, Poland; Ro, Romania.
H, high (high concentration in the communism era as the channels were owned by the state); L, low (low concentration in the transition period due to privatization, with the emergence of many small companies); D, domestic; F, foreign.

Review of the situation in the case study countries provides interesting insights into changes in the retailing sector. The ratio of the top ten retailers shows the ever-quickening pace of concentration in the Hungarian food retail business. Between 1997 and 2003 the proportion of total sales for the ten largest food retailers increased by 37%. In both 1997 and 2003 the top ten retailers' share from total sales (52 and 89%, respectively) had been realized in around 20% of the stores, which means that those retailers could capture a larger market share without considerably increasing the number of stores.

Looking for reasons one has to take into account an important characteristic of the Hungarian food retail sector. In Hungary, from those ten retailers, one (Co-op/ÁFÉSZ) in 1997 and four (Co-op Hungary, CBA, Honiker and Reál) in 2003 had been so-called buying associations, some of them operating almost as a franchise system formed from a considerable number of relatively small (mostly 51–200 m² floor area) stores with independent ownership, or forming mini-chains.

In 1997, two other chains (Hungarotabak and Tobaccoland) had the same type of small-shop structure. The presence and development of these buyer associations is the main reason for the much slower decrease in the number of stores. These small-shop networks, according to GFK Hungary, were characterized by quite high (69.6%) penetration and frequency (35.3%) of shopping, but the consumer spending per shopping trip was quite low.

The review of developments in Romania shows a lesser degree of transformation of the retail sector. When looking at the top five in the Romanian grocery trade, things may, at first glance, look similar to the situation in Central and Eastern Europe: there are many foreign companies at the top of the tree. However, the situation is fundamentally different from markets such as Hungary and the Czech Republic, where Western retailers are involved in some aggressive business techniques: in Romania, there is only one grocer with a double-digit percentage market share (Metro Group).

In Poland, the proportion of modern distribution channels in retail sales, which includes hypermarkets, supermarkets and discount stores, has been increasing rapidly. This share increased from 18% in 1998 to 32% in 2002. According to experts' predictions, retail chains will control 50–60% of retail sales in the next 3–4 years (Retail & Consumer Worlds, 2004).

The intermediary trading system

Under central planning, farms delivered their products either directly to processing companies or to state-owned independent procurement organizations, which specialized in a number of commodities and had monopolistic positions. These purchasing organizations were the typical suppliers of the retail system, and often had their own retailing outlets as well.

As a result of reforms, wholesale organizations have become privatized and markets competitive. Wholesale markets were also created to facilitate the trade of mainly perishable farm products, fruit and vegetables. A relatively large number of wholesaling organizations now deal mainly with the unorganized small farmers. Their operation is often non-transparent, monopolistic and rent seeking. Their influence, however, has been challenged by the increasingly direct relationships between farmers and processors and by changes in the procurement practice through:

- shifting from local store-by-store procurement to nationally centralized purchasing centres;
- moving toward regionalization of national procurement systems;
- switching from traditional wholesalers to new, specialized wholesalers;
- increasing use of local logistical networks of multinational companies;
- switching to preferred supplier systems; and
- moving to higher private standards, quality and safety.

On the whole, the wholesale phase of the vertical flow has changed a lot. Most traditional wholesalers have been downsized or broken up and transformed. Changes in trade structure were also enforced by the rapid development of large international super- and hypermarket chains. The entrance of super- and hypermarket chains has increased competition, strongly influencing the situation of wholesale companies: these chains then started to purchase products directly from producers and to import directly from countries of origin, neglecting home wholesale companies.

In Hungary, the international chain, METRO, offers 7 days delivery a week, which is a challenge for other wholesalers who wish to keep their clients. This is a very competitive sector of the vertical chain, as foreign businesses are tough competitors in CEECs. If food imports are significant then there is a need for wholesalers to stock the required range of goods for customers. At this level, international chains do have the advantage over domestic.

Due to deregulation of the storage sector at the beginning of the 1990s, there was a dynamic development of small, independent wholesale companies in Poland, which are currently dominating the market. There are around 3800 such companies for which fruit and vegetable trade is the main activity (see Fig. 16.2). The small wholesale companies usually deliver fruit and vegetables to fruit-processing companies, as well as to local markets in towns. After a boom in small, local markets at the beginning of the 1990s, resulting from liquidation of traditional distribution channels, their role is currently diminishing.

Evolving Relations in Selected Supply Chains

In the three countries, six product chains have been analysed and major changes in the vertical line addressed. In the case of milk it was even possible to make a comparison between Hungary and Romania.

Wheat: Romania

Wheat production has a large share of gross agricultural outputs in all three countries, uses significant agriculture sector resources and provides raw materials for food processing as well as for animal feed. With a share of about 22% of arable land representing about 32% of the area under cereals, wheat is the main cereal for human consumption cultivated in Romania. Generally, about 10% of wheat production

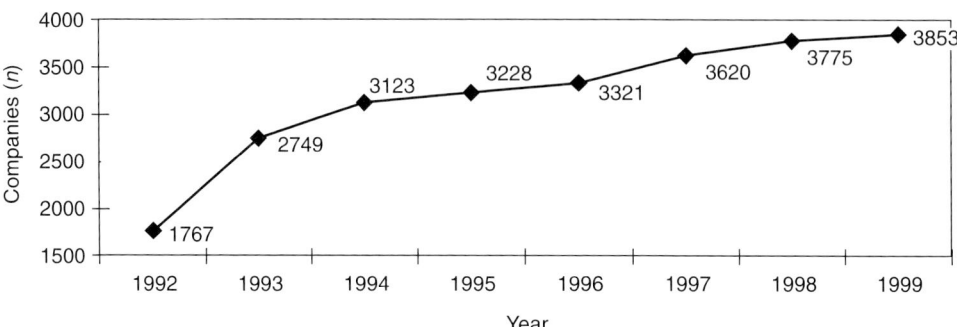

Fig. 16.2. Number of companies specializing in wholesale fruit and vegetable activity in Poland (from Pizlo, 2001).

is used for seed, another 10% for animal feed, about 20–25% for bread-making in rural households and thus only 55–60% enters the market chains.

The demand for wheat in Romania in the period 1989–2002 has been relatively constant, with the average consumption varying between 153 and 178 kg per capita, 30% higher in urban areas than in rural. Bread is considered to be the major staple food in the Romanian nutrition model, and therefore self-sufficiency in wheat is considered to be a matter of national security.

The wheat sector has gone through a significant restructuring in terms of ownership and farming. The share of the private sector in the area under wheat and rye in 1990–2000 amounted to 75–85%, and this had increased to 90% by 2001. Among the farms cultivating wheat, those with a utilized agricultural area (UAA) of up to 5 ha represent 84% of the total number and were cultivating only 27% of the area under wheat.

The way farms use their wheat production depends on how much they consume on the farm. The private agricultural associations are selling about half of their wheat production (38–59%) to storage and processing companies. Agricultural enterprises with a majority of state ownership are currently in various stages of privatization. They sell a little more than half (40–62%) of their wheat production to the storage and processing units.

Agricultural producers can sell wheat on the basis of specific contracts negotiated with certain beneficiaries after the price of the crop has been fixed. The individual, smaller households use the output of wheat for their own needs. If they have a larger area, they prefer to lease the land to local large farms. Because of privatization of the storage network and liberalization of tariffs there is no supervision by the government in this sector any more.

Price fluctuation has been a problem, but providing better coordination – at least at regional level – would help producers to avoid this. Partnerships of small producers with processors, although addressing quality requirements, have some disadvantages such as low farm gate prices, price fluctuation and poor productivity. If they sell under the coordination of producers' organizations, then a direct partnership with processors might be established, resulting in a better farm gate price based on stronger bargaining position. However, to avoid price fluctuations demands coordination of the supply side, at least at regional or even at national level.

The market for bread and bakery products is mostly domestic. There are the specialized companies producing bread and bakery products and belonging to agricultural commercial companies, to village mills and bakeries to cooperatives and all the various types of general food shops (hypermarkets, supermarkets, cash and carry, mixed shops, specialized shops, etc.). The large bakeries and bread-makers sell their products through their networks of specialized shops, supermarkets and mixed shops in large cities. The small-sized bakeries are still active today, mostly in small towns and in rural areas; in addition, cooperative-owned bakeries are also important in providing supplies in small towns and villages.

There are several chains through which producers can sell their primary products. Some of them work on a contractual basis or without it, but this brings higher risks for producers. Besides, one model of a vertically integrated chain has also appeared covering all phases of the vertical line from the buying of raw materials to production of the final product bought by consumers. This is the most advanced organizational form yet for increasing profitability and decreasing risks.

Data on added expenditure and price transmission in the chain can be seen in Tables 16.3 and 16.4. The greatest contribution in the chain relates to the agricultural sector (29%), but this provides, at the same time, the lowest profit (2.8%); the most profitable sector is trade, with profitability rates between 27 and 39%, rates that represent, at the chain level, between 39 and 60.6%.

The farming pattern for wheat did not change significantly during the transition period: the largest part of production (47%) came from small-size farms (private households). The medium-sized and large size farms produced 28%, and the state farms about 19%. Privatization of the state farms is presently ongoing, so this pattern is expected to change in the coming years. However, there are still many channels through which to sell wheat: because of efficiency problems small producers are not interested in selling.

Fruit and vegetables

Apple: Poland

Poland is the largest apple producer in Central and Eastern Europe, with production levels now 1.6–2.4 million t per year

Table 16.3. Expenditures added to the vertically integrated chain, Romania 2000 (from Gavrilescu et al., 2004).

	Free chain		Vertically integrated chain	
Sector	(Expense/unit)	(%)	(Expense/unit)	(%)
Agriculture[a]	3,046	29.0	3,046	29.0
Storage[a]	914	8.7	867	8.2
Milling[b]	1,990	18.9	1,267	12.1
Bakery[c]	1,713	16.3	1,540	14.7
Trade[c]	2,846	27.1	3,789	36.0
Total	10,509	100.0	10,509	100.0

[a] lei/kg wheat; [b] lei/720 g flour; [c] lei/kg bread.

Table 16.4. Profits obtained by the vertically integrated chain, Romania 2002 (from Gavrilescu et al., 2004).

	Free chain		Vertical integrated chain	
Sector	(Profit/unit)	(%)	(Profit/unit)	(%)
Agriculture[a]	−388	−9.0	146	2.8
Storage[a]	557	12.9	510	9.9
Milling[b]	775	17.9	680	13.3
Bakery[c]	1149	26.6	690	13.4
Trade[c]	1697	39.2	3117	30.6
Total	4330	100.0	5143	100.0

[a] lei/kg wheat; [b] lei/720 g flour; [c] lei/kg bread.

(2.43 million t in 2003). The largest share of apple production is from Central Poland (51%). Currently, production of fruit is widely dispersed. Small farms constitute the majority of fruit-growing farms, while most orchard land belongs to larger farms, these having, on average, > 5 ha. There is a trend for increasing specialization of market-oriented farms. While the number of fruit farms is diminishing, the total area of farmland under fruit production is increasing. In 2002, there were around 320,000 farms[2] with an orchard. Most of them (> 65%) were very small (< 5 ha), covering only 34% of the total orchard area of the country.

There are two important factors influencing apple production: farm size and membership of a producers' group. The smaller farmers, usually not associated with any producers' group, tend to perceive their situation as being difficult, mainly because of the lack of capital necessary for investment and a lack of influence in the market. Despite the existence of many branch organizations and associations, a very low level of economic cooperation between producers characterizes fruit and vegetable markets. Current producers' associations and horticultural cooperatives very often have organizational and financial problems and they do not fulfil their statutory tasks.

During the transition period, the apple market could be characterized as unorganized, with the widely dispersed structure of purchasers causing many problems for producers.

A new breed of purchasers, such as supermarket chains and foreign processing companies, then entered the field, changing business conditions substantially. Fruit exchanges (*gieldy*) ceased to play an important role, while platforms of market chains (*platformy*) took over their tasks. Also, producers started to sell directly to supermarket chains and to fruit processing companies. A monopolist in the foreign fruit trade (Hortex) lost its dominant position. Currently, in the central region of Poland there are around 300 exporting companies that compete all strongly.

The developing market can also be characterized by the creation of producers' groups, which currently have only a marginal share in agricultural raw material distribution. According to members of these groups, the most important problems with purchasers are connected with delayed payment and the necessity of meeting high quality requirements. Producers have very tight deadlines for delivering products, they have to provide their own transport, pay high advertising costs and a large share of the delivered products' value is deducted (on account of spoiled fruit).

In order to improve cooperation in the vertical chain, one of the interviewed processing companies plans to start close cooperation with producers and to support them in producing given subspecies of apples needed for juice extract production. This support could include training and finance credit. However, producers would have to guarantee supply.

Onion: Hungary

In Hungary, the fruit and vegetable sector is very important. Consumption in 2002 amounted to 203.2 kg per capita. There has been a decrease in production during recent years caused by declining fruit consumption, especially that of domestic fruits (–18%). Vegetables make up 55% of this consumption. Onion accounts for around 20% of the total fresh vegetable consumption and is a traditional product of Hungarian agriculture. Production goes back to the Turkish occupation of the country in the 16th century. Traditionally, onion production was based on the use of baby onions (first-year baby onions were produced from seed and these baby onions were planted the following year to grow red onion), but since the 1970s onion production has been based mainly on planting onion seed.

Two regions have a leading role in the production: the Northern Great Plain (31%) and the Southern Great Plain (46%) region, the Makó area. Onion, but especially Makó onion because of its good storability, excellent quality and high dry matter content. It traditionally had been a successful, mainly export product of Hungary which, unfortunately, has changed in recent years. Production of Makó onion has gone through a difficult period because of shortage of budget for R and D.

Table 16.5 shows that the private farmers' share of onion production in the analysed period was always close to 90%. This means that the production of onion is mainly by farmers producing on a small scale and, despite some production by producers' organizations (POs), onion production is one of the most fragmented sectors in Hungarian agriculture.

To gain a better market position an increasing number of small producers decided to join POs during recent years. For example, the onion PO, Makó was founded in February 2003 and registered later in that year with an agenda of vegetable production. Among members one can find small producers (10%), entrepreneurs (20%) and partnerships (70%). Makó manages 500 ha, of which 300 is for onion production. The total number of producers involved amounts to 140, with a total annual turnover of HUF 500 million, HUF 300 million of which goes toward onion production. To improve their bargaining power, Makó – along with 20 other POs – have established a joint stock company providing an example of increasing cooperation between small producers. After a cautious beginning, this venture is now gaining momentum. Onion POs have considerable influence within the Onion Produce Council, founded in 1993.

Dramatic changes have taken place in the vertical flow of onion production between 1998 and 2002. In 2002, 85–88% of onion production came from private farmers, a drop in output compared to that in 1998, due to a decline in the onion-producing area. Total fresh sales amounted to 45 and 47%, respectively.

At retail level there was a strong shift in volume (from 26 to 39%) to modern and traditional retail store formats through wholesale markets and a decrease, from 28 to 21%, to consumer markets. At the same time, consumption from own production dropped from 47 to 30%.

Subsequently, upon joining producers' organizations, the position of small producers started to become stabilized; however, producers have not yet become fully efficient players in the vertical chain. POs have changed the procurement system by taking over a wholesale function and representing small producers when making deals with other wholesalers, processors or retailers. POs mean an umbrella for small farmers to coordinate supply and establishing stronger bargain power for marketing.

Fruit and vegetable processing, with the top ten companies capturing 41% of the net sales, is not as concentrated a position as in the dairy industry, and increased by only 1% between 1998 and 2002. Despite a number of structural changes already established in both the dairy and the fruit and vegetable processing sectors, EU accession has certainly brought more challenges.

As with processing, FDI has been significant in altering the structure of, and buyer relationships at, the retail level. These

Table 16.5. Smallholders' (individual farmers') share (%) of production and cultivation area of onion and other vegetables, Hungary, 1998–2003 (from Fertö et al., 2004).

	1998	1999	2000	2001	2002	2003	Increase, 1998–2003 (%)
Production							
Onion	88.4	90.3	87.6	84.4	85.3	89.5	+1.24
Vegetables	82.5	86.8	77.2	75.6	71.7	73.1	−11.40
Area*							
Onion	81.1	83.6	76.5	83.2	77.0	84.3	+3.95

investors have developed along Western European lines by introducing and developing warehouse point distribution, own brands and systems for electronic data interchange (EDI). The structural changes in recent years are the most evident in the retail sector. Based on estimations in the case of HORECA, onion consumption increased by about 8%. One important trend is the absolute and relative decline of the consumption from own production (26 and 18%, respectively) and from farmers' markets (28 and 21%, respectively). This portion of the onion market is now mostly bought in the modern and traditional retail formats (see Fig. 16.3).

Pigs: Poland

The number of pigs in Poland in 1986 totalled 13.4 million, in 1996 15.2 million and in 2003 approximately 19.0 million. Pork consumption has stabilized at a level of 40/kg per capita. Pig production in Poland is concentrated on private family farms, usually of small area and therefore having limited production capacity (see Table 16.6). Within 10 years, the number of pig producers has dropped from 1.66 million to 1.09 million (−35%), but it is still very large. In years 1986–1996, the average ratio of pigs to producer increased by 75% from 8 to 14, but this level is still low. It is caused by the small scale of pig production on farms with an area of less than 10 ha, but this type of pig production predominates in Poland.

In the early 1990s small trade companies were created on the basis of cooperative and state-owned outlets, as well as new private entities. Freedom to create market relationships and lack of administrative restrictions allowed for the development of new distribution channels in the pork market. Concerning the status in the vertical chain, members of producers' groups are in a better position vis-à-vis meat-processing companies than are independent farmers, by having beneficial, negotiated contracts.

The transformation process has resulted in changes in the ratio of registered to unregistered animal procurement in Poland. In the first phase of transformation, integration relationships between pig producers with meat-processing companies based on the contracting system collapsed. Entrepreneurship of small companies, lack of entry barriers for new entities and their better accessibility to a dispersed retail network conspired to the effect that the state sector lost its dominating market position in a very short time, partly due to delay in the restructuring of state-owned companies.

Meat processing is also dispersed within Poland. There are 4200 firms involved in the pig industry: 2800 dealing with slaughtering and cutting up of animals, 2650 processing red meat, 650 producing minced meat and 70 dealing with meat storage. Eight hundred and seventy of these processing plants employ over five people each and 350 plants each have more than 50 employees. Large and medium-sized plants control 41% of slaughtering and 60% of meat processing. The level of specialization in the meat industry is relatively low. Utilization of production capacity in meat-processing plants, in most cases, does not exceed 60%, and technical and technological standards of the Polish meat industry are very differentiated.

Contracts between farmers and meat-processing companies can cover one or more years, and usually include: minimum number of deliveries/procurements per year, monthly or quarterly number of deliveries, minimum of pigs per delivery and payment time limits for delivered pigs. Prices differ according to the quality of meat specified in EUROPE classification.

The major difficulty for small scale pig producers is providing the quality and quantity that processors need and, in addition, they find the farm gate price very low. For small producers adjustment of specialization and concentration in production would be a solution but, however, due to high input costs and having no economy of scale, small producers, in this subsector, cannot be competitive in general. One

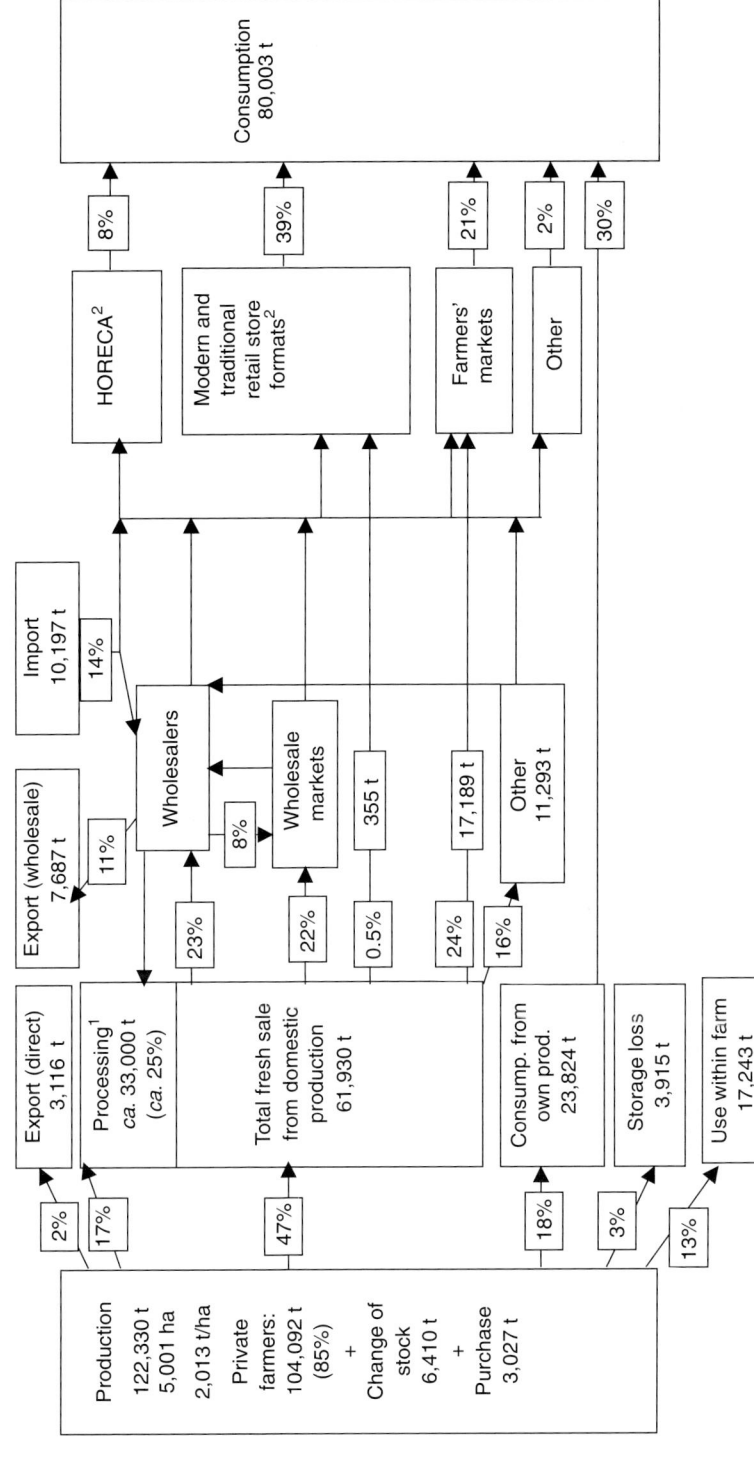

Fig. 16.3. Vertical integration for onion production in Hungary, 2002 (from Fertö et al., 2004). Production level (100%), 131,762 t; wholesale level (100%), 71,169t; retail level (100%), 80,003 t.

Table 16.6. Pig production on individual farms in Poland by size of herd, 1986 and 1996 (from Wilkin *et al.*, 2004).

Herd category by number of pigs	Farms (*n*)		Structure of farms (%)		Pigs (*n*)		Structure of pig production (%)	
	1986	1996	1986	1996	1986	1996	1986	1996
1–10	1,277	687	76	63	4,581	2,924	34	16
11–50	368	349	22	32	7,144	7,029	53	46
50–99	16	38	20	4	1,051	2,549	8	17
100 and over	4	14	0	1	626	3,150	5	21
Total	1,665	1,088	100	100	13,402	15,152	100	100

would expect that their share in pig production will decrease over time.

Regarding wholesale activities in the distribution of food products, it is known that there are 14,000 local wholesalers employing more than five people; this accounts for 80% of all wholesalers in the market. Regarding bigger wholesalers, these include: five nationwide wholesale networks, five procurement groups, 60 regional wholesale networks and 500 regional wholesale firms.

In the rationalization process of the vertical chain, processors try to eliminate middlemen and set up direct links with primary producers. However, as regards small producers, the process of purchasing pigs from producers has not yet been taken over by processors from middlemen and agents. On the other hand, producers' associations can initiate negotiations with processors and coordinate the supply chains of small producers, thus achieving a better farm gate price for pigs.

Besides the quantity and quality aspects, it is more demanding for small producers to use selected varieties of pig and reduce production costs. For producers of pork it is very important to be integrated with meat-processing companies: those who do not contract with the companies receive at least 10% less for their pork deliveries. There is also an economy-of-scale benefit for bigger producers.

There are several factors causing problems in the vertical chain (see Fig. 16.4).

In the 1990s a brokerage of private wholesale companies became one of the basic distribution channels of purchase of pigs for slaughter for processing companies. Private wholesale companies usually cooperate with small and medium-sized pig producers and with medium-sized and large-scale meat-processing companies.

In the retail trade there are 15,000 meat stores, 90,000 grocery stores, 1800 large network stores and 65,000 catering units. The share of large network shops in the distribution of meat and meat products is around 33% (Przemiany, 2004). Large retailers have the most noticeable impact on the improvement in product quality, on vertical and horizontal integration and on rationalization of the delivery system; however, price fluctuation is still a severe problem and has a strong impact on procurement and retail prices (see Fig. 16.5).

In the food chain in Poland one can observe a growing structural asymmetry. At both ends of the food chain there are a large number of actors: 1.1 million producers of primary products (farmers) and 12 million consumers (households). These groups form a highly competitive environment. In the middle there are processing plants and traders where concentration is growing quickly. In some regions there are food processors or procurement companies with quasi-monopolistic positions where they can dictate delivery prices and increase profits at a cost to agricultural producers.

Milk: Hungary and Romania

In Hungary, the consumption of milk declined constantly in the first half of the 1990s, but then from 1995 to 2000 it started

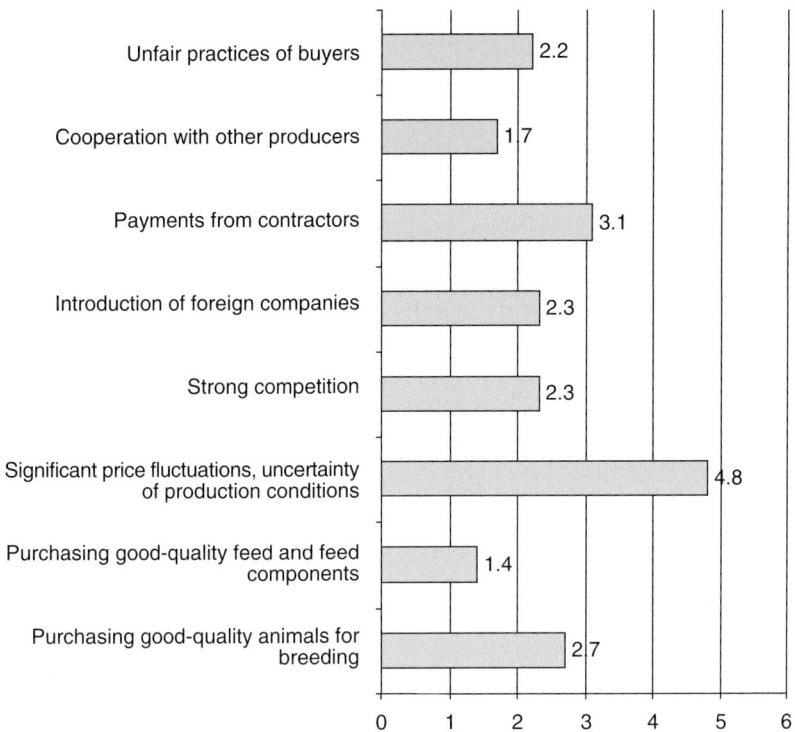

Fig. 16.4. The main problems affecting the production and procurement of pork, according to farmers surveyed (from Wilkin et al., 2004). Scale: 1, least important; 5, most important.

to increase again, with a decline of 10.2%. Milk production has fluctuated at around 2 billion l/year in response to the changing economic and political conditions between 1993 and 2003.

In contrast, in Romania the average annual per capita domestic consumption increased continuously during the transition period (1990–2000) from 144 to 194 l of dairy products, where processed milk represents only a fraction of the total milk output. Almost 80% of the total output is either consumed on-farm or sold on the peasant markets as fresh milk, cheese or cream. The remaining 20% is sold to processing units.

In Hungary the structure of milk production has changed considerably during the previous 14 years. The number of dairy farms decreased dramatically between 1996 and 2003 – by 45% for private farms, but the fall for agricultural enterprises was much more modest, at 12%. Surprisingly, during the period analysed, the average herd size decreased from 326 to 298 in agricultural enterprises, whilst it increased from 2.9 to 4.4 on private farms.

Nowadays, around 700–800 agricultural enterprises and 20–25,000 private farmers keep dairy cows. Milk production, on the other hand, has shown a slight tendency to increase over the last decade. The production in 2003 was 2.02 million t, with an average lifetime yield per cow of 6168 kg. Compared to the EU-15 countries, yields are still 5–20% lower, but higher than in other NMS (New Member State) countries.

The dairy farm structure differs between agricultural enterprises and private farms. Ninety-five per cent of private farms have fewer than ten cows, while 74% of agricultural enterprises have more than 100. The proportion of farms having fewer than ten cows is 71% for private farms and 0.1% for agricultural enterprises.

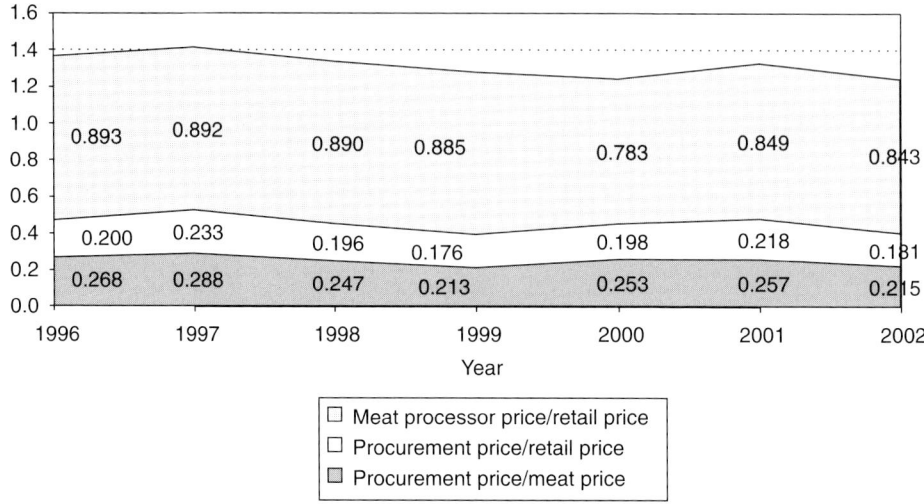

Fig. 16.5. Price relations in vertical integration in the Polish ham industry, 1996–2002 (from Wilkin et al., 2004).

Foreign direct investment has played a dominant role in the Hungarian food industry. Although the number of foreign-owned companies decreased between 1995 and 2002, their role in owners' equity represents > 70%, and their share in net sales exceeds 50%. Concentration in the milk processing sector started in the middle of the 1990s, but the number of processors is still around 80, although, the top ten companies commanded almost 80% of the net sales and the top five 57%. The concentration in the dairy export sector has already reached a fairly high level, the largest ten processors capturing 89% of the total export market.

From the three channels (sales to wholesalers, to retailers and other sales) the processors–retail sector is by far the most important (~ 60%). An important trend is the absolute and relative decline of: (i) the consumption from own production (−40 ml; −2%), to 1%; and (ii) direct sales to consumers (−70ml; −4%), to 4%, between 1998 and 2002.

The larger processors that relied on sizeable numbers of small producers for raw milk have rationalized the number of actors they deal with. Frequently, dairies ensure their supplies via long-term skeleton contracts with the larger milk producers, annually agreeing prices and quantities to be supplied. Contracting allows dairies to have greater control over the agricultural production process. The processors determine quality requirements and enforce them through the procurement system. Farmers are paid according to the quality of milk, with bonus payments for 'extra quality' milk and penalties for, or refusal to purchase, milk below certain quality thresholds. These quality thresholds have had the effect of excluding small-scale producers who cannot preserve the quality of their milk due to the lack of adequate cooling facilities.

During the transition period in Romania, significant changes occurred in the cattle sector, the state dairy farms almost disappearing. By 2001, 98.3% of cattle were in private ownership. The herds are, however, not equally distributed all over the country. There has been a shift from large dairy farms, state-owned or former cooperatives, to very small-sized private households. The latter shift has resulted in continuously increasing yields and total milk production. Of total milk production, about 95% was being produced by households (small-sized farms) in 2000. The average annual per capita domestic consumption increased continuously during the transition period (1990–2000), from 144 to 194 l of milk and milk products, while the butter consumption dropped dramatically from 2.1 kg (1990) to 0.3 kg (2000).

The high percentage of family consumption (40%) certifies that most dairy farms are producing for self-consumption: it is the main channel through which milk reaches the consumer. Seventy per cent of the milk quantity consumed in Romania is represented by non-processed milk. There are two distribution channels for processed milk: industrial or at peasant household level (artisan processing).

Concerning distribution of industrially processed dairy products, this is organized on a contract basis between milk processors and retail outlets (stores) on the one hand and, with the intermediary distribution firms, delivering products to large stores/supermarkets in the larger towns on the other. Another type of distribution channel for fresh milk, cheese and sour cream is a type of direct sale – typically from small farms.

The milk sector saw more fundamental changes during the transition period. The private agricultural associations with dairy farms emerging after de-collectivization organized their own collection points with basic cooling facilities (if any), on the premises of the old ones. The large dairy companies organized their collection system in collection centres, sited around factory locations. These are supplied with milk from the collection points located in villages.

Privatization of the state-owned enterprises has been slow (it had reached only 75% in 1999) and was completed only by the end of 2000. In the same period, a large number of new, private, small and medium-size enterprises for milk and dairy emerged. In 2002, the milk and dairy-processing sector comprised a total of 835 enterprises. There are some very large processors that operate in the dairy industry (SC Napolact SA, Cluj Napoca and SC Friesland Romania SA processing about 300,000 l/day; SC Danone SRL, 130,000 l/day, SC Parametru SRL, 100,000 l/day, etc.).

Processed milk represents just a fraction of the total milk output. Almost 80% of the total output is either consumed on-farm or sold on the peasant markets as fresh milk, cheese or cream. The small and medium-sized processing units (yearly average processing capacity of 1000–5000 hl) processed 90% of the total milk purchased by the processing industry in 2002. On the other hand, their accumulated turnover reached only 30% of that of the large enterprises.

Small, private milk and dairy-processing units emerged, producing mainly drinking milk with higher fat content and packed in plastic bags, and cheese (white and yellow). These were supplied with raw milk by the local agricultural and family associations. The SMEs in the milk and dairy industrial sector are very volatile, the number of processing units changing significantly from year to year.

Since 1997, important foreign investors have entered the industry (Danone, Hochland, etc.). Their arrival has meant important investments in machinery and tehnologies, new products on the markets and significantly improved quality, packaging, management and marketing of the products. These investments in the large enterprises in the milk and dairy industry have resulted in a significant increase in concentration and a decline in imports, due to the fact that they have started to produce various products locally.

The newly emerged small-sized milk-processing enterprises paid the farmers lower prices than did the controlled ones, but some of the farmers were happy to be paid less, but with no delay, in comparison with the higher price-plus-bonuses scheme of the state-owned milk-processing companies. This latter method of payment often meant a time lag for payment of up to 6 months, during which time the value of money frequently became considerably devalued due to high inflation rates. Some of the former state-owned milk-processing companies recreated a part of their collection network, by paying reasonable prices to farmers and – most importantly – with little or no delay. Some of them make contracts directly with the farmers, other deal with collection centres.

Small Farmers in the Changing Market

Changing the patterns of vertical coordination have a significant impact upon small farmers in the region, mainly through their links with processing and wholesaling, but also by the changing structure of retailing. There are both positive and negative impacts. On the positive side, the increased demand for quality products and the improved competitive input supply need first to be mentioned. The assessments of the negative consequences are somewhat more complicated.

A key concern is that the emerging new vertical chains will exclude a large proportion of farmers and, in particular, small farmers. There are a number of important reasons for this:

- Transaction costs favour larger farms in supply chains; it is more difficult and costly to procure products from a larger number of producers.
- When a certain amount of investment is needed in order to contract with or supply to the company, small farms are often more constrained by their financial means from making the necessary investments.
- Per unit of output, small farms typically require more assistance from the company.
- Small farmers are often conservative and unable to recognize the need for quality and changes in production methods.
- Small farmers are suspicious and biased against any form of cooperation that would improve their bargaining position and their access to markets in general.
- Small farmers are also handicapped by the state of rural infrastructure and the level of communication facilities available.

These case studies show a largely consistent picture and confirm the main hypotheses (Swinnen, 2005) that transaction costs and investment constraints are a serious consideration and that companies express a preference for working with relatively fewer, larger and modern suppliers.

However, our initial observations also show a very mixed picture of actual contracting, with many more small farms being contracted than was initially predicted, based on the arguments above. Small farmers are not fully excluded from the supply chains and more major companies also contract with small farmers. More sophisticated supplier assistance programmes, however, tend to be more readily available for larger farms. Often, supplier programmes fail to address the characteristics of the entire range of farm types. For example, in case studies of dairy processors, investment support for larger farms included leasing arrangements for on-farm equipment, while assistance programmes for smaller dairy farms included investments in collection units with micro-refrigeration units.

According to our investigation, the degree of integration of small farmers into vertical product chains depends on the actual farming structure in a given country. In countries like Hungary, where larger farms dominate the supply of primary products, there is less encouragement for processors and traders to deal with small farms and these, to a large extent, are excluded or unable to integrate into new vertical chains.

In countries with a preponderance of smallholder agriculture, despite the apparent disadvantages noted earlier, the empirical evidence suggests that vertical coordination with small farmers is widespread. Furthermore, empirical evidence presented in the World Bank study (2005) indicates that companies, in reality, work with surprisingly large numbers of suppliers and of surprisingly small size.

Our case studies suggest also that company preferences for contracting with large farms are not as obvious as one might think. While processors may prefer to deal with large farms because of lower transaction costs in, e.g. collection and administration, however, contract enforcement may be more problematic, and hence costly, with larger farms. Processors repeatedly emphasized (Swinnen, 2005) that farms' 'willingness to learn, take on board advice and a professional attitude were more important than size in establishing fruitful farm–processor relationships.

In some cases, small farms may have substantive cost advantages. This is particularly the case in labour-intensive, high maintenance, production activities with relatively small economies of scale. Processors may prefer a mix of suppliers in order not to become too dependent on a few large suppliers. This situation is, to a large extent, due to the fact that during the first period of the transition Central and Eastern Europe has been a supplier's market.

The collapse of farm output has created a gap between processing capacity and supply: hence there has been excess demand based on processing capacity. This situation has, however, changed quickly. Hungary and Poland – and even Romania – in recent years are already experiencing strong competition between farm suppliers, and product quality is constantly improving. If this competition between suppliers increases, or if demand falls, pressure on processors may lead to a consolidation of the supplier base. This suggests that one should not be complacent, despite the observations of significant contracting with small suppliers taking place.

Small farmers often cannot make the necessary upgrades, and will depend on farm assistance. If there is sufficient (quality) supply, this will be a problem, because the processor is unlikely to come up with adequate support packages. Hence,

we have the paradoxical situation that small, poor farms may be better off (in the context of 'supply chain-driven development') if they are in an environment that is dominated by small, poor farms. In a more competitive and supply-dominated environment, however, cooperation between small farmers is an essential precondition of survival and active participation in the product chains.

Case studies indicate that small farmers in the region are rather slow to recognize the necessity of cooperation in the marketing of their products. The negative experience with collective farming from the Communist period has made a significant negative impact upon farmers' attitude toward any form of cooperation. Those who finally decided to join POs were able to increase their bargaining power, and thereby could maintain their production level; even their adjustment to increased quality requirements was easier.

Apple producers in Poland even asked for government support to stabilize the market prices by contracting and applying minimum prices. Those apple producers who had joined POs – as well as the big independent wholesalers – gained significant advantages over those not involved in any cooperative arrangements.

During the transition, product markets were not well organized for some years. It was true for apple markets in Poland as well as for the onion and milk markets in Hungary. In recent years producers have had to cope with ever-stronger competition forced by super- and hypermarkets, which forced them to enter into some form of cooperation in marketing.

However, there also seem to be differences between processing companies in their willingness to work with small farms. Some processing companies continue to work with small local suppliers even when others do not. These companies have been able to design and enforce contracts which both the small farms and the companies find beneficial. This suggests that small-scale farmers may have future prospects when effectively organised. Companies willing to invest in upgrading small farms only go so far, and tend to have a strategy in the long term to upgrade part of their supply to larger, more efficient and fewer suppliers.

Conclusions

At the end of the day, the question has to be asked: how has the emergence of large retail outlets, the so-called retail revolution, impacted upon small producers? Farm leaders and the public media often blame supermarket chains for the increased difficulties of small farms and persistent rural poverty. In reality, as our case studies indicate, the situation is much more complex. The difficulties of small farmers are the result of a number of problems, and supermarkets are only one of them. Further research would be needed to gain insights into these factors and establish fully verifiable conclusions on the impacts of the retail revolution upon small farmers.

The majority of small farms in this region are subsistence oriented and have only marginal contacts with markets. Most of these contacts are with local markets or in the form of direct sales from the farm. They have practically no direct relations with large retailing systems. Beyond local markets they sell to wholesalers and to the processing industry. Impacts of the retail revolution can be felt by them via increased demands and pressures from the wholesaling and processing side.

The integration of small farms into vertical chains requires fundamental change on the side of small farms as well. However, a large proportion of them are unwilling or unable to make these changes. These farms will either maintain their part-time, subsistence nature, providing only additional income or else disappear, providing scope for consolidation of the remainder. Many of these small farmers will, however, become more commercial, increase their farm size, improve their technology and will cooperate in order to cope with the challenges of vertical chains. Policies should target these farmers, supporting them in this process.

Notes

1. This study is based upon the IIED project Regoverning Markets (Phase I). Specifically, the following references were used as major source materials: Csaki et al. (2004) – Regional Summary, 2004; Fertö et al. (2004) – Country Study, Hungary; Gavrilescu et al. (2004) – Country Study, Romania; Wilkin et al. (2004) – Country Study, Poland.
2. This represents around 11% of the total number of farms in Poland.

References

Csáki, C., Forgács, C. and Kovács, B. (2004) CEE – *Regional summary. Regoverning markets* (Phase 1).

Fertö, I., Forgács, C., Juhász, A. and Kürthy, G. (2004) *Country study – Hungary. Regoverning markets.* (Phase 1).

Forgacs, C. (2004) The challenge of integrating CEEC agriculture into the EU. Presidential address, *EAAE Congress, Studies in Agricultural Economics*, Zaragoza, Spain, 2002. AKII, Budapest, (100), pp. 19–38.

Gavrilescu, D., Grodea, M., Serbanescu, C. and Turtoi, C. (2004) *Country study – Romania*. Regoverning markets (Phase 1).

Pizło, W. (2001) Rynek owoców w Polsce i wybranych krajach Unii Europejskiej – ujęcie teoretyczne i empiryczne. Wydawnictwo SGGW, Warsaw.

Przemiany przemyslu spozywczego w latach 1988–2003 (2004) R. Urban (ed.), IERGZ, Warsaw.

Reardon, T. and Swinnen, J.F.M. (2004) *Agrifood Sector Liberalization and the Rise of Supermarkets in Former State-controlled Economies: Comparison with Other Developing Countries*. Development Policy Review.

Retail & Consumer Worlds (2004) *Winning Strategies in Russia and Central and Eastern Europe, 2003/2004*. Price Waterhouse Coopers, International.

Swinnen, J.F.M. (2005) *Changing Market Relations in Central and Eastern Europe*. World Bank Manuscript, Washington, DC.

Wilkin, J., Juchniewicz, M. and Milczarek, D. (2004) Country study – Poland. Regoverning markets (Phase 1).
World Bank (2005) *Comparative Analyis of Vertical Relations in Agriculture in Selected ECA Countries*. World Bank, Washington, DC.

17 The Impact of Retail Investments in the Czech Republic, Slovakia, Poland and the Russian Federation

L. Dries, T. Reardon, and E. Van Kerckhove

Introduction

One of the main characteristics of the retail market in Central Eastern Europe (CEE) is the dominant position of international retail companies. In 2003, the five companies that generated the highest aggregate sales revenue in the region were all foreign owned: Metro, Tesco, Rewe, Tengelmann and Auchan (PMR, 2005).

Furthermore, six CEE countries are in the top ten of most attractive investment sites for retailers, according to AT Kearney's 2005 global retail development index. Finally, both in 2003 and 2004, Russia was leading the top ten of countries receiving the highest share of foreign direct investments (FDI) by global retail chains.

An important global discussion exists on the impact of FDI in general and rapid food retail investments in specific on local suppliers. Case studies in the CEE region suggest that foreign investors have played an important role in solving specific transition problems caused by the breakdown of exchange systems and contract enforcement mechanisms through vertical coordination throughout the supply chain (Foster, 1999; Gow *et al.*, 2000). In some cases at least, such FDI-induced vertical coordination has contributed to improved access to finance and inputs, and productivity growth of suppliers (Gow and Swinnen, 2001; Dries and Swinnen, 2004).

On the other hand, there exists a wide body of literature pointing to the dangers of increased (foreign) investments in modern food retailing for local (especially small) suppliers. For example, Farina and Reardon (2000) and Reardon and Berdegué (2002) show, using the example of retail investments in Latin America, how this can lead to the rapid exclusion of thousands of small suppliers.

The reason for this exclusion can be found in the fact that foreign investors in the food supply chain prefer to deal with a few large suppliers to minimize transaction costs, forcing consolidation of the supplier base and hence separating many small suppliers from their traditional outlets (Runsten and Key, 1996; Holloway *et al.*, 2000; Winters, 2000). Higher standards for quality and food safety are other factors that limit the opportunities for local suppliers that have difficulties in complying with these requirements in order to survive in a rapidly changing trading environment.

The success of the CEE region in attracting investments from the main global retailers in recent years makes this region an interesting case for identifying the impact of food retail investments on the local supply base. The evidence presented in this chapter is based on interviews in the Czech Republic, Poland, Slovakia and the Russian Federation. The first section discusses the methodology and data collection process. In the second section, we draw on evidence from various statistical sources to describe investments in the retail sector in the different countries that are covered in our study. Next, we discuss the effect that these investments have had on restructuring the procurement system for food. Finally, we present evidence of the impact of the changing procurement systems for local food suppliers. This evidence is presented in two case studies, dairy products and fresh fruit and vegetables (FFV).

Methodology and Data

This chapter is based on interviews with players at different levels in the food supply chain: primary producers (farmers and farmers' organizations), processors, wholesalers and food retailers (both large-scale, i.e. hypermarkets, supermarkets and discount stores and traditional retailers). The interviews focused on the one hand on the dairy sector (Poland and Russia) and on the fresh fruit and vegetables chain (Czech Republic and Slovakia) on the other.

The four selected countries present an interesting mix. According to Dries *et al.* (2004), the Czech Republic and Poland are considered front-runners in terms of the modernization of the retail sector. In the Russian Federation, on the other hand, the retail transformation has lagged behind significantly compared to developments in the front-runner countries.

Supermarkets tend to penetrate fresh food (such as fresh fruits and vegetables) retail markets and make changes in their procurement systems in these markets more slowly than for processed/packaged food products, which lend themselves more easily to these kinds of changes. Because the retail transformation in the Russian Federation has started relatively recently compared to that in the Central European countries, we decided to focus on the Russian processed food sector (more specifically, dairy).

Another factor is that the dairy sector is more important than the FFV sector in the Russian Federation, both in terms of output and employment. As a result, procurement system changes in the dairy sector have a potentially larger impact on the rural population than changes in the FFV sector.

Similarly, the dairy sector is of crucial importance for the livelihood of many rural families in Poland. Moreover, the Polish dairy sector presents an interesting case, as the recent developments in the retail sector and procurement systems have coincided (or interacted) with adjustments caused by a combination of transition elements, foreign investments in the processing sector and the European integration process. The latter may have had a specific impact on the dairy sector, on top of possible external factors that are driving dairy sector restructuring in the Russian Federation, through the imposition of EU hygiene and food safety rules, pre-accession investment support, etc.

In the Czech Republic and Slovakia we have opted to study the FFV sector. This sector is of special interest because the supply chain is generally shorter than in the case of processed products. This means that changing procurement systems will have a direct impact on primary producers of FFV, because there is no processor in the chain to buffer the effect.

Retail Investments

The spread of the large-scale retail sector

Figure 17.1 illustrates how the share of the large-format retail sector in total retail has increased rapidly in the Czech Republic and Slovakia. For example, in the Czech Repub-

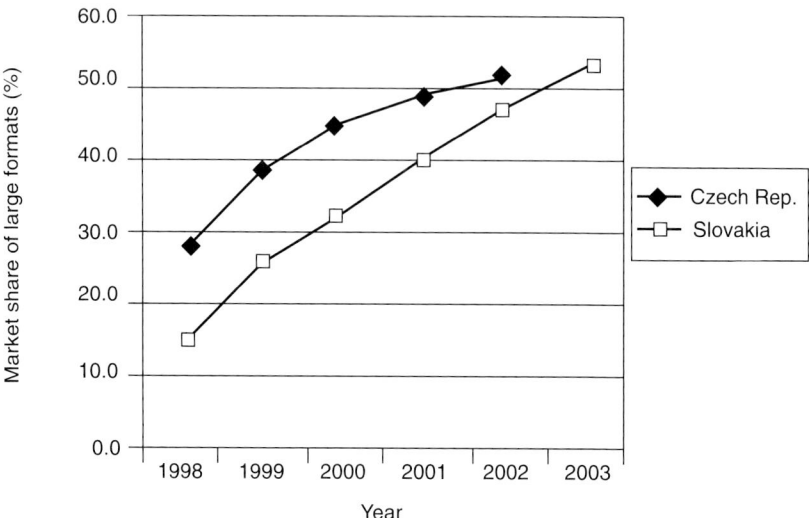

Fig. 17.1. Change in total market share of large-format retail sector in the Czech Republic and Slovakia, 1998–2003 (from Shopping Monitor CE (INCOMA Research)).

lic, this share has grown from around 30% of the total retail market in 1998 to more than 50% in 2002. Notice how the market share of the large-format retail sector was already higher in the Czech Republic in the late 1990s, but that the Slovakian large-scale retail sector has continued its rapid growth in the ensuing 5 years.

The share of large formats in overall food retail has also increased dramatically in the past 6 years (since the economic crisis of 1998) in the Russian Federation. The overall share of supermarkets in national food retail rose from virtually zero to 10% during this period.

Furthermore, Fig. 17.2 shows that large formats are the-fastest growing retail format in the Moscow region. Between 2001 and 2003, the share of large formats in total food retail has increased from less than 10% to 30% of the Moscow market. At the same time, the market share of traditional retail outlets has decreased substantially.

Internationalization of the retail sector

Table 17.1 shows the entry year and location of investments by the leading retailers in Central Europe. First, these eight retail companies together comprise almost 28% of the €59.4 billion grocery sales in the region (IGD, 2004). Secondly, the table shows that the major retailers have first invested in the Czech Republic, Hungary and Poland before venturing into the Slovakian grocery market. This observation is in line with the late entry of foreign investors in other Slovakian food sectors. This was due to the poor political environment in the mid-1990s in Slovakia. Finally, we remark that all of the major retail chains have invested in more than one of the Central European countries.

When we look at FDI in the retail sector in individual CEE countries we see a confirmation of the strong position held by international retail companies. The number of foreign companies in the top ten retailers in 2004 is ten in the Czech Republic (approximately 62% market share); nine in Poland (30%); six in Slovakia (38%); and three in the Russian Federation (6%) (IGD, 2004; LZ, 2005).

Move to secondary cities and rural towns

In the same way that foreign chains move from the competition in their home coun-

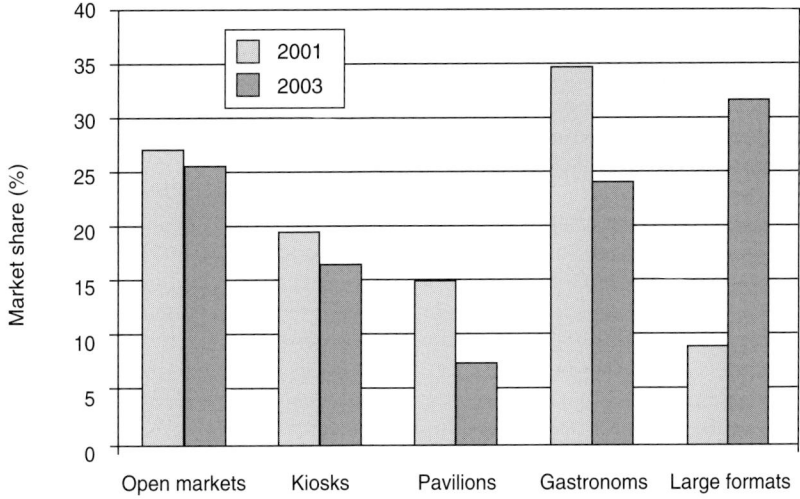

Fig. 17.2. Change in food market share of large-format retail sector in the Moscow region, 2001 and 2003 (from IGD, 2004).

Table 17.1. Expansion of major retailers in Central Europe by entry year and location (from IGD, 2004).

Retailer	Sales* (€ million)	1989	1990	1991	1992	1993	1994	1995	1996	1997	1998	1999	2000	2001
Metro	4961						Hu, Pl		Cz				Sk	
Tesco	2815						Hu	Pl	Cz				Sk	
Rewe	1845					Pl	Sk		Hu	Cz				
Ahold	1680			Cz				Pl						Sk
Auchan	1416								Pl		Hu			
Lidl & Schwarz	1310									Cz			Sk	Pl
Tengelmann	1296	Hu			Cz			Pl						Sk
Carrefour	1240									Pl	Cz	Sk		

* Sales in the Czech Republic (Cz), Hungary (Hu), Poland (Pl) and Slovakia (Sk) in 2003.

tries to less saturated markets, the main retail chains are also moving their investments within countries: both from large cities to smaller cities and towns and from richer neighbourhoods to middle- to lower-income neighbourhoods.

In Russia, there is a rapid penetration by the leading chains into 'the provinces'. At first, the emphasis is on the south-western and western areas, more densely populated and richer than the central and eastern parts of Russia. For example, we have seen Pyaterochka move from their base in St Petersburg to Moscow in 2001 and into the regions since 2002.

Other examples are: (i) Perekriostok, moving from Moscow City into the Moscow region in 1999, to St Petersburg in 2002 and into the regions in 2003; (ii) Ramenka-Ramstore (Migros Turk) invested first in Moscow, moved to the Moscow suburbs in 2003 and started investing in the regions in that same year; and (iii) Metro moved from Moscow into St Petersburg and has opened several stores in the regions in 2004.

Consolidation

As competition is soaring in the CEE retail markets, companies are not only relocating to less developed markets and rural areas, but we also see a rebalancing of power among the existing market players through mergers and acquisitions, asset swaps and market exits. Figure 17.3 shows the market shares of the top five players in the Central European retail sector. We see that, on average, the CE markets are still more fragmented than, for example, the UK market.

Especially in Poland, the consolidation process is lagging behind. The latter was also confirmed in a recent study by the OECD (2005), which claimed that, after EU accession, consumer prices had risen only in those markets where competition in the processing and retail sector was still low. According to this study, retail prices had gone up in Poland, while they actually decreased after accession in countries like the Czech Republic, Hungary and Slovakia, where competition between retailers is much stronger.

New legal restrictions introduced in 2002 have made it more difficult to construct shopping centres in Poland, and competition between major retail chains has therefore shifted to mergers and acquisitions. In 2002, two spectacular buy-outs took place: Ahold bought Jumbo hypermarkets from Jeronimo Martins and Tesco acquired the HIT chain of shops. In 2005, Tesco also bought Julius Meinl supermarkets as the latter exited the Polish market.

This recent wave of mergers and acquisitions has not been limited to the Polish retail market. In the second half of 2005, Tesco and Carrefour agreed to a large-scale asset swap in which Tesco acquired 15 hypermarkets from Carrefour in the Czech Republic and Slovakia, in return for six hypermarkets and two development sites in Taiwan. Apart from Carrefour, also Julius Meinl has exited the Czech market and Edeka is planning to do so. Earlier that year another player, Delvita, had sold its Slovakian stores to Rewe in order to focus on its core market, the Czech Republic.

Procurement System Change

Centralization and regionalization of procurement

Centralization of procurement through the use of distribution centres (DC) can lead to a more efficient buying process for the retailer, through the reduction of coordination costs, by generating economies of scale through buying in larger volumes and by having tighter control over product consis-

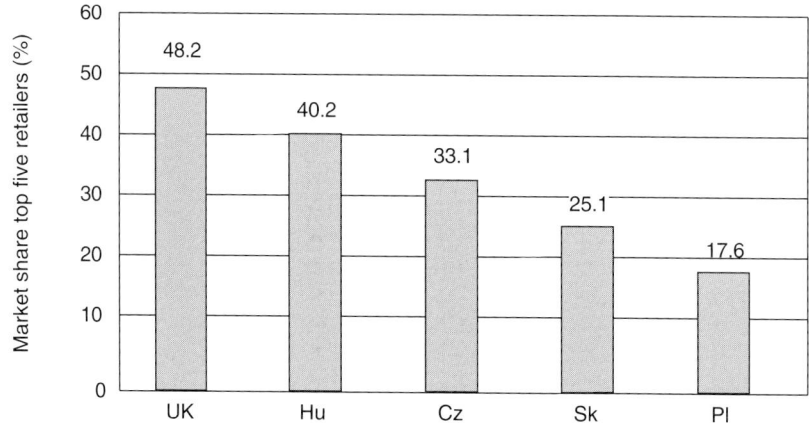

Fig. 17.3. Market share of top five retailers in the UK and Central Europe (from IGD, 2004). UK, United Kingdom; Hu, Hungary; Cz, Czech Republic; Sk, Slovakia; Pl, Poland.

tency. Typically, chains make this move when they reach a certain volume threshold where it becomes markedly more efficient to shift to DC.

In the examples of both FFV (Czech Republic and Slovakia) and dairy products (Poland), we find a recent tendency to shift from per-store procurement to a centralized system. For example, in the Czech Republic, Ahold opened its first DC for FFV in 2001 and opened a second one in 2002. Delvita was already operating a DC by 1995 and opened a second in 2003. Tesco has built its first DC in the Czech Republic at the end of 2003.

The logical extension which has been taken by various chains in the CEE region is to move to cross-border sourcing — coordinating procurement over a chain's DCs in the set of countries in which it operates. These systems allow the procurement of the cheapest and best-quality products from the various countries. This process is related to EU accession, which increases opportunities for cross-border procurement. In Central Europe, for example, Ahold announced in October 2002 the formation of Ahold Central Europe (ACE), an integration of its operations in Poland, Czech Republic and Slovakia undertaken over 2003. This integration is organized by category so that, for example, there is an 'ACE Fresh' for FFV procurement.

In Russia, several factors still inhibit the centralization of procurement for dairy products. In all our interviews with retailers, interviewees emphasized that fresh logistics (for fresh and semi-processed products) is a major constraint to centralization. They noted that Russian food logistics had been geared — even in Moscow, and more so in the other areas — to frozen and dry/processed products. Exacerbating the lack of adequate infrastructure to handle perishables, interviewees noted that road congestion is a major problem in food logistics in Moscow and St Petersburg. Outside of those areas there are major transport costs, but due more to long distances, poor roads, and so on, rather than to congestion.

Rationalisation of the supply chain

From the interviews in Poland we find that wholesalers are rapidly losing the strong position that they had in the distribution of dairy products at the beginning of the 1990s. Supermarket chains have shifted to buying mostly directly from dairy-processing companies. As a consequence of this rapidly disappearing market opportunity, wholesalers are consolidating and increasingly becoming dedicated wholesalers for the traditional retail sector. If this happens, they do not often specialize in dairy products alone, but try to offer a wide range of food products that are sold in the small-scale traditional shops.

Also in the Czech Republic we find an increasing rationalization of the FFV supply chain. The leading chains are shifting from traditional wholesalers to 'specialized/dedicated wholesalers' that are specialized in a product category and dedicated to supplying supermarkets. That means that the wholesaler is more responsive to the quality, safety and consistency requirements of supermarkets than are traditional wholesalers, who aggregate products over many producers and qualities with little capacity for segregation.

Shortening the supply chain is also established through the 'direct' purchase from growers/processors, through a preferred supplier programme. This is done in order to select producers capable of meeting the quality and safety standards of the supermarkets, thus lowering transaction costs for the chain both by lower search costs and by reducing the number of suppliers per unit sold. The retailer or the wholesaler acting on its behalf then provides incentives (negative and positive) to meet the retailers requirements — such as via explicit or implicit contracts, lower risk and sometimes price premiums, as well as resolution of certain idiosyncratic factor market failures facing the producers.

As an example of the latter, an interview with one of the leading banks in the Czech Republic showed that farmers who wish to apply for a bank loan must show that they have a contract with the buyer of their products. This contract then serves as a collateral substitute for producers.

The role of wholesalers in the dairy procurement system is also changing in the Russian Federation. There have been some general changes over the past 3–4 years, initiated by the leading domestic and foreign chains (with the second- and third-tier chains still using the more traditional procurement systems, i.e. reliance on general wholesalers): (i) a shift from general to specialized wholesalers; (ii) a shift from wholesalers to direct sourcing from second-stage processors; and (iii) a reduction in the number of suppliers, whether wholesalers or processors.

Use of global logistics multinationals

A related trend is for leading chains to use the services of global multinational logistics firms. In this way, large retailers induce a rapid transfer of world-class logistics technology into the local wholesale sector. This allows the leading chains to reduce their costs, become yet more competitive, further distance themselves from weaker local chains and accelerate the consolidation process. For example, in April 2003, Tesco signed an agreement with the US-based global multinational ProLogis for lease of a large ProLogis DC in the Czech Republic.

In Russia, the centralization of procurement is still underdeveloped due to several problems (see above). As a result, several large chains in Russia are doing what many leading chains in other regions are doing: turning to multinational logistics companies that have set up shop in Russia to alleviate these constraints.

For example, Auchan (and Danone) use the services of F&M Logistics. The latter has a distribution centre near the Moscow airport, where Auchan rents space (among several other warehouse spaces it rents). The interviewees in general complained of insufficient logistic company services in Moscow, but even more so in other major cities and provinces. This is a major challenge which needs to be addressed in order to help both retailers and suppliers – and thus consumers and food sector growth.

Shift towards private standards and labels

Leading chains are shifting toward higher quality and increasingly safe products through private standards imposed on suppliers. There are several reasons for this, as revealed in our interviews: (i) higher product quality and safety are being used to attract consumers, as competitive tools against the remaining small shops and markets; (ii) standardization reduces costs and allows more efficiency of product flow in the procurement system; (iii) bringing the attributes of local supply into conformity with the private standards of European retailers, several of whom are also the leading chains in CEE (such as Tesco, Ahold, Carrefour and Metro); (iv) centralized purchase (with better monitoring ability), qualified, specialized wholesalers and preferred supplier programmes of selected producers raise the capacity of retailers for applying higher standards; and (v) in general, public food regulations for the domestic market are not easily enforced by governments in the region, so private standards and private enforcement are the main means by which food safety at retail outlets is imposed, at least at the present time.

Furthermore, retail companies are also increasingly shifting towards the use of private-label products. For example, Tesco introduced its first private-label dairy products in Poland in 2000. The 'TKZ' label offers standard-quality products at prices that are 30–40% lower than the price of the market leader in that product category and includes a range of 30 dairy products like milk, cream, yoghurt, spreadable cheese and Brie. The 'TBC' label – high-quality products at prices 10% lower than that of the market leader – covers an additional 15 dairy products like milk, yellow cheese and margarine.

Similarly, in Russia the large-format retailers have recently started to introduce private-label dairy products. Ramenka (Ramstore) is one of the first large retailers to have introduced private-label dairy products, e.g. 'Ramstore milk'. At this moment the private-label UHT milk is sold only in Ramstore's Moscow-based outlets, because transportation of the product to other regions would diminish this product's cost advantage and make it uncompetitive with locally produced milk. Private label products already constitute 9–10% of total dairy product sales.

Auchan has also put out a tender for companies to start producing a number of Auchan private-label dairy products. The tender is open to dairies that already have products in the Auchan assortment and that, according to the retailer, will be able to meet the requirements.

Impact on Upstream Suppliers

In general, the procurement system changes of the leading chains imply the following changes in conditions facing suppliers in the agrifood system: (i) centralization and regionalization favour suppliers who can deliver larger volumes on a consistent basis; they also mean that local producers now have to compete with producers around their countries and in their regions; and (ii) higher standards for product quality and safety will put additional pressure on suppliers to invest in upgrading technologies in order to comply with these requirements.

The dairy sector

We found that, in order to stimulate the restructuring and upgrading of the supply base, all the interviewed Polish dairies have programmes that assist their supplying farms. There are four such programmes:

1. An input (especially feed) supply programme. The companies provide access to inputs such as feed, seeds and fertilizers for on-farm feed production. Farmers purchase the inputs through company shops and the inputs are paid from the milk revenues.
2. Assistance in making dairy-specific investments through credit programmes. Investment assistance takes the form of leasing of equipment and cattle, with payments deducted from future payments for milk deliveries, as well as loans for buying new or second-hand cooling and milking equipment.
3. Extension service.
4. Bank loan guarantees for bank loans to farmers. In order to obtain a bank loan, the farmer needs collateral. However, in many cases land or buildings are not accepted as a bank guarantee. Therefore, most interviewed dairies provide an additional service to their suppliers by co-signing the bank loan. In this way the dairy provides the bank loan guarantee and facilitates its farmers' access to bank credits.

Dries and Swinnen (2004) showed that improving milk quality had been a crucial aspect of the dairy companies' policies in Poland over the previous decade. For example, as an incentive to upgrade the quality of milk deliveries, all interviewed dairy companies were paying price premiums to farmers that were able to deliver high-quality milk.

Interviews with two of the main dairy processors in the Russian Federation (Wimm Bill Dann and Campina) showed that there are significant entry barriers and survival requirements for processors in the new 'supermarketized' dairy products market. This spills over into pressure on farmers to upgrade to become preferred suppliers to the leading processors. For now, this pressure is felt more keenly in western Russia, where competition between retailers is strongest, and less so in central and eastern Russia. At the same time, as mentioned several times in the interviews, the increased competition for milk by the main dairy processors may also create important opportunities for Russian milk producers.

Campina noted that the milk supply

conditions were inadequate when they entered the market in 2001. For example, even the large farms (such as their largest supplier with 2400 cows) had outdated facilities and no cooling tanks. The company noted that it is hard, if not impossible, for farmers to get credit from government or commercial banks for upgrading.

Starting in that year, Campina began financing (as an input credit, pre-financed with the help of Rabobank) cooling tanks for the farms – as well as supplying training, quality control and Dutch cattle. Both to control quality and to provide an incentive, they also instituted annual contracts with the farmers (from whom they buy directly). Most of their 18 farmers are local, although some are in other areas; their closest relations (in terms of assistance) are with the six large farms near the Stupino plant. The pay-off to Campina was that their preferred suppliers' production of second-class milk dropped from 36 to only 9% in just 4 years; concomitantly, production of premium-class (Campina-class) milk rose from 6 to 55% of premium class (see Fig. 17.4).

The question remains whether supermarkets are driving this structural change at the farm level or whether other factors are more important. In the case of Poland, we found no evidence during our interviews that the implementation of dairy assistance programmes was directly linked to the increasing importance of the supermarket sector. Rather, dairy processors frequently stated that upgrading their supplier base was guided by their wish to gain access to the EU market.

In Russia, the picture is somewhat different and the supermarket sector is having a real impact throughout the dairy supply chain. Interviews with the dairy-processing companies – who feel under cost and quality pressures from the supermarket chains – show that they are moving in the same direction as the supermarket chains in terms of increased requirements for their supply base. This implies that they are selecting dairy farmers able to meet the requirements, and they are helping that subset of their suppliers with the greatest potential to upgrade (such as making investments, credit from the processor, cooling tanks).

In summary, in countries close to the EU (either in terms of accession or in terms of trade), the restructuring of the dairy chain was mostly driven by investments in processing, while in countries further from the EU and less advanced in transition, retail investments are now playing a more

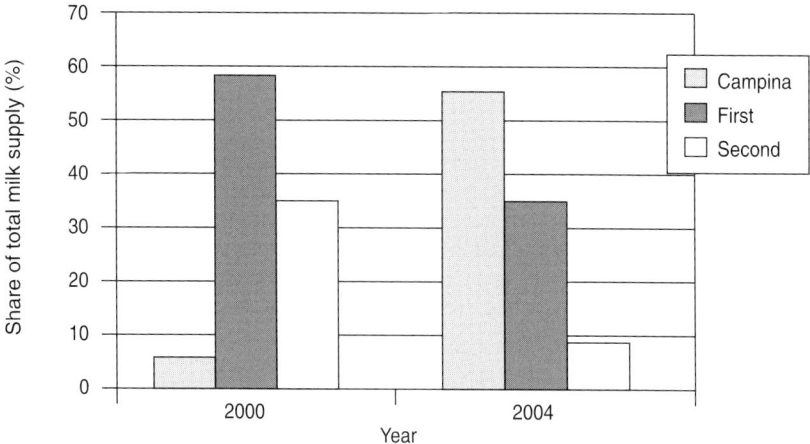

Fig. 17.4. Categories of milk supplied to the Campina factory in Stupino, Russia, 2000 and 2004 (from company interview). The Campina-class milk includes milk complying with Campina's international quality standards as well as Premium milk (the top class, by quality, in the Russian classification system).

important role in driving change throughout the dairy chain (Swinnen et al., 2006).

Fresh fruit and vegetables

In order to shed some light on the impact of the retail transformation and changing procurement systems, we present results from a survey of 250 fruit and vegetable growers that was conducted in the spring of 2004. Respondents were randomly selected in the three main FFV areas in the Czech Republic (Stredocesky, Vychodocesky and Jihomoravsky) on the basis of a list of producers from the fruit and vegetable growers unions, as well as on membership lists from producer organizations.

To increase the representativeness of the survey, a certain number of the observations were selected randomly in the areas where interviews were being taken, on the condition that these additional observations were not already present in the main list above.

Figure 17.5 shows how the average quality of products from growers in the survey differs according to the marketing channel that is used. The quality of products supplied to supermarket chains is much higher than the quality of products sold elsewhere: the share of extra-class products sold to supermarket chains is almost 40%, while this share is below 20% for all other marketing channels. We should note that the average quality of produce sold through a producer marketing organization (PMO) is also very low (only 15% extra-class).

Furthermore, the survey shows not only that the quality of products sold to supermarkets is higher, but also that there has been a continuous growth in the share of highest-quality produce in the period 2000–2003 for growers that sold products to supermarkets in that period. On the other hand, growers that sold most of their produce on the local market have seen a significant decline in the average quality of their products in that same period.

From the survey we also find that a lot of the growers have made investments in the last 10 years to upgrade their farming operations. According to experts at VUZE (the research institute for agricultural economics in Prague), FFV producers will invest first in irrigation and storage facilities to improve and preserve the quality of their products, and last in services like washing, sorting, packing and transport equipment. Most of these investments are made by using own resources.

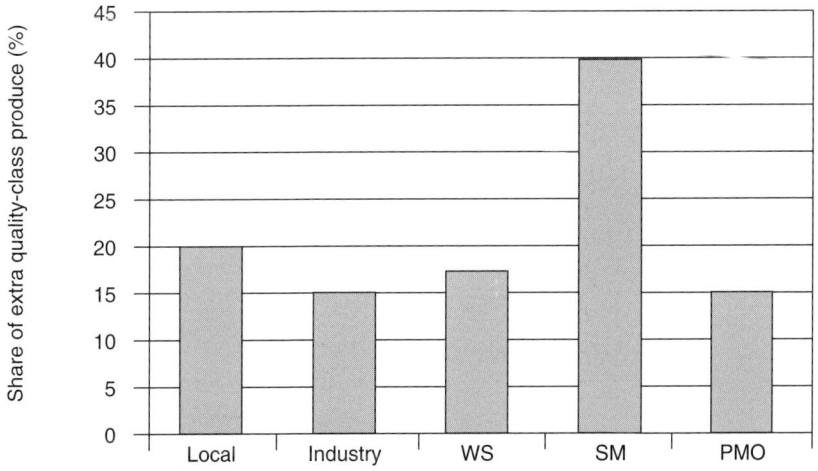

Fig. 17.5. Proportions of extra-class FFV produce for different marketing channels in the Czech Republic (from farm survey). WS, wholesale; SM, supermarkets; PMO, producer marketing organizations.

We found no evidence of forward credit or loans from the buyers of the products, and bank loan guarantees are given only rarely (and in the few cases that we found included mainly the PMO, never a wholesaler or supermarket chain). This contrasts with the substantial buyer–supplier investment assistance that was found by Dries and Swinnen (2004) in the example of the dairy sector in Poland.

Growers that supply their products to PMO or wholesalers seem to make significantly more investments than other growers, while producers that supply the local market are making significantly less. However, there is no significant evidence that farmers who sell their products to either wholesalers, PMO or supermarket chains grow faster than other producers.

Because of the importance of small producers in the Czech FFV sector, and as it may be especially difficult for these producers to comply with the requirements from supermarkets in terms of quality and volume of delivered produce, we also interviewed the main PMOs in the FFV sector. The rapid changes that have occurred in the food retail sector in the past decade (aided by financial support from the EU as part of the accession programme) have been the main driving force behind the organization of farmers. Four out of five of the interviewed PMOs indicated that the main reason for their establishment was to gather sufficient quantity and product varieties to satisfy the requirements of the large supermarket chains.

The potential benefits of a PMO for its members include increased bargaining power vis-à-vis the buyer of FFV products and services provided by the PMO to its members. It is interesting to note that these PMOs – like the dairy processors in the previous section – are providing various services to their members. For example, the growers in the survey that were a member of a PMO had access to all of the following: extension service; storage, sorting and packaging facilities; information service.

Furthermore, the interviews with PMOs showed that some also assist their members in having facilitated access to inputs through a payment guarantee programme between the PMO and the input supplier. Finally, from an interview with one of the main banks in the Czech Republic, we found that members of a PMO were also in a preferred position to apply for a bank loan because the PMO would provide some kind of payment security.

Conclusions

This chapter adds to the discussion on the impact of FDI in general, and rapid food retail investments in specific on local suppliers. On the one hand, there is an extensive literature that points at the positive role of foreign investors in solving transition-related problems – such as contract enforcement problems – through increased vertical coordination in the supply chain (Foster, 1999; Gow et al., 2000; Gow and Swinnen, 2001; Dries and Swinnen, 2004).

These studies contrast sharply with work done by, for example, Farina and Reardon (2000) and Reardon and Berdegué (2002), who showed that retail investments in Latin America could lead to the rapid exclusion of thousands of small suppliers.

The success of the CEE region in attracting investments from the main global retailers in recent years makes this region an interesting case in which to identify the impact of food retail investments on the local supply base.

The retail transformation through foreign direct investments and increased competition has created the need for retailers to reduce costs, to have consistent volumes and to increase quality of supplies to gain marketing advantage over competitors.

As a result, the procurement system has changed in several ways: (i) increased centralized procurement and regionalization of the buying process; (ii) consolidation upstream in the supply chain and shortening of the supply chain (through direct supplies and a system of preferred suppliers); (iii) focus on the core business and the use of global logistics companies; and (iv) a shift towards private standards and labels.

These changes have had a substantial impact on upstream suppliers and we present evidence on this impact based on case studies in two different sectors: dairy products (in Poland and the Russian Federation) and fresh fruit and vegetables (in the Czech Republic and Slovakia).

We find that, under certain circumstances, small farmers are included in procurement systems of large-scale agro-processors and supermarket chains. The case study of dairy products shows a substantial involvement of small milk producers in Poland, but a low level of participation of small producers in the Russian Federation. Swinnen (2004) finds that small farmers are more likely to be included in cases where there is the incentive (they must, due to lack of sufficient supply from larger firms) and the capacity (sufficiently low transaction costs are in place due to effective associations). Where the capacity is insufficient but the incentive is high, large firms often try to resolve idiosyncratic market failures facing small growers by providing technical assistance and input credit (Reardon, 2005).

Furthermore, the FFV case study gives evidence of the important role of producer organizations. Both consistency and volume requirements put small producers in a disadvantaged position which they might be able to overcome when there are well-functioning producer marketing organizations. We have found that, in the Czech Republic, these PMOs provide additional services to their members under the form of: extension services, storage, sorting and packaging facilities, information service, etc.

In conclusion, we can state that the pressures on the supply chain caused by changing procurement systems of the main retail chains are leading to the restructuring of the supply base. However, this restructuring may be less dramatic than has been found in certain other regions (Farina and Reardon, 2000; Reardon and Berdegué, 2002).

An important role is played by dairy processors that have implemented assistance programmes for their suppliers to upgrade milk quality and facilitate on-farm investments. In the FFV sector, this role is potentially taken over by the PMOs which, in many cases, have been established as a direct result of mounting pressures from the retail sector.

Acknowledgements

The authors would like to thank Artan Qineti for his help with the interviews and data collection; Professor Jan Pokrivcak and his colleagues at the University of Nitra (Slovakia), researchers at VUZE (Czech Republic) and IERIGZ (Poland); Dr. Eugenia Serova from AFE (Moscow) and Dr. Andrei Golokhvastov, Agriconsult (Saint Petersburg) for useful insights on the issues discussed in this chapter. They also thank Professor Pavel Zufan and his students from the Mendel University of Agriculture and Forestry in Brno for the assistance they provided with the survey in the Czech Republic. This research was made possible through funding from the United Nations Food and Agriculture Organization and the European Bank for Reconstruction and Development.

References

Dries, L. and Swinnen, J.F.M. (2004) Foreign direct investment, vertical integration, and local suppliers: evidence from the Polish dairy sector. *World Development* 32 (9), 1525–1544.

Dries, L., Reardon, T. and Swinnen, J.F.M. (2004) The rapid rise of supermarkets in Central and Eastern Europe: implications for the agrifood sector and rural development. *Development Policy Review* 22 (5), 525–556.

Farina, E.M.M.Q. and Reardon, T. (2000) Agrifood grades and standards in the extended Mercosur: their role in the changing agrifood system. *American Journal of Agricultural Economics* 82 (5), 1170–1176.

Foster, C. (1999) The impact of FDI in the upstream and downstream sectors on investment in agriculture in the NIS. In: OECD (ed.) *Agricultural Finance and Credit Infrastructure in Transition Economies.* OECD, Paris.

Gow, H. and Swinnen, J.F.M. (2001) Private enforcement capital and contract enforcement in transition countries. *American Journal of Agricultural Economics* 83 (3), 686–690.

Gow, H., Streeter, D. and Swinnen, J. (2000) How private contract enforcement mechanisms can succeed where public institutions fail: the case of Juhocukor A.S. *Agricultural Economics* 23 (3), 253–265.

Holloway, G., Nicholson, C., Delgado, C., Staal, S. and Ehui, S. (2000) Agroindustrialisation through institutional innovation. Transaction costs, cooperatives and milk-market development in the East African Highlands. *Agricultural Economics* 23, 279–288.

IGD (2004) *Central Europe and Russia. Assessing the Opportunities.* IGD, Watford, UK.

LZ (Lebensmittelzeitung), 2005 (available at http://www.lz.net).

OECD (2005) *Agricultural Policies in OECD Countries. Monitoring and Evaluation.* OECD Publications, Paris.

PMR (2005) *Retailing in Russia and CEE 2004/2005* (available at http://www.ceeretail.com).

Reardon, T. (2005) *Retail Companies as Integrators of Value Chains in Developing Countries. Diffusion, Procurement System Change and Trade and Development Effects.* GTZ, Eschborn, Germany.

Reardon, T. and Berdegué, J.A. (2002) The rapid rise of supermarkets in Latin America: challenges and opportunities for development. *Development Policy Review* 20 (4), 317–334.

Runsten, D. and Key, N. (1996) *Contract Farming in Developing Countries: Theoretical Issues and Analysis of some Mexican Cases.* Report LC/L.989, UN-ECLAC, Santiago, Chile.

Swinnen, J.F.M. (2004) *When the Market Comes to You: or Not. The Dynamics of Vertical Co-ordination in Agro-food Chains in Europe and Central Asia.* The World Bank, Washington, DC.

Swinnen, J.F.M., Dries, L., Germenji, E. and Noev, N. (2006) *Foreign Investment, Supermarkets and the Restructuring of Supply Chains: Evidence from Eastern European Dairy Sectors.* LICOS discussion paper 165/2006, LICOS, KULeuven, Leuven, Belgium.

Winters, A.L. (2000) *Trade Liberalisation and Poverty* (available at http://www.worldbank.org/poverty/wdr-poverty/winters.htm).

18 Vertical Coordination in the Dairy Sector: a Comparative Analysis of Romania and Slovakia

S. van Berkum

Introduction

A major problem in the agricultural sector and in rural areas in countries in transition is the breakdown of the relationships of farms with input suppliers and output markets (Swinnen, 2003). The simultaneous privatization and restructuring of farms and of the up- and downstream companies in the agri-food chain has caused major disruptions (Macours and Swinnen, 2000). The outcome is that many farms and rural households face serious constraints in accessing essential inputs and in selling their products. The problems are made worse by the lack of public institutions necessary to support market-based transactions, such as those for enforcing property rights and contractual agreements.

In the absence of appropriate public institutions, private contractual initiatives – often from large food and agribusiness companies – are emerging to overcome these obstacles (see World Bank, 2001, for conceptual issues on private institutions and Swinnen, 2003, for an overview of case studies). Large traders, agribusinesses and food processing companies, often as part of their own restructuring, began contracting with farms and rural households to provide basic inputs in return for guaranteed and quality supplies. This process of interlinked contracting is growing rapidly in most Central and Eastern European agriculture and rural areas.

This chapter provides an analysis and documentation of changes that have occurred during the transition in the vertical coordination of the dairy supply chain in Romania and Slovakia, and its effects on the various agents in the chain. The analysis focuses on Romania and Slovakia.[1] These two countries represent interesting contrasts with respect to several relevant issues. Slovakia joined the EU in 2004 and is therefore more advanced in the EU integration process than Romania, which is aiming for EU membership in 2007. Small-scale household production dominates in Romania, while dairy farming in Slovakia is mainly large-scale. Similarly, the processing sector is much more fragmented in Romania than in Slovakia. In both countries dairy production represents a significant share of total agricultural production.

This chapter starts with a brief description of the structure of the dairy supply chain in both countries. Next, emerging vertical relations are described based on interviews with dairy companies in Slovakia and

Romania. The interviews focus on the types of and conditions for vertical coordination between farms and processors. The penultimate section analyses the consequences of vertical coordination for various agents in the chain, while the chapter concludes with a summary of the main findings.

Structural Features in the Dairy Supply Chain

Industry structure at the primary level

Romanian milk production has, traditionally, been concentrated in the private sector. In 1989 state-run farms accounted for 18% of production, with other large farms accounting for 28% and family farms for 56%. By 2002, the share of individual family farms had grown to over 99%, with other large farms (cooperative units or associations) accounting for less than 1%. Milk production is, therefore, very much focused on small-scale family units.

The privatization process at the farm level resulted in a very fragmented farm structure. Almost 96% of farms have one to two cows (see Table 18.1), and these farms have 84% of all milking cows in Romania. Only 0.26% of all farms – around 3100 in number – have 10 cows or more. Around 75,000 milking cows, or 5.4% of the total herd of milking cows, are on these larger farms.

The structure of the Slovak dairy farm sector contrasts sharply with that in Romania: over 90% of Slovakia's milk production is produced on large corporate farms (both joint stock and cooperatives), while individual farms account for only a small proportion. Almost half of all 1200 dairy farms have a herd size of between 100 and 500 cows, the national average of dairy farms being 183 cows (see Table 18.2).

Industry structure at the processing level

Romania

At the processing level, the current dairy industry in Romania consists of ex-state firms that have been privatized plus a

Table 18.1. Dairy farm size, Romania, 2002 (from NIS, 2005a).

Size category (cows/farm)	Farms		Cows		Average head/farm
	n	%	n	%	
Total	1,180,801	100	1,583,065	100	1.34
1–2	1,131,733	95.85	1,326,891	83.82	1.17
3–9	45,940	3.89	170,501	10.77	3.71
10–19	2,153	0.18	27,520	1.74	12.78
20–29	446	0.04	10,248	0.65	22.98
30–49	245	0.02	8,900	0.56	36.33
50–99	148	0.01	9,847	0.62	66.53
> 100	136	0.01	29,158	1.84	214.40

Table 18.2. Dairy farm size, Slovakia, 2003 (from World Bank, 2006).

Size category (cows/farm)	Farms		Cows		Average head/farm
	n	%	n	%	
0–10	257	749	3	0.3	3,563
11–30	91	1,711	19	0.8	4,553
31–50	51	2,035	40	0.9	4,161
51–100	159	12,095	76	5.5	4,098
101–500	547	129,852	237	58.9	4,962
> 500	102	74,097	726	33.6	5,280
Total	1,207	220,540	183	100	5,010

developing small-scale private sector, which has matured since 1990. By the end of 2003, most formerly state-owned enterprises had been privatized or liquidated, while ten were still in the process of privatization. Simultaneously, many new dairies had been established over the years, but many had also ceased to exist (NIS, 2002).

Data from 1999 indicate that, at that time, there were 973 dairy processing enterprises in total. Most of them were very small in terms of number of employees: 909 enterprises were reported to have less than 50 employees, while 64 dairies had more than 50 employees. Since the end of the 1990s the number of dairies (in operation) has fallen to around 600, with a drop of 40% in the number of smaller dairies with less than 50 employees by 2004.

Nevertheless, the structure of the processing sector remains very fragmented. Comparing the 1999 to 2004 data on employment shows that the size distribution in the industry remains very skewed: more than 90% of the units have fewer than 50 employees. In 2004, around 250 dairies each had a production capacity of less than 1000 t of milk per year (MAPAM, 2004).

One important development is that some foreign investment has entered the sector, especially from France, the Netherlands, Greece, Germany and Switzerland. Some of the foreign-owned companies belong to the larger dairy processors in Romania. Table 18.3 lists a number of companies that are estimated to have processed more than 20,000 t in 2003. Most of these companies have several factories and produce in different locations across the country. The six largest dairy companies of the country account for around 25% of the dairy processing sector intake. Three out of the six largest dairies are foreign owned: Friesland, Hochland and Danone. Furthermore, Friesland has been the majority shareholder of Napolact since mid-2004, after having acquired 40% of the shares in 2002.

The structure of the Romanian dairy industry may change very rapidly in the coming years. The outlook of EU accession calls, among others, for compliance with EU quality norms and standards. In 2004, only 17 dairies' production was in accord with EU standards, these factories representing 15% of the milk-processing capacity in Romania (MAPAM, 2004).

Around 75 dairies – representing 25% of the industry's production capacity – are subject to restructuring investments with Phare or SAPARD[2] assistance in order to enable them to fully adopt the EU requirements. The remaining companies do not produce according to EU norms and are not included in support programmes for improvements. The majority of these firms – around 500 in total – will have to close down their operations by accession, because they lack the financial means to invest in the necessary modernization of equipment.

Slovakia

At the processing level, the industry structure in Slovakia differs strongly from that in Romania. Slovakia counts only 34 dairy companies. Table 18.4 lists the 18 main dairy-processing companies in Slovakia that, altogether, held about 87% of the market share at the beginning of 2003. The top three companies combined occupied 27% of the total market.

Table 18.3. List of large dairy companies in Romania, 2003 (from MAPAM, 2004).

Company name	Majority owner	FDI since year	Estimated intake (t)
Friesland România	Friesland, Netherlands	2000	80,000
S.C. Napolact	Friesland, Netherlands	2002	80,000
Hochland România	Hochland, Germany	1998	30,000
Danone	Danone, France	1998	25,000
Prodlacta	Domestic		25,000
Raraul	Domestic		23,000

Table 18.4. Financial structure of the Slovakian dairy-processing sector, 2003 (from Dries and Noev, 2006).

Company name	Majority owner	FDI since year	Market share[c] (%)
Mliekospol[a]	95% Sole, Italy	2002	8
Tamilk[a]	100% Sole, Italy	2001	4
Sole Slovakia[a]	99% Sole, Italy	2001	4
Rajo[a]	51% Meggle, Germany	1993	13
Liptovska Mliekaren[a]	97% Bongrain, France	2000	6
Zvolenska Mliekaren[a]	100% Bongrain, France	2001	4
Milex Nové Mesto nad Vahom[a]	51% Cooperative (49% Bongrain, France)	2001	4
Zempmilk[a]	91% Fromageries Bel, France	2000	7
Prievidzska Mliekaren[a]	95% Artax, Austria	2000	4
Milsy[a]	95% Artax, Austria	2001	4
Nutricia Dairy[b]	100% Friesland, Netherlands	2000	4
Laktis[a]	(9% Friesland, Netherlands)	2002	5
Senicka Mliekaren[a]	67% Cooperative		4
Levicka Mliekaren[a]	Domestic		4
Milkagro[a]	Domestic		4
Humenska Mliekaren[a]	Domestic		4
Tvrdosinska Mliekarin[b]	???		4
Other			13

[a] Corporation; [b] limited liability company; [c] estimated.

There is considerable foreign investment in the dairy sector. Eight different international dairy companies are present in the Slovakian market: Sole (Italy), Meggle (Germany), Bongrain, Danone and Fromageries Bel (France), Artax (Austria), Friesland Foods (the Netherlands), and Amine Aour (Lebanon). A 2003 report of the Slovak Dairy Union showed that 77% of milk purchased in Slovakia was processed by foreign-owned dairy companies (Dries and Noev, 2006).

Table 18.4 also shows that most of the foreign investments, with the exception of the entry of Meggle in 1993, have taken place since 2000; compared to other CEECs, this is relatively late. The sudden attractiveness of Slovakia can, at least partly, be attributed to a shift in the political environment in previous years when, after the 1998 elections, the new government moved quickly to implement key reforms, creating a more attractive investment climate.

Milk flows in the supply chain

A major feature of the current Romanian dairy sector is the low utilization of total milk production by processing enterprises, with only 21% of estimated milk production being delivered for processing, compared with 86% in Slovakia (see Table 18.5). In Romania a high proportion of milk is retained on farms for family and livestock usage, and significant quantities are sold directly to consumers, frequently through street markets. Farm family consumption is

Table 18.5. Milk utilization in Romania[a] and Slovakia[b].

Milk usage (percentage of total milk production)	Romania	Slovakia
Processing	21	86
On-farm human consumption	41	6
On-farm animal feed consumption	12	5
Direct sales	26	3
Total milk production (t million)	5088	1142

[a] From Leat and van Berkum (2003); [b] from World Bank (2006).

estimated at approximately 41%, farm feeding of animals at 12% with a further 26% being sold directly by producers through street markets and direct sales to low-income consumers.

The high level of farm usage and direct selling in Romania is a consequence of several factors, including: (i) the small-scale structure of production; (ii) a consequential lack of commercial orientation amongst many producers; (iii) an underdeveloped milk collection system; (iv) the big difference between the procurement price and the street market price; and (v) the unreliability of milk payments made by some processors, with delays in payment to producers of up to 3 months (see Leat and van Berkum, 2003).

It is also likely, however, to be the result of difficulties in regulating direct sales – especially those on the street. A major challenge in the commercial development of the Romanian dairy sector will be to increase the supplies of good-quality raw milk to the processing sector in a cost-effective manner.

Since the start of transition, Romania has been a net importer of dairy products. Yet, the level of imports has always been very modest (1–2% of total consumption), while exports have never played an important role. Slovakian imports of dairy products total less than 10% of total domestic production (in milk equivalents), but the country is a net exporter of dairy products: its export of around 300,000 t of milk equals 25–30% of domestic milk production. The milk is processed into various dairy products, yet the share of fluid milk products, butter and milk powder is substantial, indicating that the domestic industry is processing mainly relatively simple products.

Vertical Coordination in the Dairy Chain

Dairy companies

The four companies interviewed in Romania comprise two foreign and two domestic. The two foreign companies – Friesland Romania and Danone – are among the largest dairies in the country (see also Table 18.3). The Romanian companies are one large- and one small-sized dairy. The large-sized company, Raraul, is a former state company, privatized in 1994 with 67% of the shares owned by one family. The small-sized dairy, Promilch, located in Iasi county (north-east Romania), was started as a private company by three local people. Since 1999, ISPA Eco SRL, a limited liability company fully owned by the ISPA members, has gradually expanded its share to 65% of the total shareholding.

The sample of Slovakian dairies consists of nine companies. These dairy companies represent 30% of all high-capacity dairies. Dairies in the sample differ considerably in size, but all companies interviewed belong to the larger dairies in the country. The overall average processing capacity of the dairies in the 2003 sample was 58,000 t, while the average capacity in Slovakia was 48,700 t. Milk processed by the dairies in the 2003 sample was 42,000 t on average, and the national level was 29,500 t per dairy. The sample records an average capacity utilization of 72%, against an overall capacity utilization of 61% in the Slovak dairy companies.

Contract, contract partners and collection arrangements

Romania

All four companies take in milk from individual farmers. Most of the milk is delivered based on a written contract, in which in most cases the price setting and payment system are arranged. Promilch has a written contract with the farmers' association ISPA, its major shareholder and by far its most important milk supplier, and not with individual members of ISPA (which number around 2000).

Next to individual farmers, Friesland also contracts intermediate traders, but only to a very small (< 5%) proportion of Friesland's total intake. All four companies conduct business with the very small farmers having only one or two cows. The two foreign-owned companies. Friesland and Danone, also contract with larger farms (which are farmers with more than five cows in the Romanian context), some of which can supply 300–400 kg of milk daily on average.

In general, dairies in Romania do not document milk delivery contracts with small-scale farmers in a notary's deed because transaction costs are too high. Friesland, for instance, has about 40,000 small farmers, Raraul having approximately 8000. Usually, dairies readjust farm prices three to four times a year, because of inflation and the market situation (due to high seasonality of the production there is a big difference between summer and winter production, and thus prices).

Farmers, therefore, consider contracts as rather non-committal; terms change frequently, and every time the terms change farmers enjoy the freedom to switch dairies, especially when one dairy offers better conditions than the other. Dairies, however, do make up contracts in a notary's deed with the larger farms, in an attempt to bind them. This is certainly the case if dairies provide farms with development assistance (see below).

The small farmers either deliver their milk to collection points by themselves or their milk is transported to a collection point by a milk collector. The larger farmers are visited by a tanker collection. Collection and transport costs/kg of milk are estimated as being relatively high, especially in the winter when production is seasonally low. It is interesting to note that the four companies use different systems in organizing their milk collection and transport.

Raraul and Promilch, for instance, take care of the collection and transport by themselves. Estimated collection costs of these companies are between 10 and 20% of all costs (depending on the season). Friesland and Danone have outsourced the transportation of milk (and their products) to independent conveyors.

The collection points and centres that supply Danone are all owned by private entrepreneurs. Friesland owns collection points/centres, in which it has recently invested much in milk-cooling and quality-testing equipment. Also, Raraul and Promilch/ISPA invested in cooling facilities and milk control equipment in milk-collection centres. Before the companies made these investments, the centres did not exist or they were only very poorly equipped. Table 18.6 summarizes the contract partners and collection arrangements of the four companies.

Slovakia

Of the nine Slovakian dairies in our sample, six had drafted contracts with individual farmers, in combination with corporate farms. Contracts are in written form. Dairies indicated that 50% of their contracts had a long-term validity (4–5 years), while the other half consisted of 1-year contracts. This suggests that relationships between processors and farmers in the Slovak dairy sector are rather stable.

The number of suppliers to each of the selected Slovak dairies ranges from seven farmers in the lowest case to 91 farmers at the opposite end. This number is very low compared to the Romanian cases.

Regarding farm size, dairies show a pre-

Table 18.6. Contract partners and collection arrangements in Romania (from van Berkum, 2006).

Arrangement	Danone	Friesland	Promilch	Raraul
Contract small farmers	X	X	X	X
Contract large farmers	X	X		X
Own collection centres		X	X	X
Arrange transport from farm to collection centre			X	X
Arrange transport from collection centre to dairy			X	X

X, 'yes' or 'applicable to'.

ference for the larger farms. The preference is based on the idea that large suppliers are more reliable as a regular supplier than are small dairy farms. Furthermore, the larger farms are considered stronger economic units, having property (land, dairy cows, buildings), while their size assures lower transaction costs due to relatively high volumes that can be loaded at once. In this context it is important to note that one dairy started collaboration with a producer association representing a group of small suppliers. Membership in a producer association is important for small, individual farmers wishing to become attractive to dairies.

Quality improvements through payment and control system

Romania

Improving the quality of milk delivered is of key importance to further development of the Romanian dairy sector and in the interests of every company wanting to produce high-quality dairy products. The companies interviewed encourage the improvement of the milk quality, mainly through its milk payment system, linking the payment to quality grades. Friesland pays the small farmers according to fat content, measured at the collection points by the company itself. The larger farmers are paid on the basis of fat and protein content, density and bacterial counts. The latter farms are included in the company's quality system and the milk supply is regularly controlled at the farm.

Danone offers a relatively low base price (10% below the market price), but offers bonuses when a farmer delivers milk of above-average quality according to protein content and bacterial count, and also for constant delivery. In this way farmers can reach a mark-up of 35% above the average market price. Milk quality controls take place at the (larger) farm and at the collection points.

Prices paid by Raraul to farmers are linked to the quality of the milk delivered. Milk samples are taken at the farm through the collector, and these samples are analysed at the collection points.

Promilch's payment to ISPA-farmers is also determined according to quality and is based on individual samples tested through modern equipment available at the association-owned milk collection centres. Facilities at the milk collection centres allow for measurement of fat content, density and acidity grades for each individual supplier. This system motivates and stimulates farmers to improve their milk quality. For the bigger farmers, a premium price based on increased volume delivered is negotiated within the contract with Promilch.

Higher prices for better quality milk should encourage farmers to deliver their milk to the dairy that is paying for quality. However, there are signs that the four selected dairies face a tough competition for milk. All interviewed companies indicated that, although price arrangements are set in a contract, prices are negotiated frequently as farmers claim they can sell their milk at higher prices elsewhere.

Friesland claims it is almost continuously negotiating with its suppliers about the milk price and points to the farmers' attitude that contracts are not considered binding. ISPA reports that prices are established monthly, taking into account market developments. Promilch/ISPA has a 1-year contract for those farmers with more than ten cows but renegotiates prices (at least) every 6 months.

If prices (or even deliveries) depend on quality, the organization of quality control is of key importance to the trust farmers have in the system. In the case of our selected dairies, milk collectors perform quality control before the milk is mixed with other farms' milk. Subsequently, the milk is further analysed in milk collection centres and in the dairy laboratories.

Friesland claims it has a transparent system. The samples for determination of the quality of the milk are made available for testing and checking by the responsible public inspection services. Promilch/ISPA reports that there are several stages of quality control: the milk collector controls at the farm on density and acidity of the milk, while the farmers' association (through the laboratory staff in the field) also controls the proportions of fat, protein, dry matter and added water at the collection centre. Furthermore, the factory controls the entire intake itself through its own laboratory. On top of that, at least monthly, the laboratory of the Veterinary Direction and, periodically, the laboratory of the Consumers' Protection Office, control milk quality. Danone and Raraul indicate they use a similar quality control system and are governed by external inspection.

The interviewees, however, complain that the public inspection services are not accurate enough to control every dairy in operation. It seems to the interviewed companies that public inspection discriminates against the dairies that are most quality-aware, by applying higher standards to them than to others. Furthermore, the public authorities are accused of poor inspection levels at open-air street markets where milk and cheese are sold non-cooled and not checked for their basic food safety requirements.

Slovakia

Contract agreements refer mainly to quality. All dairies in the sample define exactly the raw milk quality requirements in their agreements. All of them applied general (public) quality standards (e.g. protein content, bacterial counts). Dairies control quality, while a third independent party may check the results. Quality is generally tested on the farm as a sampling (three cases) and in combination with the control at the gate of the dairy plant (five cases). Usually, the processor determines the quality criteria and sets the agreement on this issue. Only one dairy replied that the company's client sets the requirements.

In four dairies, quality requirements refer only to the raw material, while in the other dairies in the sample quality requirements were also set with respect to the production process of raw milk. Quality in dairy processing is guarded by the HACCP system, by daily intra-operational controls and prevention measures. Supervision of the quality control of milk and dairy products at the farm and processor level is carried out by the SVFA (State Veterinary and Food Administration) branch office in respective regions and by the Central Testing Laboratory (in Žilina). These institutions carry out inspections randomly.

The contracts consist of explicit agreements on the volumes of delivery. Agreements on pricing are explicitly expressed in contracts, but eventual payment depends on the actual quality upon delivery while prices are negotiated regularly. In seven cases processors provided logistics. One dairy shares the logistics responsibilities with the farm. An independent carrier was used in some cases.

Only one dairy indicated that it calls for requirements with respect to the use of inputs. This dairy recommends to his supplying farmers that they purchase certified inputs. The dairy pre-finances these inputs in exchange for raw milk delivery.

General

Improving the quality of the milk has been a crucial element in the dairy companies' policy in the two countries. For example, the dairy companies pay price premiums to farmers who are able to deliver high-quality milk. However, in contrast to the situation in Slovakia, quality awareness among dairy companies and farmers in Romania is still rather low. Companies that demand high-quality milk face tough competition for milk with companies that are less demanding in terms of quality – and relatively well-paying – while many farmers prefer direct sales at street markets where they are paid in cash and quality requirements are low. While in Slovakia the public inspection seems to function well, public authorities in Romania are accused of discrimination against dairies that are most quality-aware and criticized for poor inspection levels at open-air street markets.

Support for dairy farms

Romania

The dairy companies surveyed use several ways to support their farmers with the aim of improving the quality of milk supply and guaranteeing a stable supply (see Table 18.7). Most support is in the area of extension service. For instance, Friesland and Danone have staff out in the field, who visit and advise farmers on milk hygienic circumstances, cleaning practices and fodder management. This service is in principle open for every farmer who delivers milk to these two dairies.

The ISPA farmers' association, majority shareholder of Promilch, employs staff providing extension services to its 2000 members. Services provided are various: from supporting farmers in compiling feeding plans for their herd to a full business plan. In its early days, much extension work focused on convincing farmers to improve hygiene in their milking practices. The association distributes leaflets with practical information and hints on cultivating feed, storing milk at the farms, cleaning practices, and so forth. ISPA staff pays visits to farmers individually and organizes meetings, trainings, on-farm demonstrations and trials through which knowledge exchange is enhanced.

Raraul has made several efforts to improve farming conditions in order to improve milk quality. One example of this is that the company buys in fodder supplements and sells these at reasonable prices to its farmers. Another example occurred some years ago, when Raraul distributed pregnant heifers to farmers. This programme, however, was not successful because only a few farmers qualified for receiving the animals. In order to acquire a heifer, farmers had to prove they had good husbandry practices. Those farmers who were successful financed the purchase by pre-financed milk supply to the factory. Raraul has also invested in cooling facilities at its collection points.

Friesland and Danone – the two large foreign-owned dairies – are willing to pre-finance inputs (such as feed compounds or fertilizers) and provide loans for cooling facilities or milk parlour updating, but they support only the larger and most loyal farmers. Farmers who apply for pre-financed inputs have to deliver good-quality milk for at least 6 months.

In addition to pre-financed inputs, Danone is willing to provide farmers with medium-term credits for investments in, for instance, milking installations and animal purchases. A farmer can qualify for investment credits if he is a stable supplier to the company and if his farm is of a certain minimum size. In principle, Danone offers investment credit assistance only to the medium and larger farms, targeting farms that can deliver around 400 kg/day (in due course).[3]

Furthermore, together with his requests for support, the farmer sends in a business development plan. If Danone accepts this plan, the company and the farmer make up a contract in which the conditions for the

Table 18.7. Elements of a farm assistance programme offered by the surveyed Romanian dairies (from van Berkum, 2006).

Element offered	Danone	Friesland	Promilch	Raraul
Extension services	X	X	X	X
Provide good-quality inputs financed by deducting milk money	X	X	X	X
Support for purchases of simple inputs by prepayment of milk deliverance	X	X		
Investment support by small loans	X	X	X	
Support in receiving bank loans (e.g. loan guarantee)	X	X	X	

X, 'yes' or 'applicable to'.

loan are laid down. Danone normally takes the farm housing and/or land as guarantee for non-deliverance of milk or breach of contract. The contract is signed in a notary's deed.

ISPA also plays a role in helping farmers with credit, but as its members are predominantly small-scale farmers and borrowers are largely farmers with only a few milk cows. The association uses a Dutch fund – based on very attractive terms – and provides small loans to farmers who want to invest in animals, (re)construction of animal housing and/or equipment. Farmers qualify for a loan through an interview in which they have to present their business plan. An average loan is around €400, with a maximum of €2000. ISPA loans are to be repaid after a 6–18 month grace period for animals, and a 4-year grace period for construction investments. Farmers do not have to provide any collateral: the milk delivered is considered the collateral.

Eligibility criteria for loans include several elements. First, the farmer needs to have a durable relation with ISPA. In practice, ISPA requires a delivery period of at least 6 months, but preferably 12. It is important that a farmer uses an appropriate fodder base at his farm and agrees upon a commitment to further expanding the farm. The requirements are, however, not too strict and are subject to ISPA staff assessments. Trust and reliability are important. ISPA deals with the default risk by having a solidary liability of both the loan beneficiary and the milk collection centre staff, who guarantee the reliability of the borrower.

Slovakia

The majority of dairies in the sample provide some form of assistance to their suppliers (see Table 18.8). Two dairies support farm investments (in quality-improvement measures and milking and cooling equipment), with a maximum amount per farm. Other dairies provide assistance programmes to farmers that include the pre-financing of inputs purchased or bank loan guarantees. These programmes are applied selectively to their large suppliers that deliver high-quality milk.

In competition for milk, some dairies offer shorter payment periods and quality price premiums to their best suppliers. One dairy (whose size is above the sample average) replied in the affirmative to all the questions on support as an expression of interest in its suppliers and their economic viability. The type of support most frequently offered relates to quality improvements, mainly through extension. Dairies expressed that every farm is, in principle, eligible to this type of support.

General

All companies surveyed in the two countries apply some kind of support to the farmers that deliver their milk. This support is mainly in the area of extension service. Credit availability is low in the Romanian case, especially for small-scale farmers. The Romanian dairy companies are reluctant to provide farmers with pre-

Table 18.8. Elements of the farm assistance programme offered by the surveyed Slovakian dairies (from World Bank, 2006).

Element offered	Share of dairies in the sample offering assistance (%)
Support concerning production and storage	22
Support concerning improving quality	78
Support concerning management	44
Provision of credit	44
Support in receiving bank loans (e.g. loan guarantee)	22
Advice concerning investments	22
Support concerning purchase of farm inputs	22

financed inputs and loans; only the larger and loyal ones are offered these services. The exception is the farmers' association that provides its small-scale members with a full package of services, including credits.

Dairy companies in Slovakia are also rather selective in providing credits to their farmers, focusing their services mainly on the larger farmers. On the other hand, credit availability is less of a problem for the generally large-scale Slovakian farms, which have better-established technological bases from which they started (e.g. milking equipment and know-how), compared to other countries where a more radical reorganization of the supply system or collapse of the supporting institutions has caused greater problems in responding to high-quality requirements by processors. Furthermore, the Slovak dairy chain was given the opportunity to use EU Sapard funds for restructuring and modernization in the course of becoming member of the EU.

Effects of Vertical Coordination

Quality improvement: driving forces and obstacles

Romania

Companies surveyed indicated that improving milk quality was the main driving force behind their farm assistance programmes. Both the modern retail demand for guaranteed supply of high-quality products and EU integration drive have engineered changes in the quality awareness in the supply chain. Presently, milk quality norms set by the Romanian government refer only to minimum requirements in guaranteeing that the milk is safe for human consumption. These Romanian standards are generally lower than EU standards. Moreover, the number of dairies that use quality norms (fat and protein content, density and somatic cell count) as a base for milk payments is, according to the interviewed dairies, still low.

At the same time, efforts of those dairies that are trying to encourage farmers to improve the quality of milk delivered are undermined in several ways. Most (small) dairies accept low-quality milk and yet pay farmers attractive prices. These dairies generally do not invest in quality-improvement measures and do not request quality-improving investments from the farmers. Consequently, farmers are not encouraged to make any investment in quality improvements. Low-quality products can still be sold, because the majority of consumers are not yet so discerning. There are even accusations that inspection institutions apply double standards, allowing dairies to operate without production licences, to sell their products without paying taxes and to produce without obeying basic quality standards.

This has a very destructive impact on the industry's efforts to increase the quality of milk delivered. Interviewees indicate that the price differences between high- and low-quality milk is not so great during the winter months, when production is seasonally low. During these months there is much competition between the 'good' and 'bad' dairies in order to secure their supply. Contract enforcement is a problem because most agreements with the smaller farmers are not in a notary deed, while frequent price adjustments incite farmers to reconsider their business relation with their dairy and to switch dairies.

Street market selling is another obstacle to rapid improvement of the quality of dairy products in Romania. An estimated one-quarter of all milk production is sold directly to consumers at typical peasant street markets as fresh dairy products, including cheeses (see Table 18.5). Formally, the issues of health of the animals used to produce the products and the hygiene quality of the products sold are controlled by veterinary and local authorities, Yet, interviewees indicate to having serious doubts about the functioning of these authorities and about the effectiveness of the implementation of veterinary and health regulations in the country.

The quality of products sold at street markets is generally considered to be far below EU standards (Leat and van Berkum, 2003). As long as such outlets exist and the terms on which products are sold accepted, farmers have little incentive to improve milk quality.

Slovakia

The impacts of vertical coordination are difficult to assess, as the survey was limited and focused on present relations rather than on developments over time. Yet, there are developments in the dairy supply chain that point to positive effects of vertical relations. For instance, there are indications that the quality of milk produced by Slovakian farms has improved in recent years. For instance, the share of milk in the highest quality classes has increased from an already satisfactory level in the late 1990s up to 95% of all milk delivered (see Table 18.9). Milk of that quality is acceptable according to EU standards. Although there is still some scope for improvement,[4] quality of milk is no longer considered a major problem in the Slovakian milk sector.

The high proportion of EU-quality milk in Slovakia relatively early on in the transition period may be due to the fact that the large farms in Slovakia already had in place the basic investments in on-farm cooling equipment and milk-lines. In recent years, dairies have also invested a lot in new technologies to improve their production efficiency as well as to improve their production facilities in order to comply with EU-quality standards and market distribution requirements.

Also at farm level, the sector has benefited from investment support through the EU Sapard Funds, aiming at improving the quality of milk delivered (World Bank, 2006). This had major results. Following a spring 2004 investigation by the EU and Slovak Veterinary and Food Inspection of dairies on requirements and standards fulfilments, all high-capacity dairies are certified to export into the EU market.

Low-capacity dairies (with less than 2000 t/year production capacity), however, can release their product only on the domestic market and are assumed to be ceasing trading soon, as they are not expected to be able to invest in the required facilities to meet the hygienic and quality criteria necessary to serve foreign and domestic markets in the near future.

Impact on yields and production

Romania

Impacts of the contractual arrangements at the farm level are difficult to indicate, because this brief research did not include interviews with farmers. Yet, it may be assumed that when a farmer takes the given advice, uses better fodder and is granted small loans for investments in more productive cows, housing and/or milking parlour equipment, his cows will yield more milk and production will increase (see Leat and van Berkum, 2003).

In the same vein, relatively small changes in the industry's practices can have a major impact at farm level. An example from Friesland is illustrative in this respect: in 2001 the company bought a Romanian dairy, which utilized less than 50% of its capacity and had a bad reputation with respect to paying its farmers. Without changing anything but payments on time, Friesland succeeded in processing 20–30% more milk within a time span of 3 months. If farmers are convinced that a processor is reliable in making its milk payments,

Table 18.9. Milk deliveries in Slovakia by grade, 2003 (from World Bank, 2006).

Grade	Quantity (t million)	(%)
Total	506	100
Q class + 1st class[a]	480	95
Q class	271	53
1st class	209	41
Non-standardized	27	5

Q and 1st-class milk are of acceptable quality according to EU standards.

producers are generally prepared to deliver (more of) their milk to that processor.

The general picture for the Romanian dairy sector is that yields are increasing but slowly, with some acceleration in growth in the first years of the 1990s and since 2000 (see Fig. 18.1); total production did not increase much between 1995 and 2000, because the total dairy herd had decreased slightly over the years, but more recently yield improvements have pushed up total production.

Whether assistance programmes have contributed to these countrywide results is very doubtful: the initiatives – as reported by the four surveyed companies – seem too few to have any noticeable impact on the average yields in the country. Also, at dairy company level, it is hard to identify any impact on intake per farmer. Again, the number of farmers receiving assistance is fairly low. Furthermore, the supply base of most dairies changes continuously, as a significant proportion of small-scale farmers deliver milk to dairies on a on–off basis, selling part of their production on the street markets and switching from one dairy to another.

Slovakia

Milk production in Slovakia decreased by around 15% during the period 1993–2001 (see Fig. 18.2). This is mainly due to the decline in the total number of animals which, in 2003, was only 40% of the 1989 figure. However, yields per cow have increased significantly since 1993, indicating that farms have been investing in yield-increasing measures (better feed, better genetics, etc.) soon after the economic transition took off.

Conclusions

This paper provides an analysis of the dynamics of vertical coordination in the dairy supply chain in Romania and Slovakia. A major contrast between the two countries is that small-scale household production dominates in Romania, while dairy farming in Slovakia is mainly large-scale. The surveys indicate that there is extensive vertical coordination in Slovakia: almost the whole dairy sector is based on

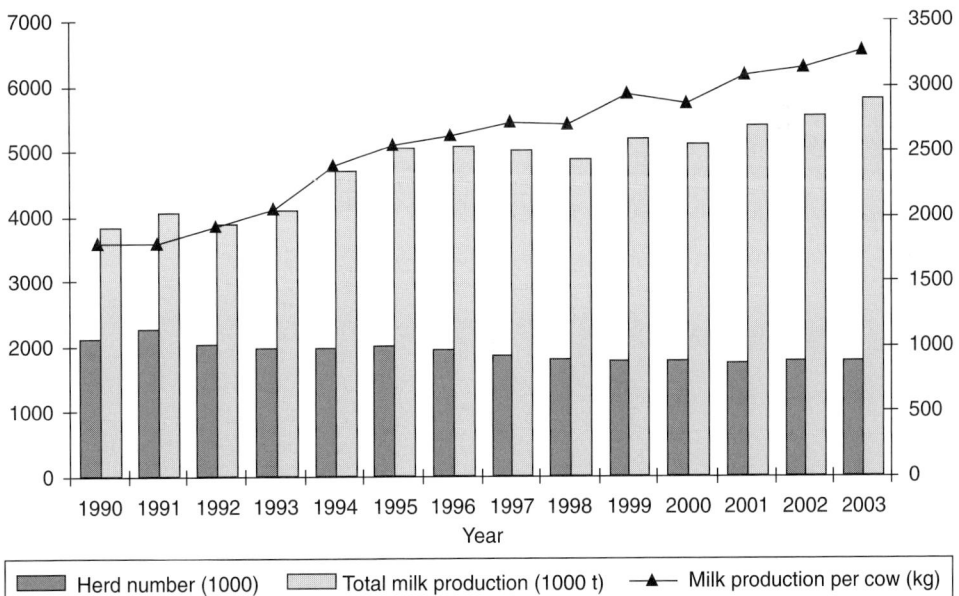

Fig. 18.1. Milk production, yield and herd numbers, Romania, 1990–2003 (from NIS, 2005b).

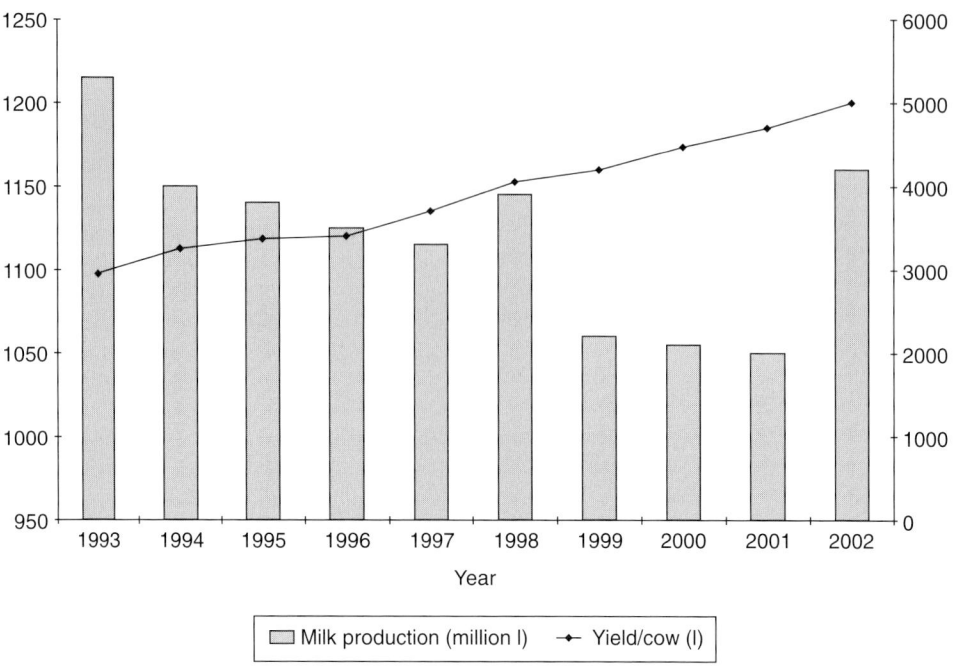

Fig. 18.2. Milk production and yield, Slovakia, 1993–2002.

supply contracts, including elements of farm assistance.

In Romania, however, only a few dairy companies apply vertical coordination. Years of macroeconomic instability, a weak public inspection authority and poor contract enforcement are among the explanations for the limited use of supplier assistance programmes in the Romanian dairy supply chain. Other key findings of the surveys are summarized below.

Improving the quality of milk

This has been a crucial element in the dairy companies' policy in the two countries. For example, the dairy companies pay price premiums to farmers that are able to deliver high-quality milk. Farm assistance programmes include extension, training and advice with respect to fodder management, hygienic circumstances and other issues aimed at improving the quality of milk.

In Slovakia, the quality of milk is no longer considered a major problem. This may be due to the fact that the large farms that dominated Slovak agriculture early on in the transition period had basic investments in cooling facilities, milk-lines and so on, while in more recent years they could benefit from EU Sapard Funds. However, in Romania, the low and unstable quality of milk is a key problem for sector development. Investments for quality improvement in Romania are seriously hampered by the typical small-scale structure with its poorly productive holdings.

Weak public inspection authorities and a lack of uniformly applied quality standards

These factors reduce the effectiveness of vertical coordination in Romania. Industry efforts to increase the quality of milk are undermined by dairies that accept low-quality of milk and by street market selling. These alternative outlets to farmers also contribute to the poor enforcement of contracts in Romania: farmers may switch rather easily to one of the many other dairies in operation without any negative image consequence of breaching the contract, or sell their produce on the street market.

In contrast to this situation, public inspection in Slovakia functions properly. Moreover, the fact that the sector consists of low numbers of farms and dairy companies may play a role in Slovakia, with the effect of making widely known the instance of any farmer who breaches his contracts. Having been shown to be unreliable, that farmer loses his reputation and this may limit his chances of acquiring a contract with another processor.

Effects of vertical coordination have been positive

In Slovakia, investments in new processing technologies, improved hygiene conditions at factory and farm level, etc. have further improved milk quality. Milk yields per cow have shown a rather rapid increase since 1993. Vertical coordination has contributed to these positive developments. Those companies in Romania that apply assistance support also report positive effects on yields, production and quality of milk delivered by those farmers receiving assistance.

The survey in Romania and in Slovakia indicates that vertical coordination improves the access to inputs for farmers. The support applied by the companies surveyed in the two countries is mainly in the area of extension. The Romanian dairy companies are reluctant to provide farmers with pre-financed inputs and loans; only the larger and loyal ones are offered these services. The exception is the farmers' association, which provides it small-scale members with a full package of services, including credits. In Slovakia, dairy companies are also rather selective in providing credits to their farmers, focusing their services mainly on the larger farmers. In general, however, access to (commercial) credits is not a major problem for the large-scale farms in Slovakia.

Although the larger farmers have some privileges in assistance programmes with respect to investment fund eligibility, there are no signs that the present vertical coordination arrangements in the Romanian dairy supply chain exclude small farmers.

Despite high transaction costs, dairies are willing to collect the milk from small plots, largely through collection points. The two foreign dairies interviewed in the survey explicitly indicated their main aims of reducing the number of small-scale suppliers and working with larger suppliers.

Yet, the problem is that there are still very few dairy farms with more than five cows in Romania. For the moment, dairies have to accept this situation until restructuring and consolidation in the sector kicks in. In the meantime, the larger dairies are keen to assist their supplying farmers in improving their conditions for producing higher-quality milk by providing advice, improving access to inputs – including investment means – and enhancing access to output markets. Farmers who are willing to learn and develop get opportunities to further grow their business.

Foreign investment

This has been important for the development of the sector, mainly as an initiator of change and institutional innovation. In Romania, for example, increased competition from internationally operating companies has encouraged the tendency of specialization in the sector and initiated further efforts to implement strict quality standards along the entire the dairy chain.

A stable macroeconomic environment and strong public (inspection) institutions

These conditions are of crucial importance for supplier assistance programmes or chain-based finance. Since vertical coordination is primarily a financial activity, instability may undermine contract enforcement. Romania has endured many years with rather high inflation rates, while the Slovak economy been more stable in recent years. Furthermore, the process of institutional development necessary for a well-functioning market economy is at a more advanced stage in Slovakia than in Romania.

Notes

1 This chapter expands upon two reports with case studies on Romania and Slovakia (van Berkum, 2006; World Bank, 2006).
2 The Phare programme is a financial instrument of the EU's pre-accession strategy for the candidate countries of Central Europe. From 2000, Phare has been complemented by (among others) SAPARD, the Special Accession Programme for Agriculture and Rural Development. For further details see http://www.ec.europa.eu/ enlargement
3 In the interview, the company's representative mentioned that Danone's assistance programme is targeted at farms with 20 cows or more. According to available statistics, this would apply to fewer than 1000 farms throughout Romania.
4 For instance, according to the results of controls conducted by the SVFA in 2003, 6.7% of milk samples and dairy products did not meet quality requirements (mostly microbiological indicators).

References

Dries, L. and Noev, N. (2006) A comparative analysis of vertical coordination in dairy chains in Poland, Slovakia and Bulgaria. In: Swinnen, J.F.M. (ed.) *Case Studies on Vertical Coordination in Agri-Food Chains in Eastern Europe and Central Asia*. ECSSD Working Paper No. 42, The World Bank, Washington, DC.

Leat, P. and van Berkum, S. (2003) Dairy sector analysis. In: van Berkum, S., Davies, S. and Popov, S. (eds) *The Romanian Agri-food Chain: on the Road to Accession*. Ministry of Agriculture, Forests, Water and Environment, Bucharest.

Macours, K. and Swinnen, J. (2000) Causes of output decline in economic transition: the case of Central and East European agriculture. *Journal of Comparative Economics* 28 (1), 172–206.

MAPAM (Ministry of Agriculture, Forests, Water and Environment) (2004) *Statistical Information on the Situation in the Dairy Processing Industry*. MAPAM, Bucharest.

National Institute for Statistics (NIS) (2002) *Romanian Statistical Yearbook*. NIS, Bucharest.

National Institute for Statistics (NIS) (2005a) *Agricultural Census*. NIS, Bucharest.

National Institute for Statistics (NIS) (2005b) *Annual Statistics 2004*. NIS, Bucharest, Chapter 13.

Swinnen, J.F.M. (2003) Vertical integration, interlinking markets, and growth in the Central and East European Agri-food sectors. In: Van Huylenbroeck, G. et al. (eds) *Importance of Policies and Institutions for Agriculture*. Academia Press, Ghent, Belgium, pp. 101–118.

Van Berkum, S. (2006) Vertical coordination in ECA supply chains: evidence from the dairy sector in Romania. In: Swinnen, J.F.M. (ed.) *Case Studies on Vertical Coordination in Agri-Food Chains in Eastern Europe and Central Asia*. ECSSD Working Paper No. 42, The World Bank, Washington, DC.

World Bank (2001) *Building Institutions for Markets*. World Development Report 2002. World Bank, Washington, DC/Oxford University Press, Oxford, UK.

World Bank (2006) *Market Linkages in the Slovak Agri-food Sector*. World Bank Slovakia Agricultural Policy Dialog Project (TA-P082205-TAS-BB). World Bank, Washington, DC.

Part III

The Policy Agenda

19 Global Supply Chains, Standards and the Poor: some Conclusions and Implications for Government Policy and International Organizations

J.F.M. Swinnen and M. Maertens

The previous chapters in this book provide a vast amount of insights on how the globalization of supply chains, the unprecedented increase in foreign investment in agricultural commodities and food markets worldwide, the rise and spread of food quality and safety standards and the rapid growth of high-value food systems are all affecting producers in developing, transition and emerging economies. We will not attempt to summarize all these findings. Instead, we will identify what we think are some key conclusions and present a series of policy implications.

Some Conclusions

First, agri-food markets globally experience rapid changes with major implications. Food standards become increasingly important and are driving vertical coordination in agri-food supply chains. Modern, large-scale retail chains and multinational processing companies play a central role in these vertically coordinated high-value food supply chains.

Most authors in this book agree that the increasing importance of high-value agricultural markets, increased standards and modern supply chains: (i) create important opportunities for enhancing agricultural productivity, for increasing rural incomes and for reducing poverty in developing and transition countries; while (ii) also imposing major challenges for these countries and the most resource-constrained households.

Second, there is large variation between countries in both the progress of these changes and their implications. Whilst in some countries – often the richest ones – modern supermarkets and large food processors have taken over almost the entire processing and marketing sectors, in other countries marketing is still largely organized through small, local companies, or through local markets. For example, in China, India, and many African countries, the produce handled by modern processing companies and retailers is still only a very small share of total volume traded – often only a few percentage points.

Third, there is large variation between countries (and sectors) in the extent of participation of small and poorer farms and households. In some countries, e.g. China, Madagascar, several Asian countries and some Eastern European countries such as Poland, high-value supply chains are based on contract farming with small farmers.

Nevertheless, there is also evidence that small – and especially the poorest – farmers are excluded from high-value supply chains, e.g. in some transition and Latin American countries. In Senegal, a shift is observed from a system of contract farming based on small-scale production in the late 1990s towards more large-scale estate production and integration of small farmers as estate wage workers.

Fourth, several studies show that small farmers and fishermen are much more evident in modern supply chains than would be expected based on the arguments of: (i) too-high transaction costs; (ii) difficulties in monitoring food quality and safety; and (iii) too-high investment and human capital demands, given the constraints of small farmers.

This is the case in many transition countries and in South Asia. However, in Africa too, many small farmers are involved in contracts with modern supply chains. For example, in Madagascar high-value vegetable exports are based on contracting with thousands of small farmers. In China, also, procurement from large numbers of very small farms plays a dominating role in the rapidly growing vegetable markets.

Fifth, rural households which are integrated in high-value supply chains, either as contracted producers or as workers, often benefit strongly from the gains in high-value markets. Many authors find that small farmers in Asia (China, Philippines, India and Thailand), Central America (Costa Rica, Guatemala, El Salvador, Honduras and Nicaragua), Africa (Senegal and Madagascar) and Central and Eastern Europe (Poland, Romania, etc.) do gain from integration in high-value supply chains in terms of higher productivity, higher profits and higher incomes.

Sixth, the benefits for small farmers arise through the direct income effects of contracts and wages and through household and farm spillover effects. An illustrative example of such spillover effects is found in Chapter 12 (Madagascar), where contracts for FFV production have technical and managerial spillover effects on rice productivity, reduce income variability and hence household vulnerability.

Finally, despite these important potential opportunities, several authors also point at important challenges for small farmers and poor households and the dangers for them in becoming marginalized in high-value food supply chains. This marginalization can come from their exclusion from supply chains as well as from unequal power relationships in the chain and extraction of rents by large processing and trading companies.

These dangers appear most acute in countries and sectors where there is a substantial heterogeneity in farm structures, such as in several Eastern European and former Soviet transition countries and in Latin America, where there is a mixture of large, medium and small farms.

The Policy Agenda

These conclusions point to important areas for a development policy agenda. High-value agricultural markets and modern supply chains have the potential to bring about pro-poor economic growth in developing and transition countries. However, to ensure that the poor are not excluded and do share in the benefits, it is crucial that policy initiatives address the main constraints which prevent modern supply chains working with the poor or, vice versa, that constrain poor producers from participating in high-value supply chains.

The authors of the chapters in this book have identified a wide variety of important policy issues for ensuring and maximizing the potential beneficial effects of high-value agriculture and modern supply chain developments. These policy issues include: (i) the role of investment policy; (ii) public standards; (iii) macro-economic reforms;

(iv) capital market and trade liberalization; (v) privatization; and (vi) competition policy, etc. It would be impossible to address all these policy issues here.

In the remainder of this chapter we concentrate on a series of key messages and implications that relate directly to the analyses on supply chain restructuring, standards and contracting as presented in the previous chapters. A government strategy for stimulating domestic growth in a supply chain-driven development process, while ensuring the inclusion of local producers who face major constraints in this process – and an equitable distribution of rents in the chain – should include several policy components, encompassing changes in the regulatory environment and public investments.

These policy issues and components can be classified, roughly, into three groups – although some of the policies could fit into more than one of these groups: (i) the enabling environment for high-value supply chain development; (ii) policy and programmes for addressing equity and efficiency concerns in supply chains; and (iii) implications of supply chain development for public interventions and for agri-business development.

Before discussing these in detail, it is important to emphasize more general policy issues, which are arguably the most important policy implications. The first is the recognition of the importance of supply chain development and the vertical coordination phenomenon in global and domestic agri-food chains and, therefore, the need to explicitly integrate these developments into policy thinking and programme strategies.

One of the key findings of this volume is that structural changes and vertical coordination in high-value agri-food chains are extremely important developments in low-income countries, in the light of economic growth as well as of poverty reduction and rural development. Policies, in general, have not integrated these structural developments so far.

The second is that there is significant variation across countries and sectors. The implication is that there is no one-size-fits-all strategy but, instead, several models of supply chain coordination reflecting commodity characteristics, stages of transition and development. Instead, optimal policies and policy components will also need to differ and change to reflect these differences.

In the rest of this chapter we discuss in more detail the three groups of policy issues we have identified above. We also refer the reader to the final chapters (Pingali *et al.*, Chapter 20, van der Meer, Chapter 21 and Gow and Cocks, Chapter 22) in the final part of this book. These chapters focus specifically on some of the key policy issues that are particularly relevant and provide a series of specific and detailed lessons and recommendations.

Enabling and Stimulating the Development of High-value Supply Chains

Increasing the capacity for high-value production and food standards management

International and domestic competition in agricultural markets is moving beyond the capacity of supplying products at market prices. Products need to comply with food quality and safety standards, which emphasize the strengths and weaknesses in high-value supply chains. Many developing and transition countries have substantial weaknesses in food safety and quality capacity and the key element for them is to overcome these weaknesses and exploit their strengths. There is evidence of low-income countries being able to establish the regulatory, technical and administrative arrangements to meet tightening standards in high-value agricultural markets.

In addition to increasing the supply capacity for high-quality and safe food, there is a need for creating the capacity to respond quickly to emerging food safety issues, changing legislation and a variety of private standards. Building capacity for compliance to food standards is discussed at length in Chapter 21; here, we indicate some key elements.

Improving administrative, technical and scientific capacity for food quality and safety

The public sector can also play a role in improving the administrative, infrastructural, technical and scientific capacity for the production and marketing of high-standard food products. The development of food safety management and control systems is essential for participation in the growing high-value agricultural markets and involves attention to the legal system, institutional transformations, human capital formation and physical infrastructure.

Government investment in projects, institutions and technical assistance to stimulate higher quality and strengthen public sector quality testing is necessary to establish food quality and safety capacity. This could include: (i) the development of systems for accreditation, conformity assessment, labelling and certification; (ii) the establishment and maintenance of monitoring and control systems; (iii) investment in laboratory units and scientific human resources; (iv) laying down directives for 'good agricultural practice'; (v) promoting better postharvest practices; and (vi) developing better traceability systems, etc. However, investments such as in cold-storage capacity and transport facilities are more efficiently dealt with by the private sector.

Farm and business assistance programmes

High-value global and domestic supply chains are based on high quality and standards. Therefore, preparing suppliers for quality- and standards-driven markets will make it easier for them to be integrated into high-value agricultural markets. Farmers and smaller agri-food businesses, in particular, face substantial constraints to gaining access to information on changing food safety legislation and quality standards in global markets, to translating that information into specific investment needs and to realizing those investments and managing high-quality production.

Farmer and business assistance programmes can play a crucial role in providing technical and market information, appropriate credit schemes and technical assistance for high-value production. In addition, there is a potential role for the government and international organizations in establishing and developing sustainable trading relationships through specific marketing assistance programmes. An example of how such programmes can be successful is described in Chapter 22.

Demonstrating capacity for producing high-quality food

In order to participate in high-value global supply chains, developing countries must demonstrate their capacity for high-standard food production. It is not enough to comply with stringent food standards; this compliance also needs to be demonstrated such that specific food products from specific countries are perceived as safe and high-quality products by domestic and foreign consumers.

Therefore, conformity in quality and compliance with food safety standards is important. Even if individual private firms are able to comply with strict requirements, a country as a whole will not be able to gain market access and significant market shares if there is no conformity. This requires specific measures such as labelling, certification and promotion of high-value products, which involves public as well as private investment.

Enabling and stimulating vertical coordination

High-value chains are typically characterized by vertical coordination (VC) to guarantee quality and food safety throughout the supply chain. Therefore, to stimulate the development of high-value chains, to guarantee the participation of small farmers in the chain and to assure an equitable distribution of rents in the chain, it is crucial to enable and encourage vertical coordination.

Institutional innovations

Enabling and stimulating VC in agricultural supply chains may entail institutional changes. It is necessary to remove policies that impede VC and stimulate innovative VC systems through the creation of the right juridical systems and the support of contract-enforcement mechanisms.

Refraining from direct intervention

It is important to refrain from direct intervention. Direct government intervention in the supply chains may crowd out alternative financing systems or cause defaults. Companies are willing to incorporate temporary defaults due to unforeseen shocks such as the weather, but not systemic risks due to government intervention.

Stimulating investment

Probably one of the most essential elements for the integration in, and the development of, high-value food supply chains and VC in those chains is that of encouragement of private investment – domestic as well as foreign investment – in the agri-food industry.

Creating the right conditions for investment

The two general conclusions in the World Bank's World Development Report *Improving the Investment Climate for Growth and Poverty Reduction* are that: (i) a good investment climate is the driving force behind economic growth and poverty reduction; and (ii) policy uncertainty is the primary concern of firms in developing countries. There is ample evidence that a poor policy environment has a negative effect on investment in the agri-food industry and on VC programmes. As such, it constrains integration in high-value supply chains and the beneficial effects of VC.

Ensuring macro-economic stability

Macro-economic stability is a key condition for stimulating domestic investment and attracting foreign investors but, even more so, for supplier assistance programmes or other forms of chain-based finance in vertically integrated supply chains. Since VC is primarily a financial activity, significant economic instability may cause coordination and enforcement failures, culminating in a collapse of contract schemes and obstructing the development of high-value supply chains.

Attracting FDI in the agri-industry

FDI in the agri-food industry could increase developing countries' supply capacity for high-quality agricultural production and facilitate their integration into global supply chains. Because of the link with their home economies and subsidiaries in other countries, foreign investors and multinational companies have better access to high-value agricultural markets, better knowledge of food safety and quality issues and enhanced financial and technical capacities to meet compliance with food standards. This might develop the supply and marketing capacity of the host economy as a whole and improve, through spillover effects, the capacity of domestic firms.

Improving Efficiency and Equity in High-value Supply Chains

For policy-makers concerned with pro-poor economic growth, enhancing efficiency and equity in high-value agricultural supply chains is a key point. Therefore, it is crucial to ensure the participation of the rural farm population in these supply chains and an equitable distribution of rents in the chain.

Reducing transaction costs

The main disadvantage for small farmers in high-value supply chains is partially due to transaction costs. Therefore, there is a need for government policy to focus on reducing those transaction costs. This can be done in several ways.

Investment in intermediary institutions could reduce the number of transactions and hence the associated costs. Intermediary institutions reduce the cost of exchange between farmers and processors or input suppliers. Specific investments in this could include the creation of farm associations and collection points, where processors and retailers can source from many small suppliers at low transaction costs. The issue of transaction costs is further dealt with by Pingali *et al.* (Chapter 20, this volume), who examine in more detail the relation between transaction costs and the potential for trading in high-value agricultural markets.

Investment in infrastructure

Improvements in rural infrastructure can reduce transport costs and, more generally, the cost of including supplies from remote areas. Rural infrastructure is identified as a serious constraint to VC, and particularly to integrating smaller producers in more remote areas. For example, bad roads, regular electricity interruptions, poor communication, etc. impede the coordination between producers, traders and processors, and constrain investments. Public investment in such infrastructure would stimulate: (i) agri-business investment; (ii) VC with suppliers; and (iii) inclusion of small farmers in remote areas.

Investment in farmers' associations

Farmers' associations have several advantages, such as reducing transaction costs, enhancing suppliers' bargaining position vis-à-vis both suppliers and governments and serve as an instrument for communication and information distribution. Stimulating farmers' associations is a frequently mentioned policy. In fact, it is hard to find a policy document which does not mention this as an important aspect. However, the creation of farmers' associations that are integrated in the coordination system of supply chains might require innovative approaches. This is particularly the case in transition countries where historical factors have created an aversion by private farmers to working in 'associations' and 'cooperatives'.

Enforcing competition

Competition in high-value supply chains is of great importance, both for efficiency and equity (see Chapter 7, this volume). Competition induces processors, retailers and input suppliers to provide more supplier assistance programmes and it constrains rent extraction of suppliers by up- or downstream companies. Given these strong benefits of competition for farmers in the chain, ensuring competition is an important role for the government.

Competition should be enforced through both domestic policies (e.g. competition policies, lower barriers of entry) as well as external policies (e.g. liberal trade policies). The importance of competition applies not only to private companies, but also in cases when the government is directly or indirectly imposing a monopoly system and thereby extracting rents from farms.

Moreover, competition is also important on the input side. The existence of alternative channels of credit or inputs will constrain rent extraction in the supply chains. Therefore, investments in alternative sources of farm finance, such as cooperative credit associations, micro-credit institutions, etc. should be supported and continued.

Enhancing the bargaining power of farmers

The empowering of farmers is needed to strengthen their position in the chain and vis-à-vis governments in bargaining for better contract deals, better policies, etc. Several of the policies mentioned earlier will contribute to this objective, such as stimulating farmers' associations, investing in quality control institutions, competition policies, etc. There are a number of additional policy measures for enhancing farmers' bargaining capabilities.

First, this involves investment in institutions to assist farms in contract negotiations and dispute settlements. Measures to increase the transparency of contracts, providing for dispute-settling arrangements, providing market benchmarks for price negotiations, training farmers in their rights/obligations as contractors, etc. are all important in increasing the transparency of the contracting system, competition among contracts and, thereby, the bargaining position of farms. As it is generally either not possible or too costly to resolve disputes in court, alternative dispute settlement institutions can play an important role.

Second, empowering farmers entails investment in institutions for (independent) quality and safety control and certification. Investing in quality control centres has the additional advantages of enhancing the bargaining power of suppliers and ensuring correct payments for quality in the chain. This will lead to better investment incentives and more equal distribution of rents. Improving quality controls, e.g. by introducing an independent control institution or by letting farm representatives participate in the evaluation, has both efficiency and equity benefits.

Third, empowering farmers will also come primarily from alternative options for accessing inputs and selling their products. Hence, it is important to encourage alternatives in input and output markets. Competition and liberalization of export regimes will also enhance farms' situation. Here also, investments in projects and institutions supporting higher quality will contribute to this goal.

Rethinking the Role of Government

The development of high-value supply chains and VC requires a fundamental rethinking of the role of the government and policy-making. Large companies develop their own standards, their own extension services, their own supply channels and wholesale exchange institutions, quality testing, etc. Some of these activities are in areas where, traditionally, governments were considered to be playing an important role. Hence, there are fundamental and difficult questions on the role of the government in such a changed environment.

Policy analysis and information-gathering

Policy analysis is complicated by the emergence of VC for a number of reasons. One reason is that basic models of supply reactions to policy changes may have to be adjusted for the more complex organization of the supply system. Another reason is that traditional instruments of information collection, on which policies are typically based, do not usually include information on VC. Hence, information collection (e.g. survey instruments) may need to be explicitly designed or adjusted to account for this.

Rethinking traditional public investments

Traditional areas of public investment such as research and extension, market information systems, veterinary services and animal surveillance programmes require rethinking to take into account the role that

VC plays in these areas. Optimal government policies in a VC environment will be based on public–private partnerships.

Public–private partnerships

Since private investments and strategies play a crucial role in the supply chain process, collaboration between public authorities, international organizations and private companies should be centre stage. The cooperation between the public and private sectors requires a well-organized private sector, with representative and effective farmers' business associations supported by the government, and a forum for communication.

For example, private sector involvement in public standard setting, development of certification procedures and the establishment of control systems for food safety is important, as private companies are often better informed about technical possibilities.

There are some successful examples of where such partnerships have contributed to positive developments from each perspective. For example, a recent collaborative project, financed by USAID, between the Michigan State University-based Partnership for Food Industry Development (PFID), South African retail chains and local NGOs, has led to the creation of a framework approach; this has led to integration of small farmers' access to seeds, services, finance and output markets – much like VC in private sector-driven models – and which has led to upgrading of small-farmer supplies and integration of small farmer groups in South African supply chains. Retail chains are interested in working with USAID in Africa to replicate this system.

Innovative finance instruments

High-value supply chain developments incorporate innovative, chain-based financing instruments. These instruments are private initiatives; some with only a limited role for the government, others with a more important role. Government intervention could include the provision of the regulatory and legal system that is required for these instruments to function; or there may be a role in co-financing seed money to start up some of these innovations. The key conclusion here seems to be one of being open to innovations that explicitly take into account the supply chain as a structural aspect of the financing problem, while being critical over which role international organizations and the government should play.

Supply-chain development as part of a wider rural development strategy

Countries where small farmers make up a large share of the agricultural sector, and thus the supplier base, are typically characterized by significant over-employment in agriculture from a long-term development perspective. Significant productivity increases and growth can arise from integration of the farm sector in modern high-value supply chains and the associated inflows of inputs, technology, capital and management.

However, these beneficial developments are unlikely to solve all structural problems in the rural areas. Therefore, it is unrealistic to assume that in such countries all households currently employed or relying on agriculture could be included in such a development. For a broader pro-poor development process, ultimately, a broader process of rural development is needed, with the creation of many off-farm employment opportunities in rural areas – or at least accessible for rural households. Integration in high-value supply chains and supply chain development models, even inclusive ones, can be only one part of such strategies.

20 The Role of the Public and Private Sectors in Commercializing Small Farms and Reducing Transaction Costs

P. Pingali, Y. Khwaja and M. Meijer

Introduction

Food markets in developing countries are undergoing profound changes that are fuelled by economic development, increase in per capita incomes, changing technology and urbanization. Increasing volumes of food marketing are being handled by supermarkets, and substantial organizational and institutional changes throughout the food marketing chain are taking place (Dolan et al., 2001).

Such changes include the setting of private grades and standards for food quality and safety and the adoption of contracts between buyers and sellers at various points along the food marketing chain.[1] Subcontracting for products of specified quality and traits is likely to proliferate as a form of interaction between retail food chains and producers. If those regions where supermarket retailing is more developed (for example, Latin America) are a precursor of what will follow elsewhere, then supermarkets and large-scale distribution will progressively dominate the food marketing chain in urban areas.

However, concentration of food trade in the hands of a few retailers and large market intermediaries threatens the existence of small traders and small businesses, central 'spot' food markets and neighbourhood stores if they are unable to meet the private standards on health and safety (Dolan et al., 2001; Reardon and Berdegué, 2002).

The pressures to meet the requirements of a more exacting food system have brought with them a renewed interest in small farm welfare. For the small farmer there are difficulties with commercialization that arise from poor public good provision that hinders market exchange and a new set of transaction costs that emerge from dealing with a food system characterized by different rules, regulations and players.

The principal challenge confronting governments and the international development community is to ensure that smallholders and other rural poor benefit from commercialization, either through participation in the market or by successfully exiting agriculture and finding employment in different sectors. There is some compelling evidence to suggest that increased transactions costs deter entry of small farmers into the market. Thus, interventions aimed at reducing transaction costs could encourage increased farmer participation in competitive markets.

In this paper we consider the relationship between transaction costs of small farmers and their potential for trading in both domestic and international markets. Section 1 examines the key issues facing small farmers in the commercialization process. Section 2 identifies the constraints that prohibit market entry for many small farmers, with the emphasis on transaction costs. Section 3 looks at how the private sector can overcome costs of market participation by small farmers. In section 4 we focus on public policy interventions.

Commercial Transformation of Food Production Systems

The issue of agricultural commercialization and the small farmer is by no means new. Most developing countries have witnessed agriculture 'moving away from traditional self-sufficiency' to one where 'farm output is ... more responsive to market trends' (Pingali and Rosegrant, 1995). It has long been understood that, with increasing economic growth, small farm production systems could not remain static and would need to gear themselves to some degree of commercialization for their survival.

What is new in the story of commercialization is the focus on agribusiness, and the scale at which it is influencing the process of change. The relationships within the food chain are, nowadays, much more complex, leading to far more informational uncertainties within the food system. There is a much greater degree of integration between producers and the output market, with a strong emphasis on standards in relation to quality and safety (Boehlje, 1999). These informational requisites incur costs that tend to diminish with increasing farm size.

Thus, entering the food system on a competitive basis is problematic for small farmers not only because of the physical investments needed to enter but also because of the transactions costs associated with the new agricultural market. In this section we discuss the evolution from subsistence to commercial production systems and ask whether small farmers can be successfully integrated into the new agri-food system.

Food production systems can be characterized as subsistence, semi-commercial or commercial systems (Pingali and Rosegrant, 1995). Increased commercialization shifts farm households away from traditional self-sufficiency goals and towards profit- and income-oriented decision-making; farm output is accordingly more responsive to market needs. The returns to intensive subsistence production systems that require high levels of family labour generally decline relative to production for the market with predominant use of purchased inputs. Initially, diversification implies the addition of other crops and other enterprises to staple-based systems.

As the level of commercial orientation increases, however, one observes mixed farming systems giving way to specialized production units for the production of high-value crop and livestock products. Commercialization, while leading to an increase in the diversity of marketed output at the national level, also leads to increasing regional and farm-level specialization.

While the speed of the above structural transformation differs substantially between countries they are all moving in the same direction. Timmer (1988) provides a comprehensive discussion on the process of structural change and commercialization of agriculture. For a recent review on agricultural commercialization see Pingali and Rosegrant, 1995; Pingali, 1997; Reardon and Timmer, 2005. Empirical evidence on commercialization trends is provided by Dyck *et al.* (1993) for East Asia; Huang and Rozelle (1994) for China; and Koppel and Zurich (1988) for South-east Asia.

Implications of commercialization for the small farmer

Modern food systems are highly integrated, with greater forward and backward linkages and significantly involve the private sector in determining standards and market regulations (Rondot et al., 2004). Moreover, they are systems that exhibit an ever-increasing degree of technological and process innovation. As such, these modern food systems are much more discriminatory in terms of who is able to enter. There are two main difficulties small farmers face in trying to adapt to modern food systems. The first concerns their ability to commercialize from production systems that are often semi- or fully subsistence and the second concerns the actual crop or enterprise choice.

There is a considerable body of literature that testifies to the productive efficiency of small farms. On the basis of this, it is argued that small farms – if they can overcome some constraints – are well placed to enter markets. A number of empirical studies, including those by and Binswanger and Elgin (1992) and Van Zyl et al. (1996), conclude that small-scale family farms tend to be more productive than large farms. Eastwood et al. (2004) present an extensive review of the literature on small farm productivity. The major reason cited for higher levels of efficiency is the higher productivity of farm family labour and lower supervision costs compared to large farms.

However, this efficiency is often rooted in traditional crop production, often for own-consumption purposes. The difficulty for small farmers is whether the existing production structures can be geared towards the market and at what cost. The alternative is to remain in a form of production that is semi- or fully subsistence. Over time, subsistence farming in any form is not a viable activity for safeguarding household food security and welfare (Pingali, 1997). What policymakers then need to consider is what the best exit strategies are for farmers who cannot remain in farm production.

The rapid changes in the food system have placed increased pressures on small farmers to diversify away from staples and to harness the lucrative gains that derive from the production and trade of high-value crops. This often seems to imply that small farmers face an either/or option in terms of their crop choice. Small farms either stay in staples, which are regarded as unprofitable, or they make the changes to shift to alternative high-value production.

The potential gains from high-value crops tend, on average, to be higher than those for staples, even though production of high-value crops can be accompanied by greater uncertainty and risk. For small farmers specializing in high-value output, a critical question remains as to whether their size can profitably support these activities long-term.

In addition, to a large extent, crop choice is determined a priori by the land potential available to small farmers. So, while high-value crop production may promise higher rewards, this option is not open to all small farmers. For some small farmers, commercialization can offer, at best, the possibility of some diversification into non-staples, but not a total specialization. So called high-potential lands may be able to make a permanent transition to high-value crops, but low-potential and marginal lands tend to be best suited to traditional crops which are often staples (Pingali, 1997). Moreover, for some farmers any kind of production on marginal lands may not be feasible long-term, in which case the emphasis needs to be on developing non-farm rural employment to support production.

Transactions Costs in Modern Agri-food Systems

The issue of transaction costs has always featured in agricultural markets. In many instances they explain the presence of missing markets, for example, in credit markets (Besley, 1994), labour markets

(Bardhan, 1984) and land (Carter and Mesbah, 1993), as well as in product markets (Holden and Binswanger, 1998; Stiglitz, 1998). These failures can result in alternative institutional arrangements (Binswanger and Rosenzweig, 1986; Timmer, 1997) such as sharecropping and interlinked markets (Bardhan, 1980; Braverman and Stiglitz, 1982; Binswanger et al., 1993a). Before elaborating on the new set of transaction costs that has arisen with the appearance of modern food system, we will briefly elaborate on how transactions costs can be defined.

Williamson (1979, 1993, 1996) defines transactions costs as a trade-off between the costs of coordination within an organization and the costs of transacting and forming contracts in the market. This trade-off will depend on the magnitude of the transaction costs. According to the seminal work of Coase (1937), it is precisely because of the presence of transaction costs associated with information, negotiation, monitoring, coordination and enforcement of contracts that intermediary firms emerge to economize on these costs. A substantive volume of literature has built on this work and been applied to agricultural markets.

Building on Coase's work, Hobbs (1997) classified transaction costs into information, negotiation and monitoring or enforcement costs. Information costs, for example, arise *ex ante* of an exchange. Negotiation costs are the costs of physically carrying out the transaction, while monitoring costs occur *ex post* of a transaction and include the costs of ensuring that the terms of the transaction (quality standards and payment arrangements) are adhered to by the other parties involved in the transaction. Others have distinguished transaction costs between tangible (transportation costs, communication costs, legal costs, etc.) and intangible (uncertainty, moral hazard, etc.) costs. (Cuevas and Graham, 1986; Birthal et al., 2005).

In addition to the above, with the rise of modern food systems, a new set of transaction costs has arisen because of the standards that are required in terms of quality, size and delivery. Private companies, in order to capture markets and differentiate their products, put ever more stringent conditions on the suppliers. Customers are increasingly willing to pay for product attributes that include convenience, taste, variety, high quality and low caloric intake (Napier, 2001).

It is precisely because many small farmers are locked into traditional modes of production far removed from meeting the requirements demanded by modern food systems that transaction costs have tended to become prohibitive. These factors go some way to explaining why smallholder farmers do not participate fully in commercialized agricultural markets. This section considers the nature of transaction costs and how they constrain the possibility of entering those markets.

Transactions costs are faced by all actors in the food system. We focus in particular on small farmers trying to integrate into the modern food supply chain. The tendency is to move away from the spot market to other forms of vertical coordination (Boehlje, 1999). This is because there is a continuous need for information-sharing on consumers' changing preferences, on quality requirements through grades and standards and on high post-production and service value addition, which requires specific investments. Open-access markets can no longer meet consumer needs for accurate information on quality and safety attributes (Van der Vorst, 2005).

The transactions costs that specifically emerge from dealing with large numbers of small farms comprise (Hayes, 2000):

- The bureaucratic costs associated with managing and coordinating integrated production, processing and marketing.
- The opportunity cost of time used in communicating with farmers and coordinating them.
- The costs involved in establishing and monitoring long-term contracts.
- The screening costs linked to uncertainties about the reliability of potential

suppliers or buyers and the uncertainty about the actual quality of the goods.
- The transfer costs associated with the legal or physical constraints on the movement and transfer of goods. This also includes handling storage costs, transport costs, etc.

Farm-specific transaction costs

For farmers, transactions costs are those associated with participation in the – increasingly vertically coordinated – markets. These costs can be household-specific, such as access to assets, or they can be the same for all farmers in a particular location, such as land quality or producing a specific product, such as perishable fruit and vegetables. It is the bundle of transactions costs that farmers face that determine market participation. Interactions between the unique features of food system participation and other household- and location-specific characteristics can further exacerbate transaction costs. Farmers will not enter markets when the value of participating is outweighed by the costs of undertaking the transaction (Sadoulet and de Janvry, 1995).

Specific transaction costs can arise in both the input and output market and affect market participation. Evidence from Bangladesh (Ahmed, 1989) found that transaction costs resulting from loans from formal lenders were higher than those of loans from informal lenders, because the borrower was usually known. In contrast, transaction costs per unit of loan decreased with loan size, and this was much faster for formal than for informal loans.

Transaction costs in output markets, for example, can affect the choice of market channel farmers use. In Ethiopia, grain brokers have been shown to be the preferred choice among small farmers (Gabre-Madhin, 1999). Farmers identify where to trade and then decide on whether to use a broker to search on their behalf. High transaction costs were linked to increased broker use because farmers spent time searching for information on markets and prices. Where farmers had better information on prices and market because of social networks, broker use was significantly less.

Location-specific transaction costs

Variances across regions matter in determining the level of transaction cost. Farmers in high-potential areas may experience a lower total level of transaction costs than those in low-potential areas. First, higher-potential areas have more reliable access to production inputs and markets and hence face lower costs and risks associated with the switch to high-value crop production. The exception here is the irrigated rice lowlands, where the drainage costs associated with growing non-rice crops tend to limit short-term movement between rice and other crops, particularly in the wet season (Pingali et al., 1997).

Second, high-potential areas generally have better transport and communication infrastructure and hence relatively lower search and information costs. Where road density is low (often the case in low-potential areas), transaction costs associated with accessing markets and information tend to be correspondingly high. Poor road infrastructure increases transportation time, and therefore costs. The price that farmers receive will be net of some of these costs – if not all – reducing the incentive to enter commercial agriculture.

Distance to a paved road can have a significant negative effect on fertilizer use because of the transactions costs associated with the time it takes to search for inputs (see Strasberg et al., 1999). Poor communication prevents efficient access to market information, increasing search and monitoring costs.

Crop-specific transaction costs

Transaction costs also vary by product. High-value crops that are often perishable – such as fish and vegetables – are typically associated with high transaction costs. On the one hand, these stem from transportation costs due to poor infrastructure such as rural roads and a lack of a cold chain. These costs can be further exacerbated the greater the distance to markets. On the other hand, intangible transaction costs arise when an asset-specific investment has been made – such as a milk-cooling tank – or when the seller is facing a monopsonistic buying structure. This increases the risk of buyers behaving opportunistically and defaulting on the contract.

Household-specific factors that influence transaction costs

There are a number of household-specific variables that are not so much transaction costs *per se*, but significantly impact on them, such as: (i) aversion to risk and uncertainty; (ii) social networks and organization; (iii) age, gender and education; and (iv) intra-household interaction. These variables all influence the costs of information-seeking, negotiating, monitoring and enforcement.

The prevalence of social networks and organizations may substantially reduce transaction costs. Often, these networks ensure cooperation between farmers in the use of scarce and communal resources such as water. Moreover, small farmers may be better placed to understand their local environments in a way that ensures best use of existing resources in an environmentally sustainable way. The use of cooperatives or farmers' organizations to overcome marketing related difficulties will be addressed in Section 3.

Age, gender and education can impact on transaction costs in different ways. Age can often be indicative of farming experience, which renders certain informational and search costs easier and thus cheaper. Transaction costs related to accessing land and credit are much more variable for women than for men. Education matters in terms of reducing the costs of searching for information. Moreover, the time taken to process and act upon information decreases with more education.

Internal transaction costs occur within the dynamics of intra-household interaction and can represent a constraint to the decision-making process in households. In some cases, this may reduce the incentive to enter competitive markets. Zaibet and Dunn (1998) argued that farm households may require a premium to overcome these costs, which is assumed to be proportionally related to the size of the household. Large or extended families may face higher negotiation costs.

Risk and uncertainty play a pivotal role in explaining the household decision to enter commercial markets. Participation in the market can reduce uncertainty as long as this is supported by better information, communication and increased access to market outlets. On the other hand, uncertainty may be exacerbated by greater market participation, as the security of subsistence is replaced by the insecurity of unstable markets and adverse price trends.

Small farmers are unlikely to exchange a known set of risks associated with subsistence for an unknown set of risks that is a function of commercialization. Households will allocate their limited resources to subsistence and commercial production such that the disutility of risk is balanced against the utility of market goods (Von Braun *et al.*, 1991). Hence, the case for the coexistence of various levels of market participation in a location in any given time period.

Overcoming Transaction Costs: the Role of the Private Sector

Because transaction costs vary among households and enterprises, commodities and regions, there is no single innovation or intervention, public or private, which can reduce them. However, there are a number of ways in which market entry by small farmers can be developed. These include: (i) contract farming; (ii) the development of farmer organizations for marketing; and (iii) development of the supply chain for high-value exports produced by smallholders through an appropriate mix of private and public sector initiatives and the facilitation of private sector provision of market information via improved telecommunications (Kydd and Poulton, 2000).

The role of government is crucial in specifying property rights and enforcing contracts in order to promote specialization and reduce the costs of market exchange (North, 2000). Moreover, government policy needs to create incentives and send signals that encourage private sector participation in developing rural economies.

Vertical coordination in overcoming costs

The widespread proliferation of supermarkets in the developing world has been seen as an important feature of modern food systems. Their growth potentially enables many small farmers to bypass market failures and substantially reduce their transaction costs. Contractual arrangements with supermarkets can enhance farmer access to credit and finance, modern inputs and technologies as well as access to managerial expertise. Reardon and Berdegué (2002) and Reardon and Swinnen (2004) have shown the positive effects for small farmers of contractual arrangements with supermarkets in Latin America, Africa and many transition economies.

The development of managerial and technical expertise, which is usually crop-independent, gives farmers a comparative advantage in terms of moving across crops when market conditions change. Even when technological conditions change, these farmers are more likely to adapt because of lower transaction costs than farmers who are using technologies for the first time.

Though there are some observed benefits to small farms that have managed to be included in vertically coordinated food systems, it is perhaps too early to conclude whether supermarkets benefit small farmers long-term or not. What is clear, however, is that in the heterogeneous cohort of small farmers, supermarkets tend to target those small farmers whose transaction costs are initially lower because of their asset base, human capital and proximity to markets.

Agribusiness, with its emphasis on quality and output, favours high-potential areas and large farmers precisely because of the need for consistency in supply and quality, but equally because of the need to reduce transaction costs (Key and Runsten, 1999). Evidence from elsewhere shows that contract farming in general favours scale because of the administration costs associated with monitoring (Reardon and Barrett, 2000; Stanton, 2000).

Swinnen (2005) has provided some compelling evidence that contract farming has proved highly successful for small farmers in some transition economies where the prevailing production structure does not feature large farms. In the absence of choice, the critical issue is not simply that farmers will be able to enter markets, but whether those farmers that are party to contracts are farmers whose initial endowments meant they faced lower transactions costs to begin with. Supermarkets pick winners.

Horizontal coordination in overcoming costs

For outsiders, the underlying market failures still remain and their transaction costs can, indeed, become higher as seeking alternative contractual arrangements outside the system becomes even more costly than before. By its very nature, commercialization demands higher output and quality. The inverse relationship that can exist between scale and transaction costs makes for a powerful incentive for small farmers to coordinate their activities so that they can jointly benefit from reduced transaction costs that are at similar levels for larger production units.

Nevertheless, collaborative action brings with it a whole new set of transaction costs. It is likely that farmers' associations will occur only if the benefits from collaboration cover the value of the required investment: not enough is yet understood about the potential benefits or, particularly, costs. Benefits can be described in terms of increased productivity and increased negotiating power. More information is needed however, to understand an actor's rationale for participating in producer groups. Better prices are often mentioned; nevertheless, some argue that receiving a better price is not the main concern, but that having a secured market outlet and access to technical assistance and credit are more important (Swinnen, 2005).

Concerning potential costs, even less is known. Successful association requires management and entrepreneurial skills, 'soft' assets that many small producers with little education are unlikely to have. Extension agents and NGOs are working hard to build capacity in these areas, but no systematic information is available as to the impact and the characteristics of farmers that benefit from these trainings.

Examples abound of instances of farmer cooperation. In Andhra Pradesh, India, the development of labour–water exchange allows marginal farmers to obtain irrigation water from neighbouring farmers with tube wells and to pay with labour services (Deshingkar et al., 2003). The availability of water has enabled year-round production of vegetables.

Contract leasing has enabled small and marginal farmers to lease out their lands to outsiders, who then supply the land with a tube well and grow a variety of crops ranging from carrots to chillies. The growth of village cooperatives in the dairy and poultry industries in Asia has pointed toward a successful way of integrating landless, small and marginal farmers into the changing food market.

In spite of these successes, we need to exercise some caution. Even where small farmers have coordinated their activities, the underlying trend is that as the process of commercialization advances, there is convergence towards large-scale production. The poultry industry in India started off with numerous small-scale units and was hailed as a victory for the small producer.

Over time, the situation has become very different. The industry is now characterized by increasing average holding size (Pingali and Khwaja, 2004). The pertinent issue is to understand which particular markets give small farmers a comparative advantage.[2] Niche and organic markets may provide a solution for a few farmers, but many farmers are still likely to be excluded.

Options and concerns for the private sector

Thus, working together – both horizontally and vertically – can improve the stability of prices/returns, provide better financial returns, improve each actor's ability to supply what the market requires and provide economies of scale and marketing support (Boehlje, 1999; Van der Vorst, 2005). Transaction costs diminish as partnerships and trust reduce the need for contracts and expensive negotiation. Vertical coordination contributes to a more efficient system, but two concerns warrant more careful examination.

First, as more efficient systems reduce the need for large numbers of suppliers, policies need to be put in place that facilitate the exit of those producers who will be left out of the system. It needs to be underlined that the issue is not the survival of small farms as such, but ensuring the livelihood and food security of people, including current small-scale producers. A major question is that of the risk of exclusion of small farmers from the supply chain.

Second, despite having an economic rationale for working together, actors remain competitors. Point of departure should be to admit that productive units, both in agriculture and industry, pertaining to one of the links in the chain, at the end of the day are looking for the highest returns (Roldán and Espinal, 2000). Any marketing system represents a field of conflicting interests between the actors, and an efficient system necessarily needs to find the balance between the economic interests of each of the actors in the system.

Small farmers in that respect find a very skewed structure in the food system, facing on the one hand a small and reducing number of large food companies and food retailers. On the other hand, at the point of input supply to farmers, large chemical and seed companies are creating patented input supply systems controlled by a small number of companies (e.g. Monsanto and Dekalb Genetics Corporation/Delta & Pine Land, DuPont and Pioneer HiBred) (Napier, 2001). Facing this structure, agricultural producers will find it increasingly difficult to negotiate favourable contract terms.

The most popular generalized formulae, such as associativity, are at best necessary but not sufficient. A generalized formula does, and will not, exist due to product/chain-specific market requirements; therefore, any option will need to consider a set of strategic actions and investments, differing by subsector, by the actors themselves in combination with public sector interventions.

For example, studies done by Berdegué demonstrated that, in the dairy sector, at a minimum there is a need for heavy investments in cooling tanks. In the vegetable sector, there is a need for management of chain coordination, cold chain infrastructure, strategic market knowledge and farm investments such as greenhouses.

Overcoming Transactions Costs: the Policy Focus

Whilst transaction costs are clearly important, a policy focus aimed at reducing the transactions costs of small farmers per se is difficult. Transaction costs tend to be highly context-specific and, because they are not always separable from production costs, this makes identifying policy priorities difficult. The prevalence and level of individual farmer transaction costs is a function of both the food system itself and the stage of economic development prevailing in the agricultural/rural sector. Furthermore, transaction costs are very difficult to measure, making it difficult to understand precisely the sources of the costs and hence the corrective action required.

It makes more sense for the public sector emphasis to be on public good provision, generating market efficiencies and institutional reform to encourage private sector participation. It is the combination of both public and private action that enables farmers to enter competitive markets, whilst also generating rural growth to stimulate non-farm employment. Agricultural transition must be managed within a framework of rural development.

In the following section we consider the type of public good provision and the institutional reform that is necessary to create a more level playing field, where many more small farmers are able to trade in competitive markets.

Public good provision

Policies aimed at the provision of better education, rural infrastructure and communication have a number of benefits for small farm welfare. For those who can successfully remain in production there is a clear link between public good services and reduced transaction costs. In terms of facilitating exit strategies, public good provision is vital to re-orient the rural economy towards alternative employment opportunities that support changing agricultural systems.

Education substantially reduces informational and search costs but, in a wider context, education has to be seen as a fundamental policy priority. As commercialization proceeds, exits from small-scale agriculture are bound to occur. Education is necessary not only for the development of non-farm sectors in the rural economy, but it is critical in facilitating labour movements across sectors.

Rural infrastructure investments play a crucial role in inducing farmers to move towards a commercial agricultural system. The emphasis for public investments should be on improving general transport, communications and market infrastructure, while allowing the private sector to invest in commodity-specific processing, storage and marketing facilities.

Accessible and cost effective communication systems such as mobile telephones can help generate information and other market-related services. The internet explosion and related technologies have drastically reduced exchange and search costs in many OECD countries and may be highly indicative of the benefits to developing countries (Bussolo and Whalley, 2002).

Institutional reform

While economic liberalization provides opportunities for diversification and commercialization, it requires farmers to be highly efficient in their use of water, land and other resources in response to changing prices (Rosegrant et al., 1995). Efficient land markets and secure property rights are essential in capturing agricultural growth (Binswanger et al., 1993b). Where land rights are secure, farmers have greater incentive that is needed for investment in land improvements. Secure land rights also make long-term investments more likely. Moreover, land ownership is an important source of collateral that can improve the credit status of farmers, leading to easier access to funding for inputs, etc. (Feder et al., 1988).

Individual farmers and households need to be assured of 'stable engagement' with land and water resources, meaning land tenure and water use rights that are flexible enough to promote comparative advantage in food staples and cash crops. These rights must be matched by access to rural credit and finance, and the dissemination of technology and good practices in water use (De Haen et al., 2003).

Government schemes to certify quality and safe food according to public regulations are required. This is important for domestic consumption and food safety, and even more so if a country wants to access foreign markets. If a country wants to export, it is necessary that an independent body guarantee that the produce adheres to the required quality and safety standards.

The Codex Alimentarius Commission, jointly serviced by FAO and WHO, is charged with the responsibility of developing a food code. Its recommendations are based on the principle of sound scientific analysis and evidence, involving a thorough review of all relevant information. Codex international food standards are developed to protect the health of the consumers and ensure fair practices in the food trade. The SPS Agreement of the WTO cites Codex standards, guidelines and recommendations as the preferred international measures for facilitating international trade in food. The focus of the Codex is shifting to take account of the changing global food system.

Competition and trade policy needs to address the constraints faced by small farmers. Often such policies favour scale because of the emphasis on growth. Incentives need to be placed where the costs of setting up agriculturally related businesses are reduced. Liberalization of domestic markets through removal of quantitative restrictions on trade and the opening up of economies to internal trade opportunities are often both key steps in starting or accelerating the process of commercialization.

However, the opening up of markets also exposes producers to increased risk due to the greater volatility of world prices. Governments have historically intervened heavily in domestic markets to protect and stabilize the prices of agricultural commodities, with the result that domestic producer prices have varied substantially less than international prices. The relationship between diversification and risk is thus crucial in the context of trade and macroeconomic reform designed to align domestic prices more closely with international prices.

Many low-volume markets are associated with high-price volatility. Moreover, the diversification 'start-up' phenomenon, of high prices for several seasons leading to over-supply and a consequent collapse of prices, is all too common. This can be countered by measures to expand the market by lowering transaction costs, improving external linkages or providing storage and processing technologies. Effective rural financial institutions will also assist in risk-spreading and in the sharing of the benefits of commercialization more widely across the community and region.

Conclusion

The transition process is painful. Before we target transactions costs as a remedy for increased small farmer participation we need to bear in mind two points. First, while a reduction in transaction costs should, in principle, allow for a greater number of farmers to trade, the ability to enter is not the same as the ability to stay. This is as much a function of other factors as it is of transaction costs. Therefore, interventions need to be cost-effective. Public money should not be spent in declining and non-competitive sectors.

Second, transaction costs are household-, commodity- and location-specific and are subject to constant change. Interventions aimed at targeted reductions in specific costs should not be in the public domain. Public sector interventions are best left for public good provision and institutional reforms for the correction of incomplete or absent markets. The reduction of transaction costs associated with the specificities of the food system is best left in the hands of the private sector.

In order to better target interventions and take corrective action, a holistic view is required that analyses the relationships between agricultural commercialization, chain efficiency and the small farmers. Transaction costs have shown to play a key role in this, but our understanding is still insufficient, both in terms of analysing their relationship with production costs and whether they can be reduced over time.

It is combinations of transactions costs that determine market entry and, very often, the sources of transaction costs are not be separable, which makes targeting policy difficult. Because of measurement problems we do not yet know how to address these issues. Some critical issues that require further research include the following:

- Emphasizing the heterogeneous nature of the small farmer, identifying who wins and who loses and what can be done to reduce the transitional costs of the losers.
- Taking a broader look at the whole value chain. How are contractual arrangements determined? What and where are the bottlenecks that ultimately impact small farmers?
- Identifying more specific policy recommendations beyond the generalized interventions listed above; this requires more context specific research. Lessons learned from these specifics should then be brought back up to the more general level.

Notes

1 See Reardon and Timmer (2005) for a more comprehensive coverage of the issues related to the proliferation of supermarkets.
2 From case studies in Central America, one can deduce that subsectors requiring large investment – such as beef and milk – seem to exclude small producers (see Schütz et al., 2004). On the other hand, labour-intensive production for, e.g. fruit and vegetables, seems to favour small farmer participation. This argument is based on the lower transaction costs involved in supervising family labour. One may question how this comparative advantage holds in areas where there is a shortage of labour.

References

Ahmed, Z.U. (1989) Effective costs of rural loans in Bangladesh. *World Development* 17 (3), 357–363.
Bardhan, P.K. (1980) Interlocking factor markets and agrarian development; a review of issues. *Oxford Economic Papers* 32 (1), 79–98.
Bardhan, P.K. (1984) *Land, Labour and Rural Poverty: Essays in Development Economics.* Oxford University Press, Delhi, India.
Besley, T. (1994) How do market failures justify interventions in rural credit markets? *World Bank Research Observer* 9 (1), 27–47.
Binswanger, H.P. and Elgin, M. (1992) What are the prospects for land reform? In: Maunder, A. and Valdez, A. (eds) *Agriculture and Governments in an Interdependent World.* International Association of Agricultural Economists, Buenos Aires.
Binswanger, H.P. and Rosenzweig, M. (1986) Behavioural and material determinants of production relations in agriculture. *Journal of Development Studies* 22 (3), 503–539.
Binswanger, H., Khandkar, S.R. and Rosenzweig, M. (1993a) How infrastructure and financial institutions affect agricultural output and investment in India. *Journal of Development Economics* 41, 337–366.
Binswanger, H., Deininger, K. and Feder, G. (1993b) Power, distortions, revolt and reform in agricultural land relations. In: Behrman, J. and Srinivasan, T.N. (eds) *Handbook of Development Economics*, Vol. 3. Elsevier Science, Amsterdam.
Birthal, P.S., Joshi, P.K. and Gulati, A. (2005) *Vertical Coordination in High-Value Food Commodities: Implications for Smallholders.* IFPRI. MTID Discussion paper No. 85, April 2005, IFPRI, Washington, DC.
Boehlje, M. (1999) Structural changes in the agricultural industries: how do we measure, analyse and understand them? *American Journal of Agricultural Economics* 5, 1028–1041.
Braverman, A. and Stiglitz, J.E. (1982) Sharecropping and interlinking of agrarian markets. *American Economic Review* 72 (4), 715.
Bussolo, M. and Whalley, J. (2002) Globalisation in Developing Countries: The Role of Transaction Costs in Explaining Economic Performance in India. DFID project paper, DFID, London.
Carter, M.R. and Mesbah, D. (1993) Can land market reform mitigate the exclusionary aspects of rapid agro-export growth? *World Development* 21 (7), 1085–1100.
Coase, R.H. (1937) The nature of the firm. *Economica* 4, 386–405.
Cuevas, C.E. and Graham, D.H. (1986) Rationing agricultural credit in developing countries: the role and determinants of transaction costs for borrowers. In: Maunder, A. and Renborg, A. (eds) *Agriculture in a Turbulent World Economy.* Grower Publishers, Hampshire, UK.
De Haen, H., Stamoulis, K., Shetty, P. and Pingali, P. (2003) The world food economy in the twenty-first century: challenges for international cooperation. *Development Policy Review* 21 (5/6), 683.
Deshingkar, P., Kulkarni, U., Rao, L. and Rao, S. (2003) Changing food systems in India: resource-sharing and marketing arrangements for vegetable production in Andhra Pradesh. Development Policy Review, ODI 21 (5/6), 627–639.
Dolan, C., Humphrey, J. and Harris-Pascal, C. (2001) Horticulture Commodity Chains: the Impact of the UK Market on the African Fresh Vegetable Industry. IDS Working Paper Number 96. IDS, Sussex, UK.
Dyck, J.H., Huang, S.W. and Wailes, E. (1993) Structural change and competitiveness of the Asian rice economies in Taiwan, Korea and Japan. Proceedings of the First Asian Conference of Agricultural Economists, Seoul, South Korea, 10–13 August 1993.
Eastwood, R., Lipton, M. and Newell, A. (2004) Farm size. Paper prepared for Volume III of the *Handbook of Agricultural Economics.* University of Essex, UK.
Feder, G., Onchan, T., Chalamwong, Y. and Hongladarom, C. (1988) *Land Policies and Farm Productivity in Thailand, The World Bank.* The Johns Hopkins University Press, London.
Gabre-Madhin, E.Z. (1999) *Transaction Costs and Market Institutions: Grain Brokers in Ethiopia.* MSS Discussion Paper No. 31. Market and Structural Studies Division, International Food Policy Research Institute IFPRI, Washington, DC.
Hayes, D. (2000) Transaction-costs economics and the evolving structure of agricultural production. In: Schmitz, T.G., Moss, C.B., Schmitz, A., Kagan, A. and Babcock, B. (eds) *E-Commerce in Agribusiness.* Florida Science Source, Inc., Florida.
Hobbs, J.E. (1997) Measuring the importance of transaction costs in cattle marketing. *American Journal of Agricultural Economics* 79, 1083–1095.

Holden, S.T. and Binswanger, H.P. (1998) Small-farmer decision making, market imperfections and natural resource management in developing countries. In: Lutz, E. (ed.) *Agriculture and the Environment: Perspective on Sustainable Rural Development.* A World Bank Symposium, Washington, DC.

Huang, J. and Rozelle, S. (1994) Environmental stress and yields in China. *American Journal of Agricultural Economics* 77, 853–864.

Key, N. and Runsten, D. (1999) Contract farming, small-holders, and rural development in Latin America: the organization of agroprocessing firms and the scale of outgrower production. *World Development* 27 (2), 381–401.

Koppel, B. and Zurick, D. (1988) Rural transformation and the future of agricultural development policy in Asia. *Agricultural Administration and Extension* 28, 283–301.

Kydd, J. and Poulton, C. (2000) *Globalisation, Agricultural Liberalisation and Market Access for the Rural Poor.* Wye College, London.

Napier, R. (2001) Global trends impacting farmers: implications for family farm management. Paper presented at *Pulse Days 2001*, Saskatoon, New South Wales, Australia.

North, D.C. (2000) Revolution in economics. In: Menard, C. (ed.) *Institutions, Contracts and Organisations: Perspectives from New Institutional Economics.* Edward Elgar, Cheltenham, UK.

Pingali, P.L. (1997) From subsistence to commercial production systems: the transformation of Asian agriculture. *American Journal of Agricultural Econonomics* 79, 628–634

Pingali, P.L. and Khwaja, Y. (2004) Globalisation of Indian Diets and the Transformation of Food Supply Systems. ESA Working Paper Nos. 04–05, FAO, Rome.

Pingali, P.L. and Rosegrant, M.W. (1995) Agricultural commercialization and diversification: processes and policies. *Food Policy* 20 (3), 171–185.

Pingali, P.L., Hossain, M. and Gerpacio, R.V. (1997) *Asian Rice Bowls – the Returning Crisis?* CAB International, Wallingford, UK.

Reardon, T. and Barrett, C.B. (2000) Agroindustrialization, globalization, and international development. An overview of issues, patterns and determinants. *Agricultural Economics* 23, 195–205.

Reardon, T. and Berdegué, J. (2002) The rapid rise of supermarkets in Latin America: challenges and opportunities for development. *Development Policy Review* 20 (4), 317–334.

Reardon, T. and Swinnen, J.F.M. (2004) Agrifood sector liberalization and the rise of supermarkets in former state-controlled economies: a comparative overview. *Development Policy Review* 22 (5), 515–523.

Reardon, T. and Timmer, C.P. (2006) Transformation of markets for agricultural output in developing countries since 1950: how has thinking changed? In: Evenson, R.E., Pingali, P. and Schultz, T.P. (eds) *Volume 3 Handbook of Agricultural Economics: Agricultural Development: Farmer, Farm Production and Farm Markets* {In press}

Roldán, D. and Espinal, C.F. (2000) *¿Son Posibles los Acuerdos de Competitividad en el Sector Agroproductivo?* Colección de documentos IICA Serie Competitividad No. 3. IICA, San José, Costa Rica.

Rondot, P., Biénabe, E. and Collion, M. (2004) Rural economic organization and market restructuring: What challenges, what opportunities for small holders? A global issue paper, presented at international seminar *Regoverning Markets*, November 2004, IIED/RIMISP/KIT, Amsterdam.

Rosegrant, M.W., Scheleyer, R. and Yadav, S.N. (1995) Water policy for efficient agricultural diversification: market-based approaches. *Food Policy* 20 (3), 203–223.

Sadoulet, E. and de Janvry, A. (1995) *Quantitative Development Policy Analysis.* Johns Hopkins University Press, Baltimore, Ohio.

Schütz, P., Balsevich, F. and Reardon, T.A. (2004) Acceso de pequeños productores a mercados dinámicos: el caso de la carne vacuna en Nicaragua. *MSU, Regoverning Markets.* International Livestock Research Instiute (ILRI), Washington, DC.

Stanton, J.V. (2000) The role of agribusiness development: replacing the diminished role of the government in raising rural incomes. *Journal of Agribusiness* 18 (2), 173–187.

Stiglitz, J. (1998) Markets, market failures and development. In: Eicher, C. and Staatz, J. (eds) *International Agricultural Development*, 3rd edn. Johns Hopkins University Press, Baltimore, Ohio.

Strasberg, P.J., Jayne, T.S., Yamano, T., Nyoro, J., Karanja, D. and Straus, J. (1999) Effects of Agricultural Commercialisation on Food Crop Input Use and Productivity in Kenya. MSU International Development Working Paper No. 71, Department of Agricultural Economics, Michigan State University, East Lansing, Michigan.

Swinnen, J.F.M. (2005) When the market comes to you – or not. The dynamics of vertical coordination in agri-food chains in transition. Final report of The World Bank (ECSSD) ESW on *Dynamics of Vertical*

Coordination in ECA Agrifood Chains: Implications for Policy and Bank Operation. World Bank, Washington, DC.

Timmer, C.P. (1988) The agricultural transformation. In: Chenery, H.B. and Shrinivasan, T.N. (eds) *Handbook of Development Economics.* North Holland, Amsterdam.

Timmer, C.P. (1997) Farmers and markets: the political economy of new paradigms. *American Journal of Agricultural Economics* 79, 621–627.

Van der Vorst, J.G.A.J. (2005) Performance measurement in agrifood supply chain networks: an overview. In: Ondersteijn, C. (ed.) *Quantifying Supply Chain Performance.* Kluwer Publishing, Dordrecht, Netherlands.

Van Zyl, J., Millor, B. and Parker, A. (1996) *The Agrarian Structure in Poland: The Myth of Large Farm Superiority.* World Bank Policy Research Working Paper No. 1596, World Bank, Washington, DC.

Von Braun, J., De Haen, H. and Blanken, J. (1991) *Commercialization of Agriculture under Population Pressure: Effects on Production, Consumption, and Nutrition in Rwanda.* Research Report 85, International Food Policy Research Institute (IFPRI), Washington, DC.

Williamson, O.E. (1979) The transaction costs economics: the governance of contractual relations. *Journal of Law and Economics* 22, 233–261.

Williamson, O.E. (1993) The evolving science of organization. *Journal of Institutional and Theoretical Economics* 149, 36–63.

Williamson, O.E. (1996) *The Mechanisms of Governance.* Oxford University Press, New York.

Zaibet, L.T. and Dunn, E.G. (1998) Land tenure, farm size, and rural market participation in developing countries: the case of the Tunisia olive sector. *Economic Development and Cultural Change* 46 (4), 831–848.

21 Building Capacity for Compliance with Evolving Food Safety and Agricultural Health Standards

K. van der Meer[1]

Background

Food safety and agricultural health standards, or more specifically sanitary and phytosanitary (SPS) measures, in international trade have become increasingly important for developing countries.[2] They are an important subject in trade negotiations. With the gradual liberalization of trade, technical barriers to trade and, especially, SPS measures are increasingly seen by developing countries as new protective barriers.

The challenge of meeting SPS measures for developing countries is real. Not only are sanitary and phytosanitary requirements tightening, as will be discussed below, they are also generally much more important for high-value products than for other, mainly bulk products. International trade from developing to industrial countries in high-value food products – fruit, vegetables, fish, meat, nuts and spices – has expanded to over 50% of developing country exports. Traditional tropical products – coffee, tea, cocoa, sugar, cotton and tobacco – have declined in the past 20 years from a level of ~ 40% to < 20%, and temperate and other products have remained stable at slightly over 30%. Failure to meet SPS requirements means exclusion from that growing market segment.

The aim of this chapter is to discuss the challenges developing countries are facing in meeting SPS requirements and their need for support in capacity building. First, there is a brief discussion of the range of SPS requirements that exporters from developing countries are facing when they seek to access developed country markets. Secondly, attention will be given to the dynamics in consumer markets in industrial and developing countries, with particular attention to food scandals, which are driving the tightening of food safety requirements. Third, there is a brief discussion of the findings in a recent World Bank study (2005) on compliance efforts and their costs and benefits and some impact of SPS measures on equity. Finally, the complexity of capacity building and options for improving effectiveness of efforts in this area is discussed.

Sanitary and Phytosanitary Requirements and Enforcement

Requirements

Under the WTO SPS Agreement, countries can impose restrictions on imports of agricultural and food products for the protection of the health of humans, plants and animals. However, these restrictions should be reasonable, not disrupt trade unnecessarily and not be discriminatory for foreign producers. The WTO recommends members to harmonize their requirements by using standards formulated by three international standard setting bodies: (i) the CODEX Alimentarius for food safety; (ii) the Office International des Epizooties (OIE, or World Organization for Animal Health) for animal diseases; and (iii) the International Plant Protection Convention (IPPC) for plant pests and diseases.

Countries may use other standards, but they have to provide scientific justification for doing so, and accept the same standards for imports from elsewhere. However, for many potential hazards no international standards have been formulated and for these areas countries have more room to impose their own restrictions.

A common restriction regarding food safety prescribes that residues of pesticides, veterinary drugs and harmful chemicals in food remain below a maximum residue level (MRL). Importing countries can reject products with levels of residues that exceed the MRL. Violations of MRLs are the most common grounds for rejection by industrial countries. Several countries also forbid products treated with veterinary drugs and pesticides that are internationally banned or not allowed in the importing country.

There are examples where the detection of even small traces of these forbidden chemicals led to rejection. A few years ago, the detection of traces of nitrofuran – a prohibited antibiotic – in shrimp from China, Vietnam and Thailand led the EU to impose a suspension of shrimp import from these countries. Japan put a ban on frozen spinach from China after shipments were found with traces of forbidden pesticides. Contamination with heavy metals, dioxin and other chemical pollutants can occur because of air, soil and water pollution – and during transport in unclean containers.

Contamination with bacteria and other pathogens is the most important concern regarding foods of animal origin and can lead to tight controls not only on the prevalence of pathogens, but also on freshness, the disease status in the country of origin and hygiene conditions at production sites, processing plants and during transportation. The presence of zoonoses – animal diseases that form human health risks, such as mad cow disease (BSE) and avian flu – can easily lead to bans of trade as evidenced in recent years in the trade in beef between Canada and the USA and chicken exports from Thailand.

Another particular health risk are the cancerous aflatoxins and ochratoxins – microtoxins produced by fungi in products like maize, coffee and nuts if stored with too high a moisture content. Tight aflatoxin norms form special obstacles for exports, especially for exports to the EU of pistachio nuts from Iran, Brazil nuts from the Amazon countries and peanuts from Africa.

Many animal diseases pose no risk to human health but are an economic risk for the importing country, since diseases may cross borders with infected live animals or animal products. Industrial countries have strong pre-requirements for health surveillance and control for certain diseases, such as foot-and-mouth-disease, before import permits can be obtained. These requirements include health certificates issued by the veterinary service of the exporting country.

For imports of breeding stock of animals, including aquatic species, health safety requirements are often stringent. The standards for the animal health control system, as set by the OIE, date back to the time before the WTO agreements and assume a well-funded, capable veterinary service. Many developing countries have endemic animal diseases, which are hard to eradicate, and they lack the resources to meet pre-requirements for export of most animal products to industrial countries (Perry *et al.*, 2005). Since developing countries have lower requirements, and also the inability to control cross-border trade, the export of livestock and livestock products from most developing countries goes to other developing countries, often as informal trade.

Plant exports are also subject to many pre-conditions about disease prevalence, surveillance and pest control. In many cases, importing countries require for each shipment from the National Plant Protection Organization of the country of origin a phytosanitary certificate guaranteeing that imported products are free from certain pests and diseases. In contrast to the situation with animals, the number of plants and plant materials traded and the number of possible pests are far bigger.

The number of international standards is limited, which leaves much room for countries to restrict imports. Most countries have a list of products, specified by country of origin, that cannot be imported unless permission is obtained. In many cases countries require pest risk assessments (PRAs) before permission for imports is granted. However, in many developing countries, the data on prevalence of pests and diseases that are required for PRA is insufficiently available and difficult to collect. Negotiations and requests for import permission can drag on for many years without results – and also between industrial countries if there is no agreement on the acceptable risks.

For imported fresh products, importing countries can require fumigation or vaporization, which is costly and reduces the quality of the product. Some countries – for example, Japan – have a zero tolerance policy for any insect found in shipments of fresh produce, regardless of whether the species constitutes any economic risk for domestic crops. The inability of inspectors to distinguish hazardous from harmless insects can be used as an excuse for delays and rejections. A recent international standard on controlling possible diseases transferred with packing wood (ISPM 15, International Standard for Phytosanitary Measures) can have important economic impacts for exporters from developing countries.

SPS requirements between countries differ greatly. Requirements for food safety are, in many respects, highest in the EU, followed by Japan and the other industrial countries. Countries of the former Soviet Union and the Middle East often have less stringent requirements. Many developing countries have no fully fledged food safety system in place. For animal and plant health there are also clear differences between countries, with Japan and Australia taking the lowest risks and highest precautions, followed by the USA and the EU.

SPS measures are non-tariff barriers against imports. A measure can be a justifiable barrier if it meets all WTO SPS requirements, or it may just be used to protect the domestic industry against competition. Many of the existing SPS measures of individual countries are not be based on a proper risk assessment and good science. Risk for the spread of a hazard may be highly exaggerated by the importing country, while in practice it is insignificant. Administrative and technical procedures by the importing country may cause delays and unnecessary high costs for the importer.

The SPS Agreement calls for recognition of regionalization, which means that pest- and disease-free zones of exporting countries are recognized. Similarly, risks for hazards in importing countries may apply to certain areas only and import restrictions need not apply to the entire country. Regionalization could ultimately open large new markets, but many countries show no interest to cooperation on implementation of regionalization principles. The ultimate way of challenging the legitimacy of SPS measures is to initiate a WTO panel case. However, that requires a long procedure with significant technical and financial resources. So far, panel cases have almost exclusively been initiated by the richer countries, especially the USA and the EU nations.

Enforcement

In most countries there is a considerable gap between safety requirements and enforcement. In food safety, many standards and products are not, or hardly, inspected because of limited technical facilities and resources. Because of increased public concerns about food safety there is a tendency in many countries to expand controls to areas formerly not controlled, which sometimes leads to new food scandals. The availability of more and better equipment contributes to a greater detection of violations.

In Japan, the detection of the use of prohibited pesticides in frozen Chinese spinach was the result of the expansion of testing to more groups of pesticides (Chen *et al.*, 2004). The recent increase in the number of detected violations of aflatoxin requirements in the EU resulted more from intensified enforcement than from the tightening of requirements. In the Netherlands, control of pesticide residues in grapes was intensified after non-governmental organizations (NGOs) complained about frequent non-compliance. The detection in the EU of nitrofurans in shrimp from China, Thailand and Vietnam was the direct result of the purchase of more powerful testing equipment.

Enforcement differs greatly between countries. In the EU, there has been much discussion on differences in enforcement between northern and southern member countries, presumably leading to redirection of some imports to ports with relatively lenient testing regimes. In particular, in developing countries there is often a lack of basic facilities to test for most food contaminants and plant and animal pests and diseases, which leaves requirements unchecked. In many cases, animal health and phytosanitary certificates are issued without the ability to check the presumed facts. The gap between requirements and enforcement can easily result in disruption of trade when some problem occurs. In the case of detected non-compliance, bans can be imposed on imports, resulting in considerable cost to the exporters.

Whereas protection of animal and plant health is heavily dominated by government measures, the private sector plays an increasingly important role in setting standards for food safety. Many food companies individually or collectively set protocols for the ways in which food safety is to be ensured. Since companies have different market strategies, their requirements differ as well. This adds to the large range of food safety requirements for different countries and market segments. The most complex aspects of the private protocols are not the food safety requirements as such, but the requirements on production conditions and methods and certification.

In a generic sense, there are not only huge information problems about SPS requirements but there is also much uncertainty as to how rules will be interpreted and enforced. Publicly funded institutions are important sources of information, but they face many limitations because of the sheer number of public and private requirements. Specialized international traders are often best informed about the rules for particular products and the ways they are implemented and enforced in various markets. Moreover, they know what retailers and other private buyers demand. This is one of the reasons why they – and not public agencies – are often the most important source of information for small-scale producers and enterprises in developing countries, and one of the reasons why the private sector can play crucial roles in organizing supply chains for export.

Dynamics in Food Markets

Rapid changes have taken place in global food markets in recent years. Changes in consumer demand, food safety concerns, trade liberalization and the rise of modern retail and logistic systems are the main drivers for these changes. With higher income and changing lifestyles, there is increased demand for more variety, higher quality, year-round supply of fresh produce, 'healthy' food, 'ready-to-eat' food, convenience and value added. And, last but not least, consumers require safe food, and have increasing concerns about the social and environmental conditions under which food is produced.

Food industries, supermarkets and food services compete for market shares and market power by trying to meet consumers' preferences. They have become important buyers in global markets and ask for specifications that meet consumer demands. Food industries serve consumers with attractive processed products. Supermarkets try to offer an attractive assortment of products at one-place-to-shop. Food services – restaurants, canteens, fast food outlets – offer direct service to consumers that bypasses supermarkets. In many countries the market share of food services is growing faster than that of supermarkets.

Information technology, logistics and advances in food processing and postharvest handling have greatly enhanced the development of global sourcing and retailing. Trade liberalization has contributed to a rapid growth of international trade in food, especially for fruit, vegetables and fisheries products (FAO, 2004; World Bank, 2005). Removal of constraints on foreign investment has facilitated the growth of supermarkets in developing countries.

Economies of scale are important in retailing, transport, logistics and processing, and there is a clear concentration among retailers, food services and food processors. Yet, there is heavy competition from which companies try to escape through strategies of product differentiation, product branding and product and market innovation.

Food safety concerns have been an important accelerator of changes in food market development in high-income industrial countries. Many countries have seen food scandals and food scares. Most important examples are BSE, high residues of pesticides and antibiotics, dioxin and toxic chemicals in the food chain, listeria, salmonella and other microbiological hazards, hepatitis and, recently, avian flu.

These scandals and scares have attracted major attention in the media and contributed to consumers' concerns and a fall in the perceived trustworthiness of food regulators, scientists and the food industry. In many countries this has resulted in political pressure to strengthen public control. Fears of bio-terrorism have added to this. As a result, food laws and regulations have been revised in Japan, the EU, the USA and elsewhere; responsibilities have been sharpened and border controls intensified.

The private sector has been significantly affected by food safety crises over the last decade. Food companies and traders – exporters as well as importers – sometimes experienced heavy losses because of stocks that had to be discarded, interrupted supplies and loss of business.

As a result, most food companies now treat food safety as an important commercial risk, but also as an opportunity to distinguish themselves from competitors. They deal with food safety risks through increased control of the supply chains from farm to table, abandoning open markets with anonymous suppliers and turning to vertically integrated or coordinated supply chains. This usually involves reliance on preferred suppliers who assure safety through tracking and tracing, and independent certification of good agricultural and good manufacturing practices.

The trends in consumer demand, retailing and food safety management described here are most visible and pronounced in high-income countries, although in developing countries the same trends can also be observed in the urban areas with relatively high incomes, albeit with a lesser impact. Whereas there is clear market segmentation with regard to quality and food safety, the differences between the top and bottom ends of the market are much smaller in industrial countries than in developing countries.

In developing countries, generally, a three-tier system of production and marketing is emerging, as summarized in Table 21.1 for fruit and vegetables in China. At one end of the spectrum, there are traditional local production and market systems characterized by lack of standardization and coordination within the supply chain, easy access by small-scale producers and low prices.

Table 21.1. Characteristics of the three production and market segments for fresh produce (from World Bank, 2006).

Characteristic	Traditional local	Modern urban	Export
Food safety awareness and compliance	Low	Emerging	High
Supply chain organization	Scattered, supply-driven	Efforts to control by processor, retailer	Demand-driven, controlled by exporter
Price, value added and standardization	Low	Increasing	High
Participation of small-scale producers	No constraint	Emerging constraints; new role for producers' organizations	Contract farming; need for producers' organizations
Factors driving competitiveness	Low cost	Sufficient quantity, consistent quality	Quality, volume, flexibility, innovation
Trust between buyers and sellers	Not very important	Emerging role	Crucial factor

The export market segment, at the other end of the spectrum, has to meet high international requirements for quality, safety, consistency, scheduled supply and value added which, in most cases, can only be achieved by vertical integration or durable coordination within commercially organized supply chains. High prices provide remuneration for successful supply chain coordination. The involvement of smallholders depends much on supply chain arrangements with contract farming made by the private exporters.

Between these two segments there is a third segment consisting of production for retailing in the domestic modern urban sector, where the demand for quality, safety, consistency and value added is increasing but much lower than for top-end international markets, and constrained by the lesser willingness of consumers to pay for such services. Since prices in this sector are also lower, its supply chain coordination develops much more slowly than that of the export sector. This means that in developing countries the requirements for food safety vary greatly with the market segment.

In nearly all developing countries the traditional market segment is by far the largest, with often over 90% of the volume of production. Except for some countries specialized on one commodity (shrimp in East Asia, bananas in Central America), exports rarely constitute more than a small percentage of volume of production.

Supermarkets are growing rapidly, especially in middle-income countries (Reardon and Berdegué, 2002), but the share of the modern urban sector is still only a small segment, with relatively low food safety requirements as compared to the export sector. In the process of economic development this sector will gradually replace the traditional sector, but in most countries this will take several decades, especially in the case fresh fruit and vegetables (Shepherd, 2005), depending mainly on the rate of growth and urbanization (Tschirley and Ayieko, 2005; World Bank, 2006).

Costs and Benefits of Compliance

Measurement problems

Measurement of the costs and benefits of compliance, which include both private and public sector costs and benefits, involves a range of conceptual and empirical problems. First, the cost of production can differ significantly between producers, not only because of differences in comparative advantages, efficiencies and resource endowments but also because of the large range of product–market combinations and inter-seasonal differences.

Also, prices received can differ between product–market combinations and seasons. There are high-cost/high-return and low-cost/low-return combinations. Compliance with new sanitary and phytosanitary requirements can involve different kinds of additional costs for different situations, and benefits of compliance can vary considerably from case to case.

Second, in many cases costs and benefits of compliance cannot be isolated from other improvements being implemented at the same time. For example, protocols like EurepGAP[3] and BRC[4] contain a package of measures aimed at improving quality, safety, the environment and labour conditions. Entrepreneurs who have introduced HACCP-based process control often report savings in operational cost because of better process control, which initially they did not expect.

Third, compliance with new requirements often involves learning and innovation. Use of pesticides is often much higher than technically necessary because of lack of knowledge of the biology of pests, proper techniques of application and Integrated Pest Management. Savings can be made in reducing pesticide use, but shifting to lower use of pesticides requires education, experimentation and adjustment to growing technology. The cost of such learning and innovation is real, but difficult to express in monetary terms.

Empirical findings

The empirical evidence from the pilot studies shows that, in many instances, costs are less than assumed, especially relative to the value of exports (World Bank, 2005). Costs for introducing EurepGAP to tomato growers in Morocco were reported at about 12% of the cost of production and 4% of the export value. Improvements in shrimp production in Bangladesh and Nicaragua were 3.3 and 1.9%, respectively, of export value. Costs are often more readily apparent than benefits. Many potential benefits of standards compliance are long-term, intangible or accrue to stakeholders who do not incur the associated costs.

From interviews, it appeared that industry leaders, such as citrus and tomato exporters in Morocco, understand the benefits far better than do small-scale producers. Benefits of compliance depend much on the market conditions. In a 'buyers' market', the competitive pressure may squeeze nearly all benefits. For example, a producer, detected as having used cheap banned pesticides, can solve the problem by using a more expensive pesticide. In this case there will be cost of compliance but little direct benefit, other than maintaining market access.

In a 'suppliers' market', insufficient supply can lead to significant price premiums for 'safe' food. In coordinated supply chains for exports, contracted small-scale producers often receive 10–25% higher prices for compliance than those paid in local markets (Van der Meer, 2005; World Bank, 2006).

Developing countries as a group do not suffer from the tightening of SPS standards. More importantly, there is no evidence that new measures discriminate systematically against developing countries. Most of the costly trade disputes are between industrial countries. Yet, costs and benefits of compliance with new sanitary and phytosanitary measures can have profound distributional impacts on consumers, farmers, labourers and entrepreneurs.

For example, most new measures have impact on the comparative advantage of producers in different locations because of differences in natural conditions, pest and disease pressure and endowments with capital, institutions and human skills. This can lead directly to relative changes in profitability, competitiveness and market share and, indirectly, to structural changes.

Larger, incumbent suppliers tend to have an incremental advantage because they can realize economies of scale, have better access to information and can benefit from well-established reputations. Yet, there are examples of smaller players in middle-income countries such as Thailand (see Box 21.1) and low-income countries such as Ghana (FAO, 2004) that have maintained or even enhanced their competitiveness and market share during this period of more stringent standards.

Some of these have succeeded individually, others in well-organized industries and well-managed supply chains. The tightening of standards appears to be giving rise to opportunities for value added, resulting in increased off-farm employment opportunities, especially in product cleaning, handling, processing and packing, and in a broad array of process controls. The terms and conditions of this employment in the formal supply chains, although not optimal, are almost certainly better than those in the informal sector, in part because many foreign buyers are imposing labour and environmental standards.

The general conclusion about the impact of tightening requirements is that there are winners and losers and that outcomes depend much on initial conditions and capacities for managing food safety and agricultural health.

The Need for Capacity Building

In many cases, the inadequate capacities for managing food safety and agricultural health form a bottleneck for achieving optimal benefit from participation in agricultural trade or for provision of optimal protection to human health and the health of crops and livestock. In particular, poor countries and small producers tend to have more problems with acquiring optimal capacities. Managing food safety, agricultural health and, more particularly, SPS requirements, is complex: it crosscuts many professional fields and involves various public agencies and private sector stakeholders.

What does capacity for managing SPS requirements involve?

The first and most basic requirement for a country is to have a proper policy and legal and regulatory framework that gives direction and provides rule of law for managing food safety and animal and plant health. This includes a large amount of regulation. Industrial countries and transition economies typically have thousands of regulations in this area. Risk management plays an important role in the science-based measures demanded by the WTO SPS Agreement. Significant levels of funding are required in managing food safety and plant and animal health and, often, a choice has to be made between many alternative strategies. Therefore, the analysis of cost

---

Box 21.1. Thailand Western Region GAP Cluster (from World Bank, 2006).

After several Thai companies had shown that small-scale farmers under contract-farming arrangements could be successfully included in supply chains for exports of vegetables such as asparagus, baby maize and okra, a partnership between stakeholders was set up in 2002 to expand this model. The partnership, named Western Region GAP Cluster, includes private exporters, distributors, private input companies, farmers, government services and Kasaetsart University. The objective of the GAP Cluster is to seek synergy in ensuring safety and quality production from farm to table. Kasaetsart University helps in identifying Good Agriculture Practices, solving problems in the field and developing training courses for farmers, farm advisers and farm inspectors.

Companies take the lead in initiating training courses, since the expansion of contract farming schemes depends on the company's ability to identify markets. Company and University staff, and officers of Government services, jointly provide the training courses, which are financially supported by government grants. Training facilities are provided by the University. The Cluster, with grant funding from the government, provides synergy among the cooperating stakeholders by reducing high costs and technical limitations which individual companies would otherwise be facing. In this way, more small-scale farmers have access to profitable supply chains.

and benefits should contribute to priority setting in policy preparation and in implementation.

Policy making is only useful if there are capable agencies in food safety and in animal and plant health charged with the enforcement of regulations, testing and inspection. Applied science is important for performing a range of basic functions such as:

- diagnosis of plant and animal pests and diseases;
- diagnosis of food- and water-borne human health problems;
- monitoring and surveillance of the prevalence of animal and plant pests and diseases, food- and water-borne human health problems and the collection of information in databases;
- regulation of the chemical composition of pesticides, veterinary drugs and other agrochemicals in markets;
- testing of food and agricultural products for harmful levels of residues of agrochemicals, contamination by hazardous chemicals, microbiological contaminations and pathogens; and
- designing good agricultural practice, good manufacturing practice and good laboratory practice.

Given the trade-related nature of SPS measures, there are many international functions to be carried out. Some functions are carried out in the context of the WTO SPS Committee and the standard-setting bodies – CODEX Alimentarius, IPPC and OIE – such as participation in standard-setting activities, provision of basic information about a country's pest and disease situation and notification of changes in regulations. Most work, however, concerns bilateral issues with trading partners, such as negotiation about market access, exchange of information and bilateral agreements.

Private sector capacities form the crucial factor in market performance. Private companies and farmers must be able to meet public and private safety and quality requirements in foreign and domestic markets. Their production facilities should be adequate and they should be able to apply good manufacturing practice and good agricultural practice that includes the appropriate technology for pest and disease control and proper use of agrochemicals.

In addition, they need knowledge about markets and access to resources to perform competitively. Much of this is private sector responsibility, yet there are many factors that depend on investment climate and government policies. They need a proper regulatory framework for SPS and for doing business in general. Public inspection services and the issuance of certificates should be effective, on time and at low cost.

The most important capacity of a country in successfully managing complex food safety and agricultural health systems is not necessarily the technical and legal one, but rather the capacity to make holistic assessments of its long-term self-interests and, periodically, a comprehensive strategy and action plan for its capacity building. This requires, first of all, a good understanding of international markets and the role of standards, the ability to assess costs and benefits of various measures, and a clear view of proper public and private responsibilities in various fields. On the basis of a strategic framework founded on such well-understood self-interests, effective efforts can be made to increase policy-making and implementation capacity in specialist areas. However, in most developing countries, the reality is far removed from this.

Deficiencies often encountered in developing countries' capacities

Developing and transition economies have many difficulties in managing complex food safety and agricultural health systems. A holistic policy-making capacity is often absent. In fact, experiences from project proposals for capacity building submitted to international agencies often show that countries still have major difficulties in articulating their needs.

Overlapping responsibilities between agencies and ministries, in particular, and between agencies for food safety and veterinary services, cause competition and duplication and thwart cooperation. Such institutional problems appear difficult to solve. A single agency for food safety is often propagated as a solution, and it may be so for policymaking. However, the implementation of policies for each specific area – food safety, animal and plant health – remains necessarily the responsibility of specialized agencies such as the respective inspectorates and laboratories for food safety, veterinary control and plant protection, all of which have broader tasks than SPS; thus, coordination and cooperation between these agencies remains a major challenge.

Because of the specialist technical nature of their work, the veterinary services, national plant protection organizations and food safety departments in health ministries often have an information and policy monopoly for their particular fields, with limited external accountability. These units rarely carry out analysis of costs, risks, opportunities and benefits. Generally, they are driven by technical concerns and bureaucratic interests and not able to convince budget bureaux to provide resources for their work.

The general emphasis on the costs of imposed SPS measures and the lack of assessment of opportunities and benefits is not conducive to the mobilization of additional resources. The resultant underfunding has self-perpetuating consequences. The basic information on food- and waterborne human health hazards – and on plant and animal pests and diseases of national and international importance – needed for the formulation of a strategic policy and action plan is often not available or unreliable. The units responsible for preparing and maintaining such databases are underfunded and lack skills and testing facilities.

A common weakness in many countries is a deficient regulatory system. Laws on food safety, animal health and plant protection often have limited provision for enforcement and implementation, and the required regulatory framework is mainly missing, even in WTO member countries. When countries are accepted for WTO membership they receive support for the harmonization of their laws with international principles. This support is often not extended to analyses of what kind of legal provisions and regulatory framework would best serve the country.

As a result, many WTO member countries are stuck with a major backlog of work in overhauling their insufficient and outdated laws and regulations, for which they, especially the small and poor ones, lack the expertise. This is evident in transition economies that have entered the WTO where, generally, the regulatory system of the plan economy is still applied, which is certainly not in compliance with WTO/SPS principles. For small and poor developing countries, lack of knowledge is a huge obstacle to enacting a regulatory framework that both meets international requirements and serves the national interest.

Regardless of whether they have a good strategy or not, nearly all countries do have implementation programmes for managing food safety, animal health and plant health. The effectiveness of these programmes is often low because of weak policy and regulatory frameworks, poor design and prioritization, underfunding and weaknesses in human skills and laboratory capabilities. The lack of rule of law and the underfunding lead easily to rent-seeking activities.

Examples include: (i) inspections biased toward earning fees rather than controlling health risks; (ii) mandatory inspections and issuance of licences and certificates for which there is no international requirement; and (iii) ineffective border controls and issuance of certificates which are not based on adequate inspections. Public sector controls often add to costs rather than to compliance (see Box 21.2).

In many developing countries, the agencies mandated with food safety, plant health and animal health are in a vicious circle of low effectiveness, poor governance and poor reputation, and lack human skills, testing facilities and an operational budget. It is fair to say that many countries lack the ability to perform the science-based SPS management as required by international agreements. Moreover, laboratory results and certification lack independent accreditation and international recognition. Consequently, trading partners can easily reject data on the pest and disease situation that are provided for risk assessment in negotiations for market access. And, last but not least, the health of consumers, livestock and crops is often poorly served.

Capacity-building efforts

Because of the complexity of SPS management systems and the interrelations of many factors, capacity building is also complex. There is no easy fix or blueprint for capacity building. The situations and interests of countries vary with their level of development, endowments and institutions. Therefore, most SPS capacity building must be tailor-made.

Many improvements may be necessary but may not be sufficient if pursued in isolation. Provision of training and laboratory equipment, for example, has proved to be of low impact in cases where more basic obstacles for managing food safety and agricultural health were ignored. Participation in standard-setting bodies and the WTO SPS Committee work has low impact on most of the national capacities that are of importance for the promotion of exports and the protection of domestic health.

The focus in capacity building is often on public agencies but ignores the fact that, in many countries, private exporters have managed to develop exports even where public agencies have little to offer. The reason for such successes is simple. Many products have low food safety standards and no phytosanitary risks, such as frozen and processed fruits and vegetables, and many developing country markets, in general, have low or modest requirements. In this context, too, it is wise to remember that South–South trade is likely to grow faster than South–North trade for many perishable foodstuffs.

For several kinds of product, exporters can develop their own arrangements. Even for the demanding top-end export markets for fresh fruit and vegetables, exporters have often shown the ability to develop good agricultural practice and to organize supply chains with contracted small-scale producers. In fisheries, private companies have also shown their ability to meet the requirements and access export markets. Foreign buyers regularly provide advice and assistance in meeting requirements, and, in some reported cases, they have even supported governments in fixing their regulations for export to certain markets.

There is much scope for improved compliance in exports by helping companies to overcome obstacles with limited and selective government support. Requirements for government cooperation in the issuance of certificates are, for most markets, not difficult to meet. Where economies of scale play a role, such as in cold chains and laboratory facilities, public support can help in overcoming bottlenecks.

Innovation, training, technology and getting things started can also be areas for government support. The public role can

---

Box 21.2. Public tests add to the cost of doing business (from author's fieldwork)

An exporting company is required by its foreign buyers to provide certified tests on certain food safety parameters. The tests are performed at an accredited laboratory of the mother company in a third country. However, the food safety authority in the home country of the exporter also performs mandatory tests for the issuance of export permits, although it lacks the capability of doing the tests required by the foreign buyers. Therefore, these public tests only add to the costs of doing business.

be indispensable in meeting international requirements and bilateral agreements for market access. In instances of specific obstacles for exports, targeted capacity-building efforts in the public and private sectors can be much more cost-effective than non-prioritized generic capacity-building efforts. This applies in particular to small countries. Neverethless, there is often unjustifiable preference for capacity building in generic fields and for demanding product–market combinations.

Because of underfunding, agencies engaged in food safety and agricultural health and their laboratories are highly dependent on support from donors and international agencies, such as FAO, WHO or UNIDO. A common practice is to ask for whatever support is available, regardless of real priorities; and given the lack of comprehensive planning and prioritization this is often no more than a shopping list shared with all potentially interested donors and agencies.

Donor support for SPS capacity building is about US$75 million per year; about one per thousand of the value of developing country exports to industrial countries (World Bank, 2005). This is certainly a limited amount in the light of the major deficiencies in developing countries. The effectiveness of donor support is mixed. It is constrained for a couple of reasons.

Capacity building for SPS is a relatively new topic since it has become a major issue only in recent years because of the SPS agreement and tightened safety requirements. Much of the generic SPS expertise is in agencies of industrial countries, but many specialists in these agencies have technical background and little relevant experience in developing countries. The impact of capacity-building support by donors and international agencies is poorly and inadequately evaluated and little effort goes into good practice formulation. Most support is not based on a comprehensive analysis of the bottlenecks, there is often no strategic plan, support given is ad hoc and, hence, often turns out to be ineffective.

Examples are the provision of laboratory equipment in situations where there are no operational budgets or no well-designed surveillance programmes. A frequent weakness is the lack of donor coordination, or even donor competition. Because of possible repercussions from trading partners, public agencies often impose secrecy about the real situation regarding the prevalence of food safety hazards and data on plant and animal health, and their control capacities. Documents and statistical data prepared by donors, international agencies and governments are not readily available. This impairs the effectiveness of work, results in much duplication and complicates project design for capacity building.

By the nature of the weaknesses in many countries, capacity building requires a sustained effort over a long period, covering different services and activities. However, most donor agencies and international organizations are also severely limited by short timeframes for the delivery of support. In addition, donors are often constrained by the thematic scope of the support they can provide in a particular country. Sometimes they are also biased toward their own preferences and political agendas rather than toward the interests of the recipient countries.

For example, the support of animal registration systems by the EU is generally not justified by assessment of costs and benefits and effects on poor producers and poor consumers, but would help the EU in the case of a disease outbreak in the recipient country. Obviously, the effectiveness of donor support could greatly improve with donor coordination, joint cooperation on strategy formulation and the acceptance of some discipline with regard to the assessment of costs and benefits and evaluation.

Governments' core role is to provide the proper framework within which the private sector can operate effectively. This includes a proper legal and regulatory framework that meets international requirements and agreements with trading partners, has easy procedures and enhances good governance. In most cases, priority support is needed for developing a proper policy framework and action plan with priorities. Assessments of costs, risks, opportunities and benefits – even if only qualitative assessments are possible – should be guiding strategic choices and priorities. In expanding SPS management measures, priority should be given to measures that have attractive cost–benefit estimates.

A general misconception is that developing countries need to copy SPS regulatory systems from the industrial countries. This would go far beyond their resources and priority needs. International agreements recommend harmonization, but it is up to countries to assess to what extent this harmonization is beneficial or feasible. Much will depend on the requirements of trading partners and the answer will be selective harmonization.

In countries with an extensive informal sector, full enforcement of international food safety standards, such as those of the CODEX Alimentarius, is in general not possible and not desirable in the foreseeable future. The costs for the public sector would be prohibitive and the impact on the cost of living of the poor detrimental. Food safety priorities here should be risk-based, which will often mean priority for particular food- and water-borne health hazards and parasites.

Developing countries should, for their domestic strategies, look more at outcomes of human health and analyse from there what interventions are most recommendable, rather than be guided by technical parameters such as residue levels or microbiological contaminations. In order to prevent trade conflicts, priority should be given to safety enforcement of risky imports and products from domestic companies that compete directly with importers for the same market segments. Priority for import control for plant and animal health should be given to a limited number of product–market combinations that entail significant risk of import of hazardous pests.

Conclusions

In many cases, the inadequate capacities for managing food safety and agricultural health form a bottleneck for achieving optimal benefit from participating in agricultural trade or for providing optimal protection to human health and health of crops and livestock. In particular, poor countries and small producers tend to have more problems with acquiring optimal capacities. There is much scope for increasing the quality, effectiveness and quantity of capacity building. Main areas for improvement are comprehensive holistic planning and donor coordination. Priority setting for capacity building should be guided by assessments of costs, benefits, opportunities and risks.

Notes

1. The author thanks Cees de Haan and Laura Ignacio for their valuable contribution and advice.
2. Managing food safety and agricultural health (i.e. animal and plant health) includes a broad range of activities, and sanitary and phytosanitary (SPS) measures are a subset of these activities subject to the WTO Agreement on Applications of Sanitary and Phytosanitary Measures. Food safety or agricultural health measures are considered SPS measures subject to the Agreement if they affect trade, and this often depends on the particular context. This chapter refers in general to food safety and agricultural health and to SPS in a more specific context, but both terms can frequently be used interchangeably.
3. EurepGAP is a set of standards and certification procedures on Good Agricultural Practices (GAP), now globally recognized and applied, developed by a partnership of agricultural producers and retailers belonging to the Euro-Retailer Produce Working Group (EUREP) (http://www.eurep.org).
4. The British Retail Consortium (BRC), an association of retailers, introduced the BRC Food Technical Standards in 1998 to set the criteria for best practice in the food industry. The group has also developed a Packaging Standard and a Consumer Products Standard. (http://www.brc.org.uk).

Acronyms and Abbreviations

BRC	British Retail Consortium
BSE	Bovine spongiform encephalopathy, or mad cow disease
CODEX	CODEX Alimentarius, standard-setting body for food safety
EU	European Union
EurepGAP	Euro-Retailer Produce GAP
FAO	Food and Agriculture Organization
HACCP	Hazard Analysis and Critical Control Point
IPPC	International Plant Protection Convention, standard-setting body for plant protection
ISPM	International Standard for Phytosanitary Measures
MRL	Maximum Residue Level
OIE	Office International des Epizooties (or World Organization for Animal Health), standard-setting organization for animal health
PRA	Pest Risk Assessment
SPS	Sanitary and phytosanitary
UNIDO	United Nations Industrial Development Organization
WHO	World Health Organization
WTO	World Trade Organization

References

Chen, K.Z., Chen, Y. and Shi, M. (2004) *Globalization, Pesticide Regulation and Supply Chain Development: a Case of Chinese Vegetable Export to Japan.* Working paper. FAO, Rome.

FAO (2004) *The Market for Non-traditional Agricultural Exports.* FAO, Rome. (Linking farmers to markets web site: http://www.fao.org/ag/ags/subjects/en/agmarket/linkages/index.html).

Perry, B., Pratt, A.N., Sones, K. and Stevens, C. (2005) *An Appropriate Level of Risk: Balancing the Need for Safe Livestock Products with Fair Market Access for the Poor.* Pro-Poor Livestock Policy Initiative (PPLPI) Working Paper. FAO, Rome.

Reardon, T. and Berdegué, J.A. (2002) The rapid rise of supermarkets in Latin America: challenges and opportunities for development. *Development Policy Review* 20 (4), 317–334.

Shepherd, A.W. (2005) *The Implications of Supermarket Development for Horticultural Farmers and Traditional Marketing Systems in Asia.* Agricultural Management, Marketing and Finance Service. FAO, Rome.

Tschirley, D. and Ayieko, M. (2005) Changing horticultural supply chains in Africa: implications for government and donor investments; evidence from Kenya and implications for Africa. Presentation made at the World Bank, 6 April 2005.

Van Der Meer, K. (2005) Exclusion of small-scale farmers from coordinated supply chains: market failure, policy failure or just economies of scale? In: Rubern, R., Slingerland, M. and Nijhoff, H. (eds) *Agrofood Chains and Networks for Development.* Kluwer/Springer Verlag in cooperation with Frontis – Wageningen International Nucleus for Strategic Expertise, Wageningen, Netherlands, pp. 209–217 (http://library.wur.nl/frontis/agri-food_chains/index.html).

World Bank (2005) *Food Safety and Agricultural Health Standards. Challenges and Opportunities for Developing Country Exports.* Report No. 31207. World Bank, Washington, DC.

World Bank (2006) *China – Compliance with Food Safety Requirements for Fruits and Vegetables. Promoting Food Safety, Competitiveness and Poverty Reduction.* World Bank, Washington, DC. (Standards and trade web site: http://web.worldbank.org/WBSITE/EXTERNAL/TOPICS/TRADE/0,,contentMDK:20629901~menuPK:222955~pagePK:148956~piPK:216618~theSitePK:239071,00.html).

22 Public Sector Initiatives to Facilitate Small Farmer Access to International Marketing Channels: Lessons from Marketing Assistance Programmes in Armenia[1]

H.R. Gow and J. Cocks

Introduction

With continued globalization of the food industry, consolidation of international procurement channels and increasing regulatory requirements, many international development specialists fear that small agricultural producers will rapidly become excluded from the international agri-food marketing system (Dries and Swinnen, 2004; Reardon, 2005). Consequently, governments and international agencies alike are re-evaluating the design of their assistance programmes. In particular, they are searching for new delivery mechanisms that can overcome the inherent weaknesses of the traditional technology-push systems.

Their challenge is in designing appropriate third-party assistance programmes that can successfully facilitate the establishment of economically sustainable, market-driven business models that provide financially-distressed small-scale producers with the necessary access to markets, technological know-how and capital resources required to successively compete in this new international business environment.

Although not theoretically required, recent Central and Eastern European (CEE) empirical evidence indicates that foreign direct investment (FDI) and the entry of multinational enterprises (MNE) are necessary catalysts for the successful integration of small farmers into international food marketing channels (Gow and Swinnen, 1998, 2001; Dries and Swinnen, 2004). By entering markets with sufficient capital, know-how and reputation to ensure contract enforcement and support investment, MNE overcame the pervasive hold-up and underinvestment problems plaguing the sector, thereby stimulating investment and growth in agricultural production (Gow and Swinnen, 1998, 2001; Dries and Swinnen, 2004).

For numerous reasons, access to sufficient FDI or MNE may not be a viable option for many developing and transition economies. Consequently, public policymakers are attempting to identify viable alternative public or third-party solutions instead of the private solutions usually found in Central and Eastern Europe. Glover and Kusterer (1990), Porter and Philips-Howard (1997), Coulter *et al.* (1999), Eaton and Shepherd (2001) and Simmons (2001) all allude to the benefits of public agencies in facilitating farmer access. However, none of these authors identify the critical processes and/or factors required in the appropriate design, development and establishment of long-term, economically sustainable business models that facilitate small producers' access to international food markets.

In this research we examine the processes involved in the successful 'public facilitation' of economically sustainable marketing channel formation in assisting small producers and agro-processors access markets. The USDA Market Assistance Program (MAP) Goat Industry Development Project (GIDP) in Armenia provides an instrumental case study for examining these issues.

In general, the recovery of Armenia's livestock sector has lagged behind that of other CEE countries. A key constraint has been the lack of FDI-initiated solutions so successfully employed elsewhere (World Bank, 1997, 2000a, b). Without the presence of FDI-catalysed private solutions, the Armenian agricultural sector has remained in a suboptimal equilibrium characterized by deep financial distress and limited investment. The goat sector is the one exception, having recently increased in size by 300% (FAO, 2002). The USDA MAP's GIDP has been an important catalyst of growth in this sector. The GIDP appears to provide an instrumental case study of a public – rather than a private – solution, successfully overcoming the pervasive underinvestment problems plaguing economic development in agricultural transition.

Recognizing the instrumental nature of the case on which we focus in this chapter (Stake, 1995), we used a grounded theory approach for the synthesis and extraction of the key lessons and processes that provide insights into the greater phenomenon, the public facilitation of economically sustainable inter-organizational marketing channel relationships in transition agriculture (Strauss and Corbin, 1994). This approach is recognized as the appropriate methodology when researchers want to gain conceptual insights into the dynamics present within a single setting or outlier (Eisenhardt, 1989).

Our analysis draws upon an iterative mixed methods data collection and evaluation process from 2002 to 2005 that combined secondary data, unstructured and semi-structured interviews, participant observation and a detailed survey of 341 goat farmers. This mixed method approach allowed for data triangulation, clarification of meanings and verification of the repeatability of observations or interpretation (Stake, 1998). This triangulation process is critical when attempting to draw generalizable lessons from a single case.

The Armenian Goat Industry

The Armenian livestock industry underwent a rapid contraction in the early 1990s – upwards of 50%. The World Bank (1995) identified three principle causes: (i) producer input cost increases; (ii) extreme payment delays by state-owned agro-processing enterprises; and (iii) depressed consumer demand and prices. Similar livestock declines were observed across all of the CEE countries (Gow and Swinnen, 1998).

However, against this trend, Armenian goat numbers have increased by 300% during transition (FAO, 2002). Several factors underlie this trend: (i) Armenia's mountainous rocky terrain favours goats and their low-input forage-grazing style of agriculture; (ii) goats provide an economically viable source of nutrition for many newly independent small farmers (Sardaryan, 2001); and (iii) goat milk provides a regular cash flow source for rural households.

Nevertheless, the Armenian goat industry remains at a rudimentary level of development, with production primarily concentrated in mountainous regions (Hutchens, 2001), where goats are grazed during the day in mixed ownership herds on common land and at night housed in farmers' buildings. These poorly defined common land property rights have led to overgrazing, reduced pasture yields and environmental degradation. Additionally, the predominant Armenian goat breeds are traditionally for meat rather than for milk production. This causes problems as they are older, smaller and breed later in life than most milking breeds, hence they are less efficient or profitable when used for milk production (Hutchens, 2001).

Goat milk does, however, provide a possible source of regular cash flows for these impoverished rural households, but this assumes one can transform the milk into a viable marketable, storeable and shippable product. But how does one achieve this? Traditionally, households have used their goat milk to produce cheeses, curds and yoghurts for private consumption. Rarely have they marketed these products outside the household – only when surpluses are available, and certainly not in a systematic manner.

Thus, for these rural households to have any chance of extracting themselves from their current poverty trap, it is critical that an economically sustainable marketing channel be established that provides them with a profitable cash flow stream. The development of an economically viable goat cheese marketing channel provides such an opportunity.

The USDA Market Assistance Program

In 1992, the US government placed a policy advisor with the Ministry of Agriculture in response to an Armenian request and later, in 1993, assisted in the creation of an extension service. After 3 years, however, it was recognized that the traditional technology-push extension efforts were not meeting industry needs. This prompted a substantial project review that resulted in the establishment of the USDA MAP[2] in 1996 and a shift in focus from the farm to the agro-processor and market. With this change, the project essentially moved from being production-driven to market-driven, and the relevant question changed from 'what can we produce?' to 'what does the market demand and how can we profitability meet this demand?'.

The Marketing Assistance Project mission statement perhaps best represents this change:

> MAP will assist farmers and agribusinesses in production, marketing and exporting food and related products to increase incomes, create jobs and raise the standard of living for Armenians working in the agro-processing sector. This assistance will come in the form of timely technical, financial and marketing support to farmers and farmer groups, agribusinesses as well as education, extension services and applied research.
>
> (USDA MAP, 2003)

The USDA MAP approach can be characterized as an integrated enterprise development approach encompassing technical, marketing and financial assistance for selected clients in sectors that are believed to have the potential to be internationally competitive. This integrated approach enables MAP project staff[3] to: (i) assist clients identify market demand and develop appropriate market supply channels through marketing assistance; (ii) develop specific products to meet demand through technical assistance; and (iii) provide the financial resources necessary to initiate and facilitate the establishment of economically sustainable businesses and marketing channels.

Since its establishment, MAP has achieved the following: (i) assisted more than 65 different processing firms employing (in total) more than 2600 full-time and 1100 seasonal staff and purchasing raw materials from over 18,000 farmers; (ii) facilitated the establishment of over 30 farmers' marketing associations;[4] (iii) established 48 production credit clubs;

(iv) provided specific technical assistance to farmers; and (v) established various research, youth development, agribusiness and extension education programmes.

The Goat Industry Development Project (GIDP)

In 1998 Gagik Sardaryan, USDA MAP economic development advisor, recognized the economic development potential of the Armenian goat industry. Goats were one of the few economically, environmentally and socially viable farming systems[5] for Armenia's mountainous rural communities (Scarfie, 1999).

At the time of Sardaryan's proposal, no formal marketing channels existed for selling goat-derived products, apart from direct sales and barter within the local village markets. Consequently, he proposed that USDA efforts should initially emphasize the rapid development of a sustainable dairy goat industry in these rural mountainous regions through genetic improvement, and later focus on the establishment of farmers' marketing associations, cheese factories and extension programmes (Scarfie, 1999).

The USDA MAP conducted market research to assess demand for Armenian goat cheese; this indicated low domestic interest. However, it uncovered substantial interest abroad. Based upon this, the USDA MAP marketing manager supported the project's development, as he intuitively believed there was sufficient domestic demand, despite research indicating the opposite.

The Yeghegis valley, Vayots Dzor region, was selected as the initial target region, for the following reasons: (i) Vayots Dzor's Yeghegis valley was Armenia's poorest region; (ii) there was a substantial Azerbaijan refugee population;[6] (iii) its mountainous, rocky terrain limited alternative farming system options; and (iv) goat numbers were high and increasing faster than elsewhere (goat numbers had increased sixfold since land privatization).

The USDA MAP management decided to exclusively fund the whole project, thereby maintaining ownership and control over the project's strategic direction, even though most of the other key donor agencies were willing to provide financial support.

While the initial proposal appeared sound, it omitted many factors that were later recognized as necessary for success. Most importantly, market potential was based upon: (i) speculative interest from a highly developed Western European export market with extremely high costs of entry; and (ii) the intuition of the marketing manager. Additionally, there were the traditional development challenges of product marketing, dairy technology, dairy processing, farm management practices, genetic selection, zoonotic diseases, association organization and leadership and cooperative development (Scarfie, 1999). These issues would later cause incentive and sequencing problems.

The GIDP began over the summer of 1999 when David Scarfie, an ACDI VOCA volunteer and Langston University goat production scientist, assisted the USDA MAP implement a traditional 'technology-push' model, combining new genetics and extension to increase goat production. The breeding programme began in late 1999 with a collaborative Artificial Insemination (AI) programme that recorded a 50% conception rate – which was considered an excellent result.

A late-1999 survey discovered a latent farmer demand for goat ownership. At that time, approximately one-third of the region's average household income was derived from goats, with the majority indicating that small ruminants provided their best income source. Consequently, in May 2000 USDA MAP imported 20 does and 10 bucks.

When placed under the management of the Vayots Dzor region Agricultural Support Center (ASC),[7] the goats initially suffered numerous health problems. It was only the introduction of appropriate animal husbandry and management techniques that alleviated these problems. Nevertheless, it did raise a serious concern amongst some staff about the appropriateness of a technology-push model. Scarfie (1999), however, argues that the technology-push efforts provided a critical platform for later industry development and technology transfer, but was the sequencing correct?

The Golden Goat Association

In early 2000, the United Methodist Christian Relief (UMCOR) NGO initiated the formation of a farmers' marketing association and cheese factory in Goghtanik village, Yeghegis valley. UMCOR soon realized its limitations and passed responsibility for the endeavour on to USDA MAP 'along with the promises it had made'.[8]

Thus, in June 2000 the USDA MAP assumed leadership and assisted in the establishment of the 'Golden Goat' milk marketing association in Goghtanik village. A jointly owned marketing association was preferred over alternative organizational structures for farmers to collectively market milk as this provided: (i) a central milk collection centre to collect, cool and store milk; (ii) improved distribution; (iii) increased bargaining power; and (iv) minimal opportunistic behaviour by downstream processors.

Various issues arose during the association's formation that would later cause conflicts. First, a downstream market was still under development, but not available. Second, an appropriate association leadership and governance development programme was not available. Third, appropriate incentive, investment and ownership structures were missing. Finally, the initial NGO's promises would later cause incentive problems and conflict.

The process of the Golden Goat Association's formation was problematic. Given that the initial impetus behind its formation had come from donor organization needs (UMCOR) as opposed to the collective internal economic needs of the members, farmers never enjoyed a feeling of ownership, control and self determination. Instead, there was an expectation of continued USDA MAP involvement and financial support based upon earlier promises. This reinforced a dependency culture and constrained efforts to create entrepreneurial spirit and economic sustainability.

The USDA MAP argued that a strong leadership and governance structure was essential to ensuring success; hence, an association president and board of directors were democratically elected from the membership. Various factors, however, adversely affected the association's internal dynamics and governance. First, while the Golden Goat Association president initially held villagers' respect, his very autocratic leadership style greatly impeded democratic decision-making. This led to membership conflicts, as farmers perceived that their needs were not being fairly addressed. Consequently, any social capital that the president had previously held with farmers was quickly destroyed.

Second, farmers were not required to make equity investment in the association, so they held no ownership stake or commitment toward the association. Finally, membership lacked sufficient training in operating democratic board meetings, transparency and effective leadership.

The starting point for the association's establishment was the construction of a jointly owned milk collection centre, where the farmers' milk was to be held before transportation to a downstream market. The USDA MAP encouraged farmers to pool their goats in a collective herd, milked daily in a controlled, mechanized milking parlour by trained milkmaids.

This increased efficiency ensured consistency in milk handling, saved on transportation and increased quality. A milk-cooling tank was leased to the association by Agroleasing, and USDA MAP provided an in-kind grant to build the collection centre.[9] Once established, technical assistance was provided for milk production, animal husbandry and forage management.

Once a downstream market was identified and established, a pricing system was developed. A fixed margin was established between the prices the cheese factory paid the association for milk and those that the association paid its farmers. This margin was set with limited economic analysis and optimistic projections of expenses and production. Consequently, USDA MAP was forced to top up the association's revenue over the first 3 years in order to pay farmers the agreed and promised price. This reinforced, rather than diminished, the dependency culture.

During the association's establishment, the newly elected association president saw an opportunity to privately establish a cheese factory to purchase milk from the association and approached USDA MAP with a request for assistance. USDA MAP agreed and provided two small grants in August 2000 to assist in the establishment of the 'Golden Goat Plus' cheese factory.

Once established, USDA MAP provided marketing and technical assistance on an as-required basis. Marketing assistance first focused on assisting with local promotion, product development and packaging but, when the company began exporting to Russia in 2001, USDA MAP provided export promotion and distribution assistance for the company's products. Technical assistance came in the form of training in cheese-making, sanitation and food safety.

The Armenian Improved Dairy Center (ARID)

Recognizing the need for a central focal point for farmers, the Armenian Improved Dairy Center (ARID) was established in September 2000 as a registered, non-profit, cooperatively owned breeding centre designed to provide farmers with genetics, education, veterinary services, medicines and extension. The ARID Center also provided the base for dissemination of GIDP and USDA MAP marketing, technical and financial assistance. Consequently, farmers co-identified the GIDP and USDA MAP initiatives with the separate ARID Center.

This would later cause problems, as there was no obvious separation in identity between ARID and GIDP. Terry Hutchens and Armen Harutunyan initially managed the ARID Center[10] and its staff. Langston University[11] provided technical assistance and training to the centre's staff on genetic improvement, AI and general farm management. The breeding programme was mostly implemented through AI, although some purebred bucks were released into villages in 2001.

The project's progress over the 2000/2001 period was hampered by a lack of technical expertise and poor management within the centre. First, the project needed a full-time trained animal scientist who possessed the necessary knowledge and skills to advance the genetic improvement, nutrition, education and extension programmes at a basic grassroots level. Langston University was unable to bridge this technical expertise gap, as they were restricted to short-term, in-country assignments where longer-term assignments were required.

Second, poor management, leadership and corruption hampered the centre's development. The autocratic Armenian director lost the earlier vision of the centre's initial intent to assist farmers. Instead, he focused on building 'his centre', which resulted in staff losses, reduced effectiveness and reduced community contact.

In March 2002, Justen Smith, an animal scientist and Assistant Professor in rangeland sciences from Washington State University, USA, was employed on a 6-month advisory contract on goat breeding, nutrition and extension. Upon arrival, Smith assisted three local veterinarians in developing an effective extension programme comprising educational seminars, personal farm visits and field trials. Smith also assisted in the establishment of youth educational programmes in conjunction with the Vayots Dzor ASC to meet the long-term human capital development requirements of rural Armenia.[12]

Following his assignment, Smith recommended that a long-term animal scientist be appointed and the centre's management be restructured to eliminate corruption and improve effectiveness. Recognizing the need for implementation of his recommendations, USDA MAP convinced Smith to return as Director of the ARID center and Project Leader for the GIDP. Within this role, Smith reorganized the centre to streamline leadership, consolidate and reduce duplication of goat industry efforts, reduce costs and eliminate corruption. Smith also initiated three important projects in 2003 that he believed critical for the long-term economic sustainability of the centre.

First, he worked toward the establishment of a critically needed meat processing facility at the centre to process the region's large population of male goats, sheep and cattle.[13] Second, he hired an Armenian assistant director to be trained in assuming the directorship of the centre once Smith had left. Third, he purchased the land on which the centre is situated. If this had not occurred, the long-tern economic sustainability of the centre would always have been under threat.

Expansion of the Goat Industry Development Project

During 2002, the GIDP underwent a substantial expansion. This process began when the mayor of Khachik village approached the USDA MAP in the spring of 2002 about establishing an association and cheese factory in their village. Recognizing the issues and difficulties related to the association's first venture, the USDA MAP management team decided to take a slightly different approach to the establishment of future associations.

Initially, the USDA team would visit the interested villages and explain very clearly the mapping-out of the association, the necessary investment commitments (in time and capital) and the relevant costs, benefits and risks involved. The villages recognized the potential of the idea, understood the risks and commitment, yet still decided to go ahead with the formation of a new association.

The new association was granted a milk-cooling tank and received milking machines via Agroleasing.[9] USDA also supported the entrepreneurial mayor in the development of a cheese factory by providing similar grants and support – as they had previously done with other entrepreneurs.

A problem with the Khachik association – like many USDA MAP-assisted associations – is that the leader who first approaches USDA MAP or is elected as president often has involvement in both the association and the local entrepreneurial cheese factory start-up, in addition to possibly being village mayor and owning a substantial herd of goats.

While this combination of leadership, vision and economic need is initially necessary to create sufficient private enforcement capital to support the venture. At a later date this combination also creates serious conflict of interest, as the entrepreneurial leader may have difficulty working in the best interests of both his farmers' association members and his own privately owned cheese factory. Recognizing this, once the association and marketing relationships are established, the USDA MAP works swiftly to impose an ex post management reshuffle to remove or alleviate, any potential conflict of interest.

During 2002, the Golden Goat Association was also expanded to include the villages of Yeghegis and Hermon. Collection centres were established at each village in the same manner as the original Goghtanik collection centre. Each collection centre had a manager, who was also a director on the association board. This expansion increased goat numbers by 200%. The original Golden Goat Association, however, struggled to achieve its anticipated potential due to poor leadership and low milk quality.[14] It was only with a leadership restructuring,[15] intensive staff training and wage subsidization that the problems were overcome.

Over this same period of time, the Golden Goat Plus cheese factory went from strength to strength, increasing cheese production from 0.5 t in 2000 to 12.5 t in 2002. The two cheese varieties, buried and feta – initially produced and marketed in Armenia and Russia – were expanded to eight varieties in 2003 in an effort to provide a broader product range. By 2004, the plant manager believed around half of the Goghtanik village had a connection with the cheese factory, either through goats in the association or through employment in the factory.

During 2002, a third association was added. Levon Gharzayan, former manager of a Soviet collective farm from Salli village, had observed Golden Goat Plus and the Golden Goat Associations. He approached USDA MAP with a proposal to form an association and cheese factory modelled on these organizations. The new factory, named Selim, anticipated processing 65–70 t of milk per year, equating to ~ 6 t of cheese.

An estimated 40 farms in three villages – Salli, Aghnjadzor, and Hors – entered 500 goats in the new association for the 2003 season. A milk collection centre supported by a herd cooperative was established in each village. Gharzayan noted that, once the villagers had learnt more about the association's principles, they became very positive toward the concept, especially when they learnt that they would own and control the association. Prior to the USDA MAP intervention there was no market for goat milk in the area, apart from barter and trading within the villages.

Market-driven Expansion

Throughout the development and expansion of GIDP, USDA MAP personnel have been extremely conscious not to establish a large industry without a profitable and sustainable downstream market capable of profitably absorbing the industry's production.

In the latter part of 2002, a considerable market potential for Armenian goat cheese was recognized in California, home to a large Armenian Diaspora population and, to a lesser extent, to people from the neighbouring Republic of Georgia.[16] The estimated demand for the two markets was upward of 200 t. These new markets were in addition to servicing the Armenian market – which had been steadily growing at the rate of 50–100% per annum since the beginning of the project – and a growing Russian market.

This discovery accelerated the expansion of the GIDP through: (i) increasing existing associations' size by adding more villages and/or increasing current herd size; (ii) establishing new associations; (iii) improving cheese quality to adhere to US and EU standards through technical assistance and provision of pasteurizers; and (iv) strengthening the leadership and management teams.

The impact of the project is self-evident. By the 2005 milking season the total number of goats within the project was estimated at 3599 (see Table 22.1), and farmer numbers at 248 (see Table 22.2). The increase in goat numbers had resulted both from new villages joining current associations and from the formation of new associations. However, we have recently observed goat numbers decreasing within associations as farmers replace less productive, native, meat breeds with more productive crossbreeds.

Concurrently, additional cheese factories were provided with assistance in 2002, 2003 and 2004, bringing the total number of cheese facilities to seven (see Table 22.3). Further, several cheese factory, association and credit club establishment projects are currently under way with the aim of further expanding milk collection and processing capacity.

Accessing international export markets requires that factories substantially upgrade their production processes to international grades and standards requirements. For example, the US market requires that all dairy products be pasteurized. The USDA MAP facilitated this process with technical

Table 22.1. Goat numbers in associations (from USDA MAP, 2002; USDA internal documents).

Association	2000	2001	2002	2003	2004	2005
Golden Goat	na	300	660	1220	970	855
Goghtanik	na	300	320	400	300	340
Hermon	0	0	180	300	250	180
Vardahovit	0	0	0	320	220	185
Yeghegis	0	0	160	200	200	150
Khachik	0	0	144	214	280	392
Salli	0	0	0	500	540	669
Aghnjadzor	0	0	0	160	120	204
Hors	0	0	0	140	220	180
Salli	0	0	0	200	200	285
Balaqi Lchak					180	120
Agarakadzor – individual farm					50	70
Rind – individual farm	98	184	206	280	250	208
Gomk					450	380
Gavar					80	165
Lchashen					220	250
Eghipatrush					100	120
Meghrashen						100
Vernashen					120	180
Gnishik						90
Total	na	300	804	2184	3420	3599

na, not available.

Table 22.2. Farmer numbers in associations.

Association	2000	2001	2002	2003	2004	2005
Golden Goat	na	40	111	119	119	119
Goghtanik	na	40	43	43	43	43
Hermon	0	0	26	26	26	26
Vardahovit	0	0	0	8	8	8
Yeghegis	0	0	42	42	42	42
Khachik	0	0	41	41	41	41
Salli	0	0	0	40	40	46
Aghnjadzor	0	0	0	na	13	15
Hors	0	0	0	na	15	17
Salli	0	0	0	na	12	14
Balaqi Lchak farmers' group					3	4
Agarakadzor – individual farm					1	1
Gomk farmers' group					6	8
Vernashen cooperative					5	6
Gavar farmers' group					3	3
Lchashen farmers' group					3	5
Eghipetrush farmers' group					2	3
Meghrashen farmers' group						4
Gnishik farmers' group						8
Total	na	40	152	200	223	248

na, not available.

Table 22.3. USDA MAP-assisted goat cheese processing facilities (from USDA MAP, 2002; USDA internal documents).

Processing facility	Year of formation	Output			
		2002 (t)	2003 (t)	2004 (t)	2005 (t)
Golden Goat Plus	2000	10.26		15.0	16.0
Spitak Aghbyur	2002	5.20		5.0	3.5
Selim	2002	0.2t		5.0	4.5
Balaki Lchak	2003	na	2	2.1	2.3
Gomq/Vayots Dzor/	2004	na		1.5	3.7
Gavar/Urashta/	2004	na			1.5
Lchashen/Ranchpar/	2002				1.5
Total		20.75		28.6	33

na, not available.

advice, new product and procedure development assistance and leasing pasteurizers through Agroleasing. However, once achieved, producers like the Selim processing facility in Salli village have developed the ability to produce pasteurized goat cheese of equivalent quality to that of the EU or the USA. Nevertheless, it is critical that firms continue to meet and exceed their HACCP and food safety standards, as the consequences in not so doing so can be devastating.[17]

Finally, toward the end of 2003, GIDP's success spurred procurement competition between local processors. The success of Selim and continued problems at Golden Goat resulted in Vardahovit farmers threatening to withdrawing from the Golden Goat association in 2004 and switching to direct sale via Selim. This was significant because, for Selim to purchase from Vardahovit, the milk would have to travel directly past the Golden Goat Plus factory and all of the other Golden Goat Association villages to reach the Selim factory.

Recognizing that additional GIDP expansion would stretch their human resource capacity and that poor management and leadership had previously constrained some associations, USDA MAP management instigated various innovations. First, they established a Center for Cooperative Development in 2003 in cooperation with the Armenian Academy of Agriculture to shift the responsibility for cooperative development away from USDA MAP and to Armenian specialists within the Academy.

Second, a medium-term consultant on cooperative development was hired to provide training to the Academy, association presidents, boards of directors and collection centre managers on cooperative leadership, governance and management. And finally, a SME business development office was established with the task of developing management, leadership, accounting and financial and strategic planning for the cheese factories.

Lessons and Implications

Our analysis of the USDA MAP Goat Industry Development Project yields several important lessons for policy initiatives and project designs in this area. We distinguish key lessons for two different phases of the process.

Establishment phase

1. Adopt a market-driven value proposition approach that is driven by real, observable and concrete market opportunities – this is fundamental to project success. Without taking this approach, no progress can result.
2. Ensure that communities and producer groups self-select themselves. This will ensure that they assume collective owner-

ship of the enterprise and marketing associations and minimize the situation where individuals or groups are looking for free handouts. Allow them to find and approach you.

3. Provide appropriate education and information on the programme's investment requirements and costs and benefits. Discuss these openly with group members. Do not oversell the concept or benefits. Everyone needs to have realistic expectations from the beginning; this will minimize later conflicts if the enterprise hits difficulties. Provide the group members with sufficient time to digest the information and commitment requirements before voting on the formation of an association.

4. Establish a democratic and transparent leadership and governance structure. Immediately following a positive group decision to pursue the formation of an enterprise or association, a formal and transparent governance structure needs to be established. This should include the election of a board of directors and officers, development of by-laws and legal registration of the organization.

5. Identify and develop a local entrepreneurial business/community leader. Every project needs a business leader; this is an individual who not only recognizes and understands the market value proposition from an entrepreneurial perspective but also possesses sufficient social capital to ensure he can effectively engage and lead the association members during the association's initial establishment.[18] This can be an extremely volatile process fraught with difficulties, and the leader will probably need all of his social capital to lead the association through this process. Just being an entrepreneur or leader alone is not enough: the selected individual must possess a sufficient amount of both attributes.[19]

6. Focus on the domestic market while initially establishing the production, management and marketing systems. Only allow firms to step up to the international market with its increased private grades and standards requirements once they have established an economically viable channel that returns positive value to all participants. This will ensure that all channel participants independently commit to make the necessary additional investments.

7. Ensure value flows directly through the marketing channel. This will correctly align channel members' incentives to their vertical channel partners above and below them and, assuming sufficient value is created, ensure long-term economic sustainability. Do not provide any subsidies or supports that can affect the cash flow stream of the proposed value proposition or enterprise: this will build a dependency mentality within the organization or channel.

8. Provide assistance through customizable, flexible and linked packages (Marketing, Finance and Technology), purposely designed to meet each client's specific requirements.

9. Minimize financial grants and supports. Use grants only for one-off, definable investments that provide a focal point for the association to bind group members together and assist in establishing an initial collective buy-in to the common cause – establishment of the association. However, if used, strict match-and-payment requirements need to be imposed. For example, grants can provide construction materials, but the association must provide labour for the construction wotk. Similarly, cooling tanks or movable plant may be provided on a 6-month, interest-free lease initially, to reduce the cash-flow demands on the association.[20]

Moving towards independence

1. Empower clients and associations to make their own independent business decisions. It is critical that all channel members take full ownership and responsibility for their individual economic and business decisions. The facilitators can assist in providing training on decision-making and analysis processes, but must separate themselves from the decisions.

Under no circumstances should any facilitator attempt to influence the decision.
2. Separate the entrepreneurial business leader from the association leadership once the association gains economic stability. At such time as the association and marketing chain are established and producing stable economic returns, work to ensure a rapid transition to new democratic and transparent leadership and governance structure independent of the previous entrepreneurial business leader. This will minimize conflicts of interest for the business leader between the entrepreneurial, profit-making requirements of his private enterprise and the leadership requirements of the marketing association.
3. Provide financial resources through enforceable mechanisms (credit clubs and leasing programmes) that are interlinked to the market value proposition, thereby correcting incentive and repayment problems.[21]
4. Ensure separation of support structures and assistance programmes vertically and horizontally from each other and each level of the marketing channel to maintain visible independence, thereby ensuring that agents recognize the public agency's activities are independent from the channel's economic activities.
5. Institutionalize programmes, structures and organizations by rapidly integrating and empowering local staff to take ownership in management and leadership. Develop suitable succession systems to transfer leadership and ensure long-term economic sustainability.

Conclusions

This paper examines the structure and processes by which third-party agencies can successfully facilitate the establishment of economically sustainable marketing channels based upon implementation of flexible and customizable packaging of marketing, financial and technical support programmes for both commercial entrepreneurial processors and local, farmer-owned, milk-marketing associations.

The USDA MAP and the Armenian goat industry provided an instrumental case study to gain a greater understanding of the issues, responses and impact involved in this process. The Armenian goat industry provides a natural experiment for this evaluation as there has been neither FDI, MNE nor external ODA before the USDA MAP GIDP began in 1999.

Although small in scope, this case provides numerous useful lessons that policy advisors and programme designers should note when implementing assistance in the agribusiness sector. As Jason Smith noted in our exit interview: 'the key to the [long-term economic] sustainability of the project is ensuring that farmers continue making a profit and the associations continue making a profit without outside funding'.

These profits should flow through the chain separately from the project and devoid of subsidizes, thereby providing all chain participants with transparent market incentives. Once an economically viable market is identified, a customizable, flexible and linked package of financial, technical and marketing support programmes should be provided only to self-selected villages and business leaders who can provide sufficient commitment, vision and collective social capital between members to ensure success.

All programmes should be designed to minimize incentive problems and issues and within and outwith the chain. If done correctly, as this case study shows, third-party international development agencies can successfully create facilitation programmes to assist impoverished small farmers establish economically sustainable marketing chains.

This case study is important as it provides an instrumental case documenting how third parties can successfully imitate FDI and MNE in facilitating the establishment of economically sustainable marketing chains. Numerous theoretical and empirical questions still remain to be answered with respect to programme design, structure of incentives and impact on farmers.

However, that said, this case study does provide a unique longitudinal analysis of programme design, implementation, expansion and change. Based upon this analysis, fourteen basic rules have been synthesised to assist policymakers in the design of future programmes.

Notes

1. The opinions within this chapter are those of the authors and not necessarily those of the USA Department of Agriculture or the University of Illinois. We wish to thank the staff and management of the Goat Industry Development Project, USDA Marketing Assistance Program and Center for Agribusiness and Rural Development in Armenia, members of the University of Illinois impact assessment team and reviewers for their assistance, advice and comments during the development of this chapter.
2. The Office of International Programs in the USDA CSREES managed these efforts and provided overall strategic direction. The project was funded under the Freedom Support Act (1992) and administered by the US embassy in Armenia. The ambassador has overall control. Funding has been consistent year on year, at around US$7.5 million per annum.
3. The project draws upon three human capital pools: (i) permanent Armenian staff; (ii) American university faculty and professional consultants; and (iii) American volunteers via organizations such as ACDI VOCA. The two latter groups are contracted for specific assignments ranging from 2 weeks to 9 months in duration. Short-term consultants address specific MAP client needs, whereas longer-term personnel provide consistency and continuity in programme assistance and greatly contribute to their Armenian counterparts' development.
4. They are called 'associations' as apposed to 'cooperatives' in an attempt to disassociate them from the Soviet era cooperative farms and the stigma still associated with these farms.
5. Modern breeds of dairy goat actually have feed conversion rates 25–30% higher than cows in situations where feed resources are scarce (FAO, 2002).
6. Previously, substantial aid had been provided to these war refugees, thus creating a dependency culture.
7. The ASC is a regional extension centre overseen by the Armenian Extension Service located in Yerevan.
8. These promises would later cause numerous difficulties, as farmers never accepted association ownership.
9. When providing financial assistance, USDA MAP tries to avoid providing grants as they believe they provide perverse economic incentives. Whenever possible, they lease equipment to firms and farmers' groups. The enforcement of leases is better than direct loans and the incentives are enhanced compared with direct grants.
10. Hutchens, an American extension plant pathologist working for USDA MAP on seed potatoes in the Vayots Dzor region, was technical advisor to the centre. Hutchens split his time evenly between seed potatoes and providing technical assistance to the ARID Center. Harauturyan, who was manager of the Vayots Dzor ASC, was appointed director of the ARID Center.
11. E Kika de la Garza Institute for Goat Research at Langston University, Oklahoma, is the one of three goat research institutes in the USA.
12. The initial programme consisted of two villages in Vayots Dzor, with five youths in each. The ARID Center provided technical expertise to the youths on how to raise and care for goats, with USDA MAP providing funding for the project. At the end of the summer the goats were auctioned off, with the money earned by the youths being used for starting their own goat herds and to help other children start a goat project the following year. After the success of the first two clubs, youth programmes expanded significantly in 2003. By the end of 2003 there were six youth clubs, with 60 youngsters involved. Smith created a full-time staff position at the ARID Center to develop the youth programme, with the goal that each year ten new young people would join each group and those from the previous year would use their goats to start their own herds.
13. The concept was that an entrepreneur would be identified to operate the facility, and a proportion of the revenue stream would provide a cash flow stream to the ARID Center to fund the breeding and education activities. Smith recognized that various governance and enforcement issues existed based upon previous USDA MAP experiences with the Golden Goat association; however, he thought that the benefits far exceeded the costs.
14. Low milk quality was caused by poor milking technique, poor milk handling and inadequate

transportation from the collection centre to the cheese factory.
15 The manager of Golden Goat Plus stepped down from his role as president of the Golden Goat marketing association, with one of the farmer members replacing him as the new association president.
16 The Californian market was identified by the USDA MAP marketing manager on a market research trip to the USA.
17 A potentially devastating problem arose in the early part of 2003 when a consumer found glass in some Armenian cheese that had been exported to Russia. A change in cheese production procedures away from glass jars to plastic jars was implemented to avoid this happening in the future. None the less, it reiterated to USDA MAP the vulnerability of the cheese processing sector when exporting and also its stage of development.
18 This is similar to developing private enforcement capital between farmers and the MNE; see Gow et al. (2000) for further details.
19 Note that this individual may expend all of his social capital during the establishment process.
20 This can be thought of as a private enforcement capital shifter or expander. See Gow et al. (2000) for further details.
21 See Abrahamyan et al. (2006) for a complete discussion of USDA MAP credit programmes.

References

Coulter, J., Goodland, A., Tallonaire, A. and Stringfellow, R. (1999) Marrying farmer cooperation and contract farming for agricultural service provision in Sub-Saharan Africa. In: *Guide to Developing Agricultural Markets and Agro-Enterprise Series*. World Bank, Washington, DC.
Dries, L. and Swinnen, J.F.M. (2004) Foreign direct investment, vertical integration, and local suppliers: evidence from the Polish dairy industry. *World Development* 32 (9), 1525–1544.
Eaton, C. and Shepherd, A.W. (2001) Contract farming: partnerships for growth. *FAO Agricultural Services Bulletin 145*. Food and Agricultural Organization (FAO), Rome.
Eisenhardt, K.M. (1989) Building theories from case study research. *Academy of Management Review* 14 (4), 532–550.
FAO, (2002) *A Strategy for Sustainable Agricultural Development* (http://www.fao.org/tc/tca/docs/ARMENIA-strategy.pdf, accessed 15 December 2003).
Glover, D. and Kusterer, K. (1990) *Small Farmers, Big Business: Contract Farming and Rural Development*. St Martin's Press, New York.
Gow, H.R. and Swinnen, J.F.M. (1998) Up- and downstream restructuring, foreign direct investment, and hold-up problems in agricultural transition. *European Review of Agricultural Economics* 25, 331–350.
Gow, H.R. and Swinnen, J.F.M. (2001) Private enforcement capital and contract enforcement in transition economies. *American Journal of Agricultural Economics* 83 (3), 686–690.
Gow, H.R., Streeter, D.H. and Swinnen, J.F.M. (2000) How private contract enforcement mechanisms can succeed where public institutions fail: the case of Juhockur a.s. *Agricultural Economics* 23, 253–265.
Hutchens, T.K. (2001) *Close-out Report for ARID Center Goat Breeding Program*. USDA MAP TDY consultant report, USDA, Washington, DC.
Porter, G. and Philips-Howard, P. (1997) Comparing contracts: an evaluation of contract farming schemes in Africa. *World Development* 25 (2), 227–238.
Reardon, T. (2005) *Retail Companies as Integrators of Value Chains in Developing Countries: Diffusion, Procurement Systems Change, and Trade and Development Effects*. GTZ Trade Programme, GTZ, Eschborn, Germany.
Sardaryan, G. (2001) *Regional Agricultural Intervention and Development Project*. USDA MAP internal staff report, USDA, Washington, DC.
Scarfie, D.A. (1999) *Armenian Goat Breeding Project 1999: Report and Recommendations*. USDA MAP TDY consultant report, USDA, Washington, DC.
Simmons, P. (2001) *Overview of Smallholder Contract Farming in Developing Countries*. Working paper. Graduate School of Agricultural and Resource Economics, University of New England, Australia.
Stake, R.E. (1995) *The Art of Case Study Research*. Sage Publications, California.
Stake, R.E. (1998) Case studies. In: Denzin, N.K. and Lincoln, Y.S. (eds) *Strategies of Qualitative Inquiry*. Sage Publications, California, pp. 86–109.
Strauss, A. and Corbin, J. (1994) Grounded theory methodology: an overview. In: Denzin, N.K. and Lincoln, Y.S. (eds) *Handbook of Qualitative Research*. Sage Publications, California, pp. 273–285.

USDA MAP (2002) *USDA MAP 2002 Marketing Audit.* USDA MAP internal document, USDA, Washington, DC.
USDA MAP (2003) *USDA MAP Mission Statement* (http://www.usda.am/mission.html, accessed 7 March 2003).
World Bank (1995) *Armenia: The Challenge of Reform in the Agricultural Sector.* World Bank, Washington, DC.
World Bank (1997) *Armenia Agricultural Reform Support Project.* World Bank, Washington, DC.
World Bank (2002a) *Transition: the First Ten Years. Analysis and Lessons for Eastern Europe and the Former Soviet Union.* World Bank, Washington, DC.
World Bank (2002b) *Growth Challenges and Government Policies in Armenia.* World Bank, Washington, DC.

Index

acquisitions *see* mergers and acquisitions
Africa: Nile perch exports 36–39
agro-holdings ("new operators" *see under* Russia
animals: welfare
  consumer concerns 6
  private standards *vs.* regulations 13
apples 215–216
Argentina: role of multinationals 65
Armenia *see also* CIS (Commonwealth of Independent States)
  Armenian Improved Dairy Center (ARID) 300–301
  farmer associations 303(fig)
  goat industry characteristics 296–297
    quality and safety problems 307(n14) 308(n17)
  Golden Goat Association 299–300
  slow recovery of livestock sector 296
  USDA Market Assistance Project 297–298
    Goat Industry Development Project (MAPGDIP) 298–299, 301–304
    lessons for policy and project design 304–306
  USDA Market Assistance Project, Goat Industry Development Project (MAPGDIP)
  market-driven expansion 302–304
associations
  of buyers 7
  of farmers 303(fig)

  Golden Goat Association 299–300
  need for 264, 273–274
  policy recommendations 305
auctions 124–125, 131–132

bananas 61
Bangladesh
  food export trends 94(tab)
  foreign direct investment 93
  GDP 1990–2002 92
  growth in food processing 98
  lower rice demand with urbanization 92
  shrimp exports 32–33
  supermarkets 96
BASIS project 202, 203(fig) 204
beans, French 149
beans, green
  EU regulations 163
  exports from Senegal 161–162
    supply chains 165–167
    welfare effects 168–170
Benin 81
Bio-terrorism and Response Act (USA) 21
Brazil 65
British Retail Consortium (BRC) Standard 10, 293(n4)
broilers 193–194(box)

cancer: and pesticide use 142
carcinogens, fungal 282

CEE countries *see also* individual countries
  dairy sector
    changes in vertical organization of supply chains 220–224, 233, 234, 235–237
    dairy companies 245
    drivers and obstacles for quality improvement 251–252
    farm structure 242
    impact of contracts on yields and production 252–253, 254(fig)
    milk flows in the supply chain 244–245
    patterns of contracting 245–247
    positive effects of vertical coordination 255
    processing industry structure 242–244
    support for dairy farmers 249–251
    systems to improve quality 247–248
  farm structures 210(tab)
  food processing industry: impact of reforms 210–211
  foreign direct investment *see under* investment, foreign direct
  horticultural products 215–218, 219(tab) 233–234, 237–238
  importance of FDI and multinationals 295
  intermediary trading system 212–213, 214(fig)
  multinationals: negative impact 211
  pork and ham production 218, 220, 221(fig)
  primary agriculture 210
  retail sector
    impact of FDI *see under* investment, foreign direct
    impact of reforms 211–212
    market share of top five retailers 232(fig)
  small farmers 224–226
  wheat 213–215
Central America 136–139
Central Asia: cotton production 82–86
centralization: of procurement 137
certifications, third party 6
chemicals: use in horticulture 142
Chile: effect of competition on credit provision 79–80

China
  farmers: challenges of supermarket procurement 110
  food export trends 94(tab)
  food processing 98
  food share of household budget 93
  foreign direct investment 93
  GDP 1990–2002 92
  high-value agriculture 95–96
  production and market segments for fresh produce 286(tab)
  supermarkets 96, 97 109
    impact on smallholders 104
  survey on horticultural goods
    conclusions 117–120
    dominance of small traders 114–115, 116(tab)
    impact of supply chains on quality 116
    methodology 111
    participation by poor farmers 113–114, 117
    patterns of production 111–113
    statistics for households and villages 118(tab) 119(tab)
  Zheijang Plums Association 105
CIS (Commonwealth of Independent States)
  contracting survey
    conclusions 185–186
    contract support measures 178–180
    econometric models 182–185
    methodology 176–177
    procurement from small farms 180–181
    product quality 181–182
    sample characteristics by country 177(tab)
    sources of supply 177–178
coalitions, retailer 9
cocoa 61
Codex Alimentarius 156(n8) 276, 282
  recognition of HACCP 20
coffee 61
commercialization
  implications for small farmers 269
  increases regional and farm specialization 268
commission agents 125, 132
competition
  effect on input and credit programmes 79–80

effects on interlinking
   experience in Central Asia 82–86
   insights from the literature 78–82
   theoretical considerations 77–78
 should be enforced 264–265
Competition Commission (UK) 63
competitiveness
 of CIS agriculture 185
 imperfect in vertical coordination 61, 63–64
 price transmission 65–67
compliance
 benefits 30–31
 capacity for managing requirements 288–289
   capacity-building efforts 291–293
   deficiencies in developing countries 289–291
 case studies on costs and benefits
   fish product exports: Kerala 33–36
   shrimp exports: Bangladesh and Nicaragua 32–33
 costs
   affect both public and private sectors 28
   empirical findings 287–288
   estimation 29–30, 31–32, 286–287
   non-recurring vs. recurring 28–29
   tangible vs. intangible 29
 efficiency of achievement 29–30
 EU support programmes 243
 monitoring 13–14
 policy implications 262
composting 151, 152(tab)
consumers
 demands and expectations 5, 6–7, 21–22, 284–285
contamination 282
contracts
 advantages of contract schemes 102–104
 animal production 99
 contract farming in CIS countries see CIS (Commonwealth of Independent States)
 contract farming in India
   illegal in many states 126
   lacking for non-staple crops 125–126
 contract farming in Madagascar see under Madagascar
 contract farming in Senegal 165–166, 168–170
 enhancing farmer bargaining power 265
 EU supermarkets and farmers in Madagascar see under Madagascar
 interlinked see interlinking
 marketing vs. production 43, 44(tab)
 milk 99
 and quality improvement 101–102
 self-enforcing 49–51
 types 175–176
 typical contract farming commodities 99–100
cooperatives, marketing 123
coordination, vertical see vertical coordination
Costa Rica 109
 centralized procurement 137
 stomach cancer and pesticide use 142
 supermarkets 136
costs, transaction see transaction costs
cotton
 avoidance of side-selling 81–82
 contract motivation for farms 82(tab)
 effects of competition 79, 80, 86–87
 efforts to make interlinking sustainable 81–82
 strategies in Central Asia 83–86
 motivations for contracting 48, 49(tab)
 patterns of contracting 44–45
 private vs. private sector involvement 82–83
Country of Origin Labeling (COOL, USA) 21
credit: to farmers
 advantages of contract schemes 102–103
 African cotton industry 81–82
 bank loans dependent on contract with buyer 233–234
 Central American tomato and lettuce growers 140–141
 Central Asian cotton industry 82–85
 dairy sector 52–53, 235
 effect of competition 79–80
 and interlinking 75–76
 types of assistance in Senegal 165–166, 169–170
Croatia 51
Czech Republic
 consolidation of retail sector 232
 contract motivations for farms 48(tab)
 impact of procurement changes 237–238
 late payment problems 45

Czech Republic *continued*
  producer marketing organizations 237, 238
  spread of large-scale retailing 229–230
  supply chain rationalisation 233–234
  use of global logistics multinationals 234

dairy products
  Armenian goat industry *see under* Armenia
  concentration in the industry 211(fig)
  consumption 93, 220–221, 222–223
  contract farming 99
    impact on yields and production 252–253, 254(fig)
    patterns of contracting 43, 44, 51, 52, 245–247
    positive effects of vertical coordination 255
    relationship to product quality 181–182, 222, 247–249
    support measures 180, 249–251
  dairy companies 245
  drivers and obstacles for quality improvement 251–252
  farm structure and size 221, 222, 242
  foreign direct investment 222
  impact of procurement changes on dairy farmers 235–237
  loans for investment 52–53
  milk flows in the supply chain 244–245
  payment delays 46, 223–224
  private labels 234–235
  processing industry 242–244
  role of wholesalers 233, 234
  use of distribution centres 233
dependence, avoidance of 305
developing countries
  certification requirements of retailers 11–12
  deficiencies in capacity for SPS compliance 289–291
    capacity-building efforts 291–293
  effects of increased concentration on exports 68–70
  effects of tariff escalations on market access 70–71
  emerging 3-tier system of production and marketing 285–286

factors driving high-value agriculture 91–93
fish product exports
  economic significance 26
  and governance in vertical markets 71–72
  increasing participation in trade of horticultural goods 159, 171(n2)
  role of B2B standards 10
diseases, animal 282–293
diseases, plant 283
'due diligence clauses' 8–9

e-choupal scheme (India) 102
efficiency
  improvement 263–265
  of small farms 269
Efficient Consumer Response system 8, 22
EFSIS (European Food Safety Inspection Service 10
Engel's Law 93
environment
  benefits of contract farming 153
  consumer concerns 6
  eco-labels 21
  future impact of standards on manufacturing 14
  and globalization 147
  private standards *vs.* regulations 13
equity, improvement of 263–265
EurepGap 9, 11, 164, 293(n3)
European Union
  Euro-ecolabel 21
  food processing sector: product concentration 61–62
  General Food Law 2002 163–164
  green bean imports 163(fig)
  pesticide and other phytosanitary legislation 156(n8) 163
  procurement from Africa *see under* Madagascar; Senegal
  Regulation 912/2001 for green beans 163
  Regulations 2081/92 and 2082/92 (geographical identifications) 20
  regulations for fish products 27–28
    case studies of supplier countries 33–39
  retailers: concentration 62–63

support programmes for compliance
    243, 252, 256(n2)
  tariff escalation 71(tab)
  vertical coordination 43
exclusion: from vertical coordination
    277(n2)
  of small farms 53–55, 224, 260
  of small suppliers 228–229
Export Inspection Council (EIC, India) 34

fish and fishery products
  consumption in Asia 93–94
  economic significance for developing
    countries 26
  food safety standards *see under* safety,
    food
  production in Asia 95–96
Food and Veterinary Office (FVO, EU) 27
Food Safety Act 1990 (UK) 8
foreign direct investment *see* investment,
    foreign direct
Freedom Support Act (USA) 307(n2)
fringe markets
  importance to smaller suppliers 8, 16
fruit *see* horticultural products

GDP: driver of high-value agriculture 92
genetically modified (GM) foods 20–21
Georgia *see* CIS (Commonwealth of
    Independent States)
Germany: *Blauer Engel* (Blue Angel) eco-
    label 21
Ghana 81
Global Food Safety Initiative (GFSI) 9–11
globalization 59–60, 63, 147
Goat Industry Development Project (USDA)
    see under Armenia
goats *see under* Armenia
Good Agricultural Practices (GAP) code
    10, 17(n6)
Good Manufacturing Practices (GMP) code
    10–11, 17(n6)
governance: in vertical markets 71–72,
    263, 305
grain
  consumption in Asia 93
  motivations for contracting 49
  patterns of contracting 45, 51
  wheat production in Romania 213–215

Guatemala 109
  centralized procurement 137
  characteristics of tomato and lettuce
    growers 140–143
  supermarket procurement systems
    138–139
  relationships with tomato and lettuce
    growers 139–140

HACCP (Hazard Analysis Critical Control
    Point) 10–11
  in EU legislation 163
  international recognition 20
ham 222(fig)
harmonization: of standards and
    compliance 14–15
horticultural products
  consumption in Asia 93
  effect of competition 80
  extent of world trade 171(n1)
  onions in Hungary 216–218, 219(fig)
  patterns of contracting 45, 50–51
  Pepsi project for tomato paste 102
  Poland 214(fig) 215–216
  procurement systems
    impact on growers 139–143, 237–238
    types of systems and changes
      136–139, 232–233
  producer marketing organizations 237,
    238
  production and market segments in
    China 286(tab)
  production in Asia 95
  supply chain rationalisation 233–234
  survey of Chinese production *see under*
    China
  survey of Senegal exports to EU *see*
    under Senegal
  survey on non-staple crops in India *see*
    under India
  vegetable production for EU in
    Madagascar *see under* Madagascar
Hungary
  concentration in dairy industry 211(fig)
  contract motivations for farms 48(tab)
  dairy farming 220–222
  foreign direct investment 211, 217–218
  intermediary trading system 213
  late payment problems 45
  onion production 216–218, 219(fig)

Hungary *continued*
  retail sector changes 212
  role of producers' organizations 217

independence, promotion of 305–306
India
  advantages of contract farming 103–104
  changing patterns of domestic demand 122
  e-choupal scheme 102
  farmers' income 101
  fish product exports 33–36
  food export trends 94(tab)
  foreign direct investment 93
  GDP 1990–2002 92
  growth in food processing 98
  growth in high-value agriculture 95
  illegality of contract farming in many states 126
  increased focus on agricultural exports 122
  lower rice demand with urbanization 92
  Pepsi project 102
  sanitation problems 124, 130
  supermarkets 97 130
  survey on non-staple crops
    conclusions 128–129
    market infrastructure and organization 123–126
    policy recommendations 129–132
    production 123
    quality control 126–128
Indonesia
  food export trends 94(tab)
  food share of household budget 93
  growth in food processing 98
  growth in high-value agriculture 95
  lower rice demand with urbanization 92
  supermarkets 96, 97
institutional reform 276–277
interlinking
  conceptual framework 76–77
  effects of competition
    empirical insights 78–82
    theoretical considerations 77–78
  examples 75–76
  lacking in India 125–126
International Food Standard (IFS) 10
inventory management 8

investment
  to improve efficiency and equity in supply chains 264
  incentives and problems in Russia 192–195, 204
  policy implications 263
investment, foreign direct 64–65
  benefits and problems 228–229
  catalyst for contracting 183, 184, 185
  driver for high-value agriculture 92–93
  food processing in CEE countries 210–211, 243, 244
  Hungary 217–218, 222
  Romania 211, 223, 243
  Russian agriculture 192(fig)
  study of CEE retail sector
    consolidation 232
    cross-border procurement 233
    impact of changes on dairy farmers 235–237
    impact of changes on fruit and vegetable growers 237–238
    internationalization 230, 231(tab)
    methodology and data 229
    move to secondary cities and rural towns 230–231
    shift to private standards and labels 234–235
    spread of large-scale retailing 229–230
    supply chain rationalisation 233–234
    use of distribution centres 232–233
    use of global logistics multinationals 234
  supermarkets in Asia 97
ISO 9000 20

Japan
  tariff escalation 71(tab)
  zero tolerance for insects in produce 283
Just in Time system 8

Kazakhstan
  contract motivations for farms 48, 49(tab) 82(tab)
  integrated farm companies 46(box) 48–49
  vertical coordination for cotton 82–83, 84–85
  vertical coordination for grain 45, 51

Kenya
  horticulture 80, 148, 155(n6)
  importance of input finance in farming 75
  Nile perch exports 36–39
  organization of cotton supplies 81
Kerala: fish product exports 33–36
Kyrgyzstan: cotton production 82–83, 85

labelling: GM foods 20–21
labels, private 234–235
labour
  definition of standards 14
  in developing countries 12–13
leadership 305
lettuce 139, 141–143
liability: of food retailers 8–9
  impact on private standards 11
  retailer concerns 13
liberalization, trade 276
  driver for high-value agriculture 92
  effects on cotton producers 79
  policy recommendations for India 129–131
  price transmission with imperfect competition 65–67
  in a vertically related market: model 67–68
losses, postharvest 124, 126

Macedonia 50–51
Madagascar
  extent of poverty 148
  organization of cotton supplies 81
  vegetable sales to EU
    assistance to suppliers and contract enforcement 151
    characteristics of contracting farm households 149–150
    contract monitoring and supervision 150–151
    impact on technology adoption and land use 151–152
    nature and extent 149
    policy implications 154–155
    spillover effects 152–154
    standards and contracts 150
maize 123
mangoes 124, 125

Marine Products Export Development Authority (India) 35, 40(n7)
markets
  dominance of small traders in China 114–115, 116(tab)
  dynamics in food markets 284–286
  interlinking see interlinking
  wholesale
    decreased use in Central America 136–137
    infrastructure and organization in India 123–126
Maximum Residue Levels 150–151, 156(n8) 282
mergers and acquisitions 64–65
Mexico 65
Minimum Quality Standards 9
models: of contracting and contract support 182–185
Moldova see CIS (Commonwealth of Independent States)
Motion Picture Association 24
Mozambique 80
multinationals
  for global logistics 234
  in Latin America 65
  negative impact in CEE countries 211

"new agricultural operators" see under Russia
Nicaragua
  characteristics of tomato growers 140–143
  shrimp exports 33
  supermarkets 136
    relationships with tomato growers 139
Nile perch 36–39
nitrofuran 282

OGO grain company, Russia 193–194(box) 200(box) 201(fig)
oilseeds 51
ONAPES (Organisation National des Producteurs Exportateurs de Fruits et Légumes de Sénégal 161, 164, 166, 171(n4)
onions 216–218, 219(fig)
organic food standards 22

Pakistan
  cotton 79, 82
  food export trends 94(tab)
  foreign direct investment 93
  GDP 1990–2002 92
  growth in high-value agriculture 95
  lower rice demand with urbanization 92
  supermarkets 96, 97
partnerships, public-private 266
payments: problems in transition countries 45–46
Pepsi project 102
perch, Nile 36–39
pesticides
  and cancer 142
  Maximum Residue Levels 150–151, 156(n8)
pests, plant: risk assessment 283
Philippines
  costs of loans 103
  credit from wholesalers to farmers 75
  farmers' collectives 105
  food export trends 94(tab)
  foreign direct investment 93
  GDP 1990–2002 92
  supermarkets 96, 97
    impact on smallholders 104
pigs 218, 220, 221(fig)
Poland
  consolidation of retail sector 232
  dairy farming 52–53
    impact of procurement changes 235, 236
    private label products 234
  foreign direct investment 210
  fruit and vegetables 214(fig) 215–216
  intermediary trading system 213, 214(fig)
  retail sector changes 212
  supply chain rationalisation 233
policy
  implications of sales to EU 154–155
  important issues
    enabling high-value supply chains 261–263
    innovative finance instruments 266
    need for rural development strategy 266
    policy analysis and information gathering 265
    public-private partnerships 266
    summary 260–261
  to overcome transaction costs 275–277
  recommendations on support programmes 304–306
  recommendations on trade liberalization 129–132
  vertical coordination in transition countries 49, 50(fig)
pork 218, 220, 221(fig) 222(fig)
poultry 193–194(box)
poverty
  and globalization 147
  impact of high value agriculture 113–114, 153–154
power, economic
  retailers as holders 5
  and supermarket concentration 7
prices: transmission with imperfect competition 65–67
privatization
  agro-holdings in Russia 198(box)
  CEE countries 210–211
  Romanian dairy industry 223
processing, food
  dairy products 242–244
  growing demand for products 94
  in India 126
  product concentration
    Asia 98
    effect on developing countries' exports 68–70
    EU and USA 61–62
Proctor & Gamble 22
producer marketing organizations 217, 237, 238
production: management system approach to monitoring 9–10
protected designation of origin (PDO) 20
protected geographical indications (PGI) 20
public good, provision of 275–276
public-private partnerships 266

quality
  consumer attitudes to regulation 6–7
  driving forces and obstacles 251–252
  impact of supply chains 116
  Minimum Quality Standards 9
  premium product lines 12, 21
  QC of Indian non-staple crops 126–128
  role of contracts 101–102, 181–182, 247–249

reform, institutional 276–277
regulations
    for fish products in EU 27–28
    geographical identifications 20
    organic food 22
    reasons for enactment 21–22
    in relation to private standards 9, 11, 13
    retailer liability and due diligence 8–9
    on wholesale markets 124
retailers
    coalitions 9
    concentration 7
        in Asia: causes and consequences 96–98
        EU vs. USA 62–63
        impact on developing countries' exports 68–70
        impact on smallholders 104–105
        via mergers and acquisitions 64–65
    differences in local and international requirements 11–12
    foreign direct investment see under investment, foreign direct
    holders of economic power 5
    liability 8–9, 13
    market shares of top five in UK and CEE 232(fig)
    response to Wal-Mart threat 22
    survey on private standards 11–15
rice
    effects of vegetable contract growing in rice productivity 152, 153(fig)
    reduced demand with urbanization 92
Romania
    dairy sector 46, 51, 52, 221
        changes in vertical organization of supply chains 222–224
        compliance with EU standards 243
        contracts with suppliers 245–246
        dairy companies 245
        drivers and obstacles for quality improvement 251–252
        impact of contracts on yields and production 252–253
        industry structure: primary level 242
        industry structure: processing level 242–243
        low availability of milk for processing 244–245
        positive effect of vertical coordination 255
        systems to improve quality 247–248

foreign direct investment 211, 223
privatization 223
retail sector changes 212
wheat 213–215
Russia see also CIS (Commonwealth of Independent States)
    agrarian reform, early 1990s 189–191
    centralized procurement problems 233
    dairy sector
        impact of procurement changes on farmers 235–236
        private label dairy products 235
    effects of 1998 financial crisis 191
    gross agricultural output 189–190, 191(fig)
    integrated farm companies 46(box) 48–49
    investment in food and agriculture 192(fig)
    land use by farm category 1991 vs. 2000 189(fig)
    legislation on land 204(n1)
    move of retail chains into regions 231
    "new operators" (agro-holdings)
        access to land 198–199
        collective rents 199
        description 188–189
        impact on input markets 200–202
        investment 192–195, 204
        management structure 199–200
        motivation for expansion to primary agriculture 196–197
        operational size 195–196
        privatization 198(box)
        role of regional authorities 197–198
        training 203, 204(box)
    supply chain rationalisation 234
    use of global logistics multinationals 234
    vertical coordination
        company examples 193–194(box) 200(box) 201(fig)
        contracts for fertilizers 202(fig)
        contracts for petrol 203(fig)
        in deliveries of farm inputs 201–202
        grain 45
        not limited to agriculture 194
        problems 194–195

safety, food *see also* Global Food Safety Initiative (GFSI); sanitary and phytosanitary (SPS) measures
  consumer expectations 6
  driver for changes in food market development 285
  driver for supermarkets in China 97
  General Food Law 2002 (EU) 163–164
  lack of risk awareness in Indian markets 126
  policy implications 262
  public tests add to costs 291(box)
  response of retailers 11–12
  retailer liability and due diligence 8–9
  standards for fish and fishery products
    costs and benefits of compliance *see under* compliance
    differ from standards for other commodities 27
    EU regulations 27–28
sanitary and phytosanitary (SPS) measures
  capacity for managing requirements 288–289
    capacity-building efforts 291–293
    deficiencies in developing countries 289–291
  enforcement 283–284
  EU phytosanitary measures 163
  and risk assessment 283
  WTO SPS Agreement 281–282
seasonality, smoothing of 153–154
self-regulation 19
Senegal
  survey of horticultural exports to EU
    characteristics of agri-exporting companies 161(tab)
    characteristics of households 161(tab)
    compliance with EU food standards 164
    consolidation of exporters 165
    data and methodology 160–162
    export trends and characteristics 162–163
    extent of contract farming 166(tab)
    household participation 167
    increased vertical coordination 164–166
    welfare effects 168–170
SEPAS (Syndicat des Exportateurs des Produits Agricoles, Senegal) 161, 171(n3)

shrimps 32–33
  contamination with nitrofuran 282
side-selling, avoidance of 81–82
Slovakia
  consolidation of retail sector 232
  contract motivations for farms 48(tab)
  dairy sector
    contracts with suppliers 246–247
    dairy companies 245
    drivers and obstacles for quality improvement 252
    impact of contracts on yields and production 253, 254(fig)
    industry structure: primary level 242
    industry structure: processing level 243–244
    positive effect of vertical coordination 255
    systems to improve quality 248
  spread of large-scale retailing 229–230
  sugar production 51–52, 53
specialization: result of commercialization 268
SQF1000/2000 (Safe Quality Food) 10, 11
standards, private voluntary
  business to business (B2B) 10, 98, 138
  in CEE countries 234
  eco-labels 21
  Euro-Retailer Produce Working Group (Eurep) *see* EurepGap
  flexible response to change 22–23
  Global Food Safety Initiative *see* Global Food Safety Initiative (GFSI)
  as global tools 7–8, 15–16
  harmonization 14–15
  management system approach 9–10
  relationship to regulations 9, 11
  set by retailer coalitions 9
  strategic incentives 23–24
  survey of leading food retailers 11–15
  types of use 5–6
standards, public *see also* regulations
  ISO 9000 20
State Agricultural Produce Market Act (India_ 124, 125, 126, 130
sugar
  patterns of contracting 44, 51–52, 53
supermarkets
  growth
    in Asia: causes and consequences 96–98 109
    in Latin America 135, 136

impact on smallholders 104–105,
   109–110, 139–143
procurement systems 136–139
suppliers
   of horticultural goods in China 114–115,
      116(tab)
   importance of fringe markets 8, 16
   perspectives for small-scale farmers 54,
      104–105, 110, 224–226
   preferred suppliers 137–138

Tajikistan 82, 84
Tanzania
   cotton 79, 80, 82
   Nile perch exports 36–39
tariffs: effects of escalation 70–71
Thailand
   food export trends 94(tab)
   GDP 1990–2002 92
   growth in food processing 98
   growth in high-value agriculture 95
   lower rice demand with urbanization 92
   supermarkets 96, 97
   Western Region GAP cluster 288(box)
tomatoes
   growers in Central America 141–143
   procurement in Central America 138,
      139–140
   supply patterns in India 123, 124, 125
traceability 11, 21, 164
transaction costs 264
   associated with dealing with small farms
      270–271
   definition and classification 270
   farm-specific costs 271–272
   obstacle to small farmers 268
   overcoming
      policy focus 275–277
      role of private sector 272–275
   public tests of food safety 291(box)
transition countries see also CEE
      countries; CIS (Commonwealth of
      Independent States); individual
      countries
   vertical coordination
      benefits 51–53
      commodity-specific patterns 44–45
      factors acting as drivers 45–47
      finance sources 47
      future perspectives 55–56

general patterns 43–44
impacts on equity 53–55
models 47–48
motivations and constraints 48–49
policy environment 49, 50(fig)
response to market constraints 47
turmeric 123

Uganda
   Nile perch exports 36–39, 40(n9)
   organization of cotton supplies 81
Ukraine see also CIS (Commonwealth of
      Independent States)
   oilseed production 51
United Kingdom
   British Retail Consortium (BRC)
      Standard 10
   contractual practices and competition
      63
   Food Safety Act 1990 8
   market share of top five retailers 232(fig)
   procurement from Kenya 148
United Methodist Christian Relief
   (UMCOR) 299
United States
   Bio-terrorism and Response Act 21
   Country of Origin Labeling (COOL) 21
   eco-labels 21
   food processing sector 61, 62(tab)
   Freedom Support Act (USA) 307(n2)
   organization of cotton industry 81
   regulations for fish products 40(n3)
   retailers 62–63
   tariff escalation 71(tab)
   USDA
      Market Assistance Goat Industry
         Development Project
         (MAPGDIP) see under Armenia
      organic standards 22
   vertical coordination 43, 44(tab)
urbanization 92
USDA Market Assistance Goat Industry
   Development Project (MAPGDIP) see
   under Armenia
Uzbekistan 82, 83–84

vegetables see horticultural products
vertical coordination
   access of developing countries
      effects of tariff escalations 70–71

vertical coordination *continued*
  associated with increase in supermarket chain size 98
  and avoidance of side-selling 80–81
  and competitiveness 63–64
  concepts 43
  effects of increased concentration 68–70
  experience of Central Asian cotton industry 82–86
  farmer-buyer in Asia 99–100
  governance issues 71–72, 263
  green beans sector in Senegal 164–166
  high-value agriculture and small farmers 100–104, 259–260
  impact of trade liberalization: model 67–68
  imperfect competitiveness 61
    price transmission 65–67
  in overcoming transaction costs 273
  policy implications 262–263
  in Russia ("new operators") *see under* Russia
  in transition countries see also *under* CEE countries
    benefits 51–53
    commodity-specific patterns 44–45
    factors acting as drivers 45–47
    finance sources 47
    future perspectives 55–56
    general patterns 43–44
    impacts on equity 53–55
    models 47–48
    motivations and constraints 48–49
    policy environment 49–50(fig)
    response to market constraints 47
    self-enforcing contracts 49–51
  in USA and EU 43
Vietnam
  food export trends 94(tab)
  food share of household budget 93
  foreign direct investment 93
  GDP 1990–2002 92
  growth in high-value agriculture 95
  lower rice demand with urbanization 92
  supermarkets 96

Wal-Mart 8, 22
World Trade Organization (WTO) 281–282

Zambia 79, 80
Zimbabwe
  cotton 79, 80, 81–82
  incentives for farmers 81
zoonoses 282